DOCUMENTS OF
American Catholic History

DOCUMENTS OF
American Catholic History

EDITED BY

John Tracy Ellis

VOLUME 3
1966 to 1986

MICHAEL GLAZIER
Wilmington Delaware

About the Editor

John Tracy Ellis is Professorial Lecturer in Church History in the Catholic University of America. He is a member of the American Catholic Historical Association and the American Society of Church History. Throughout his career he has received many honors. In 1978 he was honored with the Laetare Medal of the University of Notre Dame—an award presented to the outstanding contributor to the life of the Church in the United States. Monsignor Ellis has written seventeen books over the course of his career and he is best known for *The Life of James Cardinal Gibbons, Archbishop of Baltimore, 1834-1921* (2 volumes); and *American Catholicism.*

Published in 1987 by Michael Glazier, Inc., 1935 West Fourth Street, Wilmington, Delaware 19805 ● ©Copyright 1987 by John Tracy Ellis ● All rights reserved

Library of Congress Cataloging-in-Publication Data

Documents of American Catholic History
Volumes 1-2 are reprints Originally published:
Chicago : H. Regnery Co., 1967. Vol. 3 is a new work.

Includes bibliographies and index.
Contents: v.1. 1493-1865 — v. 2. 1866-1966 —
v. 3. 1966-1986.
1. Catholic Church—United States—History—
Sources.
2. United States—Church history—Sources I. Ellis,
John Tracy, 1905-
BX1405.D63 1987   282'.73   86-80801
ISBN 0-89453-611-7 (vol. 1)
      0-89453-612-5 (vol. 2)
      0-89453-588-9 (vol. 3)

Printed in the United States of America.

CONTENTS

170. Peace and Vietnam. A Statement by the Catholic Bishops, November 18, 1966.

It is doubtful if any public policy of the Catholic bishops of the United States better illustrates the strikingly altered status of the American Catholic community than that relating to the issue of war and peace. In every conflict from the revolution of the 1770's up to and including World War II, the bishops stood stoutly behind the government, including the two armed conflicts of a gravely doubtful moral character, namely, the Mexican War (1846-1848) and the war against Spain (1898). It was a position that reflected Catholics' minority status in the midst of the traditional anti-Catholic bias of many Americans. In fact, this stance carried well into the war in Vietnam when as late as 1966 the bishops with, it is true, carefully nuanced reservations, yet maintained that "in the light of the facts as they are known to us, it is reasonable that our presence in Vietnam is justified." The greatly enhanced position of Catholics in relation to the American mainstream was a significant factor in the changed attitude represented between this document and the view expressed in the one that follows. Source: Hugh J. Nolan (Ed.) *Pastoral Letters of the United States Catholic Bishops*. Washington: National Conference of Catholic Bishops. 1983. III, 74-77.

---

1.   Our common humanity demands that all people live in peace and harmony with one another. This peace will exist only if the right order established by God is observed, an order which is based on the requirements of human dignity. Everyone, therefore, must be vitally and personally concerned about correcting the grave disorders which today threaten peace. As Catholics, we are members of the Church that Pope Paul has called a "messenger of peace."

2.   We, the Catholic bishops of the United States, consider it our duty to help magnify the moral voice of our nation. This voice, fortunately, is becoming louder and clearer because it is the voice of all faiths. To the strong words of the National Council of Churches, the Synagogue Council of America, and other religious bodies, we add our own plea for peace. Our approaches may at times differ, but our starting point (justice) and our goal (peace) do not.

3.   While we cannot resolve all the issues involved in the

Vietnam conflict, it is clearly our duty to insist that they be kept under constant moral scrutiny. No one is free to evade his personal responsibility by leaving it entirely to others to make moral judgments. In this connection, the Vatican Council warns that "men should take heed not to entrust themselves only to the efforts of others, while remaining careless about their own attitudes. For government officials, who must simultaneously guarantee the good of their own people and promote the universal good, depend on public opinion and feeling to the greatest possible extent."[1]

Peace and Modern Warfare

4.   While it is not possible in this brief statement to give a detailed analysis of the Church's total teaching on war and peace, it seems necessary to review certain basic principle if the present crisis is to be put in its proper moral perspectives.

5.   We reaffirmed at the Council the legitimate role of patriotism for the well-being of a nation, but a clear distinction was made between *true* and *false* patriotism: "Citizens should develop a generous and loyal devotion to their country, but without any narrowing of mind. In other words, they must always look simultaneously to the welfare of the whole human family, which is tied together by the manifold bonds linking races, peoples and nations."[2]

6.   But these limits on patriotism do not rule out a country's right to legitimate self-defense. While making it clear that all means short of force must first be used, the Council restated the traditional teaching regarding the right of self-defense: "As long as the danger of war remains and there is no competent and sufficiently powerful authority at the international level, government cannot be denied the right to legitimate defense."[3] And what a nation can do to defend itself, it may do to help another in its struggle against aggression.

7.   In the conduct of any war, there must be moral limits: "Any act of war aimed indiscriminately at the destruction of entire cities or of extensive areas along with their population is a crime against God and man himself. It merits univocal and unhesitating

---

[1]*Pastoral Constitution on the Church in the Modern World,* Part II, Chapter V, Section 1 (*The Documents of Vatican II,* Guild Press, New York, p. 296).

[2]Ibid., Part II, Chapter IV, p. 286.

[3]Ibid., Part II, Chapter V, Section 1, p. 293.

condemnation."[4] Moreover, as the Council also reminded us, the fact that a war of self-defense has unhappily begun does not mean that any and all means may be employed by the warring parties.

8.   While the stockpiling of scientific weapons serves, for the present, as a deterrent to aggression, the Council has warned us that "the arms race in which so many countries are engaged is not a safe way to preserve a steady peace."[5] Indeed, it is a "treacherous trap for humanity." Far from promoting a sure and authentic peace, it actually fosters war by diverting resources which could be better used to alleviate the human misery which causes war. In their urgent plea for disarmament, however, the Council Fathers understood that it will be effective only if it is universal and if there are adequate means of enforcing it.

9.   The Council commended those citizens who defend their nation against aggression. They are "instruments of security and freedom on behalf of their people. As long as they fulfill this role properly they are making a genuine contribution to the establishment of peace."[6]

At the same time, however, it pointed out that some provision should be made for those who conscientiously object to bearing arms: "It seems right that laws make humane provisions for the care of those who for reasons of conscience refuse to bear arms; provided, however, that they accept some other form of service to the human community."[7]

Principles Put to Work

10.   In the light of these principles, how are we as Americans to judge the involvement of the United States in Vietnam? What can we do to promote peace?

11.   Americans can have confidence in the sincerity of their leaders as long as they work for a just peace in Vietnam. Their efforts to find a solution to the present impasse are well known. We realize that citizens of all faiths and of differing political loyalties honestly differ among themselves over the moral issues involved in this tragic conflict. While we do not claim to be able to resolve these

---

[4] Ibid., Part II, Chapter V, Section 1, p. 294.

[5] Ibid., Part II, Chapter V, Section 1, p. 295.

[6] Ibid., Part II, Chapter V, Section 1, p. 293.

[7] Ibid., Part II, Chapter V, Section 1, p. 293.

issues authoritatively, in the light of the facts as they are known to us, it is reasonable to argue that our presence in Vietnam is justified. We share the anguish of our government officials in their awesome responsibility of making life-and-death decisions about our national policy in Vietnam. We commend the valor of our men in the armed forces, and we express to them our debt of gratitude. In our time, thousands of men have given their lives in war. To those who loved them, we express our sorrow at their loss and promise our constant prayer.

12.   But we cannot stop here. While we can conscientiously support the position of our country in the present circumstances, it is the duty of everyone to search for other alternatives. And everyone—government leaders and citizens alike—must be prepared to change our course whenever a change in circumstances warrants it.

13.   This can be done effectively only if we know the facts and issues involved. Within the limits imposed by our national security, therefore, we must always insist that these facts and issues be made known to the public so that they can be considered in their moral context.

14.   On the basis of our knowledge and understanding of the current situation, we are also bound always to make sure that our government does, in fact, pursue every possibility which offers even the slightest hope of a peaceful settlement. And we must clearly protest whenever there is a danger that the conflict will be escalated beyond morally acceptable limits.

15.   On a broader level, we must support our government in its efforts to negotiate a workable formula for disarmament. What we seek is not unilateral disarmament, but one proceeding in the words of the Council, "at an equal pace according to agreement, and backed up by authentic and workable safeguards."[8] We commend the officials of our country and others for their contribution to the proposed Treaty against Nuclear Proliferation which, hopefully, will soon become a reality.

16.   Moreover, we must use every resource available, as a nation, to help alleviate the basic causes of war. If the God-given human dignity of the people of poorer nations is not to become an illusion, these nations must be able to provide for the spiritual and material needs of their citizens. We must help them do this. The economically developed nations of the world, as Pope John

---

[8] Ibid., Part II, Chapter V, Section 1, p. 296.

insisted in his great encyclical, *Pacem in Terris,* must come to the aid of those which are in the process of developing so that every man, woman and child in the world may be able "to live in conditions more in keeping with their human dignity."[9]

"The Second Mile"

17. There is a grave danger that the circumstances of the present war in Vietnam may, in time, diminish our moral sensitivity to its evils. Every means at our disposal, therefore, must be used to create a climate of peace. In this climate, prayer, personal example, study, discussion, and lectures can strengthen the will for peace. We must advocate what we believe are the best methods of promoting peace: mutual agreements, safeguards, and inspection; the creation of an international public authority to negotiate toward peace. Above all, in its peace-making efforts, we must support the work of the United Nations which, in the words of Pope Paul, marks "a stage in the development of mankind, from which retreat must never be admitted, but from which it is necessary that advance be made."[10]

18. We ask every person of good will to support with prayer the Holy Father's plea for a Christmas ceasefire. May it open the way to lasting peace. In the spirit of Christ, the Christian must be the persistent seeker in the Gospel, the man willing to walk the second mile (cf., Mt 5:42). He walks prudently, but he walks generously and he asks that all men do the same.

19. As Catholics we walk in good company. Pope Paul, in his recent encyclical on peace, cried out, in God's name, to stop war. We pray God that the sacrifices of us all, our prayers as well as our faltering efforts toward peace, will hasten the day when the whole world will echo Pope Paul's historic words: "No more war, war never again!" [11]

---

[9] *Pacem in Terris* (NCWC, Washington, D.C., pp. 28, 29).

[10] *Address to the United Nations Assembly,* Oct. 4, 1965 (*Pope Paul VI in New York,* NCWC, Washington, D.C., p. 77).

[11] Ibid., p. 9.

171. Resolution on Southeast Asia, a Statement Issued by the National Conference of Catholic Bishops, November, 1971.

During the late 1960's the opposition within the United States to the war in Vietnam steadily mounted with repeated demonstrations by students *et al.* Meanwhile the Catholic bishops had likewise turned a corner, so to speak, in their attitude toward that conflict, and called for an end to the warfare "with no further delay." If their statement put them abreast of the growing national sentiment it still represented an unprecedented break with the traditional stance of their predecessors on matters so closely related to government policy. Source: Hugh J. Nolan (Ed.), *Pastoral Letters of the United States Catholic Bishops.* Washington: National Conference of Catholic Bishops. 1983. III, 289-291.

---

1.   In the light of the urgent appeal for justice in the world pronounced by the recent synod in Rome, we bishops of the United States address ourselves again to the agonizing issue of the American involvement in Southeast Asia. And we feel compelled to make some positive recommendations concerning the long journey ahead to peace with justice in our world.

I. The American Involvement in Southeast Asia

2.   Three years ago, in our Pastoral Letter, *Human Life in Our Day,* we raised some basic moral questions concerning the Vietnam War:

> In assessing our country's involvement in Vietnam we must ask: Have we already reached, or passed, the point where the principle of proportionality becomes decisive? How much more of our resources of men and money should we commit to this struggle, assuming an acceptable cause and intention? Has the conflict in Vietnam provoked inhuman dimensions of suffering?

3.   At this point in history, it seems clear to us that whatever good we hope to achieve through continued involvement in this war is now outweighed by the destruction of human life and of moral values which it inflicts. It is our firm conviction, therefore, that the speedy ending of this war is a moral imperative of the highest priority. Hence, we feel a moral obligation to appeal urgently to our nation's leaders and indeed to the leaders of all the nations involved in this tragic conflict to bring the war to an end with no further delay.

II. The Journey Ahead to Peace with Justice in Our World

4.   It is our prayerful hope that we in America will have learned from the tragedy of Vietnam important lessons for reconstructing a world with justice and a world at peace.

5.   First, we must be determined as never before to "undertake an evaluation of war with an entirely new attitude" (Vatican II, *Pastoral Constitution on the Church in the Modern World,* No. 80). And we reach this new attitude by attending more carefully to the spirit of the Gospel and by heeding the pleas of recent popes: "Nothing is lost by peace; everything may be lost by war" (Pius XII, Radio Broadcast of 24 August 1939); "In this age of ours which prides itself on atomic power, it is irrational to believe that war is still an apt means of vindicating violated rights" (John XXIII, *Pacem in Terris,* No. 127); "No more war, war never again" (Paul VI, *Address to the United Nations,* 4 October 1965).

6.   Second, we realize that "peace is not merely the absence of war, but an enterprise of justice" (Vatican II, *Pastoral Constitution on the Church in the Modern World,* No. 78). In this vein, we recognize our nation's moral obligation, together with other nations, to contribute mightily to the restoration and development of Southeast Asia. After World War II, our country launched an unprecedented program of economic assistance and social reconstruction of war-torn countries. Certainly we can do no less now.

7.   Third, we are convinced that the United Nations must become more effective in the promotion of world justice and peace. In saying this, we echo the words of Pope Paul VI that "the people of the earth turn to the United Nations as the last hope of concord and peace," and we recognize with the Holy Father that the United Nations "must be perfected and made equal to the needs which world history will present" (*Address to the United Nations,* 4 October 1965). Only by strengthening the United Nations as an international forum for peace and as a multilateral instrument for peace-keeping can future Vietnams be averted.

8.   Finally, we recognize a clear need at this point in history to urge upon all Americans a spirit of forgiveness and reconciliation. We recall that at a similarly critical moment in American history, Abraham Lincoln urged his countrymen to act "with malice towards none, with charity towards all." We invite our fellow Americans to let these words guide new efforts to heal wounds in our divided society and to unite our country in the years after the war in Southeast Asia.

9.   We speak with special concern for those who have borne the heaviest burden of this war: the young men who chose conscientiously to serve in the Armed Forces, many of whom lost life or limb in this conflict. We wish to express our profound sympathy to the wives and families of the soldiers who have died in Southeast Asia. We express our profound concern for our prisoners of war and their families and promise our prayers for the prisoners' welfare and release. And on behalf of the returning veterans, we urge strongly that the government increase the present benefits and educational opportunities afforded by the G.I. Bill, and that it create new programs of drug rehabilitation, vocational training, and job placement wherever necessary.

10.   Those who in good conscience resisted this war are also subjects of our genuine pastoral concern. They too must be reintegrated as fully as possible into our society and invited to share the opportunities and responsibilities of building a better nation. Hence we repeat our plea of October 21, 1971 that the civil authorities grant generous pardon of convictions incurred under the Selective Service Act, with the understanding that sincere conscientious objectors should remain open in principle to some form of service to the community. Surely a country which showed compassion by offering amnesty after the Civil War will want to exercise no less compassion today.

Conclusion

11.   In setting forth our position at this time, we realize that the task of constructing a just social order and a world genuinely at peace will never be an easy one. But we must reaffirm that followers of Christ and all men of good will must redouble their efforts to achieve this task so worthy of our best efforts.

> Otherwise, for all its marvelous knowledge, humanity, which is already in the middle of a grave crisis, will perhaps be brought to that mournful hour in which it will experience no peace other than the dreadful peace of death. But while we say this, the Church of Christ takes her stand in the midst of the anxiety of this age, and does not cease to hope with the utmost confidence. She intends to propose to our age over and over again, in season and out of season this apostolic message: "Behold, now is the acceptable time" for a change of heart; "Behold, now is the day of salvation!"(Vatican II, *Pastoral Constitution on the Church in the Modern World,* No. 82).

172. A Document on Ecclesiastical Archives, November 22, 1974.

If the statement, 'no documents, no history,' may well be thought a cliché in professional circles, like most clichés it nonetheless expresses a genuine truth. As the American Catholic community reached maturity more thought was given to its roots, but, alas, the evidence of those beginnings was often no longer extant. Accidents of nature, neglect of the written records, and all too often deliberate destruction had taken their toll. Prompted by the initiative of Paul J. Hallinan, late Archbishop of Atlanta, himself a trained historian, the bishops' Committee for the Bicentennial of 1976 sponsored a statement, written by Michael V. Gannon of the University of Florida. That statement stimulated a nationwide interest among Catholic bishops and superiors of religious communities of women and men with a notable increase in the number of fulltime archivists appointed in dioceses and religious communities for the preservation and proper ordering of the unpublished sources contained in their respective archives. If the last decade has witnessed a significant increase of scholarly books and articles on American Catholic history, that development is owed in some measure to the enlivened interest and care of archival sources that now characterizes these documentary collections. Source: *A Document on Ecclesiastical Archives. Committee for the Bicentennial, November 22, 1974.* Washington: National Conference of Catholic Bishops. 1974.

In 1976 the Catholic Church in the United States will observe, along with the national Bicentennial, its own 411th year of continuous presence on the soil of our country. That long history, beginning with the founding of the town and parish of St. Augustine in 1565, and continuing through the establishment of the first American diocese, that of Baltimore, in 1789, down to the present, represents one of the most heroic, varied, productive, and inspiring chapters in the record of the nearly two millennia of Catholic Christianity. We American Catholics are justifiably proud, as the bicentennial year approaches, of the contributions of our forebears both to the mission of the Church and to the formation of the nation.

At the same time we regret that our Church's singular role in the development of our country has not been presented as fully as it deserves to be. Although books, monographs, articles, and essays on the subject of American Catholicism abound and many of them are of high scholarly and literary quality, church historians have still not penetrated to the heart of the peculiarly American experience in all too many cases, because they have not had access to the pertinent documents of bishops, dioceses, religious orders, and institutions. The difficulty is not so much that such papers are not extant, although it is true, unfortunately, that in certain known cases large holdings of important documents have been destroyed because they were mistakenly judged to be "outdated" or "useless" or "trash." The problem is rather that in many places the papers which do exist in abundance have not yet been organized for preservation and research. Consequently, on the one hand, they are not easily accessible to church historians and, on the other, they are in danger of being lost, dispersed, or damaged through lack of proper care, fire or flood, or inadvertent disposal.

The Bicentennial has made all American Catholics more aware of their past and more conscious of their obligation to hand down to posterity the records of those accomplishments for the Church and the nation. American Catholics are a people with a tradition—apart from the Aboriginal Indians, the longest tradition in North America. The Church is an institution with a centuries-old reverence for official records. Yet American Catholics sometimes seem to be so concerned about the present that they neglect their duties to the past.

The Bicentennial is a most appropriate time to remind ourselves of this tradition of our Church and to inaugurate a nationwide effort to preserve and organize all existing records and papers that can be found in the chancery offices, general and provincial houses of religious orders, and institutions of our country. In a particular way we recommend to each of the residential bishops who have not yet done so that he appoint a properly qualified priest, religious man or woman, or lay person as diocesan archivist. Although the Code of Canon Law designates the chancellor as legal custodian of the archives (C.I.C.,c. 372), as it also lays down the strict conditions under which documents are to be safeguarded (cc. 375.2, 376.1, 376.2, 377, 378), most chancellors, it seems, do not have the time, amidst their own official duties, to undertake the highly detailed work of organizing archives. Nor, it must be added, do most chancellors and vice chancellors have the necessary background and training in archival science. The excellent organization of archives that has already been achieved by trained archivists in a few dioceses, religious orders, and institutions, however, provides a model for the rest.

In urging each bishop who does not already have a diocesan archivist to appoint one, even if that person could devote only one day a week to this work, we also propose that, for the benefit of those newly appointed, a brief training course be conducted by some of the archivists who have had long experience.

Finally, we express our sincere hope that the residential bishops may be disposed to grant access to the diocesan archives without undue limitations when properly accredited ecclesiastical historians request it. The past products of such research support, we believe, the contention that serious historians, even graduate students and doctoral candidates, have, with very rare exceptions, used such permission with honesty, fairness, responsibility, respect for the documents, and true Christian charity. Catholic historians have characteristically evinced a distinct pride in the persons and institutions of their Church of past generations, and, in our judgment, no bishop need fear that by opening his archives to scholarly examination, he will expose the Church's past to deliberate attempts at embarrassment. True, scandals and shortcomings may be uncovered, but in these matters we believe that it is still appropriate to follow the admonition of Pope Leo XIII, who in his letter on historical studies, *Saepenumero considerantes,* of August 18, 1883, quoting from Cicero, declared "that the first law of history is not to dare to utter falsehood; the second, not to fear to speak the truth; and, moreover, no room must be left for suspicion of partiality or prejudice."

173. A Call to Restructure the Parish, November, 1975.

In the 'uncertain anxious time' that followed Vatican Council II few ecclesiastical institutions received more critical scrutiny in light of the conciliar directives than the parish. One of the earliest and influential calls for structural change on a parochial basis was made by the then Auxiliary Bishop of Toledo, since 1977 Bishop of Steubenville. Reflecting his 30-year experience as a parish priest, Albert H. Ottenweller called for an approach that would accentuate the personal rather than the institutional, for the creation of instrumentalities within the parish that would link persons more closely into a community. Source: *Origins,* 5 (December 11, 1975), 394-396.

I feel very honored to be able to present to this body of bishops a concern of mine for the future of the church. I will try to be brief and to the point. From the outset I must admit that I have a prejudice in favor of priests who are in pastoral ministry.

I see the parish as the key to renewal in the church. I am not a theologian, nor a scripture scholar. For more than 30 years I have worked as a parish priest. I see myself as a journeyman pastor experienced in dealing with people and problems at the grass roots.

I think a pastor's expertise is taking theory, theological principles, and making them work on the level of where people are. I think this was Martin Luther King's genious—he drew the principles of civil rights out of the textbook, Jesus' teaching from the gospels, and took them down to a crowded basement of a Baptist Church in Selma, Alabama and brought them to birth in people there; and they marched through the streets, and theory became a *movement.*

I think priests do this in parishes. Under the guidance of the Holy Spirit the bishops at the Second Vatican Council saw a vision of what the church of our time ought to be. But that vision must be brought to life in the churches and in the market place. It is one thing to formulate guidelines for the new rite of penance—it is quite another thing to put those guidelines to work so that ordinary Catholic people may celebrate penance as a deep and satisfying faith experience.

This said, I would like to propose that a study be made of the model of parish as presently structured compared to other possible models. I think restructuring is critical because parish priests are finding it extremely difficult if not impossible to bring the directives of the Second Vatican Council to life in their parishes (especially the large parishes) as those parishes are now constituted.

I will not take up your time going over the problems of declining mass attendance, alienation of youth, lack of communication, etc., that beset large parishes in this day. They are only too well known. I would like to mention, however, the frustration of pastors and others working in parish ministry.

I see talented priests avoiding parish work in favor of specialities such as campus ministry, counselling, religious education, etc. I see pastors of larger parishes transferred to smaller parishes, having breakdowns, just waiting around for retirement. I believe that a substantial part of the problem lies in this fact that, at least, the large parishes are not fitted for the job the council is asking them to do. To coin a phrase—we're trying to put new wine into the old bottles.

Institution/Community

What do I mean by restructuring the parish? Mostly when we talk about models we think in terms of church in general.

Instead of talking about the institutional *church*, and *church* as community I would like to speak of the *parish* as institution and the *parish* as community. For our purposes I would like to define institution in this way: *Institution* is a grouping of people organized to put out a product, or deliver a service. For example, at General Motors people are organized as workers, sales people, etc. to produce and market automobiles. In an institution the product is important not the person.

I would define community as a group of people banded together not to put out a product or to deliver a service, but to grow in relation to one another. Example: the family. A family does not put out a product or deliver a service. Members are responsible for each other. They care for each other and in loving relationships they grow as persons.

Now let's refer these ideas to the parish situation. A parish is an institution. And this must not be minimized. A parish delivers services. It educates, cares for the poor, helps the missions, etc. But a parish is also a community. Members of a parish have a need and a right to be like an extended family, to know each other, care for each other and so grow in the love of God and of one another. My contention is that right now, organizationally, parishes are very heavy on institution and very light on community. We think institution. We think programs. We think service.

For example, suppose in the parish we are worried about our religious education program. It is not effective. Young people are not showing up. How do we meet the problem? Institutionally we must put out a better product. We will improve CCD teacher training. We'll buy the best film strips we can find. Perhaps, we'll even invest in a director of religious education. We'll give it one more try. After all this effort, maybe, children stay away in even greater numbers than before. Why? They are hungry for community, but we keep giving them institution. We emphasize product more than person.

The movements that seem spiritually alive and appealing are such groups as cursillo, marriage encounter, charismatic prayer groups, comunidades de base—groups that are person and growth oriented. It seems very odd that in most cases parishioners must go outside the parish structure to be a part of one of these movements.

My proposal is that parish structure be studied to find a model more adaptable to our times and to the vision of the council.

Both the crisis and the challenge it seems to me lie in the parish. We can strengthen commissions, conferences and departments on both national and diocesan levels, but unless their programs are able to be absorbed and implemented on the parish level, not much is accomplished.

I know a pastor who reads it like this. He says, "I feel like there is a big funnel above me. All kinds of programs are dumped into it from the top: new rite of penance, bicentennial observance, Holy Year, fight against abortion—and he listed some more—and they come down through the narrow end of that funnel right on my head."

It seems to me that beautiful programs have been developed for use in parishes. I call them secondary programs. Many of them, ideal as they are, never see the light of day, or at most only dimly, because the primary structure of the parish is faulty. It is not adapted to do the job we ask of it.

If we can say with Pope Paul, "The church is a mystery," we also can say, "The parish is a mystery." It is a reality imbued with the presence of God.

It lies, therefore, within the very nature of the parish to be always open to new and greater exploration. It is my proposal that the structures of the parish be explored so that it truly can be God's little flock.

174. Shared Responsibility in the Local Church. Pastoral Letter of Howard J. Hubbard, Bishop of Albany, New York, September 21, 1978.

An expression frequently heard in Catholic circles following Vatican Council II was the necessity to heed the 'signs of the times.' One of those signs in both the ecclesiastical and secular domains has been the emphasis on the individual person with its implications for the individual's rights, for the equality of women, for racial and ethnic groups' recognition, in fact, for minorities in general. Within the Church the implementation of these rights has quite naturally often centered on the parish, the ecclesiastical unit that brings together every segment of the people of God. That the effort to realize a 'shared responsibility' should have occasioned tension and strife in some parishes will come as no surprise. Bishop Hubbard found the basis for his approach in the council's principle of shared responsibility which he described as "truly scripturally based, theologically sound and pastorally oriented." His pastoral letter spelled out in detail how he thought that goal could be most effectively achieved. Source: *Origins*, 8 (March 15, 1979), 615-624.

I take this opportunity to share with you some reflections on my vision of the church in the Diocese of Albany after a year and a half of serving among you as your bishop.

First, I would like to express my sincere gratitude for the warm welcome and willing cooperation you, the people of the diocese, have afforded me since my episcopal ordination. Leaders can fulfill their task, which is a responsibility of service, only in an atmosphere of openness and respect. This I have experienced in superabundance. Your responsiveness has been a constant source of joy, hope and strength.

My leadership role among you flows from the mystery we call the church, that divine reality inserted into human history through which God reveals to us and shares with us the riches of his life.

Because the church is a mystery, it cannot be totally understood or fully defined. But, from its very beginning, the church has been revealed to be a community of people formed by the word of God, animated by the creative power of the Holy Spirit, and sustained by the worship and service of its members.

Community involves a sharing of beliefs, experiences, ideals and values. "Those who believe share all things in common" (Acts 2:44).

Christian community leads one to put aside selfish goals and private interests for the sake of the private good. It is based upon the willingness of all community members to accept responsibility, individually and corporately, for the way each lives, uses his or her talents and gifts, and responds to the needs and rights of others.

The early Christians celebrated their identity as a worshipping community in word and sacrament. "They devoted themselves to the apostles' instructions and communal life, to the breaking of bread and prayers" (Acts 2:42).

And the fruit of this sharing of word and sacraments was service to others. "None of their members was ever in want, as all those who owned land or houses would sell them and bring money from them to present it to the apostles; it was then distributed to any members who might be in need" (Acts 4:34-35).

The challenge for us today is to rekindle within ourselves, within our diocese and parish communities, and within the larger society, that spirit of worship, love and service that existed in the apostolic church.

To some, such a challenge may seem overwhelming given the complex nature of the world and society in which we live today.

While it is true, however, that we can't recapture fully the pristine simplicity of the apostolic community as described in the Acts of the Apostles, and while many of the structures of the early church are no longer relevant to our contemporary setting, nevertheless the same divine call beckons us, the same Spirit forms us, and the same activity of worship and service must be at the heart of our response.

Shared Responsibility

The Second Vatican Council has given us, I believe, a principle that enables us to respond to God's call and to fulfill his mission in our time. That principle is the concept of shared responsibility, a principle that is truly scripturally based, theologically sound and pastorally oriented.

Stated simply, shared responsibility (which also has been described as collegiality, coresponsibility and participatory involvement) means that each member of the church, by reason of baptism, has the right and duty to participate in the church's mission to make Christ present here on earth and to spread the liberating truth of his good news. All members of the church—clergy, religious and laity—are thus called to be "servants of Christ and stewards of the mystery of God" (1 Cor. 4:1).

In seeking to understand this concept of shared responsibility, focus must be placed on the mission that is given to each member of the church in the sacrament of baptism.

Through baptism, every Christian is brought into an intimate, personal and abiding union with Jesus and with all other Christians. The church, then, comprises a multiplicity of members who share a common sacramental dignity and equality. "We are brought into the one body of Christ by baptism, in the one Spirit, whether we are Jews or Greeks, slaves or freemen" (1 Cor. 12:13).

This sacramental dignity and equality unites pope, bishops, priests, deacons, religious and laity in the one body of Christ which is the church.

Shared responsibility then means that, since the laity as well as the clergy and religious are all configured to Christ by baptism and the other sacraments, they all have the responsibility and opportunity of participating in the saving mission of Christ in the world. The Second Vatican Council in its Dogmatic Constitution on the Church makes the point his way:

"Gathered together in the people of God and established in the one body of Christ under one head, the laity—no matter who they are—have as living members, the vocation of applying to the building up of the church, and to its continual sanctification, all the powers which they have received from the goodness of the creator and from the grace of the redeemer."

While this concept of shared responsibility is neither new nor revolutionary from a scriptural or theological perspective, practically it is one that needs to be relearned and experienced.

We are emerging from a period in church history during which the responsibility for the mission of the church was projected to be that of the hierarchy exclusively.

It was thought that the role of the pope and bishops (and by extension, in popular understanding, priests and religious) was to preach, to lead and to sanctify, while the laity were to be taught, to be led and to be sanctified.

The laity, in other words, were looked upon as having a more modest, passive role to play in the church, helping out only on a temporary, standby basis, when specifically called upon.

But the Second Vatican Council gives us an enriched understanding of the role each member of the church is to have. In its Constitution on the Church, the council declared:

"The pastors, indeed, know well how much the laity contribute to the welfare of the whole church. For they know that they themselves were not established by Christ to undertake alone the whole salvific mission of the church to the world, but it is their exalted office to be shepherds of the faithful and also to recognize the latter's contribution and charisms that everyone in their own way will, with one mind, cooperate in the common task. For all must 'practice the truth in love, and so grow up in all things in him who is the head, Christ.'"

All, then—laity, religious and clergy—are obliged to offer time, talent and resources so that the mission of Christ in his church might be fulfilled. This basic responsibility rests upon each one of us regardless of state of life or the differing roles we exercise.

Furthermore, this obligation of participating in the church's mission is marked by an interdependence which comes from the very nature of the church as a community in Christ. St. Paul, in the 12th Chapter of his first Letter to the Corinthians, likened us to one body, each member dependent upon the other.

"The body is one and has many members, but all the members, many though they are, are one body; and so it is with Christ. It was in one Spirit that all of us, whether Jew or Greek, slave or free, were baptized into the body." (12,13)

"The eye cannot say to the hand, 'I do not need you,' any

more than the head can say to the foot, 'I do not need you.'" (21)

We depend upon the Lord Jesus as the foundation of our Christian lives and we depend upon each other as members of the body of Christ. While we have differing roles and responsibilities, we are all under one head, Jesus Christ, and, through him, we need and depend upon each other as brothers and sisters.

To put this another way: Every member of the church has certain God-given gifts or talents that are to be used for serving Christ in building upon the community around us.

Again, St. Paul states it very precisely when he says:

"There is a variety of gifts but always the same Spirit; there are all sorts of services to be done but always to the same Lord; working in all sorts of different ways in different people, it is the same God who is working in all of them" (1 Cor. 12:4-7).

The message is clear. However humble our gift may be, it is needed. And while our gifts may be different, together, in their variety, they build up a Christian community by contributing to the sanctification and growth of others.

Shared responsibility is the proper discernment and exercise of these gifts in and through our worship of God, the proclamation of his message to others and our service on behalf of humankind.

To sum up: Responsibility for the mission of the church is shared by all the baptized—ordained and non-ordained, vowed and non-vowed, teacher, carpenter, housewife, businessman, young and old, resigned priest and religious, parent, single person, child— all bound together by a variety of gifts and ministries, and all serving the one mission, the mission of our Lord Jesus.

Shared responsibility, then, is neither a luxury nor a concession. Rather, it is necessary and perennial dimension of the life of the church, exercised by those who are rooted in a living and loving relationship with Christ.

It should be noted that the concept of shared responsibility fully respects the fact that the church is a unique community established by Christ into a hierarchic structure. The deacons, priests and bishops, joined with the bishop of Rome as successor of St. Peter, have the specific responsibilities of their offices described in the laws of the church.

This hierarchical structure, however, is to be exercised not in a unilateral way, but in a collegial way with opportunities for the various members of the church, in accordance with their gifts, talents and charisms, to participate in policies, decisions and mission.

The pope is the head of the church, but he acts in consultation with the body of bishops throughout the world.

The bishop is the chief shepherd in his diocese, but to fulfill his responsibility he needs the counsel and assistance of his priests, deacons, religious and laity in giving shape to the work of the church, hence the formation of priests senates, brothers, sisters and deacons councils, and diocesan pastoral councils, to consult with and advise him on pastoral matters.

Extending this principle of collegiality to the grass-roots level, parish members are to have responsibility for the mission of the church through the formation of parish councils and regional or deanery councils. Thus all members of the church are called to join in harmonious action with the pope, their bishops and pastors, sharing with them their knowledge, talent and other resources for the development of God's kingdom. My episcopal motto, "Rejoice, we are his people," seeks to affirm this truth and to invite all the faithful to make it a lived reality in our diocese.

Change is never easy, especially change that affects our self-image, our roles and our ministries. To embrace this challenge and opportunity of shared responsibility will demand a certain shift in attitudes and practices on the part of all our people.

Let me address the major groupings within our diocese and the special role I envision for each as this concept of shared responsibility becomes viable for our day.

To Priests

The priests of the diocese have been a special blessing to the church of Albany. Over the years you, my brothers, have labored with pastoral zeal and enthusiasm to promote the Christ life within our midst.

Your love and support for one another, your loyalty to the pope and the bishops of the diocese, and your devotion to the people entrusted to your care have been the source of great inspiration and major factors contributing to the vitality of our diocese.

The past 15 years have in some ways been difficult for you. Accustomed to one model of the church, you have been called not only to adapt to a new understanding of church and ministry but also to be leaders in implementing it. Your patience, enduring zeal and willingness to face these new challenges have been and continue to be special graces and reasons for profound gratitude.

In the days ahead I need your continued cooperation. As the Second Vatican Council states:

"Priests, prudent cooperators with the episcopal order as well as its aids and instruments, are called to serve the people of God. They constitute one priesthood with their bishop, although the priesthood comprises different functions. Associated with their bishop in a spirit of trust and generosity, priests make him present in a certain sense in the individual local congregations of the faithful, and take upon themselves, as far as they are able, his duties and concerns, discharging them with daily care. As they sanctify and govern under the bishop's authority that part of the Lord's flock entrusted to them, they make the universal church visible in their own locality and lend powerful assistance to the upbuilding of the whole body of Christ (cf. Eph. 4:12). Intent always upon the welfare of God's children, they must strive to lend their effort to the pastoral work of the whole diocese, and even the entire church." (Constitution on the Church, 28)

While your role is unique and indispensible, however, it is not and cannot be self-contained. Especially as we look to the future, you must be willing to share with the deacons, religious and laity of our diocese many of the roles and ministries you have traditionally been required to exercise.

With other persons entering the sanctuary as lectors, acolytes and ministers of the eucharist, or assuming responsibility for religious education, health care, social services and financial matters related to the life of the parish or diocese (many of which responsibilities were often viewed as your exclusive domain), there can well emerge questions about the proper role of the priest. As a result, there can develop the natural human reaction to cling to one's own identity or vested interest. But, in point of fact, what is emerging, I believe, is not a challenge to your role or identity but an opportunity for greater service, an opportunity to explore the interrelatedness of all ministries of the church and to facilitate their development.

More and more, then, I envision your role to be initiators, coordinators and facilitators of ministries, to help others to discover the unique gifts, talents and charisms with which they have been endowed by the Lord and to put these at the service of the whole body of Christ.

As leaders of the church, in other words, you must have a deep respect for the gifts that the Spirit bestows in great variety and must strive tirelessly to unify this variety of gifts for building up the kingdom.

As is pointed out in "As One Who Serves," the excellent contemporary commentary on the priesthood, "Your task might be compared to the conductor of an orchestra, trying to translate the vision of the composer into harmonious blends of sounds coming from a great variety of instruments, many of which you can't play yourselves. For the truly effective leader is one who can develop the talents of others and coordinate their efforts so that they complement each other and produce a superior collective effort."

It would probably be easier and more convenient, both personally and ministerially, to continue to operate as in the past. But if this happens, the Spirit will be stifled, gifts will be unused or abused, and there will be perpetuated a model of the church that is not in accord with the gospel spirit or the mandates of the Second Vatican Council.

Your special role, then, is to be enablers and facilitators of all the gifts and ministries within the Christian community so that the church in all its richness and multifaceted dimensions may be more visible in our diocese. This special role complements the uniqueness of your role at the table of the Lord. At the table, you gather God's people in all their variety together. Your role as enablers and facilitators is seen thus, as the extension of your liturgical ministry.

To Religious

The religious of our diocese, both women and men, have made an invaluable contribution to the mission of the church. Your magnificent legacy is evident both from the various apostolates in which you are engaged and from the diversity of gifts that you exercise, in our elementary schools, in our social-service programs, in the hospital and nursing home field, in parish ministry, in religious education, in the retreat-prayer movements and in many other apostolates.

Also, your response to the call for renewal extended by the Vatican Council has been superb. I would venture to say that no group within the church has responded more enthusiastically or seriously to this concept of shared responsibility enunciated in the council documents than communities of women and men religious—at times with pain and tension, at times with confusion and groping, and at times with resistance and conflicts, but always with the desire to be open and responsive to the Spirit moving in our times and with the goal to serve and to make the church and your own communities the alive and vibrant instruments of faith, love and service that they are meant to be. For all this, you have the profound gratitude of the whole diocese.

In the immediate future I would envision three special ways in which you can contribute to developing this concept of shared responsibility.

First, I would encourage you to continue to explore ways and means of intercommunity cooperation. One of the great problems in today's church is regionalism and parochialism. We have to get away from an exclusive notion of "our school," "our parish" or "our community" and focus on common needs and mission. Each community has an individual charism which should be preserved and respected. At the same time, the blending of these charisms for the good of the total mission of Christ's church is essential in our times. Through intercommunity planning and staffing, you can set a tone or climate that will enrich the whole diocese and truly foster mutual cooperation and support.

Second, if people are to realize their gifts and exercise their talents on behalf of the church, there is need for them to break from the depersonalization and lifestyle of excessive consumption, of wasteful depletion of resources, and of the affluent use of service and leisure that abound within our society today so that they can place themselves freely and selflessly at the service of the Lord and his people.

The vowed life you as religious embrace enables you to offer an irrefutable witness against consumerism and depersonalization by a lifestyle that is genuinely frugal and austere as evidenced by your disdain of money and power; by your simplicity of diet, clothing and transportation; and by your personal communal work among the spiritually, physically and psychologically poor.

The ability to be an effective counterwitness to the dehumanizing and debilitating trends of the times has always been a special charism of religious communities. Such a dynamic witness is imperative today if people are to be moved from lethargy, indifference and excess to embrace the full implications of their baptismal commitment to be faithful stewards of the mysteries of God.

Third, I would suggest that women religious in particular can play a leadership role in advancing ministerial and decision-making positions for women in the church.

The role of all women, religious and lay alike, must be upgraded in the church. We need to acknowledge the invaluable contribution women have made and are making in our diocese, in our homes, schools, religious education centers, day-care centers, parishes and in various diocesan departments and agencies; and to make available additional leadership roles in education, pastoral service, liturgy and administration.

You who are women religious, by background and training, have a distinct role to play in forging the way for increased participation of women in the parochial, deanery and diocesan mission of the church at Albany. However, in doing so, I would caution that you not focus exclusively or possessively on the role of women religious or on the question of ordination for women, but that you be first and foremost advocates for new and expanded opportunities in the church for all women.

To Permanent Deacons

The restored order of the permanent diaconate has been one of the most exciting and fruitful ministries to emerge in our postconciliar church. You who have accepted this call—and your families—have given generously and selflessly of your time and talent in preparing for ordination and in pioneering the implementation of this ministry in our diocese.

In a very brief time you have made your impact felt in our jails, hospitals, nursing homes and parishes, and in ministry among the poor, in rural areas and to various racial and ethnic groups.

Your ministry flows out of your family life and work experience and, in a unique way, bridges the false but all too frequent distinction that is made between the sacred and the secular, between the sanctuary and the pew.

In developing the concept of shared responsibility, you have a role to play in witnessing to that ministry of service that is at the heart of the charge you received at ordination—to imitate Christ, "who came not to be served but to serve and to offer his life as a ransom for many" (Mk. 10:45).

You and your families are living examples of the type of participation and involvement that is called for in today's church. You demonstrate publicly and in extraordinary fashion the possibility of blending family, work and community responsibility with a deep, service-oriented commitment to the mission of the church.

I hope that you will continue to expand you ministry in the days ahead into new areas of service that respond to the ever-changing needs of God's people and in ways that avoid a new clericalism which would rob your ministry of its fresh character and belie the concept of shared responsibility.

To Laity

The laity of our diocese have been outstanding in their loyalty and fidelity to the church and its work, responding generously and courageously to the many demands that are made of them to be the church in action.

You, the laity, through your life of prayer, solicitude for your family members and friends, and generosity to the needs of the church and the community around you, are a never-ending source of inspiration and encouragement.

Your openness to change, your hunger and thirst for things of the Spirit, and your willingness to sacrifice personally and financially for the demands of the Gospel have been truly remarkable.

You, in a particular way, are the target of this shared responsibility. As the Second Vatican Council explicitly states:

"The lay apostolate, however, is a participation in the saving ministry of the church itself. Through their baptism and confirmation, all are commissioned to that apostolate by the Lord himself. Moreover, through the sacraments, especially the holy eucharist, there is communicated and nourished that charity toward God and man which is the soul of the entire apostolate. Now, the laity are called in a special way to make the church present and operative in those places and circumstances where only through them can she become the salt of the earth. Thus every layman, by virtue of the gifts bestowed upon him is at the same time a witness and a loving instrument of the mission of the church herself, 'according to the measure of Christ's bestowal' (Eph. 4:7)." (Constitution on the Church,33)

The call to shared responsibility is both a privilege and a duty, the privilege of being an integral part of God's redemptive plan for humankind and the duty of revealing his love to others.

Yes, being church, being a member of God's people is an amazing grace and gives to each of you no matter what your call or state in life a great dignity and empowerment. I ask you to reflect frequently upon this.

Our world is filled with lonely, frightened, hurting people who feel lost, who need someone to share with them the joys, hopes, blessings and consolations of our Christian faith. The Lord is counting on you to mirror his kindness, his fidelity, his tenderness, and his love to our sin-wounded world where alienation, disaffection and disillusionment abound.

Christ has guaranteed through the Spirit that ecclesial

presence in the world will continue, but this does not prevent the light of his Gospel from going dim in a particular area, for example, in a local parish or diocese.

Thus the challenge is clear. You must work in cooperation with me and the priests, deacons and religious of our diocese to advance his kingdom. You must be willing to pledge that which is most dear to you—your personhood, time, talent and resources—and to invest these to make your life and the life of your parish and our diocese a true reflection of Jesus and his way of life.

I pray that you will embrace this challenge zealously and enthusiastically, and that you will be patient with me and our priests and religious as we continue to implement this collegial model of the church in our diocese.

Like all transitions, this move to shared responsibility for the church's mission will have its ups and downs, its successes and failures, but I am convinced that this is what the Spirit is calling us to and that your willingness to accept this challenge is the key to our future.

While this concept of shared responsibility applies to all aspects of the church's mission, in our diocese I would suggest three immediate areas of focus for its implementation: in the parish, in the family and in the whole area of reconciliation and evangelization.

The Parish

The parish has been and will continue to be the center of the church's life. It is the spiritual descendant of the early Christian community that was described at the outset of this pastoral letter.

The parish is meant to be a group of Christians who pray and worship together and who extend that worship in their lives by helping each other with spiritual, emotional and financial support.

Today, with the isolation of the family, massive mobility, alienation and loneliness, there is less structure in our society for people to come together and to support each other through interdependence. Yet the basis of Christianity rests on the requirements of mutual interdependence. The parish is where the interdependence should happen, where support systems for Christian service must constantly be developed.

Father Eugene Mainelli puts it this way:

"It is ultimately in the parish where God's revelation and love and people's efforts touch in a special and supportive community. All the movements of Christian life today—ecumenism, spiritual renewal, community action, and social service, and church reform itself—will take root and flourish if at all in the local communities of faith, the parishes." (Social Thought, Fall, 1975, Vol 1, No. 2)

While some predict the demise of the parish, I am convinced that the parish, be it territorial, ethnic or by commonality of interest, will remain the normal and usual way we as Catholics organize ourselves for Christian life and work. This does not mean, of course, that all parishes must function in the same manner or that the style of parish life for the future must be predicated on the past. Forms of parish life must change and be ever responsive to the changing communities they serve.

There will always be need, however, for tangible structures wherein people can experience the loving presence of the Lord and build community by sharing his redemptive and liberating love with others. That structure is the parish.

To achieve its purpose, the parish must provide a climate of mutual acceptance and support. The unique gifts possessed by every member must be promoted. The parish must demonstrate a collaborative relationship among all.

The parish council is the instrument or vehicle for ensuring this collaboration. The parish council is both a ministry and the sign of a true Chrstian community. It is a partnership that gives witness, not only to what the parish is, but especially to what the parish is called to be. It shares in setting directions and it calls the people to walk in the way of the risen Lord.

Already in our diocese we have many active and fruitful parish councils. I hope they will continue to grow and flourish. I encourage members of existing parish councils constantly to review their purposes and their manner of functioning. At times, councils can tend to function routinely, doing what has been done in the past without evaluating the effectiveness of existing activities or looking to new challenges. Continuing needs assessment, evaluation of programs and activities, and accountability for areas of responsibility are essential for an effective and alive parish council and parish community. I ask our office of pastoral planning and our diocesan pastoral council to be of assistance to parish councils that are seeking to grow and to revitalize themselves through goal planning and evaluation.

I also ask that, in those parishes where councils do not exist, some process begin to ensure the establishment of such. I strongly encourage that every parish of the diocese have a functioning, truly representative parish council or its equivalent by 1981.

Again, our office of pastoral planning and our diocesan pastoral council are requested to give leadership in this regard. A thorough process of education and parishwide consultation is the best way to begin this effort.

Parish councils are not intended to undermine or to usurp the role of the pastor or the parish staff. The pastor exercises a key role of leadership in the parish in the name and by the authority of the bishop. Together with the parish staff, the pastor has the responsibility for overseeing the development of the parish's growth and implementing policy decisions emanating from the church universal, the diocese and the parish. But the pastor and his staff can best fulfill this responsibility when a well-informed, spiritually alive, truly representative parish council can offer its best counsel and advice.

As I pointed out previously, the pastor's leadership role is more and more that of enabling and coordinating. He must facilitate the sharing of decision making and the delegation of leadership for various parish responsibilities, services and activities. He should do this in consultation with his brother priests and with the religious and the laity of the staff. Through the convening of regular meetings, joint planning and evaluation, and regular sharing of information and experience, the parish staff under the guidance of the pastor can be a real model of shared responsibility and leadership for the parish council and the entire parish.

The ultimate purpose of every parish is to foster the development of the Christ life and to promote the mission of the church. This mission has many aspects; no one of them may be isolated from the other, and every one of them serves to form and complement the others. For purposes of organization and communication, in our diocese, we suggest that all parish activity be grouped under one of four areas of mission: prayer and worship, Christian education, Christian service, and church administration.

Prayer and Worship

The whole church, baptized in Jesus, shares his priesthood and therefore has the privileged responsibility of worshiping God and joining in the celebration of the sacraments, especially the eucharist.

Every baptized member of the church is part of the holy people. When we join together for the celebration of the eucharist and the other sacraments, we do so not only as individuals, but also as people joined in faith to our brothers and sisters. To become a prayerful, worshiping community is a most essential goal for every parish.

Within this worshiping parish community, different liturgical roles are performed. The laity are called to exercise various ministries, such as reader, cantor, choir, musician, artist, usher, server and minister of communion. They are coordinated and led by the ordained priest who has the unique responsibility of providing prayerful celebrations that evoke a response of faith. It is his responsibility to pronounce the eucharistic prayers at Mass, to absolve in the sacrament of reconciliation, to administer the other sacraments and, along with the deacon, to proclaim the Gospel and offer fitting homilies.

The liturgy itself is to be expressive of the needs in the parish community, the size of the congregation, age level, cultural or ethnic backgrounds, resources of the community and much more. Parish liturgies must be responsive to people's needs and reflective of their lives. Otherwise the heart of parish life is severely crippled.

That is why liturgical planning is so important. It is essential that the priests, deacons, lectors, cantors, musicians, organists, artists and other liturgical ministers be well-trained in their roles and that the celebrations themselves be well-planned and carefully coordinated. This is best achieved by an ongoing parish liturgical team which seeks to develop a climate of prayerful and joyful celebration.

I urge formation of such a team in each parish under the auspices of the parish council and I pledge myself to form a diocesan liturgical team to be a resource and guide for local parish communities.

The parish liturgy team must concern itself not only with the eucharistic liturgy, "the source and summit of the Christian life," but also with the fostering of other forms of prayer as well since, as St. Paul admonishes, "We must pray always."

Particularly noteworthy in today's church is the growth of the charismatic renewal throughout the world and in our diocese. This movement, which highlights the presence of the Spirit in our midst and the centrality of Jesus in our lives, has much to teach all of us about the alive sense of praise, joy, hope and thanksgiving that we need to express in our prayers and worship.

I also applaud the efficacious prayer experiences fostered by the Apostolate of the Suffering in our diocese. This apostolate provides a visible witness to the type of vital contribution that can be made by shut-ins and by those confined to hospitals and nursing homes.

A rich and reverent prayer life must be at the core of every Christian's existence. Otherwise our life will be empty and our activity futile.

Karl Rahner has expressed the idea that in a world with few institutional supports for religion, the only Christians in the future will be those who have an experience of God. Prayer, however one may define it and of whatever style if may be, is the only way to gain that experience and to lead others to him.

Christian Education

The foundation of every parish is faith in God. The growth and maintenance of that faith are the responsibility of every member of the parish community. Unfortunately, faith formation or religious education has been too often reserved only for children or students and for those who have the responsibility for formal teaching, namely priests, deacons, religious and teachers of religion.

However, no one of us ever stops developing. No one of us ever reaches total assurance on deep and troubling questions. No one of us grows so mature that we do not need reflection to renew once again our commitment to God, self and fellow human beings.

That is why our approach to religious education must be total—directed to the total person in his or her concrete life circumstance and to the total parish community. That is also why I consider continuing religious education for adults—clergy, religious and laity—to be of critical importance in striving to implement the concept of shared responsibility.

The bishops of the United States stated it well in their pastoral letter, "To Teach as Jesus Did," when they defined the continuing education of adults as being "situated not at the periphery of the church's educational mission but at its center."

In the past, the parish has tended to concentrate its religious education efforts on one or two approaches—a school, a religious education program for public-school youngsters, an annual or semiannual adult discussion course or seminar. These approaches have served, and continue to serve, the ends of Christian education. But, good as they are, they constantly need to be reassessed to ascertain if they are really still preaching the good news effectively and exciting people to a love for the Lord and each other.

Furthermore, varied and flexible programs must be developed. It has become very clear that there are teachable moments in each person's life. We must seize upon those moments to address the person in the name of Jesus and his message.

The liturgy, for example, can be a prime source of deepened faith understanding through message and worship. Sacramental preparation programs provide a similar opportunity.

Parish communities must also search for ways to provide religious education and faith sharing in each apostolate and ministry. Youth groups, folk-music ensembles, prayer groups, altar boys, lay ministers, senior-citizen groups, PTAs, parish-council sessions, Altar, Rosary and Holy Names societies, Cursillo groups and Marriage Encounter circles, all provide fertile opportunities to share the meaning of religion in the life of their members.

Experiences of faith formation such as Search, PET, days of renewal, retreats, Engaged, Marriage, and Family Encounters, also offer great opportunities for growth and development.

I would note, too, the superb contribution our diocesan newspaper, The Evangelist, makes in providing for our people up-to-date news and commentary about trends, developments and movements in the life of the church. I cannot recommend highly enough regular reading of this weekly as a major tool for one's continued religious education.

We must be more than informed about our faith, however; we must also realize our responsibility to share it with others. People have this responsibility on different levels:

1. Each one of us must be willing to search out opportunities for ongoing formation through reading, study and courses, and to share with family, friends and neighbors our own convictions of faith.

2. Parents have a special and inalienable responsibility to share their faith with their children. Although Catholic schools and parish schools of religion exist to help fulfill this responsibility, they cannot substitute for it. This responsibility will be most fruitfully filled by lives lived in Christ.

3. The pastor, parish staff and parish council have the responsibility to see that a variety of formal and informal faith-formation programs such as are described above are available for all segments of the parish community. In this regard, I am especially grateful to the religious and laity who teach in our parochial schools of religion. Their willingness to update themselves and to bring the teachings of Jesus to others is one of the precious treasures of our contemporary church.

4. The bishop and his offices for schools and religious education must provide overall direction and guidance. Regional boards for religious education and school boards participate in this responsibility in a special way. So, too, do those who teach in diocesan and private Catholic high schools, our Catholic colleges and in our campus ministry programs, bringing the gospel message to these special settings.

To assist in developing that total approach to education, parochially, regionally and diocesanwide, mentioned earlier and envisioned in the bishops' pastoral "To Teach as Jesus Did," I have commissioned a task force to study and propose potential models for total education and I have asked our planning office to assist the task force with this study.

I recognize the crisis that confronts our Catholic schools today. They have had a very special place in nurturing the faith of our people and in transmitting Christian values. Increasingly, however, inflation, declining religious personnel and dwindling enrollments have necessitated the closing of some schools and the consolidation or regionalization of others.

It is obvious that the cherished ideal of a Catholic-school education for every Catholic child is not and cannot be a reality. But it is also obvious that there is need in our pluralistic society, an increasingly secular one at that, for a system of education that seeks to integrate religious truths and values with life. Our Catholic schools provide that alternative.

I encourage our people to support our Catholic schools by enrolling their children and by personal and financial sacrifices required to ensure that the vitality of our schools is not a faded dream but a pledge for the future.

I also ask our diocesan school board and office and all regional and parochial school boards to continue the exploration of concepts, such as negotiated tuition, grants in aid, clustering and shared facilities, so that the most prudent use may be made of our financial and personnel resources. In particular, I ask that ways be developed to ensure that financial criteria do not exclude the poor and disadvantaged from sharing the rich heritage of a Catholic school education.

Christian Service

In addition to being a community of faith and worship, the parish must also be a community of service, a community of caring and sharing, made up of people who seek to reach out to the poor, sick, aging, isolated and alienated.

The Synod of Bishops in 1971 reminded us that efforts on behalf of justice are a constitutive element of the Christian life, as much a part of it as the proclamation of God's word and the celebration of the sacrments.

This service dimension of the Christian life needs to be strongly emphasized. Many of us grew up with the notion that political, social and economic issues had little, if anything at all, to do with living our faith. Social involvement and efforts on behalf of justice were looked upon as either unrelated or peripheral to the core of our faith, as something optional that could be accepted or rejected at one's pleasure.

However, in our times, we have been reminded that our personal and communal lives, like the life of Jesus, must be characterized by a profound concern for people in their concrete human situation, a concern rooted in a response to the Father's love that finds its full expression in our love for and involvement with our fellow human beings.

We have been told, in other words, that a ministry of service and justice must be an integral and essential part of every Christian life, and part and parcel of the life of every parish community. The Vatican Council, for example, stated that, "The joys and hopes, the griefs and anxieties of all, especially those who are poor or in any way afflicted, should be the hopes, griefs, anxieties of the followers of Christ." (Pastoral Constitution on the Church in the Modern World, 1)

And the popes of this century, as well as statements of the National Conference of Catholic Bishops, have reminded us repeatedly of needed programs for peace, respect for life, civil reform, responsible use of the world's resources, disarmament, the elimination of drug abuse, care for the mentally and physically handicapped, legislation safeguarding the rights of the family, neighborhood preservation and many other concerns that flow from our social involvement. These programs must be directed not only toward the alleviation of human misery, but also toward changing those forces that cause such misery—toward what is referred to as "systemic change."

Our diocesan office of health and social services and our commission for peace and justice have given visionary leadership in this area. But these efforts will be effective only insofar as they are translated into tangible programs and actions in the lives of our people, especially at the parish level.

Each parish community, then, should have a committee or

group to deal with these social needs in cooperation with other parishes, other churches and synagogues, and the diocesan and community agencies established to deal with such issues.

It is the responsibility of a parish social service or social action committee to call critical social needs to the attention of parishioners and to facilitate their participation in programs to alleviate them. In all this, we must affirm our resolve to serve not only the needs of the parish but also the needs of the larger diocesan, national and world communities.

Over the years, members of parish-based organizations, such as the St. Vincent de Paul Society, the Legion of Mary, the Rosary Society and Holy Names Society, and other church-related groups such as the Knights of Columbus, the Knights of St. John, the Catholic Daughters of America, the Ladies of Charity and the Catholic Women's Service League, have responded personally, compassionately, and productively to human needs.

More recently, however, given the antiseptic, computerized society in which we live, with its greater emphasis on governmental and church bureaucracy, there has been the trend to a pocketbook mentality toward service and charity, with as little personal involvement as possible. The government, professionally staffed church organization or United Fund agencies have increasingly been looked upon to do the job in the field of human services, relieving the individual and the parish community of their responsibility for Christian service.

Such an approach has been well-intentioned; in practice, however, it has far too often contributed to polarization and alienation. It has isolated young from old, the well from the ill, the mentally stable from the emotionally troubled, the incarcerated from the free, the affluent from the poor, the well-housed from those in slums, the favored majorities from the depressed minorities. There have been notable exceptions but, for the most part, each group has grown a universe apart from its opposite, with the comfortable segment increasingly isolating itself physically and mentally from getting involved beyond writing a check or paying taxes for welfare appropriations.

As a result, people at all social and economic levels, I believe, are fed up and disillusioned with our social condition. They yearn for and are willing to invest themselves in a thrust that will involve individuals, families, parishes and the church as a whole in a truly personal ministry of love, concern and help wherever it is needed—in our hospitals, nursing homes, jails, inner cities, rural communities, and local neighborhoods, and among young and old, rich and poor, black and white, brown and red, educated and uneducated.

Therefore, I challenge all our people to do this type of personalized service and selfless utilization of their time, gifts and talents on behalf of others. I ask that this service thrust be parish based even when it is ecumenically or regionally oriented.

Further, I call for the development of a diocesan service corps composed of individuals willing to give from one to three years of their time to volunteer for a service commitment in one of our parishes or parish-oriented projects.

I am commissioning a task force composed of members from the diocesan office of health and social services, campus ministry, chancery and stewardship office to address the issues of recruitment, placement and finances, and to establish a model to be operational by 1980. I believe that the need for such is pressing, that people, especially young adults, will volunteer, and that such a corps will be a dynamic stimulant to all our people to exercise the call to service that is addressed to each of us.

I am convinced, especially given the dehumanized and depersonalized climate that prevails in our society today, that the more visible and viable our ministry of service becomes, the more credible and attractive our ministry of word and sacrament will be.

Church Administration

If there is one area of church life that we may tend to underestimate or even belittle, it is the ministry of administration—that ministry which deals with the proper management of finances, property and resources so that the worship, education and service ministry of the church might be fulfilled.

Paul, in his first Letter to the Corinthians, refers to administration as one of the gifts given to the Christian community, along with prophecy, teaching and others (1 Cor. 12:28). The prudent exercise of this gift or charism is of critical importance if the overall mission of the church is to be accomplished.

The administrative task in every parish grows larger and larger each day, as aging buildings need repairs, as new ones must be constructed, as mandatory personnel benefits change, as church and governmental structures demand more accountability, as school and religious-education costs rise, and as parish-giving and fund-raising activities struggle to keep pace with soaring inflation.

As a consequence, more and more effort and energy must be directed to these pressing matters. Unfortunately, the pastor and other parish staff increasingly find themselves devoting their labors to these efforts, detracting proportionately from their other pressing responsibilities.

This is unfortunate because pastoral staff frequently become demoralized when so much of their energy is consumed in administrative and fund-rasing areas of parish life, and because most parish staffs do not have training or expertise in the fields of budgeting, building maintenance and administrative procedures.

Administration, then, is a crucial ministry which must be shared, especially with competent lay people. It requires a commitment of people with expertise in planning, finances and management to lend their gifts to the fulfillment of the parish mission. Also to be considered is a willingness to share resources, personnel and other advantages on an interparochial, regional and ecumenical basis.

It should be stressed that the administrative component must be harmonized with gospel values and overall diocesan and parish goals so that administrative concerns do not themselves set priorities but are addressed within a context of the parish's overall mission.

What I seek to underscore is that the parish must be the hub and center of the church's life—a life that is shared with all members of the community whose unique and indispensible gifts and talents are essential to the mission of the church.

To highlight my concern for, and commitment to, the vitality of parish life, I pledge myself to visit the parishes of the diocese over the next four years, apart from the regular cycle of confirmation. I will seek out the opportunity to discuss with the pastor, parish staff, parish-council members and the entire parish community their views about the vision of parish life herein proposed, and to assess and evaluate the implementation of such at the local level.

Also, to ensure ongoing action and communication between the bishop's office and the parishes, and to stimulate interparochial planning and cooperation, I ask that in addition to the formation of parish councils, regional (or deanery) councils be formed. I request the diocesan pastoral council to oversee the development of this concept.

I believe that my role as chief shepherd will be only as effective as the advice and counsel I receive. The diocesan pastoral council is designated as the chief advisory board to the bishop in his diocese. But this collegial body will function adequately and responsibly only insofar as it is in dialogue with and truly representative of active parish and regional councils.

What is called for, then, is shared responsibility at the parish, regional and diocesan level, so that we—bishop, priests, deacons, religious and laity—are truly a people on pilgrimage together who cooperatively and collaboratively seek to advance the kingdom of God here on earth.

All this is involved in the term stewardship: the use of one's time, talent and treasure on behalf of the Gospel. That is why our recently created office of stewardship is so important: to assist parishes, in conjunction with our office of pastoral planning, in assessing needs, recruiting people and developing the financial resources to fulfill the ministry of word, sacrament and service.

There are two other special emphases I would envision for the immediate future to enhance parish life and to spark this concept of shared responsibility, namely, family life, and reconciliation and evangelization.

The Family

If the parish is the foundation of the church, the family is the cornerstone of the parish. As a matter of fact, there is a reciprocal relationship between the natural family and the parish family; these two basic units of our church and society are called to be in ministry to each other.

The family is the church in miniature. Therefore, the church, especially at the parish level, must try to minister to families with renewed understanding, compassion and competency to help family members grow and serve others. In so doing, the church herself will be revitalized and enriched.

The Call to Action Conference, sponsored by the U.S. bishops in 1976 as part of the church's bicentennial observance, revealed that family-related issues were the foremost issues surfaced from among thousands of pastoral and social concerns that were identified. Our people, then, are looking to the church as the preeminent institution in our turbulent society to help couples and family members deal with the challenges of family life such as divorce and separation, premarital and extramarital sexual activity, out-of-wedlock activities and juvenile deliquency.

The church's primary responsibility in this regard is to help families experience God's love through a prayerful, spirit-filled parish community of faith and charity—and to encourage the involvement of families in Christian service to other families in the parish and to the entire community.

The church, in other words, must articulate the message of Jesus as revealed in the scriptures and as shared through the church's tradition and sacramental life. But, at the same time, the church must recognize that ministry to and for families must essentially involve a ministry of the laity—a ministry by families.

The key to family life, then, is to be found in the family itself becoming aware of its Christian mission. The family must become an active agent within the church for renewal and change; it must foster caring and sharing among its own members which then spills over into the same type of loving, caring concern in the wider community.

In this way, there is a true complementarity between parish and family: the parish supporting families spiritually and sacramentally in their efforts to live in fidelity and peace, and challenging families to heroism and greater holiness by becoming centers of apostolic service; and families, in so responding, making the message and the mission of the parish more credible and attractive to others.

Over the years, our church had a rich heritage of support for family life. Our parishes, our schools and religious education programs, and our system of social service and health care, have served many important purposes but none more important than that of supporting the family, enriching it through contacts with other families, affirming it through preaching and sacrament, and bolstering it through programs of education.

Today we face new problems and new challenges. We don't have all the answers, but we do have the framework, the value system and the faith dimension within which viable, creative options can be developed.

Therefore, I ask our family life commission and those vital movements such as Marriage Encounter and Cursillo, which have proven so effective in strengthening marriage and family life, to assist our parish families with resources and programs that will promote personal, social and spiritual family growth and that will combat those utilitarian, materialistic and hedonistic forces that challenge the integrity of marriage and family.

Specifically, we need to offer comprehensive programs providing long-range as well as immediate marriage preparation for young people, foster family activities in parishes, ministering to hurting families, advocating public policy that will enshrine the family as a cornerstone of society, affirming the ethnic and racial character of various families, and encouraging greater experiences for married couples, single parents and functioning family units.

A special ministry to separated and divorced Catholics must also be developed. Too often these members have been neglected by the church, causing them to live painful, lonely lives, sometimes alienated from their spiritual home when remarriage has occurred. Renewed efforts must be made to assist these suffering brothers and sisters in their particular plight.

It pains me to learn how many Catholics are misinformed about the status of divorce and separated Catholics and how many myths exist about the grounds for a church annulment, the cost of pursuing such and the length of time for the process.

I ask our diocesan marriage tribunal to continue its efforts to assist those who seek annulments. I further ask all those in pastoral positions to be sensitive to the divorced and remarried, to acquaint them with the rights and opportunities available for them, and to create among all our people a climate of understanding.

I also ask our family life commission to develop support groups for the separated and divorced at the parish or regional level, especially for single parents, to provide them with the spiritual and emotional assistance they need to cope with their particular problems.

In focusing upon family life, I don't mean in any way to ignore or downplay the vocation of those who lead single lives. Theirs, too, is a unique vocation within the church and a witness to the Christian life in a special way. Most single persons, however, are part of a family system in which they can use their gifts and receive love and support. Parishes, nonetheless, must be sensitive not to exclude singles from their programs and activities and must have a special concern for widows and widowers. I am most pleased by the renewed activity of our singles group in the diocese and encourage the growth of this type of movement throughout our diocese.

There are two special contributions I would ask families to make to the larger church. The first is for parents and family members to pray for vocations to the priesthood and religious life, and to encourage family members to consider these indispensible vocations in the Christian community. The family is the domestic church. It is in the home that the Christian life is most fully lived and experienced. It is from this context that vocations must emerge.

Second, I believe that the family is the place where the church's concern about respect for human life can most effectively be taught and appreciated. This loving interaction of family members can best convey the inherent value of every human life and underscore that this value is determined not by what a person does or produces, but rather by the simple fact that each person has been called into existence by God and is loved by him.

In the life cycle of family members, there is an unparalleled opportunity to give living witness to our belief in the sacredness of human life: in the unborn, the young, the sick and the aging. Yes, the family is the best school for conveying information about sex, communicating caring attitudes toward the poor and disadvantaged, and showing respect for life that is less than perfect.

If our families can communicate this respect for life at each stage in the life spectrum, then the problems of abortion, illegitimacy and injustice at all levels wil be substantially reduced.

Reconciliation and Evangelization

The other major emphasis I envision permeating parish life and making the concept of shared responsibility come alive in the immediate future is the call to reconciliation and evangelization.

There are thousands of Roman Catholics in our diocese who need to hear anew or afresh the good news of our Lord, Jesus Christ. They differ widely in their degree of commitment to, and living of, their faith. Those Roman Catholics actively living and practicing their faith need to hear a message of hope and encouragement; they need to be nourished in their living out of their faith commitment. Those who are tepid in their faith need an invitation to come and know the Lord in a more intimate and personal way. And those who are alienated from their faith, for whatever reason, need to hear a word of welcome and healing.

There are many within our community who have fallen away from the practice of faith. This could be for a variety of reasons. Perhaps they find themselves in a situation which they believe separates them from the Roman Catholic community. Perhaps they feel they were insulted by a priest, or religious or lay person. Or perhaps they have difficulty in understanding some of the church's moral, doctrinal or social teachings, or in accepting the changes which have come about. We, as a community, need to reach out to these brothers and sisters in a gentle, loving way.

In addition, there are untold numbers in our diocese who are totally unchurched, belonging to no ecclesial community, never having heard the message of Jesus. They need someone to share with them the hopes, joys, blessings, consolations and challenges of our Christian faith.

What is needed is both reconciliation within our own

membership and evangelization to the unchurched who so desperately need to hear the saving message of Jesus.

I firmly believe that the time is ripe for such a thrust. Some may argue that we should wait for the day when our own house is in better spiritual condition, when all our diocesan and parish communities are models of what has been outlined in this letter, before reaching out in such a fashion. However, the Christian community has never been in perfect order and never will be until the *parousia*. We are pilgrim people who are always in need of reform, who always fall somewhat short of the mark as we wait for the coming of our Lord and savior, Jesus Christ. Until that day, we must live in joyful hope, sharing as best we can the good news of his kingdom.

To launch this approach, I designate Lent of 1979 as a time for reconciliation within the Roman Catholic Diocese of Albany. I propose to reach out to as many members of our diocesan community as possible by conducting a diocesan retreat during the week of March 26, using the medium of television.

The specifics of this program will be explained at a later date. But I envision this to be a program directed to and involving all our people, priests and deacons, religious and laity, practicing and alienated. My role as bishop will be to set the tone, to offer the call to reconciliation and recommitment. But the response to this call must be at the parish or regional level. This is absolutely essential for impact and follow-through.

If such a program is to be a success, it will require the application of the concept of shared responsibility. Our priests, with the aid of deacons, must present the program in their parishes and be available for discussion, counseling and sacramental ministry. Our religious must prepare those whom they serve in their apostolates to hear this call and be ready to assist them in making their response. Our laity must minister to one another in a peer-to-peer approach to arouse interest and enthusiasm. And all of us must be willing to prepare our hearts to receive God's word and to respond to the movement of the Spirit among us.

I ask then, that our people begin immediately to pray for the success of this program and that all cooperate fully so that, personally, we might become better followers of our Lord and that, communally we might be more ardent evangelists in a world that is hungering and thirsting for his message.

A detailed and specific treatment of our relations with other churches and ecclesial bodies does not fit within the scope of this letter. Where it was appropriate, however, I have alluded to the possibilities of ecumenical and interfaith collaboration. It is my abiding hope that all our efforts will be exerted as much as possible in the spirit of ecumenism, that is, with concern for Christian unity and with attention to cooperation with all persons of good will.

Conclusion

In conclusion, I express the hope and prayer that the directions presented in this pastoral letter will serve as the basis for prayerful reflection and constructive reaction on the part of all our people.

This pastoral letter is presented in the spirit of shared responsibility, not as the final word, but as a direction and as a stimulus to discussion, dialogue and action. Some may think that the considerations presented here are moving us ahead on our pilgrim journey too quickly; others may think that the directions presented do not move us forward quickly enough. We must remember, however, that the church is not and cannot be the community any one of us wants it to be. Rather, through our honest and prayerful interaction with one another, we hope it will become that community of faith, love and service described in the Book of Acts, and which the Spirit, in his own inscrutable ways, is guiding it to be.

Let us rejoice, then, that we are his people.

175. Statement on Central America. United States Catholic Conference, November 19, 1981.

With reference to the period since the independence movements of the 1820's, J. Lloyd Mecham stated, "Religion has been one of the most disturbing factors in the history of the republics of Central America," where the bitter politico-ecclesiastic conflicts have been the result of "attempts to enforce unwise policies, pro and anticlerical." [*Church and State in Latin America.* rev. ed. Chapel Hill: University of North Carolina Press. 1966. p. 308] In recent years these conflicts have intensified as they became entwined with the struggle for justice on the part of the masses, the threat of Marxist infiltration, and of United States intervention. The abuse—at times even the murder—of American missionaries in that region has naturally heightened the concern of American Catholics. Repeated statements have been issued calling for an end to armed conflict, the establishment of justice for the oppressed, and for the American government to lend assistance in ways other than arms. Probably in no part of the international scene since the 1970's has the attitude of the bishops been more closely concentrated in relation to United States foreign policy than in Central America. Source: Hugh J. Nolan (Ed.), *Pastoral Letters of the United States Catholic Bishops.* Washington: National Conference of Catholic Bishops. 1984. IV, 464-468.

---

1.   Central America has become a focal point of concern and attention in the United States. In every country of Central America the Catholic Church plays a significant role. In word and deed, in the actions of bishops, priests, religious, and lay people, the Church daily influences the flow of events precisely because it is so intimately identified with the people of those countries in their pilgrimage of faith and their pursuit of justice. In the 1979 Puebla meeting, the Latin American bishops provided a description of the fundamental force they see lying just below the surface of the sometimes confusing ebb and flow of events in their continent:

> From the depths of the countries which make up Latin America a cry is rising to heaven, growing louder and more alarming all the time. It is the cry of a suffering people who demand justice, freedom and respect for the basic rights of human beings and peoples (Puebla Document, No. 87).

2.   In responding to this cry, the Church in Central America has taken its direction from the Second Vatican Council, from Paul VI's "The Progress of Peoples" (1967), from the Medellin (1968) and Puebla (1979) conferences of the Latin American bishops, and from Pope John Paul II's addresses at Puebla and in Brazil. These sources have shaped a pastoral witness in which the Church has affirmed its own need for conversion, and has tried to respond to cries of the poor by seeking to identify with its people in their struggle for true justice. The decisions have produced a new and challenging style of ministry. In turn many have paid a heavy price: a number of priests and missionaries killed in El Salvador, including Archbishop Romero and the four U.S. women missionaries; an additional number killed in Guatemala, including Father Stanley Rother, murdered on July 28, 1981. To these and other missionaries who have given their lives, we pay tribute.

3.   The killing of these missionaries from the United States vividly reminds us of our relationship to the drama of Central America, but this is not our only bond. Those who go from the United States to serve in Central America, as well as local leadership of the Church in these countries, have often described the multiple ways in which the United States daily influences the destiny of people in these neighboring nations. The bonds between the United States and Central America are complex and diverse; they are political, cultural, economic, and religious. They are shaped by over two centuries of history and they differ in each country. This Statement cannot possibly examine these relationships in a detailed manner, but as bishops in the United States we feel a special tie to our brother bishops and to the Church in Central America. The witness of the Church there calls forth our own witness, one which seeks to address decisions taken in the United States whose consequences directly affect our sisters and brothers in the faith.

4.   There are many voices, both governmental and nongovernmental, which seek to shape our vision of Central America today. Even a cursory knowledge of the region impresses an observer with the complexity of events within each country. But some have argued that the dominant reality which must concern us is the place of Central America in the United States-Soviet global competition.

5.   In preparing this Statement, we have reviewed again the major arguments in the U.S. public debate on Central America. We have compared and evaluated them in the light of the information we have from the Church in Central America. Church leaders there speak primarily and most frequently about the internal reality of their countries: about the daily struggle of existence of the majority of their people, about the need for just social structures internally, and the right to self-determination, even as small nations, in their relationships with other countries.

6.   There is no question here of the ecclesiastical leadership in Central America being naive or confused about the threat which Soviet dominated forces could play in their societies. The Catholic Church in Latin America, as elsewhere, has hardly been complacent about communism. The Latin American Church has repeatedly stated in the last decade that external subversion is not the primary threat or principal cause of conflict in these countries. The dominant challenge is the internal conditions of poverty and the denial of basic human rights which characterize many of these societies. These conditions, if unattended, become an invitation for intervention.

7.   These conditions must be assessed country by country, but our general purpose here is to say again that the U.S. approach to Central America should be based upon an understanding of these internal realities and the way in which our policies and practices affect them. We do, of course, join our brother bishops in Central America, opposing as well any military assistance that Cuba or the

Soviet Union may provide directly or indirectly to the contending forces in that region.

8.   Any conception of the problems in Central America which is cast principally in terms of global security issues, military responses, arms transfers, and preservation of a situation which fails to promote meaningful participation of the majority of the population in their societies is, in our view, profoundly mistaken. It is to provide a different emphasis that we offer the following reflections.

9.   El Salvador: In congressional testimony and previous statements of the U.S. Catholic Conference (USCC), we have addressed the problem of El Salvador on a regular basis since February 1980 when the late Archbishop Romero called for a change in U.S. policy. Our position has been and continues to be shaped by three themes.

10.   First, following Archbishop Romero and now Bishop Rivera y Damas, we are convinced that outside military assistance from any source to any party is not a useful contribution but simply intensifies the cycle of violence in El Salvador. For this reason we have opposed and continue to oppose military aid from all sources, while supporting monitored economic assistance by the United States. We support political measures to prevent the flow of arms from other nations to El Salvador, even as we continue to oppose U.S. military assistance to the government of El Salvador.

11.   Second, we endorse and support Bishop Rivera y Damas's call for a broad-based political solution in El Salvador. At this time we wish to call attention to the crucial and creative role the United States can and should play in supporting a political rather than a military solution to the tragic conflict in El Salvador. If the United States is to play the significant role open to it, it must make efforts to persuade the major protagonists to halt the armed conflict and engage in constructive dialogue; it must assist them in healing the wounds with economic, educational, and nutritional aid. If valid elections are to be the final product of a political solution, they will come about only after appropriate preconditions are fulfilled.

12.   Third, we wish to reaffirm the position of the administrative board of the USCC regarding Salvadoran exiles now in the United States. Many have been and are being deported and others face the threat of deportation. We believe that as long as the present state of violence and turmoil exists in El Salvador, the citizens of that country, regardless of political philosophy, should not be forced to return home. Hence, we urge that a moratorium be placed on all deportations to El Salvador, at least until such time as the government in power can guarantee the safety of its citizens. We are also mindful of the suffering of large numbers of Salvadoran refugees and displaced persons in other countries; we pledge our material assistance and ask other nations also to respond to their needs.

13.   Nicaragua: The agony of war which presently ravages El Salvador is now a memory for Nicaraguans. But they presently face major political and social questions about the future direction of their society. Two central questions confronting Nicaragua are its internal direction and its external relations.

14.   Internally, Nicaragua is experiencing great difficulty in pursuing political and economic reconstruction from the devastation of war. Although stripped of essential resources, the government and people have tried to guarantee basic necessities for the population. While acknowledging these facts, we also share the concerns expressed recently by our brother bishops in Nicaragua about increasing restrictions on human rights. It is crucially important that the religious character of the society be faithfully preserved, and that the rights of free association, speech, press, and freedom of education be protected, even as the social and economic needs of the people continue to be met.

15.   The immediate question facing us as bishops in the United States is the policy of our government toward Nicaragua. We believe that a policy designed to isolate Nicaragua and prevent its access to resources crucially needed for reconstruction is neither justified by our history with Nicaragua nor useful for the Nicaraguan people. Hence we continue to support, as we have in the past, economic assistance on a bilateral and multilateral basis for Nicaragua. Such assistance should be monitored, for Nicaragua as for other countries, in terms of human rights criteria. In our view a mature, cooperative, diplomatic relationship between the United States and Nicaragua could be a force for human rights and stability in Central America.

16.   Guatemala: We deplore the escalating violence in Guatemala as described in the statement of the Guatemalan bishops on June 13, 1980: "The acts of violence among us have taken on unimaginable forms: there are murders, kidnappings, torture, and even vicious desecrations of the victims' bodies."

17.   The death toll from politically motivated murders is estimated by the U.S. Department of State to be seventy-five to one hundred per month. In a statement issued only two weeks prior to Father Rother's murder, the bishops of Guatemala asserted that they saw in the assassination of priests and religious a pattern of violence designed to silence the voice of the Church.

18.   The bishops spoke again to the violence in their land on
August 6, 1981:

> The Catholic Church. . . is today perhaps as never before in its history the
> victim of unjust attacks and of violent aggression. . . . In addition to the
> assassination or disappearance of 12 priests. . . and the violent deaths of
> numerous catechists and members of our Christian communities, it is
> known by everyone that in recent days there has been unleashed a publicity
> campaign which tends to discredit the church (Communique of the Epis-
> copal Conference of Guatemala, August 6, 1981).

19.   Numerous reports, governmental and nongovernmental,
have documented the deteriorating human rights situation in Guatemala. Pope John Paul II, in a 1980 letter to the bishops of
Guatemala, described the situation in the following way:

> I well know the anxieties you have communicated to me on more than one
> occasion, even publicly, in the last few months, for the many, far too many
> acts of violence that have racked your country, and your repeated calls for
> an end to what you have rightly called "the road to self-destruction" that
> violates all human rights—first among them the sacred right to life—and
> that does not help to solve the social problems of the nation.

20.   It is not our contention that the government of Guatemala
is responsible for all that occurs, but we do find significant the
recent human rights report of the State Department: "The
government has not taken effective steps to halt abuses or carry out
serious investigations" (U.S. Department of State: "Country
Reports on Human Rights Practices," 1981, p. 441).

21.   At this moment in Guatemalan history, U.S. diplomacy
should be directed toward enhancing the protection of human
rights and assisting the meeting of basic human needs, especially
the need for food and for capital investment for food production.
Such a policy will require a creative political vision; such vision is
not manifested by the provision of military hardware in a situation
already ridden with violence. We believe military assistance should
not be provided from any source or in any form.

22.   We offer these reflections as bishops and citizens. As
bishops we are called to teach the full dimensions of the gospel
message, including, as Paul VI said in 1975, questions involving
justice, liberation, development, and world peace *(On Evangelization, #31).* As citizens of the most powerful nation in the Western
hemisphere, we take seriously Pope John Paul II's injunction to us
at Yankee Stadium, "to seek out the structural reasons which foster

or cause the different forms of poverty in the world and in your own country, so you can apply the proper remedies."

23.   Both of these directives impel our present statement on Central America. We offer it in the hope that our continuing prayer for the church and the people of that region may be complemented by our public support in this country of their human rights and needs. We renew our special bonds with the church in Central America and we reaffirm our fraternal support to our brother bishops who serve that church.

24.   Our intention, in prayer and action, is to respond to the Lord's command heard in the prophet Isaiah: "This, rather, is the fasting I wish: releasing those bound unjustly, untying the thongs of the yoke; setting free the oppressed, breaking every yoke; sharing your bread with the hungry, sheltering the oppressed and homeless; clothing the naked when you see them and not turning your back on your own" (Is 58:6-9).

176. What the Laity Need. An Address of Dolores Leckey, May 2, 1982.

In November, 1965, Pope Paul VI promulgated the Decree on the Apostolate of the Laity of Vatican Council II. It was the first document of an ecumenical council to treat directly of the laity in the Church's history. It stated *inter alia:*

> Bishops, pastors of parishes, and other priests of both branches of the clergy should keep in mind that the right and duty to exercise the apostolate is common to all the faithful, both clergy and laity, and that the laity also have their own proper roles in building up the Church. [Walter M. Abbott, S.J. and Joseph Gallagher (Eds.), *The Documents of Vatican II.* New York: America Press. 1966. p. 514].

The implementation of this decree has not only been slow but at times painful in situations where the clergy have been reluctant to yield a meaningful voice to the laity in policy-making, as well as where the laity have shown something less than a balanced and tactful approach in parochial and diocesan affairs. It is helpful, therefore, to have the views of so well trained and highly experienced a laywoman as the Executive Director of the Bishops' Committee on the Laity in this important and delicate aspect of Catholic life as contained in a lecture at the North American College, Rome, on May 2, 1982. Source: *Origins,* 12 (May 20, 1982), 9-15.

I have titled this talk "Ministering in an Age of Apocalypse" not for dramatic effect, but because of a recent event in my own life which has affected my consciousness and my perception of my own pastoral needs.

I am, despite what you may think, a "normal" lay person. I have been married almost 25 years and am the mother of four grown children. I read; I think; I pray—and I worry—just like everybody else. I happen to work for the church, but my professional life could just as easily take place in a classroom or television studio, on a newspaper staff or perhaps in politics. The fact that I work for the church in an "administrative ministry" doesn't diminish my lay credentials.

Lay Concerns: A Sketch

One Sunday last winter when most of our family was at home for dinner, a funny thing happened to me. Somewhere between the salad and the roast, the subject of nuclear war was slipped in. My 24-year-old daughter, Mary Kate, an aspiring actress who lives in a nearby household with four other young adults, remarked in a rather pessimistic tone that our house (the one which she grew up in and in which we were all now gathered) is exactly three miles from the Pentagon. True? I looked inquiringly at my husband. "True," he said. All my maternal-preservation instincts stirred. Plans of action and salvation began to take shape. "I'd better get some bottled water and some canned goods to store in the basement," I said.

Several of "my own" looked at me in amazement. "Mother," my actress-daughter said quietly, "there won't be any basement." Her father lifted a wineglass in my direction and suggested, "I think, my dear, that if there is any warning at all we'd best go outside. We'll stand on our corner, hold each other's hand, turn in the direction of the Pentagon and face the light—and ask God to have mercy on our souls and bodies."

I looked at him in disbelief. I had not yet read a poem by Kathleen Raine which is, I suppose, a lyric of hope.

> Ah, welcome fire,
> That shall burn away
> All that I am
> But would not be.

If there be nothing
But ash of me
When the fire is out
Thy will be done.

And if there remain
Some pure star
Indestructible glory
Of what I was

Before I became
What I have been
Thy name I praise
In purging flame.

The conversation went on. My youngest son, Colum, now finishing his first year at Boston College, thought that if there were a 20-minute warning he would go to a nearby bike trail and start walking west. This would give him time to think things over, as he put it, before he died in an hour or so. On the other hand, he might want to join his father and me as we faced the light. Celia, our married daughter who is a student of Russian at Georgetown University, said that if she were in her apartment at the time she would run the two blocks to the subway, the deepest hole in Arlington. She and her husband had already discussed what to do.

Later that night, after everyone left, I knew that a new specter had taken up residence in my psyche. Now when I pray in the secrecy of my solitude, or when I'm watching birds at the feeder, or when I go to liturgy, a shadow is with me. How long it will stay I cannot say. I do find comfort in the poem and repeat like a mantra the lines, "Thy name I praise in purging flame."

I have a friend, Steven, who is a clarinetist. He and his music-teacher wife are the parents of two children. They live a very simple lifestyle for high-powered Washington. Music is not a five-figured way of life for most musicians, but for several years now Steven has had the security of a steady position with the opera orchestra.

This spring he lost that security. The economy is such that the orchestra will get by with two rather than three clarinetists. Steven is working part time in a vegetable co-op and trying to collect unemployment insurance, to which he is entitled. However, the system is so overloaded that he has been told he won't collect anything for some time.

My friend is only one of millions now without a job and literally wondering where the next dollar is coming from. In some places, I'm sure you know, the unemployment rate is 20 percent. Work is one of the essentials of a healthy life; we all know that. But a lot of people in our churches on Sunday mornings will not be going to work, as they would like to, on Monday mornings. Imagine the weight of this burden, the total weight—psychological and spiritual as well as material—that people like Steven bring with them to church.

Last summer a woman came to see me, referred by a priest we both know. I'll call her Margaret. Margaret told me she had been married for 18 years. She and her husband are professional people, and they have two teenage sons. They have had many years of marriage counseling and therapy, separately and together. Margaret said she had reached the point of wanting to live apart from her husband; she thought divorce was the only answer. Yet whenever she was at Mass she said she felt enormous anxiety, remembering her marriage vows and experiencing guilt over the action she felt she must take in order to preserve her sanity.

As we talked that summer day, I felt Margaret's exhaustion. She was worn out from the years of intense therapy, which is, as you must know, very, very hard work. I suggested to her that perhaps what she needed was a rest, a kind of sabbath; that if she could experience the healing power of solitude, which a separation, not divorce, might provide, then maybe she could see more clearly the right direction for herself and her family.

I cautioned against filling up the solitude with new projects and, especially, new relationships. Instead we talked about a period of apartness as an opportunity to pursue the inward journey, which is for everyone a lonely undertaking. It is lonely even for the married. The poet Rilke knew this well: "Once the realization is accepted that even between the closest human beings infinite distances continue to exist, a wonderful living side by side can grow up, if they succeed in loving the distance between them."

This was a new idea for her. She had never considered the solitude side of marriage. And yet solitude is as necessary to growth in God as is community. John Dunne, the theologian, says of this, "All persons committed to the inward journey must come to realize the truth that we cannot live without conflict and suffering, that we cannot avoid guilt, that we must some day die, and that in all these things we are alone and cannot make one another unalone."

Our churches hold men and women who are quietly suffering as Margaret is. Without denying the value of therapy, I would affirm the value of a genuine healing sabbath in our pastoral ministry.

My specter, Steven's unemployment, Margaret's need for solitude—these are all true stories. They tell something of the content of lay life in our time, and they say something about what is carried to liturgy, to church meetings, to all the gatherings which we name as Christian. And there are more stories. There are one-parent families, many of them headed by women courageously facing the rigors of parenting alone. They too are in our churches on Sunday mornings, at least those who have not felt completely excluded. There are childless singles as well. I have heard them tell of feeling left out of the ministerial concern of the church, which seems to them constantly to emphasize the nuclear family.

And there are other facets to lay life in the church today. Many congregations are likely to be peopled with educated, competent women and men who occupy positions of secular influence, whether that be as pharmacist or engineer or accountant. They are the people described in the Decree on the Apostolate of the Laity: "The laity, by their vocation, seek the kingdom of God by engaging in temporal affairs, and by ordering them according to the plan of God." In "Called and Gifted" the bishops of the United States elaborated on this. They said:

"The whole church faces unprecedented situations in the contemporary world and lay people are at the cutting edge of these new challenges. It is they who engage directly in the task of relating Christian values and priorities to complex questions such as those of business ethics, political choice, economic security, quality of life, cultural development and family planning." Often the more intensely people are engaged in their work, their community responsibilities, their families, the less time and energy they have for "church work." How do pastors and ministers feel about them? Are their secular vocations appreciated or understood?

Another facet of lay life today is the impact on the spiritual development of the laity. The Cursillo movement, Marriage Encounters, the charismatic renewal and others have enabled people to experience prayer and community in life-changing ways; and they bring these experiences to their Catholic congregations. And there are still other influences. For example, young people who have had important experiences with the prayer ways of the

East. They come to the Catholic community hoping to integrate their contemplative experience with their Christian heritage. They too have challenging pastoral needs.

In addition to the personal burdens which people bear and the responsibilities of life in the world and the vitality of spiritual awakening, our churches also hold people who might be described as psychologically numb. (To some extent this is true of all of us.) One understands how this can be. To be a conscious person, free and responsible, is hard work.

But the prophetic side of pastoral ministry does require moving beyond the provincialism which can harden into a "happy parish." The parish then becomes all; and we can lose the sense of being truly catholic, members of a world religion and related to the church in other parts of the world. The prophetic side of pastoral ministry must, I believe, call us to a sense of participation in the critical issues of our time: the conservation of the seas and the earth; disarmament; human rights; the needs of the disabled and the handicapped. In any congregation there is likely to be such a prophetically sensitive member. It may be the priest or it may be a student or a housewife or a civil servant. How is this voice to be heard?

What I have presented is a kind of kaleidoscope of the North American Catholic laity today, men and women who are burdened and courageous, who are lonely and discouraged, who are spiritually aware, who walk with wisdom as well as with doubt, who are settled into their numbness or who are struggling toward consciousness. This is the church in which the call to ministry is heard. It seems to me that to dare to minister to this diversity, whether one is ordained or lay, one must be radically open to what Raissa Maritain called "the adventures of grace."

Pastoral Needs of the Laity

What, in the practical order, do lay men and women need not merely to cope, but to live creatively, growing in consciousness of the love of Christ even though they—and we—are living in an apocalyptic moment? What I offer you is admittedly a limited view seen through my own particular lens. Nevertheless, I believe there is validity in the following four needs.

First is places and opportunities to tell the truth. Most of us disguise our truth in various clever ways; but nevertheless we need a safe place to grow into the true knowledge of ourselves, knowledge of our gifts and also knowledge of our defenses (unconscious as well as conscious) which keep us from genuine relationship, not only with each other but also with God. It is strange but true that in church settings people are often most reluctant to speak the truth. It may have something to do with our images of what a good churchperson is like—one who never causes any trouble, for example, by disagreeing with some parish policy or other; or one who doesn't have any trouble (perfectly compatible marriage, good financial situation and bright, obedient children); or one who never questions the meaning of life.

This image or expectation about church membership often affects the quality of contribution to parish life. Jim Anderson, an Episcopal priest who has worked extensively with parish councils, Protestant and Catholic, notes that people who know a lot about how to run a business, how to maintain mutual relationships, how to live honestly in a family, how to face adversity with courage, seem to leave their personal and professional competence in the parking lot. Anderson finds that rarely do people on church councils engage in the kind of give and take that is part of real decision making. He concludes that to speak truthfully in a spirit of dialogue (which means leaving oneself open to change) is not viewed as proper church behavior. This brings to mind the motto of the state of North Carolina, "It is better to be than to seem." Too often the converse is true in church arenas, and the motto is, "It is better to seem than to be."

I believe that the church ought to be evoking the truth from the people and not be afraid or threatened by it, remembering that Jesus taught us that it is the truth that makes us free—and remembering also that when another person speaks his or her truth to me, while it may not be my truth, there are undoubtedly echoes of myself there. The more deeply we go into our own being the more we are apt to find that we are more alike than different.

One of the most important books I've read recently is *Within the Whirlwind* by Eugenia Ginzburg. It is the second volume of her memoirs. In it she states that the reason for writing the details of her many years of political imprisonment under Stalin was simply that the truth be known. When she was imprisoned, her youngest child was only 4. It was 12 years before they were reunited. Their first night together they stayed up the whole night talking, reciting poems, connecting with each other at the level of heart and spirit. As dawn approached, her son asked her what her life had been like. She decided to tell him only the truth and not to hide anything from him. And so began her memoirs.

The publication of the first volume, *Journey Into the*

Whirlwind, brought accolades from her compatriots, artists and writers, in Russia as well as in exile. She interpreted this overwhelming reception of her work in this way: "It was perfectly clear to me that I owed this not to any special literary merit in the book, but solely to its truthfulness. People who had been starved of the simple unsophisticated truth were grateful to anyone who would take the trouble of telling them, *de profundis,* how it really was."

I think that parishes, basic Christian communities, all those places where we gathered in the name of Christ, must allow and enable people to tell their stories, their truth. This can happen only where intimacy and confidentiality and respect are present.

In our time the unemployed, the terminaly ill, the embittered, the parents of rebellious children, the divorced, the government worker with problems of conscience, the executive with mountainous responsibilities, women, blacks, the handicapped, the spiritually awakened—I could go on and on—all need a place to talk about their experience. This is the revelation of their lives. People should read, and they need to know, that their search for truth is welcomed and not suspect.

The rediscovery of the ministry of spiritual direction and counsel for all people offers one way of attending to this need. The formation of faith-and life-sharing groups is another. These two forms of religious relationship are, I suggest, vital for the life of the laity and ultimately for the life of the church. Because we are strengthened when we get in touch with the truth of our lives, other aspects of church life are affected. All of us, laity and clergy, are then freer to work toward adult relationships, using the gifts of our different experiences to help each other grow in maturity. The bishops of the United States said as much in "Called and Gifted."

The second pastoral need of lay persons is to know that they've been listened to, that they've been heard. By this I mean that there should be an effort on the part of the church's ministers and leadership to reflect on and respond to the truth that has been entrusted to them. Homilies, for example, can connect with the real life of this parish, these people. (The U.S. Bishops' Committee on Priestly Life and Ministry recently completed a statement on preaching, "Fulfilled in Your Hearing," in which the importance of the assembly and the assembly's needs are noted.)

Religious education should deal not only with doctrine and scripture, but also with the immediate life issues of a particular parish: the facts of separation and divorce, the experience of new parents, the scandal of racism, the trauma of sickness and death, and so on.

To listen to another as part of a dialogic way of being does not mean passive agreement. It means responding out of one's truth, having really heard what the other has said. Jesus and the Woman at the Well are a classic example of reciprocity, of listening to the being of each other.

A third need of today's laity, which we see in the United States as well as in the developing countries, is the opportunity to minister. That there is a decline in the number of men seeking ordination is not news. Likewise, the number of lay men and women who are eager to serve the church and the world explicitly under the aegis of the church is increasing. Active compassion— ministry—is one of the tested ways of growing beyond self-interest. It is also one of the most valuable means of discovering and enhancing one's natural giftedness, while at the same time serving the needs of others.

I meet many young people who have majored in religious studies, who have done graduate work in theology and who feel called to the ministry of the church. Some of them want and find paying positions in parishes or other religious institutions. Others volunteer for several years in the missions. (It is estimated that there are 1,500 lay volunteers in such total but temporary ministry.) I am convinced that these experiences of ministry are shaping a new kind of Catholic Christian, one who knows, really knows, what shared community life in Christ is all about.

There are many many issues surrounding lay ministry. During the next three years the U.S. bishops' Committee on the Laity intends to study various models for lay ministry training and to begin to identify criteria for discerning call along with qualifications for ministry. We will be dealing with this in depth in the deacons' class.

There is one group whose gifts are particularly needed both by the church and also by the world, especially at this historical juncture. Women. Once again, in "Called and Gifted," the bishops say:

"Special mention must be made of women, who in the past have not always been allowed to take their proper role in the church's ministry. We see the need for an increased role for women in the ministries of the church to the extent possible. We recognize the tensions and misunderstandings which arise on this question, but we wish to face these as part of a sincere attempt to become true communities of faith."

Expanding the role of women, however, is not simply for the sake of women, but for a much larger cause. Barbara Tuchman, the historian, has on many occasions contended that the making of war seems to be a preoccupation of men. Most recently (New York Times, April 18, 1982), writing about the alternative to arms control, she said:

"I am skeptical of peace. Peace has not figured among the notable achievements of mankind. It is the most talked of and least practiced of all social endeavors. Men—and in this case I mean the male gender, not the species—are always saying they hate war and war is hell and so forth, and have continued to engage in it lustily, aggressively and ceaselessly since the beginning of recorded history, and doubtless before. Historians have estimated that society has spent more time fighting than in any other activity except agriculture."

Mrs. Tuchman, incidentally, believes the only alternative to the current nuclear situation (madness, she calls it) is for the people (the *laos*) to act on their growing fear and to turn out of office those who would continue the arms buildup while every other social and cultural value is lost. She does not believe that the government of any country will do anything to redress the situation. One cannot help but note that, by and large, governments are made up of the male gender, to use the Tuchman term.

So what do women have to offer to this moment? For one thing, a cooperative way of being in life, the result of centuries of a particular kind of socialization. Before you rise up and name all the combative women in your life, let me explain.

A statement like this refers to women as a group. A school of social psychology led by Dr. Jean Baker Miller *(Toward a New Psychology of Women)* maintains that the cultural norms which have tended to keep women in restricted domestic roles have (I would add, by the grace of God) served to develop within women as a group certain behaviors which are important for all institutions of society. These are behaviors of cooperation rather than competition and also the owning of one's vulnerability. She argues that psychological and spiritual growth require awareness of our innate weakness and acknowledgment of the feelings of vulnerability which recur all through life. We need to learn in an emotional sense that these feelings are not shameful or abhorrent but rather that they present opportunities from which the individual can move on—if the feelings are experienced for what they are. Only then, according to Dr. Miller, can a person hope to find appropriate paths to new strengths. Of course with new strength will come new areas of vulnerability; for there is no absolute invulnerability, as we all know.

From a very different traditon, that of the American Indian, comes a similar perception:

"In the heart of our ancient teachings is the wisdom that woman is central to the creation and sustenance of life. It is no wonder that women are, when allowed by society and circumstance, deeply grounded in the spirit of the earth, in the essential, the deeply religious and reverent, and are profoundly thankful for the abundant gifts of creation. So it is that women are the best guides and teachers, in their inner instinctive wisdom, of the preservation and sustenance of the species."

Given Mrs. Tuchman's historical assertions, given the psychological and tribal-mystical insights into the gifts of women, given the concern of the American bishops, I can't help but think that the role of women in the church is critical not only for the church, but also for the world which God loved so much. Can it be that the church must seek out the gifts, wisdom and experience of women if there is to be a faithful ministry to the world?

The fourth pastoral need of the laity which I see as essential for our time is the affirmation of the ordinary worldly ministry of the laity (as distinct from ecclesial or designated lay ministry). This is the ongoing life of most of the members of the church, their life at home, in their professions, in culture and so on. The public school administrator, the bus driver, the architect, the farmer—they need to hear, to feel, to know that they are the church in the world.

This coming to consciousness of the fact that one's work (provided it is not of a destructive nature) is participation in the ongoing activity of God is related, I believe, to the development in people of a contemplative mood. I believe pastoral ministry ought to be attentive to this development. This will require time, energy and resources to teach ordinary people the way of contemplation. It can be done; it is being done. Essential to this task, however, are authentic and experienced teachers.

Another way is to offer people a genuine experience of sabbath, particularly through the liturgy. This insight into the needs of the laity has come to me through the work of the Grubb Institute in England. For 25 years or so the Grubb Institute has been engaged in behavioral research into the task of the church and the role of the pastor. Their work has been mostly with Catholic and Anglican groups in Britain and Ireland, but now they are beginning to test their theory in the United States. The theory is something like this.

The local expression of church, namely the parish, offers to contemporary man and woman a place of positive dependency and rest. Leaning heavily on cultural anthropology, particularly the work of Victor Turner, they name oscillation as an essential rhythm of life. This means that humans are in a kind of pendulum swing, toward activity and engagement with the world and then away from this engagement to a state of quiet, rest, dependency. They believe that supporting this second part of the rhythm is an important function of the church.

The withdrawal from engagement allows for the experience of dependency on God much like the child depends on the parent for comfort and rest after encounters with the larger world. These experiences of positive dependency, which happen chiefly in liturgy but could also occur in the occasions of intimacy mentioned earlier, strengthen and free one to be a more caring, compassionate and courageous and responsible citizen of the world. Oversimply stated, it works this way: I, active lay person, involved in family and friendship patterns, in work, a member of a village or city neighborhood, "come to church." The Mass presents to me the deepest symbols of the Christian faith, word and sacrament. Because these are such powerful symbols, symbols of ultimate reality, they have the potential to undo my prevalent societal image of God. The Mass reaches into my unconscious and, more important, the community unconscious, so that this people of God in this place gets in touch with a truer image of God—i.e., in touch with all that Jesus Christ images for us.

The effect of this "in touchness," according to the Grubb theory, is a "body of Christ" vitally committed to the fundamental biblical dynamics of freedom and responsibility. Such a community acts in the piece of the world in which it is inserted, for others. Last summer, at a meeting in Vienna on the church's responsibility for the laity, Father Yves Congar said much the same thing. He said the church in our day must be a church of transcendence and a church for the liberation of others.

The practical outcomes in a given neighborhood are that the hungry are fed, the illiterate educated, the resources of the rich shared and so on. What the Mass does, according to Grubb, is to engrave in our minds and hearts the reality of our human interdependence: Children of God. Central to this process is the experience of refreshment and rest in the worship, so that the factory worker, the busy executive, the government bureaucrat will be enabled to pursue their work in the world. Their secular vocations will be recognized and supported, but with the fresh perspective of the Gospel. The value of their Christian discipleship will not be measured by their intrachurch ministry, whether or not they usher or teach Sunday school. They may very well do these "churchly" ministries, but their Christian commitment will not be evaluated in those terms. Their teaching, their medicine, their research, whatever—that will be affirmed as primary in their lay vocation.

The problem for most lay people, however, is that they don't know or don't believe that their lay vocation is authentically Christian. Mark Gibbs, the author of *Christians With Secular Power* (Fortress Press), offers practical suggestions for expressing the church's valuing of the lay vocation with all its complexities— among them, that pastors keep track of the laity's interests and responsibilities in work, politics, leisure; and that pastors be aware of extraparochial opportunities for Christian growth and let parishioners know about them. Parishes do not have to do it all. He also suggests that "the parish get out of the way of busy laity," lamenting the fact that many prosperous suburban parishes in Britain and North America still try to entangle their laity in clubs and endless meetings. What Gibbs and the Grubb people—and others—are fundamentally concerned about is:

—The availability of good ongoing theological education for the laity, not just those who will be engaged in designated ministry.

—Resources for spiritual formation and development. What was asked of Jesus, "Teach us to pray," is still asked today. Spiritual guides and companions, "soul friends," are needed for Christians who are serious about their journey.

The Minister: Ordained and...

The needs of the laity which I have named this evening—a place to tell the truth, the experience of being listened to with respect, a chance to minister in ecclesial or designated ministry (if such be the call of God in one's life), and affirmation of the secular lay vocation and support of that vocation through theological education and in-depth spiritual formation—naturally raise questions about the capacity and role of the ordained minister, the priest. What do you need in order to care in this way for the rest of the people of God who will share life with you as gift and grace?

Based on many years of living a lay life, and now almost five years of listening to both lay people and priests, I will hazard a few suggestions about the current and future state of pastoral ministry.

Fundamentally we, i.e., you and I, need the same things. We need commitment and community to move ever more deeply into our spiritual depths, to face who we are, who God is, what the world is all about and how we participate in it all, either creatively or negatively. So, first is some kind of authentic, ongoing spiritual development—steady and reliable.

Second, the ordained minister, the priest, in today's church needs to experience and value interdependence in ministry. He needs to know, or at least to want to know, what shared ministry is all about. Not only will the people be served by a ministerial team, but the minister will grow through shared life. All of us have sharp and tenacious egos that usually die a slow death. Without the stimulus of relationships we can continue with illusions about ourselves and each other, and probably cause a lot of harm along the way.

Third, closely related to both the way of spiritual development and the interdependence of shared ministry, is what has been called willingness as opposed to willfullness. This is a basic stance in life which is marked by compassion and a kind of light touch, the opposite of possessiveness and domination. It's a John-the-Baptist attitude of "I diminish so that others may increase," an attitude which allows a priest to share the ministry in all kinds of ways. He can do this because he sees how this is a major path for Christian maturity, for the fullness of Christ. To move in this direction will mean a radical trusting in God.

Conclusion

I am back where I started with my own needs as a lay Christian, or rather, as one who desires to warrant that designation, "Christian." As I said earlier, when I think of all that probably lies ahead, a fear slides into my thought and even into my prayer. I think I need my pastors to remind me of the startling truth of Christ's love.

I had a taste of this recently in an article in Sojourners magazine. Jim Wallis, the editor, was meditating in writing on the passage from the Letter to the Romans where Paul asks, "Who shall separate us from the love of Christ?" Shall tribulation, or distress, or persecution, or famine, or nakedness, or peril or sword? Paul's answer is that nothing can separate us from this love. Wallis says that this passage is the promise of God, whether we feel it or not. Whether we accept it or not, he says, is our choice. He goes on to invite us to put in the list all that we fear could separate us from the love of God.

Wallis asks, Are you afraid that our weakness could separate you from the love of God? It can't, he says. Are you afraid that your inadequacies could separate you from the love of God? They can't. Are you afraid that your inner poverty could separate you from the love of God? It can't. Difficult marriage, loneliness, anxiety over your children's future? They can't. Negative self-image? It can't. Economic hardship, racial hatred, street crime? They can't. Rejection by loved ones? The suffering of loved ones? They can't. Persecution by authorities, going to jail for failing to pay your income tax for reasons of conscience? It can't. The Russians? They can't. War in Central America? It can't. Nuclear war? Even it can't.

At one level I believe everything St. Paul and Jim Wallis say, and yet these apocalyptic days often cloud the reality for me. I need my pastors to help me live with this truth and to learn its power. I sense they—my pastors—need me for the same reasons. We need to help each other let the cross be at the center of our lives. We need to help each other choose our lives with all their ambiguities and terrible beauties.

With the poet May Sarton, I feel:

> I am not ready to die
> But I am learning to
> trust death
> As I have trusted life.
> I am moving
> Toward a new freedom
> Born of detachment
> And a sweeter grace—
> Learning to let go.

("Gestalt at Sixty" in *Collected Poems*)

For this learning, slow though it be, I am grateful to the ministers of Christ's church: monks and parish priests, lay men and women who have been and continue to be my soul friends, religious women and men, and a bishop here and there—all of whom have gently said to me by their lives, "Let go; it's all right. Nothing can separate us from the love of Christ."

I will try to remember this when the light comes, whatever its origin.

177. Pastoral Message of the United States Hispanic Bishops, Summer, 1982.

No segment of the American Catholic community better illustrates its multiethnic composition than those of Hispanic culture and background; nor is any single ethnic group in that religious community increasing more rapidly in the United States. Taking as their point of departure the 450th anniversary of the tradition of the Blessed Virgin's apparition to the Indian, Juan Diego, in December, 1531, the bishops of Hispanic descent issued a pastoral letter in which they linked those of Hispanic ancestry in this country to the traditions that had arisen in Mexico centuries before. The beginning of that link was forged in a tentative way in 1540, only 9 years after the apparition, when Coronado launched his historic expedition into what is today the American Southwest. True, there was no uninterrupted and steady relationship; yet the intermingling of those of Spanish and Mexican birth, first with the native Indian population and later with American settlers in Arizona, California, New Mexico, and Texas became an increasingly important factor, and today the Hispanic presence has appeared in virtually every section of the United States. The implications of this development for the Church are obviously immense. The bishops here survey their problems as pastors of the Hispanics, touching upon the hardships and discrimination suffered by the latter, the need for renewed efforts in evangelization, increased vocations, as well as the Church's obligation to voice their peoples' temporal needs in such matters as employment, just wages, etc. Source: *Origins,* 12 (August 12, 1982), 145-152.

Four hundred fifty years after your apparition in our lands, we, your sons, come as the shepherds of our Hispanic people in the United States of North America. We come full of joy and hope, but we also come saddened and preoccupied with the suffering of our people.

We are the shepherds of a people on the march. Walking with our people, we come to you, Mother of God and our mother, so that we may receive a renewed spirit. We want to be filled with enthusiasm to go out and proclaim the wonders of God that have taken place in our history, that are taking place at this time in our lives and that will take place in the future.

Although the world has often misunderstood us, you do understand and hold us in esteem. You too were always a pilgrim. You were always on the march. You visited your cousin Elizabeth in the mountains (Lk. 1:39-56); your Son was born at the end of your long trek from Nazareth to Bethlehem (Lk. 2:1-7); you went on pilgrimage to the temple to present Jesus (Lk. 2:21-44); you lived in exile as a threatened and pursued stranger (Mt. 2:13-15); you returned to your land after the tyrant King Herod died (Mt.

2:19-23); and you again went on the march toward Jerusalem for the feast of the Passover (Lk. 2:41-52). You were present at the beginning and at the end of the ministry of the Lord: at Cana in Galilee, when the signs of the kingdom were first manifest (Jn. 2:1-12) and at the foot of the cross (Jn. 19:25-27). And here, at the birth of the Americas, you have appeared as a sign from heaven (Rv. 12:1), new life and new light.

You went on all of your journeys, pilgrimages and marches as a poor woman at the service of Jesus, of the kingdom of God, of the poor and those in need. The Spirit covered you. You put the word of God into practice and you shared the life of Jesus with a believing people. After the death of Jesus you hoped against all hope and you were called to the heavens as the "favored one of God" (Lk. 1:28).

> You were the faithful one. . .
> You formed the body of Jesus
> and gave him to the world. . .
> You are the Mother of God and our mother. . .
> You are the mother of all
> the inhabitants of these lands. . .
> You are the mother of the Americas!

I. Our Pilgrimage Throughout History

> *Mientras recorres la vida*
> *Tu nunca solo estas*
> *contigo por el camino*
> *Santa Maria va*

A. THE BIRTH OF A NEW PEOPLE

At a unique moment in the history of this world, three radically different and totally unknown worlds met: indigenous America, Africa and Europe.

The clash carried many of the indigenous people to slavery and death, and made them strangers in their own land. The Africans were violently wrenched from their lands and transplanted to far-off countries as slaves. This initiated a shock whose reverberations are experienced even today. There also began at that time a *mestizaje,* an intertwining of blood and culture that in effect brought about the birth of a new people.

The roots of our Latin American reality are grounded in

their threefold inheritance. It is our identity, our suffering, our greatness and our future.

Four hundred fifty years ago, at the birth of our Latin American *mestizo* race, during the deep and sharp labor pains of our people, our mother came to be with us.

A great sign came from the sky (Rv. 12:1), a beautiful woman who visited our lands and spoke to us in our native tongue with gentle love, tenderness and compassion. You are that woman.

Just as she had been chosen for her littleness and humility, so Mary chose Juan Diego, a humble Indian. From the many she could have chosen, she singled out a poor man.

The faithful child Juan Diego listened to his mother, trusted in her and accepted her command. The bishop asked her for a sign, and she gave it to him *con gusto*—not only beautiful roses but she also gave him the first flower of all flowers: her image miraculously imprinted on Juan Diego's *tilma.*

At a painful time in our history, God gave us a great gift—the portrait of his mother, who is also our mother. Her image is the visible sign of her loving presence among us. A woman with a compassionate face and heart, but whose eyes are sad because she is conscious of the suffering of her people and hears their mourning.

Ever since then you have shared our sufferings and joys, our struggles and fiestas, and all of our attempts to bring about the reign of God. You inspire us, you stir us and you continue to walk beside us. You are the source of our identity and of the unity of our people in the Americas.

Today we come to you, our mother, filled with gratitude and admiration, to bring to you the portrait of your family, to tell you of our life and to share with you the enduring dreams of the Hispanic people of the United States of North America.

B. OUR FAITH

Our ancestors had a strong sense of religiosity. Their lives were centered in their God. They were a people of spiritual values, of wisdom and humanizing customs.

The missionaries brought us the knowledge of a personal God who, through his Son, invites us to a new life. The Gospel purified and enriched the beliefs of our lands.

Because of this our faith is personal and cultural, because the word was made flesh on our land when his mother arrived on the hill of Tepeyac. Little by little the Gospel has penetrated every aspect of our life and culture. It is the alpha and omega, the center of our very being. Faith penetrates our music, art, poetry, language, customs, fiestas—every expression of our life.

Faithful to our tradition we hope that the Gospel continues to transform our life and our culture.

C. OUR MESTIZAJE

The Hispanic people of the United States of North America is a people of *mestizaje,* an interlacing of the blood and culture of the indigenous, African and European peoples. In the present reality of our people we find a new intertwining: that of the Latin American people and those of the United States. From this second *mestizaje,* the Hispanic American people begin to emerge.

We are thus a new people and within our very being we combine the cultural riches of our parents. The Virgin of Guadalupe, our *madrecita mestiza,* comes to fill with joy and blessings the painful and difficult process of our *mestizaje.*

D. OUR CULTURES

In the shaping of this people, many beautiful values from different cultures have been incorporated, all of which have enriched us today. Our culture is rich in imagery, art, music, dances, food, poetry, even to the point of embodying a certain sense of mischievousness.

Our langugage is rich in expressions that come from the Gospel. This facilitates the transmission of the word.

Our personal faith is expressed very beautifully: *Mi Padre Dios* (God my Father), *Nuestra Madrecita Maria* (Our dear mother Mary), *Nuestro Senor y Hermano Jesucristo* (Our Lord and Brother Jesus Christ), *Mis santitos* (My little saints). A true spiritual environment is fostered in our homes and many houses even become household churches. The little altar with the crucifix, your statue, *Madrecita,* and our "little saints" hold a special place in the home. The vigil lights and blessed palms speak to us of your most holy Son. Our culture is the expression of the Gospel incarnated in our people and it is a rich form of passing on the divine teachings to new generations.

E. OUR FAMILIES

It is almost impossible to explain this great gift from God. Words do not tell the whole story. For us the meaning of family is extended and includes parents, children, grandparents, aunts and uncles, "distant" relatives, neighbors, godparents and *compadres,* or intimate friends. The family is the first school of love, tenderness, acceptance, discipline and respect. In our homes we have come to experience the bonds of friendship, mutual support, concern for one another and the presence of God.

We have received from our families the thoughts and values that are the foundation and primary orientation of our lives.

The new Juan Diego who carried the message from heaven to the church of the United States was also a humble messenger: our mothers and grandmothers. They taught their sons and grandsons to pray while their fathers struggled to earn their daily bread.

Their voice has echoed insistingly: "Don't miss Mass," "Marry in the church," "May God go with you." They have marked our souls with the love of God and have caused your image of Guadalupe, full of tenderness, to blossom throughout the nation.

Madrecita, you know the miseries and faults of our families. They have not been perfect. But even with their defects they have been a great source of security, community and happiness. In the most difficult moments of our march through history, our people have never lost their joy of living. Throughout all of the burdens of life we sing—even in the midst of pain.

Faith has made us a joyful people. In our fiestas we celebrate the mystery of life that, in its successes and failures, joys and sadness, birth and even death, is a gift from God.

F. PEOPLE WHO FILL US WITH ADMIRATION

Madrecita, our history is filled with men and women who have been a great inspiration for us. They have struggled and have given their lives that we might have a better life.

We give you thanks:

—for the Indians who suffered the pain of the conquest and who fought for the good of their people.

—for the Africans, victims of slavery and humiliation;

—for the missionaries you brought from Spain, men of apostolic vision filled with courage, love and compassion;

—for our forgotten heroes, who have remained hidden in obscurity;

—for the saints who blossomed in our lands like the roses of Tepeyac.

What joy we feel, *Madrecita,* seeing so many who have brought beauty to our people with the gifts your Son has given to them:

—the artists, writers, singers and poets who dream;

—the educators, the learned and the technicians;

—the businessmen, farmers, professionals and shop owners;

—domestic and farm workers;

—migrant workers and labor unions who give strength to the voice of the worker;

—politicians who truly represent the people;

—soldiers who have fought to defend freedom.

Madrecita, a very special thanks for the priests and religious, our co-workers in the vineyard of the Lord, who have given themselves to our people and who have truly loved them.

Without the wealth of their talents and the totality of their commitment, the Gospel of your Son would not be proclaimed in all its fullness.

We give thanks to God, *Madrecita,* for having called us to be the apostles of your Son in our day. We ask you to walk with us still.

II. Our Reality

Aunque te digan algunos
que nada puede cambiar
lucha por un mundo nuevo
lucha por la verdad

Much has been gained but the suffering continues. We are conscious of the oppression and exploitation of our people. We have seen bodies disfigured by hunger and saddened by the fear of the law; we have heard the cries of abandoned children mistreated by their own parents. We sense the loneliness of the elderly ignored by their relatives and the depression of prisoners whose greatest crime has been the lack of money to pay someone to defend them in court. We have shared the pain and the heat of farm workers and domestic laborers, the invisible slaves of modern society. In the jails and the detention camps there are some who have come to our country in search of work and freedom, yet who have been considered criminals. We have seen our youth with empty eyes because they have nothing to look forward to in life. We have been with the countless victims of the violence that grows daily in our neighborhoods and even in our families. We will not rest until all injustice is eliminated from our life.

We have shared with our people the fear that comes from racism and discrimination. The knowledge that we might be rejected, ridiculed or insulted paralyzes us.

Just as Juan Diego accepted his challenge, we now accept ours: that of being artisans of a new people.

A. OUR IDENTITY

We are people twice *mestizado*. We are in the beginning stages of our life as Hispanic Americans.

Every birth is at one and the same time joy and sadness. Our birth as a people has been the same. Constant rejection has been a part of our daily life.

Nevertheless, our parents taught us to love the United States, although the struggle has been difficult. Our people have always struggled to improve themselves. We love the peace founded on truth, justice, love and freedom *(Pacem in Terris)*. We have not taken up arms against our country but instead have defended it. We have fought to eliminate the injustices that rule our lives. The road has been long and difficult, littered with many obstacles, but we have made progress and will continue ahead with firmness and determination.

B. OUR ACCOMPLISHMENTS

Morenita, we give you thanks for the many beautiful things that have been happening to us lately.

Our people are beginning to count in society. Their voice is now being heard. Each day they are becoming more responsible for the religious and social structures that shape their lives.

Your children have already celebrated pastoral conventions on a national level.

The efforts of the farm workers have brought forth their fruits. Many of our people today enjoy a better life, thanks to the heroic efforts of our leaders.

Fourteen sons of our people have been called to be successors of the apostles.

Vocations to religious life and to the priesthood are on the rise.

Catholic movements and associations have arisen, dedicated to the social and apostolic progress of our people.

We have pastoral centers dedicated to research, theological reflection, the production of materials and the formation of pastoral leaders.

The bishops have established national and regional offices to serve your people.

We give thanks to your Son for all that is being achieved. But we ask him to give us the strength and courage to continue facing the gigantic problems of our day. As John Paul II said in Mexico, "We want to be the voice of those who have no voice." The poor have the right to our love and special care.

C. CHALLENGES

There are certain challenges in our society which we must meet.

Our betterment in social life does not mean that we forget our roots—our Latin American *mestiza* tradition. The more we value our past, the more strength will we have to launch ourselves toward the building of our future.

Development of a more human life does not mean that we allow ourselves to be enslaved and destroyed by materialism, consumerism, social climbing, the desire for continuous pleasure and immediate gratification. All of this come from the idolatry of gold. These values are the cancer of society.

The modernization of the family does not mean that we abandon the greatest treasure of our Hispanic culture. The family is in great danger today. Divorce is on the rise, the elderly are forgotten and even cheated, children are abandoned and young people make the street their home. The spirit of individualism is killing the spirit of community that is the core of the family.

Christian unity does not mean religious indifference. Ecumenism must not lead us to lose our identity as Catholics. Affirming ecumenism, we reject every type of active proselytizing which is anti-ecumenical and destructive to our people. The great diversity of fundamentalist groups and their anti-Catholic spirit divide our families and our peoples. Our response is not one of fighting against these groups nor one of speaking ill of them or their intentions, but rather we will take their activities as a challenge to us Catholics to live more authentically and apostolically the life of the Gospel.

III. Artisans of a New Humanity

Ahora que estamos unidos
juntos en la verdad
danos fuerza te pedimos
fuerza para triunfar

A. A REDISCOVERY OF THE GOSPEL

The greatest strength of our people comes from the rediscovery of the Gospel that is our truth, our way and our life. The power of God in us is this:

—His light illuminating the meaning of our life and the goal of our mission;

—His love transforming our hearts of stone into human hearts;

—His compassion moving us to action;

—His hope encouraging us to continue struggling even when humanly speaking there is no hope;

—His strength transforming our weaknesses and converting them into strengths for the good.

B. A REBIRTH OF THE CHURCH

The word of the Gospel takes human form the more it penetrates, encompasses and ennobles our culture. It is expressed by means of images, symbols, music, art and wisdom. The church is born out of our response to the word of Jesus. Today we are living a true rebirth of the Hispanic American *mestizo* church.

C. THE LIFE OF THE CHURCH

Faith comes to us from the church and calls us to be church. In time and space this life of the church takes various forms depending on concrete needs and conditions. With great joy we see:

—The birth of new parish life where each member places his or her talents at the service of the community. The wide participation of parishioners in the mission of the church is the beginning of a new day and the source of great hope for the church of the future;

—In the renewed parishes the church is the natural center of the life of the community. The parish forms leaders and moves the people to work together for the good of all;

—The base communities *(comunidades eclesiales de base)* cause the individual to experience faith and to feel like church;

—New family movements and Bible study groups have brought new life to our communities;

—The resurgence of ministries has engendered a new ecclesial life that has incorporated many into the mission of the church. We are all called to actively take part in the apostolate;

—Permanent deacons, men prepared and ordained for service to the people of God, have renewed the presence of the church in many places with their dedication and apostolic zeal.

D. POPULAR EXPRESSIONS OF FAITH

The missionaries knew how to understand the Indians, discovering their desires and inclinations in order to make these the basis for evangelization. They made dances expressions of faith.

Pilgrimages and processions offered occasions for teaching Christian doctrine. They created forms such as the *pastorela,* the *posadas* and the *siete palabras* to pass on the biblical message by means of dance, drama, music and art.

These expressions of a Christian people are true gifts of the Spirit and a beautiful treasure of our people. We invite pastoral leaders and catechists to rediscover these values.

E. CATECHESIS

Religious education continues to be a most important task in the church. Through it we grow and mature in Christian commitment.

—Catechesis must take into account our Hispanic American tradition.

—Proper methods must be utilized, especially radio and television.

—The preparation and motivation of catechists merit special attention.

Catechesis today, as in the time of the missionaries, must be based on the Bible and church tradition, taking into account the concrete signs of the times, using the methods of our tradition: dramatic interpretations of the Gospel, artistic expression of the mysteries of faith and songs with catechetical content.

F. LITURGY

The community celebration of faith is the manifestation of the Christian life of the people. So that these celebrations might be authentically those of the people, they ought to incorporate:

—the local language of the people in the prayers, readings and preaching;

—the art of our people in the representations of sacred images.

Some forms of celebration are beginning to emerge today that incorporate these fundamental principles of the Second Vatican Council. We applaud these efforts and we hope that this liturgical dawning may continue glowing and that soon it may come to shine in all its fullness.

G. THEOLOGICAL REFLECTION

Theology helps to discover how to live and proclaim our faith. Every ecclesial community has the privilege and obligation of discovering the theological meaning of its life.

—We are grateful for the theological contributions of other

local ecclesial communities and, in a very special way, we value the inspiration of the theological thought of Latin America.

—Our Hispanic American people are beginning to point out the theological significance of our identity in the United States.

—We invite our people to continue this process.

Each people and every generation has the privilege and the obligation to respond to Jesus' question to Peter: "And who do you say that I am?" (Mt. 6:15). The particular response of other local churches enriches us, but at the same time inspires and encourages us to search for our own response. Who is this Jesus who lives and speaks in our Christian people? Together we must search, formulate and proclaim our answer to this question.

H. VOCATIONS

The blossoming of new vocations for our people fills us with joy. However, the number is minimal in relation to the need. This apostolate must grow. Many men and women can respond to the Lord's call.

Our Hispanic American *mestizaje* church will reach maturity when our people have enough vocations not only for our own needs but also for the universal mission of the church.

I. A MORE AUTHENTIC FOLLOWING OF JESUS

Christ is our only model and like him we ought to be ready to commit ourselves and to be steadfast in the proclamation of truth, always filled with compassion and mercy.

Our following of him demands us to raise our voice when life is threatened, defending and respecting everyone as persons created by God. We are obligated to fight for peace and justice.

Just as he opened up new horizons for us, so too must we raise up the farm worker, the migrant and the laborer. We must aid in the self-improvement of all in search of a better place in society.

IV. A Pilgrimage with Joy, Courage and Hope

The imitation of Christ allows us to see others in their dignity as children of God.

Ahora que estamos unidos
juntos en la verdad
danos fuerza te pedimos
fuerza para triunfar

!Ven con nosotros a caminar
Santa Maria, ven!

We are heading into the 21st century!

Conscious of all that God has achieved through us, we call on our people to assume an attitude of leadership to create a more human society. We are all the church, and together we can triumph.

We invite our people to be strong co-workers with us in ministry. Jesus told every one of us: "Go out and proclaim the good news." Christians, by nature, are evangelizers. The lay person, if Christian, evangelizes.

We invite young men and women especially to place their enthusiasm, their sense of commitment and their sincerity at the service of the Gospel. May they be young apostolic bearers of the Gospel to the youth of today.

We invite our brother priests to continue living their commitment. Do not be discouraged. We always walk with Jesus. We never go alone. He gives us the strength to be enduring guardians of the faith. May we also care for our traditions and language that are the means of spreading the Gospel. May we form the lay and religious ministers that God gives us, that they may be effective co-workers with us.

We congratulate them on all the good that has been done and we invite them to be the Good Shepherd with us. May they be men of prayer, devoted sons of the *Guadalupana.*

We invite our brother and sister religious to continue giving witness to the value of the life of poverty, chastity and obedience in a world that values riches, pleasure and power. We commend them because they have been a prophetic voice for justice and peace. We invite them, according to the particular charism of their community, to be united with the efforts of the local church in which they work so that in conjunction with the bishops and the people of God of that diocese they may build up the kingdom of God.

We invite the contemplative religious to continue offering to the church the strength of their prayers and good example.

We invite our brother deacons to join our efforts and those of all the clergy in the apostolate. Faithful to their vocation as deacons, may they be men of service to the people. Let them not forget that the primary field of their apostolate is their home, their community and their place of work.

We challenge seminarians to commit themselves seriously to their studies and spiritual formation. Our people need compassionate priests with thorough knowledge of the sacred mysteries and a profound sense of the urgency of the social teachings of the church.

NUESTRO ADIOS

O Mother of the Americas, just as you trusted Juan Diego, we beg you to trust in us, the Hispanic bishops. May you send us to places we are unaccustomed to visit; may you send us to proclaim your mandate: that a temple be built wherein we may feel the love and tenderness of our mother. We want to be the artisans and the builders of this new temple—a society in which all will be able to live as brothers and sisters. We want to build up the kingdom of God, where peace is found because hate, jealousy, lies, dissension and every kind of injustice will have disappeared.

Madre de Dios
Madre de la Iglesia
Madre de los Americas
Madre de todos nosotros
Ruega por nosotros.

178. The Challenge of Peace: God's Promise and Our Response, May 3, 1983.

It has become a truism to say that the issue of nuclear warfare transcends any other problem of the contemporary world, grave as many of those problems undoubtedly are. In view of that fact the Catholic bishops of the United States might be said to have forfeited their role as moral leaders had they maintained silence in face of the nuclear threat. Not only did the pastoral letter take positions contrary to those of many in high government circles, and that with a thoroughness of treatment quite beyond previous pronouncements on the subject, but what likewise distinguished the document was the unprecedented consultation that preceded its publication. In itself that process provided revealing evidence of the maturity attained by American Catholics *vis-à-vis* their own coreligionists and as well the American public in general. The result was a bishops' official pronouncement that for the first time in history achieved widespread international attention far beyond religious circles, and drew inevitable criticism from some and strong approval from others. In the latter category no one was more emphatic than George F. Kennan, described by James Reston as "probably our most thoughtful and experienced foreign policy philosopher," [New York *Times,* October 20, 1985, p. E21]. Kennan characterized the pastoral letter as:

the most profound and searching inquiry yet conducted by any responsible
collective body into the relations of nuclear weaponry, and indeed of modern
war in general, to moral philosophy, to politics and to the conscience of the
national state. [New York *Times,* Sunday, May 1, 1983, p. E21].

Source: *Origins,* 13 (May 19, 1983), 1-32.

CONTENTS

Summary

The Second Vatican Council opened its evaluation of modern warfare with the statement: "The whole human race faces a moment of supreme crisis in its advance toward maturity." We agree with the council's assessment; the crisis of the moment is embodied in the threat which nuclear weapons pose for the world and much that we hold dear in the world. We have seen and felt the effects of the crisis of the nuclear age in the lives of people we serve. Nuclear weaponry has drastically changed the nature of warfare, and the arms race poses a threat to human life and human civilization which is without precedent.

We write this letter from the perspective of Catholic faith. Faith does not insulate us from the daily challenges of life but intensifies our desire to address them precisely in light of the gospel which has come to us in the person of the risen Christ. Through the resources of faith and reason we desire in this letter to provide hope for people in our day and direction toward a world freed of the nuclear threat.

As Catholic bishops we write this letter as an exercise of our teaching ministry. The Catholic tradition on war and peace is a long and complex one; it stretches from the Sermon on the Mount to the statements of Pope John Paul II. We wish to explore and explain the resources of the moral-religious teaching and to apply it to specific questions of our day. In doing this we realize, and we want readers of this letter to recognize, that not all statements in this letter have the same moral authority. At times we state universally binding moral principles found in the teaching of the Church; at other times the pastoral letter makes specific applications, observations and recommendations which allow for diversity of opinion on the part of those who assess the factual data of a situations differently. However, we expect Catholics to give our moral judgments serious consideration when they are forming their own views on specific problems.

The experience of preparing this letter has manifested to us the range of strongly held opinion in the Catholic community on questions of fact and judgment concerning issues of war and peace. We urge mutual respect among individuals and groups in the Church as this letter is analyzed and discussed. Obviously, as bishops, we believe that such differences should be expressed within the framework of Catholic moral teaching. We need in the Church not only conviction and commitment but also civility and charity.

While this letter is addressed principally to the Catholic community, we want it to make a contribution to the wider public debate in our country on the dangers and dilemmas of the nuclear age. Our contribution will not be primarily technical or political, but we are convinced that there is no satisfactory answer to the human problems of the nuclear age which fails to consider the moral and religious dimensions of the questions we face.

Although we speak in our own name, as Catholic bishops of the Church in the United States, we have been conscious in the preparation of this letter of the consequences our teaching will have not only for the United States but for other nations as well. One important expression of this awareness has been the consultation we have had, by correspondence and in an important meeting held at the Vatican (January 18–19, 1983), with representatives of European bishops' conferences. This consultation with bishops of other countries, and, of course, with the Holy See, has been very helpful to us.

Catholic teaching has always understood peace in positive terms. In the words of Pope John Paul II: "Peace is not just the absence of war. . . . Like a cathedral, peace must be constructed patiently and with unshakable faith." (Coventry, England, 1982) Peace is the fruit of order. Order in human society must be shaped on the basis of respect for the transcendence of God and the unique dignity of each person, understood in terms of freedom, justice, truth and love. To avoid war in our day we must be intent on building peace in an increasingly interdependent world. In Part III of this letter we set forth a positive vision of peace and the demands such a vision makes on diplomacy, national policy, and personal choices.

While pursuing peace incessantly, it is also necessary to limit the use of force in a world comprised of nation states, faced with common problems but devoid of an adequate international political authority. Keeping the peace in the nuclear age is a moral and political imperative. In Parts I and II of this letter we set forth both the principles of Catholic teaching on war and a series of judgments, based on these principles, about concrete policies. In making these judgments we speak as moral teachers, not as technical experts.

I. Some Principles, Norms and Premises of Catholic Teaching

A. ON WAR

1. Catholic teaching begins in every case with a presumption against war and for peaceful settlement of disputes. In exceptional cases, determined by the moral principles of the just-war tradition, some uses of force are permitted.

2. Every nation has a right and duty to defend itself against unjust aggression.

3. Offensive war of any kind is not morally justifiable.

4. It is never permitted to direct nuclear or conventional weapons to "the indiscriminate destruction of whole cities or vast areas with their populations. . . ." (*Pastoral Constitution, #80.*) The intentional killing of innocent civilians or non-combatants is always wrong.

5. Even defensive response to unjust attack can cause destruction which violates the principle of proportionality, going far beyond the limits of legitimate defense. This judgment is particularly important when assessing planned use of nuclear weapons. No defensive strategy, nuclear or conventional, which exceeds the limits of proportionality is morally permissible.

B. ON DETERRENCE

1. "In current conditions 'deterrence' based on balance, certainly not as an end in itself but as a step on the way toward a progressive disarmament, may still be judged morally acceptable. Nonetheless, in order to ensure peace, it is indispensable not to be satisfied with this minimum which is always susceptible to the real danger of explosion." (Pope John Paul II, "Message to U.N. Special Session on Disarmament," #8, June 1982.)

2. No *use* of nuclear weapons which would violate the principles of discrimination or proportionality may be *intended* in a strategy of deterrence. The moral demands of Catholic teaching re-

quire resolute willingness not to intend or to do moral evil even to save our own lives or the lives of those we love.

3. Deterrence is not an adequate strategy as a long-term basis for peace; it is a transitional strategy justifiable only in conjunction with resolute determination to pursue arms control and disarmament. We are convinced that "the fundamental principle on which our present peace depends must be replaced by another, which declares that the true and solid peace of nations consists not in equality of arms but in mutual trust alone." (Pope John XXIII, *Peace on Earth*, #113.)

C. THE ARMS RACE AND DISARMAMENT

1. The arms race is one of the greatest curses on the human race; it is to be condemned as a danger, an act of aggression against the poor, and a folly which does not provide the security it promises. (Cf: *Pastoral Constitution*, #81, *Statement of the Holy See to the United Nations*, 1976.)

2. Negotiations must be pursued in every reasonable form possible; they should be governed by the "demand that the arms race should cease; that the stockpiles which exist in various countries should be reduced equally and simultaneously by the parties concerned; that nuclear weapons should be banned; and that a general agreement should eventually be reached about progressive disarmament and an effective method of control." (Pope John XXIII, *Peace On Earth*, #112.)

D. ON PERSONAL CONSCIENCE

1. *Military Service:* "All those who enter the military service in loyalty to their country should look upon themselves as the custodians of the security and freedom of their fellow countrymen; and when they carry out their duty properly, they are contributing to the maintenance of peace." (*Pastoral Constitution*, #79.)

2. *Conscientious Objection:* "Moreover, it seems just that laws should make humane provision for the case of conscientious objectors who refuse to carry arms, provided they accept some other form of community service." (*Pastoral Constitution*, #79.)

3. *Non-violence:* "In this same spirit we cannot but express our admiration for all who forego the use of violence to vindicate their rights and resort to other means of defense which are available to weaker parties, provided it can be done without harm to the rights

and duties of others and of the community." (*Pastoral Constitution*, #78.)

4. *Citizens and Conscience:* "Once again we deem it opportune to remind our children of their duty to take an active part in public life, and to contribute towards the attainment of the common good of the entire human family as well as to that of their own political community. . . . In other words, it is necessary that human beings, in the intimacy of their own consciences, should so live and act in their temporal lives as to create a synthesis between scientific, technical and professional elements on the one hand, and spiritual values on the other." (Pope John XXIII, *Peace On Earth*, #146, 150.)

II. Moral Principles and Policy Choices

As bishops in the United States, assessing the concrete circumstances of our society, we have made a number of observations and recommendations in the process of applying moral principles to specific policy choices.

A. ON THE USE OF NUCLEAR WEAPONS

1. *Counter Population Use:* Under no circumstances may nuclear weapons or other instruments of mass slaughter be used for the purpose of destroying population centers or other predominantly civilian targets. Retaliatory action which would indiscriminately and disproportionately take many wholly innocent lives, lives of people who are in no way responsible for reckless actions of their government, must also be condemned.

2. *The Initiation of Nuclear War:* We do not perceive any situation in which the deliberate initiation of nuclear war, on however restricted a scale, can be morally justified. Non-nuclear attacks by another state must be resisted by other than nuclear means. Therefore, a serious moral obligation exists to develop non-nuclear defensive strategies as rapidly as possible. In this letter we urge NATO to move rapidly toward the adoption of a "no first use" policy, but we recognize this will take time to implement and will require the development of an adequate alternative defense posture.

3. *Limited Nuclear War:* Our examination of the various arguments on this question makes us highly skeptical about the real

meaning of "limited." One of the criteria of the just-war teaching is that there must be a reasonable hope of success in bringing about justice and peace. We must ask whether such a reasonable hope can exist once nuclear weapons have been exchanged. The burden of proof remains on those who assert that meaningful limitation is possible. In our view the first imperative is to prevent any use of nuclear weapons and we hope that leaders will resist the notion that nuclear conflict can be limited, contained or won in any traditional sense.

B. ON DETERRENCE

In concert with the evaluation provided by Pope John Paul II, we have arrived at a strictly conditional moral acceptance of deterrence. In this letter we have outlined criteria and recommendations which indicate the meaning of conditional acceptance of deterrence policy. We cannot consider such a policy adequate as a long-term basis for peace.

C. ON PROMOTING PEACE

1. We support immediate, bilateral verifiable agreements to halt the testing, production and deployment of new nuclear weapons systems. This recommendation is not to be identified with any specific political initiative.
2. We support efforts to achieve deep cuts in the arsenals of both superpowers; efforts should concentrate first on systems which threaten the retaliatory forces of either major power.
3. We support early and successful conclusion of negotiations of a comprehensive test ban treaty.
4. We urge new efforts to prevent the spread of nuclear weapons in the world, and to control the conventional arms race, particularly the conventional arms trade.
5. We support, in an increasingly interdependent world, political and economic policies designed to protect human dignity and to promote the human rights of every person, especially the least among us. In this regard, we call for the establishment of some form of global authority adequate to the needs of the international common good.

This letter includes many judgments from the perspective of ethics, politics and strategy needed to speak concretely and correctly to the "moment of supreme crisis" identified by Vatican II. We stress again that readers should be aware, as we have been, of the distinction between our statement of moral principles and of official Church teaching and our application of these to concrete issues. We urge that special care be taken not to use passages out of context; neither should brief portions of this document be cited to support positions it does not intend to convey or which are not truly in accord with the spirit of its teaching.

In concluding this summary we respond to two key questions often asked about this pastoral letter:

Why do we address these matters fraught with such complexity, controversy and passion? We speak as pastors, not politicians. We are teachers, not technicians. We cannot avoid our responsibility to lift up the moral dimensions of the choices before our world and nation. The nuclear age is an era of moral as well as physical danger. We are the first generation since Genesis with the power to threaten the created order. We cannot remain silent in the face of such danger. Why do we address these issues? We are simply trying to live up to the call of Jesus to be peacemakers in our own time and situation.

What are we saying? Fundamentally, we are saying that the decisions about nuclear weapons are among the most pressing moral questions of our age. While these decisions have obvious military and political aspects, they involve fundamental moral choices. In simple terms, we are saying that good ends (defending one's country, protecting freedom, etc.) cannot justify immoral means (the use of weapons which kill indiscriminately and threaten whole societies). We fear that our world and nation are headed in the wrong direction. More weapons with greater destructive potential are produced every day. More and more nations are seeking to become nuclear powers. In our quest for more and more security we fear we are actually becoming less and less secure.

In the words of our Holy Father, we need a "moral about-face." The whole world must summon the moral courage and technical means to say no to nuclear conflict; no to weapons of mass destruction; no to an arms race which robs the poor and the vulnerable; and no to the moral danger of a nuclear age which places before humankind indefensible choices of constant terror or surrender. Peacemaking is not an optional commitment. It is a requirement of our faith. We are called to be peacemakers, not by some movement of the moment, but by our Lord Jesus. The content and context of our peacemaking is set not by some political agenda or ideological program, but by the teaching of his Church.

Ultimately, this letter is intended as an expression of Christian faith, affirming the confidence we have that the risen Lord remains with us precisely in moments of crisis. It is our belief in his presence and power among us which sustain us in confronting the awesome challenge of the nuclear age. We speak from faith to provide hope for all who recognize the challenge and are working to confront it with the resources of faith and reason.

To approach the nuclear issue in faith is to recognize our absolute need for prayer: we urge and invite all to unceasing prayer for peace with justice for all people. In a spirit of prayerful hope we present this message of peace.

Introduction

1.   "The whole human race faces a moment of supreme crisis in its advance toward maturity." Thus the Second Vatican Council opened its treatment of modern warfare.[1] Since the council, the dynamic of the nuclear arms race has intensified. Apprehension about nuclear war is almost tangible and visible today. As Pope John Paul II said in his message to the United Nations concerning disarmament: "Currently, the fear and preoccupation of so many groups in various parts of the world reveals that people are more frightened about what would happen if irresponsible parties unleash some nuclear war."[2]

2.   As bishops and pastors ministering in one of the major nuclear nations, we have encountered this terror in the minds and hearts of our people—indeed, we share it. We write this letter because we agree that the world is at a moment of crisis, the effects of which are evident in people's lives. It is not our intent to play on fears, however, but to speak words of hope and encouragement in time of fear. Faith does not insulate us from the challenges of life; rather, it

---

[1] Vatican II, the *Pastoral Constitution on the Church in the Modern World* (hereafter cited: *Pastoral Constitution*), #77. Papal and conciliar texts will be referred to by title with paragraph number. Several collections of these texts exist although no single collection is comprehensive; see the following: *Peace and Disarmament: Documents of the World Council of Churches and the Roman Catholic Church* (Geneva and Rome: 1982) (hereafter cited: *Documents*, with page number); J. Gremillion, *The Gospel of Peace and Justice: Catholic Social Teaching Since Pope John* (Maryknoll, N.Y.: 1976); D. J. O'Brien and T. A. Shannon, eds., *Renewing the Earth: Catholic Documents on Peace, Justice and Liberation* (New York: 1977); A. Flannery, O.P., ed., *Vatican Council II: The Conciliar and Post Conciliar Documents* (Collegeville, Minn.: 1975); W. Abbot, ed., *The Documents of Vatican II* (New York: 1966). Both the Flannery and Abbot translations of the *Pastoral Constitution* are used in this letter.

[2] John Paul II, "Message to the Second Special Session of the United Nations General Assembly Devoted to Disarmament" (June 1982) (hereafter cited: "Message U.N. Special Session 1982"), #7.

intensifies our desire to help solve them precisely in light of the good news which has come to us in the person of Jesus, the Lord of history. From the resources of our faith we wish to provide hope and strength to all who seek a world free of the nuclear threat. Hope sustains one's capacity to live with danger without being overwhelmed by it; hope is the will to struggle against obstacles even when they appear insuperable. Ultimately our hope rests in the God who gave us life, sustains the world by his power, and has called us to revere the lives of every person and all peoples.

3.   The crisis of which we speak arises from this fact: nuclear war threatens the existence of our planet; this is a more menacing threat than any the world has known. It is neither tolerable nor necessary that human beings live under this threat. But removing it will require a major effort of intelligence, courage, and faith. As Pope John Paul II said at Hiroshima: "From now on it is only through a conscious choice and through a deliberate policy that humanity can survive."[3]

4.   As Americans, citizens of the nation which was first to produce atomic weapons, which has been the only one to use them and which today is one of the handful of nations capable of decisively influencing the course of the nuclear age, we have grave human, moral and political responsibilities to see that a "conscious choice" is made to save humanity. This letter is therefore both an invitation and a challenge to Catholics in the United States to join with others in shaping the conscious choices and deliberate policies required in this "moment of supreme crisis."

---

[3] John Paul II, "Address to Scientists and Scholars," #4, *Origins* 10 (1981):621.

I

Peace in the Modern World: Religious Perspectives and Principles

5.   The global threat of nuclear war is a central concern of the universal Church, as the words and deeds of recent popes and the Second Vatican Council vividly demonstrate. In this pastoral letter we speak as bishops of the universal Church, heirs of the religious and moral teaching on modern warfare of the last four decades. We also speak as bishops of the Church in the United States, who have both the obligation and the opportunity to share and interpret the moral and religious wisdom of the Catholic tradition by applying it to the problems of war and peace today.

6.   The nuclear threat transcends religious, cultural, and national boundaries. To confront its danger requires all the resources reason and faith can muster. This letter is a contribution to a wider common effort, meant to call Catholics and all members of our political community to dialogue and specific decisions about this awesome question.

7.   The Catholic tradition on war and peace is a long and complex one, reaching from the Sermon on the Mount to the statements of Pope John Paul II. Its development cannot be sketched in a straight line and it seldom gives a simple answer to complex questions. It speaks through many voices and has produced multiple forms of religious witness. As we locate ourselves in this tradition, seeking to draw from it and to develop it, the document which provides profound inspiration and guidance for us is the *Pastoral Constitution on the Church in the Modern World* of Vatican II, for it is based on doctrinal

principles and addresses the relationship of the Church to the world with respect to the most urgent issues of our day.[4]

8. A rule of interpretation crucial for the *Pastoral Constitution* is equally important for this pastoral letter although the authority inherent in these two documents is quite distinct. Both documents use principles of Catholic moral teaching and apply them to specific contemporary issues. The bishops at Vatican II opened the *Pastoral Constitution* with the following guideline on how to relate principles to concrete issues:

> In the first part, the Church develops her teaching on man, on the world which is the enveloping context of man's existence, and on man's relations to his fellow men. In Part II, the Church gives closer consideration to various aspects of modern life and human society; special consideration is given to those questions and problems which, in this general area, seem to have a greater urgency in our day. As a result, in Part II the subject matter which is viewed in the light of doctrinal principles is made up of diverse elements. Some elements have a permanent value; others, only a transitory one. Consequently, the constitution must be interpreted according to the general norms of theological interpretion. Interpreters must bear in mind—especially in Part II—the changeable circumstances which the subject matter, by its very nature, involves.[5]

9. In this pastoral letter, too, we address many concrete questions concerning the arms race, contemporary warfare, weapons systems, and negotiating strategies. We do not intend that our treatment of each of these issues carry the same moral authority as our statement of universal moral principles and formal Church teaching. Indeed, we stress here at the beginning that not every statement in this letter has the same moral authority. At times we reassert universally binding moral principles (e.g., non-combatant immunity and proportionality). At still other times we reaffirm statements of recent popes and the teaching of Vatican II. Again, at other times we apply moral principles to specific cases.

10. When making applications of these principles we realize—and we wish readers to recognize—that prudential judgments are involved based on specific circumstances which can change or which can be interpreted differently by people of good will (e.g., the treat-

---

[4] The *Pastoral Constitution* is made up of two parts; yet it constitutes an organic unity. By way of explanation: the constitution is called "pastoral" because, while resting on doctrinal principles, it seeks to express the relation of the Church to the world and modern mankind. The result is that, on the one hand, a pastoral slant is present in the first part and, on the other hand, a doctrinal slant is present in the second part. *Pastoral Constitution*, note 1 above.

[5] Ibid.

ment of "no first use"). However, the moral judgments that we make in specific cases, while not binding in conscience, are to be given serious attention and consideration by Catholics as they determine whether their moral judgments are consistent with the Gospel.

11. We shall do our best to indicate, stylistically and substantively, whenever we make such applications. We believe such specific judgments are an important part of this letter, but they should be interpreted in light of another passage from the *Pastoral Constitution*:

> Often enough the Christian view of things will itself suggest some specific solution in certain circumstances. Yet it happens rather frequently, and legitimately so, that with equal sincerity some of the faithful will disagree with others on a given matter. Even against the intention of their proponents, however, solutions proposed on one side or another may be easily confused by many people with the Gospel message. Hence it is necessary for people to remember that no one is allowed in the aforementioned situations to appropriate the Church's authority for his opinion. They should always try to enlighten one another through honest discussion, preserving mutual charity and caring above all for the common good.[6]

12. This passage acknowledges that, on some complex social questions, the Church expects a certain diversity of views even though all hold the same universal moral principles. The experience of preparing this pastoral letter has shown us the range of strongly held opinion in the Catholic community on questions of war and peace. Obviously, as bishops we believe that such differences should be expressed within the framework of Catholic moral teaching. We urge mutual respect among different groups in the Church as they analyze this letter and the issues it addresses. Not only conviction and commitment are needed in the Church, but also civility and charity.

13. The *Pastoral Constitution* calls us to bring the light of the gospel to bear upon "the signs of the times." Three signs of the times have particularly influenced the writing of this letter. The first, to quote Pope John Paul II at the United Nations, is that "the world wants peace, the world needs peace."[7] The second is the judgment of Vatican II about the arms race: "The arms race is one of the greatest curses on the human race and the harm it inflicts upon the poor is more than can be endured."[8] The third is the way in which the unique dangers and dynamics of the nuclear arms race present qualitatively new problems which must be addressed by fresh appli-

---

[6] Ibid., #43.

[7] John Paul II, "Message U.N. Special Session 1982," #2.

[8] *Pastoral Constitution*, #81.

cations of traditional moral principles. In light of these three characteristics, we wish to examine Catholic teaching on peace and war.

14. The Catholic social tradition, as exemplified in the *Pastoral Constitution* and recent papal teachings, is a mix of biblical, theological, and philosophical elements which are brought to bear upon the concrete problems of the day. The biblical vision of the world, created and sustained by God, scarred by sin, redeemed in Christ and destined for the kingdom, is at the heart of our religious heritage. This vision requires elaboration, explanation, and application in each age; the important task of theology is to penetrate ever more adequately the nature of the biblical vision of peace and relate it to a world not yet at peace. Consequently, the teaching about peace examines both how to construct a more peaceful world and how to assess the phenomenon of war.

15. At the center of the Church's teaching on peace and at the center of all Catholic social teaching are the transcendence of God and the dignity of the human person. The human person is the clearest reflection of God's presence in the world; all of the Church's work in pursuit of both justice and peace is designed to protect and promote the dignity of every person. For each person not only reflects God, but is the expression of God's creative work and the meaning of Christ's redemptive ministry. Christians approach the problem of war and peace with fear and reverence. God is the Lord of life, and so each human life is sacred; modern warfare threatens the obliteration of human life on a previously unimaginable scale. The sense of awe and "fear of the Lord" which former generations felt in approaching these issues weighs upon us with new urgency. In the words of the *Pastoral Constitution:*

> Men of this generation should realize that they will have to render an account of their warlike behavior; the destiny of generations to come depends largely on the decisions they make today.[9]

16. Catholic teaching on peace and war has had two purposes: to help Catholics form their consciences and to contribute to the public policy debate about the morality of war. These two purposes have led Catholic teaching to address two distinct but overlapping audiences. The first is the Catholic faithful, formed by the premises of the gospel and the principles of Catholic moral teaching. The second is the wider civil community, a more pluralistic audience, in which our brothers and sisters with whom we share the name Christian, Jews, Moslems, other religious communities, and all people of

---

[9] Ibid., #80.

good will also make up our polity. Since Catholic teaching has traditionally sought to address both audiences, we intend to speak to both in this letter, recognizing that Catholics are also members of the wider political community.

17. The conviction, rooted in Catholic ecclesiology, that both the community of the faithful and the civil community should be addressed on peace and war has produced two complementary but distinct styles of teaching. The religious community shares a specific perspective of faith and can be called to live out its implications. The wider civil community, although it does not share the same vision of faith, is equally bound by certain key moral principles. For all men and women find in the depth of their consciences a law written on the human heart by God.[10] From this law reason draws moral norms. These norms do not exhaust the gospel vision, but they speak to critical questions affecting the welfare of the human community, the role of states in international relations, and the limits of acceptable action by individuals and nations on issues of war and peace.

18. Examples of these two styles can be found in recent Catholic teaching. At times the emphasis is upon the problems and requirements for a just public policy (e.g., Pope John Paul II at the U.N. Special Session 1982); at other times the emphasis is on the specific role Christians should play (e.g., Pope John Paul II at Coventry, England, 1982). The same difference of emphasis and orientation can be found in Pope John XXIII's *Peace on Earth* and Vatican II's *Pastoral Constitution*.

19. As bishops we believe that the nature of Catholic moral teaching, the principles of Catholic ecclesiology, and the demands of our pastoral ministry require that this letter speak both to Catholics in a specific way and to the wider political community regarding public policy. Neither audience and neither mode of address can be neglected when the issue has the cosmic dimensions of the nuclear arms race.

20. We propose, therefore, to discuss both the religious vision of peace among peoples and nations and the problems associated with realizing this vision in a world of sovereign states, devoid of any central authority and divided by ideology, geography, and competing claims. We believe the religious vision has an objective basis and is capable of progressive realization. Christ is our peace, for he has "made us both one, and has broken down the dividing wall of hostility . . . that he might create in himself one new man in place of the

---

[10] Ibid., #16.

two, so making peace, and might reconcile us both to God" (Eph. 2:14-16). We also know that this peace will be achieved fully only in the kingdom of God. The realization of the kingdom, therefore, is a continuing work, progressively accomplished, precariously maintained, and needing constant effort to preserve the peace achieved and expand its scope in personal and political life.

21. Building peace within and among nations is the work of many individuals and institutions; it is the fruit of ideas and decisions taken in the political, cultural, economic, social, military, and legal sectors of life. We believe that the Church, as a community of faith and social institution, has a proper, necessary, and distinctive part to play in the pursuit of peace.

22. The distinctive contribution of the Church flows from her religious nature and ministry. The Church is called to be, in a unique way, the instrument of the kingdom of God in history. Since peace is one of the signs of that kingdom present in the world, the Church fulfills part of her essential mission by making the peace of the kingdom more visible in our time.

23. Because peace, like the kingdom of God itself, is both a divine gift and a human work, the Church should continually pray for the gift and share in the work. We are called to be a Church at the service of peace, precisely because peace is one manifestation of God's word and work in our midst. Recognition of the Church's responsibility to join with others in the work of peace is a major force behind the call today to develop a theology of peace. Much of the history of Catholic theology on war and peace has focused on limiting the resort to force in human affairs; this task is still necessary, and is reflected later in this pastoral letter, but it is not a sufficient response to Vatican II's challenge "to undertake a completely fresh reappraisal of war."[11]

24. A fresh reappraisal which includes a developed theology of peace will require contributions from several sectors of the Church's life: biblical studies, systematic and moral theology, ecclesiology, and the experience and insights of members of the Church who have struggled in various ways to make and keep the peace in this often violent age. This pastoral letter is more an invitation to continue the new appraisal of war and peace than a final synthesis of the results of such an appraisal. We have some sense of the characteristics of a theology of peace, but not a systematic statement of their relationships.

---

[11] Ibid., #80.

25.   A theology of peace should ground the task of peacemaking solidly in the biblical vision of the kingdom of God, then place it centrally in the ministry of the Church. It should specify the obstacles in the way of peace, as these are understood theologically and in the social and political sciences. It should both identify the specific contributions a community of faith can make to the work of peace and relate these to the wider work of peace pursued by other groups and institutions in society. Finally, a theology of peace must include a message of hope. The vision of hope must be available to all, but one source of its content should be found in a Church at the service of peace.

26.   We offer now a first step toward a message of peace and hope. It consists of a sketch of the biblical conception of peace; a theological understanding of how peace can be pursued in a world marked by sin; a moral assessment of key issues facing us in the pursuit of peace today; and an assessment of the political and personal tasks required of all people of good will in this most crucial period of history.

A. Peace and the Kingdom

27.   For us as believers, the sacred scriptures provide the foundation for confronting war and peace today. Any use of scripture in this area is conditioned by three factors. *First*, the term "peace" has been understood in different ways at various times and in various contexts. For example, peace can refer to an individual's sense of well-being or security, or it can mean the cessation of armed hostility, producing an atmosphere in which nations can relate to each other and settle conflicts without resorting to the use of arms. For men and women of faith, peace will imply a right relationship with God, which entails forgiveness, reconciliation, and union. Finally, the scriptures point to eschatological peace, a final, full realization of God's salvation when all creation will be made whole. Among these various meanings, the last two predominate in the scriptures and provide direction to the first two.

28.   *Second*, the scriptures as we have them today were written over a long period of time and reflect many varied historical situations, all different from our own. Our understanding of them is both complicated and enhanced by these differences, but not in any way obscured or diminished by them. *Third*, since the scriptures speak

primarily of God's intervention in history, they contain no specific treatise on war and peace. Peace and war must always be seen in light of God's intervention in human affairs and our response to that intervention. Both are elements within the ongoing revelation of God's will for creation.

29.   Acknowledging this complexity, we still recognize in the scriptures a unique source of revelation, a word of God which is addressed to us as surely as it has been to all preceding generations. We call upon the spirit of God who speaks in that word and in our hearts to aid us in our listening. The sacred texts have much to say to us about the ways in which God calls us to live in union with and in fidelity to the divine will. They provide us with direction for our lives and hold out to us an object of hope, a final promise, which guides and directs our actions here and now.

1. OLD TESTAMENT

30.   War and peace are significant and highly complex elements within the multilayered accounts of the creation and development of God's people in the Old Testament.

a. War

31.   Violence and war are very much present in the history of the people of God, particularly from the Exodus period to the monarchy. God is often seen as the one who leads the Hebrews in battle, protects them from their enemies, makes them victorious over other armies (see, for example, Deut. 1:30; 20:4; Jos. 2:24; Jgs. 3:28). The metaphor of warrior carried multifaceted connotations for a people who knew themselves to be smaller and weaker than the nations which surrounded them. It also enabled them to express their conviction about God's involvement in their lives and his desire for their growth and development. This metaphor provided the people with a sense of security; they had a God who would protect them even in the face of overwhelming obstacles. It was also a call to faith and to trust; the mighty God was to be obeyed and followed. No one can deny the presence of such images in the Old Testament nor their powerful influence upon the articulation of this people's understanding of the involvement of God in their history. The warrior God was highly significant during long periods of Israel's understanding of its faith. But this image was not the only image, and it was gradually transformed, particularly after the experience of the exile, when God was no longer identified with military victory and might. Other

images and other understandings of God's activity became predominant in expressing the faith of God's people.

b. Peace

32.   Several points must be taken into account in considering the image of peace in the Old Testament. First, all notions of peace must be understood in light of Israel's relation to God. Peace is always seen as a gift from God and as fruit of God's saving activity. Secondly, the individual's personal peace is not greatly stressed. The well-being and freedom from fear which result from God's love are viewed primarily as they pertain to the community and its unity and harmony. Furthermore, this unity and harmony extend to all of creation; true peace implied a restoration of the right order not just among peoples, but within all of creation. Third, while the images of war and the warrior God become less dominant as a more profound and complex understanding of God is presented in the texts, the images of peace and the demands upon the people for covenantal fidelity to true peace grow more urgent and more developed.

c. Peace and Fidelity to the Covenant

33.   If Israel obeyed God's laws, God would dwell among them. "I will walk among you and will be your God and you shall be my people" (Lv. 26:12). God would strengthen the people against those who opposed them and would give peace in the land. The description of life in these circumstances witnesses to unity among peoples and creation, to freedom from fear and to security (Lv. 26:3-16). The right relationship between the people and God was grounded in and expressed by a covenantal union. The covenant bound the people to God in fidelity and obedience; God was also committed in the covenant, to be present with the people, to save them, to lead them to freedom. Peace is a special characteristic of this covenant; when the prophet Ezekiel looked to the establishment of the new, truer covenant, he declared that God would establish an everlasting covenant of peace with the people (Ez. 37:26).

34.   Living in covenantal fidelity with God had ramifications in the lives of the people. It was part of fidelity to care for the needy and helpless; a society living with fidelity was one marked by justice and integrity. Furthermore, covenantal fidelity demanded that Israel put its trust in God alone and look only to him for its security. When Israel tended to forget the obligations of the covenant, prophets arose to remind the people and call them to return to God. True peace is an image which they stressed.

35.   Ezekiel, who promised a covenant of peace, condemned in no uncertain terms the false prophets who said there was peace in the land while idolatry and injustice continued (Ez. 13:16). Jeremiah followed in this tradition and berated those who "healed the wounds of the people lightly" and proclaimed peace while injustice and infidelity prevailed (Jer. 6:14; 8:10-12). Jeremiah and Isaiah both condemned the leaders when, against true security, they depended upon their own strength or alliances with other nations rather than trusting in God (Is. 7:1-9; 30:1-4; Jer. 37:10). The lament of Isaiah 48:18 makes clear the connection between justice, fidelity to God's law, and peace; he cries out: "O that you had hearkened to my commandments! Then your peace would have been like a river, and your righteousness like the waves of the sea."

d. Hope for Eschatological Peace

36.   Experience made it clear to the people of God that the covenant of peace and the fullness of salvation had not been realized in their midst. War and enmity were still present, injustices thrived, sin still manifested itself. These same experiences also convinced the people of God's fidelity to a covenant which they often neglected. Because of this fidelity, God's promise of a final salvation involving all peoples and all creation and of an ultimate reign of peace became an integral part of the hope of the Old Testament. In the midst of their failures and sin, God's people strove for greater fidelity to him and closer relationship with him; they did so because, believing in the future they had been promised, they directed their lives and energies toward an eschatological vision for which they longed. Peace is an integral component of that vision.

37.   The final age, the Messianic time, is described as one in which the "Spirit is poured on us from on high." In this age, creation will be made whole, "justice will dwell in the wilderness," the effect of righteousness will be peace, and the people will "abide in a peaceful habitation and in secure dwellings and in quiet resting places" (Is. 32:15-20). There will be no need for instruments of war (Is. 2:4; Mi. 4:3),[12] God will speak directly to the people and "righteousness and peace will embrace each other" (Ps. 85:10-11). A messiah will appear, a servant of God upon whom God has placed his spirit and who will faithfully bring forth justice to the nations: "He will not cry or lift

---

[12] The exact opposite of this vision is presented in Joel 3:10 where the foreign nations are told that their weapons will do them no good in the face of God's coming wrath.

up his voice, or make it heard in the street; a bruised reed he will not break and a dimly burning wick he will not quench; he will faithfully bring forth justice." (Is. 42:2-3).

38. The Old Testament provides us with the history of a people who portrayed their God as one who intervened in their lives, who protected them and led them to freedom, often as a mighty leader in battle. They also appear as a people who longed constantly for peace. Such peace was always seen as a result of God's gift which came about in fidelity to the covenantal union. Furthermore, in the midst of their unfulfilled longing, God's people clung tenaciously to hope in the promise of an eschatological time when, in the fullness of salvation, peace and justice would embrace and all creation would be secure from harm. The people looked for a messiah, one whose coming would signal the beginning of that time. In their waiting, they heard the prophets call them to love according to the covenantal vision, to repent, and to be ready for God's reign.

2. NEW TESTAMENT

39. As Christians we believe that Jesus is the messiah or Christ so long awaited. God's servant (Mt. 12:18-21), prophet and more than prophet (Jn. 4:19-26), the one in whom the fullness of God was pleased to dwell, through whom all things in heaven and on earth were reconciled to God, Jesus made peace by the blood of the cross (Col. 1:19-20). While the characteristics of the *shalom* of the Old Testament (gift from God, inclusive of all creation, grounded in salvation and covenantal fidelity, inextricably bound up with justice) are present in the New Testament traditions, all discussion of war and peace in the New Testament must be seen within the context of the unique revelation of God that is Jesus Christ and of the reign of God which Jesus proclaimed and inaugurated.

a. War

40. There is no notion of a warrior God who will lead the people in an historical victory over its enemies in the New Testament. The only war spoken of is found in apocalyptic images of the final moments, especially as they are depicted in the Book of Revelation. Here war stands as image of the eschatological struggle between God and Satan. It is a war in which the Lamb is victorious (Rv. 17:14).

41. Military images appear in terms of the preparedness which one must have for the coming trials (Lk. 14:31; 22:35-38). Swords appear in the New Testament as an image of division (Mt. 12:34;

Heb. 4:12); they are present at the arrest of Jesus, and he rejects their use (Lk. 22:51 and parallel texts); weapons are transformed in Ephesians, when the Christians are urged to put on the whole armor of God which includes the breastplate of righteousness, the helmet of salvation, the sword of the Spirit, "having shod your feet in the equipment of the gospel of peace" (Eph. 6:10-17; cf. I Thes. 5:8-9). Soldiers, too, are present in the New Testament. They are at the crucifixion of Jesus, of course, but they are also recipients of the baptism of John, and one centurion receives the healing of his servant (Mt. 8:5-13 and parallel texts; cf. Jn. 4:46-53).

42. Jesus challenged everyone to recognize in him the presence of the reign of God and to give themselves over to that reign. Such a radical change of allegiance was difficult for many to accept and families found themselves divided, as if by a sword. Hence, the gospels tell us that Jesus said he came not to bring peace but rather the sword (Mt. 10:34). The peace which Jesus did not bring was the false peace which the prophets had warned against. The sword which he did bring was that of the division caused by the word of God which, like a two-edged sword, "pierces to the division of soul and spirit, of joints and marrow, and discerns the thoughts and intentions of the heart" (Heb. 4:12).

43. All are invited into the reign of God. Faith in Jesus and trust in God's mercy are the criteria. Living in accord with the demands of the kingdom rather than those of one's specific profession is decisive.[13]

b. Jesus and Reign of God

44. Jesus proclaimed the reign of God in his words and made it present in his actions. His words begin with a call to conversion and a proclamation of the arrival of the kingdom. "The time is fulfilled, and the kingdom of God is at hand; repent, and believe in the gospel" (Mk. 1:15, Mt. 4:17). The call to conversion was at the same time an invitation to enter God's reign. Jesus went beyond the prophets'

---

[13] An omission in the New Testament is significant in this context. Scholars have made us aware of the presence of revolutionary groups in Israel during the time of Jesus. Barabbas, for example, was "among the rebels in prison who had committed murder in the insurrection" (Mk. 15:7). Although Jesus had come to proclaim and to bring about the true reign of God which often stood in opposition to the existing order, he makes no reference to nor does he join in any attempts such as those of the Zealots to overthrow authority by violent means. See M. Smith, "Zealots and Sicarii, Their Origins and Relations," *Harvard Theological Review* 64 (1971):1-19.

cries for conversion when he declared that, in him, the reign of God had begun and was in fact among the people (Lk. 17:20-21; 12:32).

45. His words, especially as they are preserved for us in the Sermon on the Mount, describe a new reality in which God's power is manifested and the longing of the people is fulfilled. In God's reign the poor are given the kingdom, the mourners are comforted, the meek inherit the earth, those hungry for righteousness are satisfied, the merciful know mercy, the pure see God, the persecuted know the kingdom, and peacemakers are called the children of God (Mt. 5:3-10).

46. Jesus' words also depict for us the conduct of one who lives under God's reign. His words call for a new way of life which fulfills and goes beyond the law. One of the most striking characteristics of this new way is forgiveness. All who hear Jesus are repeatedly called to forgive one another, and to do so not just once, but many, many times (Mt. 6:14-15; Lk. 6:37; Mt. 18:21-22; Mk. 11:25; Lk. 11:4; 17:3-4). The forgiveness of God, which is the beginning of salvation, is manifested in communal forgiveness and mercy.

47. Jesus also described God's reign as one in which love is an active, life-giving, inclusive force. He called for a love which went beyond family ties and bonds of friendship to reach even those who were enemies (Mt. 5:44-48; Lk. 6:27-28). Such a love does not seek revenge but rather is merciful in the face of threat and opposition (Mt. 5:39-42; Lk. 6:29-31). Disciples are to love one another as Jesus has loved them (Jn. 15:12).

48. The words of Jesus would remain an impossible, abstract ideal were it not for two things: the actions of Jesus and his gift of the spirit. In his actions, Jesus showed the way of living in God's reign; he manifested the forgiveness which he called for when he accepted all who came to him, forgave their sins, healed them, released them from the demons who possessed them. In doing these things, he made the tender mercy of God present in a world which knew violence, oppression, and injustice. Jesus pointed out the injustices of his time and opposed those who laid burdens upon the people or defiled true worship. He acted aggressively and dramatically at times, as when he cleansed the temple of those who had made God's house into a "den of robbers" (Mt. 21:12-17 and parallel texts; Jn. 3:13-25).

49. Most characteristic of Jesus' actions are those in which he showed his love. As he had commanded others, his love led him even to the giving of his own life to effect redemption. Jesus' message and his actions were dangerous ones in his time, and they led to his death—a cruel and viciously inflicted death, a criminal's death (Gal.

3:13). In all of his suffering, as in all of his life and ministry, Jesus refused to defend himself with force or with violence. He endured violence and cruelty so that God's love might be fully manifest and the world might be reconciled to the One from whom it had become estranged. Even at his death, Jesus cried out for forgiveness for those who were his executioners: "Father, forgive them . . . " (Lk. 23:34).

50. The resurrection of Jesus is the sign to the world that God indeed does reign, does give life in death, and that the love of God is stronger even than death (Rom. 8:36-39).

51. Only in light of this, the fullest demonstration of the power of God's reign, can Jesus' gift of peace—a peace which the world cannot give (Jn. 14:27)—be understood. Jesus gives that peace to his disciples, to those who had witnessed the helplessness of the crucifixion and *t*he power of the resurrection (Jn. 20:19, 20, 26). The peace which he gives to them as he greets them as their risen Lord is the fullness of salvation. It is the reconciliation of the world and God (Rom. 5:1-2; Col. 1:20); the restoration of the unity and harmony of all creation which the Old Testament spoke of with such longing. Because the walls of hostility between God and humankind were broken down in the life and death of the true, perfect servant, union and well-being between God and the world were finally fully possible (Eph. 2:13-22; Gal. 3:28).

c. Jesus and the Community of Believers

52. As his first gift to his followers, the risen Jesus gave his gift of peace. This gift permeated the meetings between the risen Jesus and his followers (Jn. 20:19-29). So intense was that gift and so abiding was its power that the remembrance of that gift and the daily living of it became the hallmark of the community of faith. Simultaneously, Jesus gave his spirit to those who followed him. These two personal and communal gifts are inseparable. In the spirit of Jesus the community of believers was enabled to recognize and to proclaim the savior of the world.

53. Gifted with Jesus' own spirit, they could recognize what God had done and know in their own lives the power of the One who creates from nothing. The early Christian communities knew that this power and the reconciliation and peace which marked it were not yet fully operative in their world. They struggled with external persecution and with interior sin, as do all people. But their experience of the spirit of God and their memory of the Christ who was with them nevertheless enabled them to look forward with unshakable confidence to the time when the fullness of God's reign would make itself known in the world. At the same time, they knew that they were called to be ministers of reconciliation (2 Cor. 5:19-20), people who would make the peace which God had established visible through the love and the unity within their own communities.

54. Jesus Christ, then, is our peace, and in his death-resurrection he gives God's peace to our world. In him God has indeed reconciled the world, made it one, and has manifested definitively that his will is this reconciliation, this unity between God and all peoples, and among the peoples themselves. The way to union has been opened, the covenant of peace established. The risen Lord's gift of peace is inextricably bound to the call to follow Jesus and to continue the proclamation of God's reign. Matthew's gospel (Mt. 28:16-20; cf. Lk. 24:44-53) tells us that Jesus' last words to his disciples were a sending forth and a promise: "I shall be with you all days." In the continuing presence of Jesus, disciples of all ages find the courage to follow him. To follow Jesus Christ implies continual conversion in one's own life as one seeks to act in ways which are consonant with the justice, forgiveness, and love of God's reign. Discipleship reaches out to the ends of the earth and calls for reconciliation among all peoples so that God's purpose, "a plan for the fullness of time, to unite all things in him" (Eph. 1:10), will be fulfilled.

3. CONCLUSION

55. Even a brief examination of war and peace in the scriptures makes it clear that they do not provide us with detailed answers to the specifics of the questions which we face today. They do not speak specifically of nuclear war or nuclear weapons, for these were beyond the imagination of the communities in which the scriptures were formed. The sacred texts do, however, provide us with urgent direction when we look at today's concrete realities. The fullness of eschatological peace remains before us in hope and yet the gift of peace is already ours in the reconciliation effected in Jesus Christ. These two profoundly religious meanings of peace inform and influence all other meanings for Christians. Because we have been gifted with God's peace in the risen Christ, we are called to our own peace and to the making of peace in our world. As disciples and as children of God, it is our task to seek for ways in which to make the forgiveness, justice and mercy and love of God visible in a world where violence and enmity are too often the norm. When we listen to God's word, we hear again and always the call to repentance and to belief: to repentance because although we are redeemed we continue to need

redemption; to belief, because although the reign of God is near, it is still seeking its fullness.

B. Kingdom and History

56.   The Christian understanding of history is hopeful and confident but also sober and realistic. "Christian optimism based on the glorious cross of Christ and the outpouring of the Holy Spirit is no excuse for self-deception. For Christians, peace on earth is always a challenge because of the presence of sin in man's heart."[14] Peace must be built on the basis of justice in a world where the personal and social consequences of sin are evident.

57.   Christian hope about history is rooted in our belief in God as creator and sustainer of our existence and our conviction that the kingdom of God will come in spite of sin, human weakness, and failure. It is precisely because sin is part of history that the realization of the peace of the kingdom is never permanent or total. This is the continuing refrain from the patristic period to Pope John Paul II:

> For it was sin and hatred that were an obstacle to peace with God and with others: he destroyed them by the offering of life on the cross; he reconciled in one body those who were hostile (cf. Eph. 2:16; Rom. 12:5) . . . Although Christians put all their best energies into preventing war or stopping it, they do not deceive themselves about their ability to cause peace to triumph, nor about the effect of their efforts to this end. They therefore concern themselves with all human initiatives in favor of peace and very often take part in them. But they regard them with realism and humility. One could almost say that they relativize them in two senses: they relate them both to the self-deception of humanity and to God's saving plan.[15]

58.   Christians are called to live the tension between the vision of the reign of God and its concrete realization in history. The tension is often described in terms of "already but not yet": i.e., we already live in the grace of the kingdom, but it is not yet the completed kingdom. Hence, we are a pilgrim people in a world marked by conflict and injustice. Christ's grace is at work in the world; his command of love and his call to reconciliation are not purely future ideals but call us to obedience today.

---

[14] John Paul II, "World Day of Peace Message 1982," #12, *Origins* 11 (1982): 477.

[15] Ibid., #11-12, pp. 477-78.

59.   With Pope Paul VI and Pope John Paul II we are convinced that "peace is possible."[16] At the same time, experience convinces us that "in this world a totally and permanently peaceful human society is unfortunately a utopia, and that ideologies that hold up that prospect as easily attainable are based on hopes that cannot be realized, whatever the reason behind them."[17]

60.   This recognition—that peace is possible but never assured and that its possibility must be continually protected and preserved in the face of obstacles and attacks upon it—accounts in large measure for the complexity of Catholic teaching on warfare. In the kingdom of God, peace and justice will be fully realized. Justice is always the foundation of peace. In history, efforts to pursue both peace and justice are at times in tension, and the struggle for justice may threaten certain forms of peace.

61.   It is within this tension of kingdom and history that Catholic teaching has addressed the problem of war. Wars mark the fabric of human history, distort the life of nations today, and, in the form of nuclear weapons, threaten the destruction of the world as we know it and the civilization which has been patiently constructed over centuries. The causes of war are multiple and not easily identified. Christians will find in any violent situation the consequences of sin: not only sinful patterns of domination, oppression or aggression, but the conflict of values and interests which illustrate the limitations of a sinful world. The threat of nuclear war which affects the world today reflects such sinful patterns and conflicts.

62.   In the "already but not yet" of Christian existence, members of the Church choose different paths to move toward the realization of the kingdom in history. As we examine both the positions open to individuals for forming their consciences on war and peace and the Catholic teaching on the obligation of the state to defend society, we draw extensively on the *Pastoral Constitution* for two reasons.

63.   First, we find its treatment of the nature of peace and the avoidance of war compelling, for it represents the prayerful thinking of bishops of the entire world and calls vigorously for fresh new attitudes, while faithfully reflecting traditional Church teaching. Secondly, the council fathers were familiar with more than the horrors of World Wars I and II. They saw conflicts continuing "to produce

---

[16] John Paul II, "Message U.N. Special Session 1982," #13; Pope Paul VI, "World Day of Peace Message 1973."

[17] John Paul II, "World Day of Peace Message 1982," #12, cited, p. 478.

their devastating effect day by day somewhere in the world," the increasing ferocity of warfare made possible by modern scientific weapons, guerrilla warfare "drawn out by new methods of deceit and subversion," and terrorism regarded as a new way to wage war.[18] The same phenomena mark our day.

64.   For similar reasons we draw heavily upon the popes of the nuclear age, from Pope Pius XII through Pope John Paul II. The teaching of popes and councils must be incarnated by each local church in a manner understandable to its culture. This allows each local church to bring its unique insights and experience to bear on the issues shaping our world. From 1966 to the present, American bishops, individually and collectively, have issued numerous statements on the issues of peace and war, ranging from the Vietnam War to conscientious objection and the use of nuclear weapons. These statements reflect not only the concerns of the hierarchy but also the voices of our people who have increasingly expressed to us their alarm over the threat of war. In this letter we wish to continue and develop the teaching on peace and war which we have previously made, and which reflects both the teaching of the universal Church and the insights and experience of the Catholic community of the United States.

65.   It is significant that explicit treatment of war and peace is reserved for the final chapter of the *Pastoral Constitution*. Only after exploring the nature and destiny of the human person does the council take up the nature of peace, which it sees not as an end in itself, but as an *indispensable condition* for the task "of constructing for all men everywhere a world more genuinely human."[19] An understanding of this task is crucial to understanding the Church's view of the moral choices open to us as Christians.

C. The Moral Choices for the Kingdom

66.   In one of its most frequently quoted passages, the *Pastoral Constitution* declares that it is necessary "to undertake a completely fresh reappraisal of war."[20] The council's teaching situates this call for a "fresh reappraisal" within the context of a broad analysis of

---

[18] *Pastoral Constitution*, #79.

[19] Ibid., #77.

[20] Ibid., #80.

the dignity of the human person and the state of the world today. If we lose sight of this broader discussion we cannot grasp the council's wisdom. For the issue of war and peace confronts everyone with a basic question: what contributes to, and what impedes, the construction of a more genuinely human world? If we are to evaluate war with an entirely new attitude, we must be serious about approaching the human person with an entirely new attitude. The obligation for all of humanity to work toward universal respect for human rights and human dignity is a fundamental imperative of the social, economic, and political order.

67. It is clear, then, that to evaluate war with a new attitude, we must go far beyond an examination of weapons systems or military strategies. We must probe the meaning of the moral choices which are ours as Christians. In accord with the vision of Vatican II, we need to be sensitive to both the danger of war and the conditions of true freedom within which moral choices can be made.[21] Peace is the setting in which moral choice can be most effectively exercised. How can we move toward that peace which is indispensable for true human freedom? How do we define such peace?

1. THE NATURE OF PEACE

68. The Catholic tradition has always understood the meaning of peace in positive terms. Peace is both a gift of God and a human work. It must be constructed on the basis of central human values: truth, justice, freedom, and love. The *Pastoral Constitution* states the traditional conception of peace:

> Peace is not merely the absence of war. Nor can it be reduced solely to the maintenance of a balance of power between enemies. Nor is it brought about by dictatorship. Instead, it is rightly and appropriately called "an enterprise of justice" (Is. 32:17). Peace results from that harmony built into human society by its divine founder and actualized by men as they thirst after ever greater justice.[22]

69. Pope John Paul II has enhanced this positive conception of peace by relating it with new philosophical depth to the Church's teaching on human dignity and human rights. The relationship was articulated in his 1979 Address to the General Assembly of the United Nations and also in his "World Day of Peace Message 1982":

---

[21] Ibid., #17.

[22] Ibid., #78.

Unconditional and effective respect for each one's unprescriptable and inalienable rights is the necessary condition in order that peace may reign in a society. Vis-a-vis these basic rights all others are in a way derivatory and secondary. In a society in which these rights are not protected, the very idea of universality is dead, as soon as a small group of individuals set up for their own exclusive advantage a principle of discrimination whereby the rights and even the lives of others are made dependent on the whim of the stronger.[23]

70.   As we have already noted, however, the protection of human rights and the preservation of peace are tasks to be accomplished in a world marked by sin and conflict of various kinds. The Church's teaching on war and peace establishes a strong presumption against war which is binding on all; it then examines when this presumption may be overriden, precisely in the name of preserving the kind of peace which protects human dignity and human rights.

2. THE PRESUMPTION AGAINST WAR AND THE PRINCIPLE OF LEGITIMATE SELF-DEFENCE

71.   Under the rubric, "curbing the savagery of war," the council contemplates the "melancholy state of humanity." It looks at this world as it is, not simply as we would want it to be. The view is stark: ferocious new means of warfare threatening savagery surpassing that of the past, deceit, subversion, terrorism, genocide. This last crime, in particular, is vehemently condemned as horrendous, but all activities which deliberately conflict with the all-embracing principles of universal natural law, which is permanently binding, are criminal, as are all orders commanding such action. Supreme commendation is due the courage of those who openly and fearlessly resist those who issue such commands. All individuals, especially government officials and experts, are bound to honor and improve upon agreements which are "aimed at making military activity and its consequences less inhuman" and which "better and more workably lead to restraining the frightfulness of war."[24]

72.   This remains a realistic appraisal of the world today. Later in this section the council calls for us "to strain every muscle as we work for the time when all war can be completely outlawed by in-

---

[23] John Paul II, "World Day of Peace Message 1982," #9, cited. The *Pastoral Constitution* stresses that peace is not only the fruit of justice, but also love, which commits us to engage in "the studied practice of brotherhood" (#78).

[24] *Pastoral Constitution*, #79.

ternational consent." We are told, however, that this goal requires the establishment of some universally recognized public authority with effective power "to safeguard, on the behalf of all, security, regard for justice, and respect for rights."[25] *But what of the present?* The council is exceedingly clear, as are the popes:

> Certainly, war has not been rooted out of human affairs. As long as the danger of war remains and there is no competent and sufficiently powerful authority at the international level, governments cannot be denied the right to legitimate defense once every means of peaceful settlement has been exhausted. Therefore, government authorities and others who share public responsibility have the duty to protect the welfare of the people entrusted to their care and to conduct such grave matters soberly.
>
> But it is one thing to undertake military action for the just defense of the people, and something else again to seek the subjugation of other nations. Nor does the possession of war potential make every military or political use of it lawful. Neither does the mere fact that war has unhappily begun mean that all is fair between the warring parties.[26]

73. The Christian has no choice but to defend peace, properly understood, against aggression. This is an inalienable obligation. It is the *how* of defending peace which offers moral options. We stress this principle again because we observe so much misunderstanding about both those who resist bearing arms and those who bear them. Great numbers from both traditions provide examples of exceptional courage, examples the world continues to need. Of the millions of men and women who have served with integrity in the armed forces, many have laid down their lives. Many others serve today throughout the world in the difficult and demanding task of helping to preserve that "peace of a sort" of which the council speaks. We see many deeply sincere individuals who, far from being indifferent or apathetic to world evils, believe strongly in conscience that they are best defending true peace by refusing to bear arms. In some cases they are motivated by their understanding of the gospel and the life and death of Jesus as forbidding all violence. In others, their motivation is simply to give personal example of Christian forbearance as a positive, constructive approach toward loving reconciliation with enemies. In still other cases, they propose or engage in "active non-violence" as programmed resistance to thwart aggression, or to render ineffective any oppression attempted by force of arms. No government, and

---

[25] Ibid., #82.
[26] Ibid., #79.

certainly no Christian, may simply assume that such individuals are mere pawns of conspiratorial forces or guilty of cowardice.

74.   Catholic teaching sees these two distinct moral responses as having a complementary relationship, in the sense that both seek to serve the common good. They differ in their perception of how the common good is to be defended most effectively, but both responses testify to the Christian conviction that peace must be pursued and rights defended within moral restraints and in the context of defining other basic human values.

75.   In all of this discussion of distinct choices, of course, we are referring to options open to individuals. The council and the popes have stated clearly that governments threatened by armed, unjust aggression must defend their people. This includes defense by armed force if necessary as a last resort. We shall discuss below the conditions and limits imposed on such defense. Even when speaking of individuals, however, the council is careful to preserve the fundamental *right* of defense. Some choose not to vindicate their rights by armed force and adopt other methods of defense, but they do not lose the right of defense nor may they renounce their obligations to others. They are praised by the council, as long as the rights and duties of others or of the community itself are not injured.

76.   Pope Pius XII is especially strong in his conviction about the responsibility of the Christian to resist unjust aggression:

> *A people threatened with an unjust aggression, or already its victim, may not remain passively indifferent, if it would think and act as befits a Christian.* All the more does the solidarity of the family of nations forbid others to behave as mere spectators, in any attitude of apathetic neutrality. Who will ever measure the harm already caused in the past by such indifference to war of aggression, which is quite alien to the Christian instinct? How much more keenly has it brought any advantage in recompense? On the contrary, it has only reassured and encouraged the authors and fomentors of aggression, while it obliges the several peoples, left to themselves, to increase their armaments indefinitely . . . Among (the) goods (of humanity) some are of such importance for society, that it is perfectly lawful to defend them against unjust aggression. *Their defense is even an obligation for the nations as a whole, who have a duty not to abandon a nation that is attacked.*[27]

---

[27] Pius XII, "Christmas Message," 1948; The same theme is reiterated in Pius XII's "Message" of October 3, 1953: "The community of nations must reckon with unprincipled criminals who, in order to realize their ambitious plans, are not afraid to unleash total war. This is the reason why other countries if they wish to preserve their very existence and their most precious possessions, and unless they are prepared to accord free action to international criminals, have no alternative but to get ready for the day when they must defend themselves. *This right to be prepared for self-defense cannot be denied, even in these days, to any state.*"

77. None of the above is to suggest, however, that armed force is the only defense against unjust aggression, regardless of circumstances. Well does the council require that grave matters concerning the protection of peoples be conducted *soberly*. The council fathers were well aware that in today's world, the "horror and perversity of war are immensely magnified by the multiplication of scientific weapons. For acts of war involving these weapons can inflict massive and indiscriminate destruction far exceeding the bounds of legitimate defense."[28] Hence, we are warned: "Men of our time must realize that they will have to give a somber reckoning for their deeds of war. For the course of the future will depend largely on the decisions they make today."[29] There must be serious and continuing study and efforts to develop programmed methods for both individuals and nations to defend against unjust aggression without using violence.

78. We believe work to develop non-violent means of fending off aggression and resolving conflict best reflects the call of Jesus both to love and to justice. Indeed, each increase in the potential destructiveness of weapons and therefore of war serves to underline the rightness of the way that Jesus mandated to his followers. But, on the other hand, the fact of aggression, oppression and injustice in our world also serves to legitimate the resort to weapons and armed force in defense of justice. We must recognize the reality of the paradox we face as Christians living in the context of the world as it presently exists; we must continue to articulate our belief that love is possible and the only real hope for all human relations, and yet accept that force, even deadly force, is sometimes justified and that nations must provide for their defense. It is the mandate of Christians, in the face of this paradox, to strive to resolve it through an even greater commitment to Christ and his message. As Pope John Paul II said:

> Christians are aware that plans based on aggression, domination and the manipulation of others lurk in human hearts, and sometimes even secretly nourish human intentions, in spite of certain declarations or manifestations of a pacifist nature. For Christians know that in this world a totally and permanently peaceful human society is unfortunately a utopia, and that ideologies that hold up that prospect as easily attainable are based on hopes that cannot be realized, whatever the reason behind them. It is a question of a mistaken view of the human condition, a lack of application in considering the question as a whole; or it may be a case of evasion in order to calm fear, or in still other cases a matter of calculated self-interest.

---

[28] *Pastoral Constitution*, #80.

[29] Ibid.

Christians are convinced, if only because they have learned from personal experience, that these deceptive hopes lead straight to the false peace of totalitarian regimes. But this realistic view in no way prevents Christians from working for peace; instead, it stirs up their ardor, for they also know that Christ's victory over deception, hate and death gives those in love with peace a more decisive motive for action than what the most generous theories about man have to offer; Christ's victory likewise gives a hope more surely based than any hope held out by the most audacious dreams.

This is why Christians, even as they strive to resist and prevent every form of warfare, have no hesitation in recalling that, in the name of an elementary requirement of justice, peoples have a right and even a duty to protect their existence and freedom by proportionate means against an unjust aggressor.[30]

79. In light of the framework of Catholic teaching on the nature of peace, the avoidance of war, and the state's right of legitimate defense, we can now spell out certain moral principles within the Catholic tradition which provide guidance for public policy and individual choice.

3. THE JUST-WAR CRITERIA

80. The moral theory of the "just-war" or "limited-war" doctrine begins with the presumption which binds all Christians: we should do no harm to our neighbors; how we treat our enemy is the key test of whether we love our neighbor; and the possibility of taking even one human life is a prospect we should consider in fear and trembling. How is it possible to move from these presumptions to the idea of a justifiable use of lethal force?

81. Historically and theologically the clearest answer to the question is found in St. Augustine. Augustine was impressed by the fact and the consequences of sin in history—the "not yet" dimension of the kingdom. In his view war was both the result of sin and a tragic remedy for sin in the life of political societies. War arose from disordered ambitions, but it could also be used, in some cases at least, to restrain evil and protect the innocent. The classic case which illustrated his view was the use of lethal force to prevent aggression against innocent victims. Faced with the fact of attack on the innocent, the presumption that we do no harm, even to our enemy, yielded to the command of love understood as the need to restrain an enemy who would injure the innocent.

---

[30] John Paul II, "World Day of Peace Message 1982," #12, cited, p. 478.

82.   The just-war argument has taken several forms in the history of Catholic theology, but this Augustinian insight is its central premise.[31] In the twentieth century, papal teaching has used the logic of Augustine and Aquinas[32] to articulate a right of self-defense for states in a decentralized international order and to state the criteria for exercising that right. The essential position was stated by Vatican II: "As long as the danger of war persists and there is no international authority with the necessary competence and power, governments cannot be denied the right of lawful self-defense, once all peace efforts have failed."[33] We have already indicated the centrality of this principle for understanding Catholic teaching about the state and its duties.

83.   Just-war teaching has evolved, however, as an effort to prevent war; only if war cannot be rationally avoided, does the teaching then seek to restrict and reduce its horrors. It does this by establishing a set of rigorous conditions which must be met if the decision to go to war is to be morally permissible. Such a decision, especially today, requires extraordinarily strong reasons for overriding the presumption *in favor of peace* and *against* war. This is one significant reason why valid just-war teaching makes provision for conscientious dissent. It is presumed that all sane people prefer peace, never *want* to initiate war, and accept even the most justifiable defensive war only as a sad necessity. Only the most powerful reasons may be permitted to override such objection. In the words of Pope Pius XII:

> The Christian will for peace . . . is very careful to avoid recourse to the force of arms in the defense of rights which, however legitimate, do not offset the risk of kindling a blaze with all its spiritual and material consequences.[34]

---

[31] Augustine called it a Manichaean heresy to assert that war is intrinsically evil and contrary to Christian charity, and stated: "War and conquest are a sad necessity in the eyes of men of principle, yet it would be still more unfortunate if wrongdoers should dominate just men." (*The City of God*, Book IV, C. 15)

Representative surveys of the history and theology of the just-war tradition include: F. H. Russell, *The Just War in the Middle Ages* (New York: 1975); P. Ramsey, *War and the Christian Conscience* (Durham, N.C.: 1961); P. Ramsey, *The Just War: Force and Political Responsibility* (New York: 1968), James T. Johnson, *Ideology, Reason and the Limitation of War* (Princeton: 1975), *Just War Tradition and the Restraint of War: A Moral and Historical Inquiry* (Princeton: 1981); L. B. Walters, *Five Classic Just-War Theories* (Ph.D. Dissertation, Yale University, 1971); W. O'Brien, *War and/or Survival* (New York: 1969), *The Conduct of Just and Limited War* (New York: 1981); J. C. Murray, "Remarks on the Moral Problem of War," *Theological Studies* 20 (1959):40-61.

[32] Aquinas treats the question of war in the *Summa Theologica*, II-IIae, q. 40; also cf. II-IIae, q. 64.

[33] *Pastoral Constitution*, #79.

[34] Pius XII, "Christmas Message," 1948.

84. The determination of *when* conditions exist which allow the resort to force in spite of the strong presumption against it is made in light of *jus ad bellum* criteria. The determination of *how* even a justified resort to force must be conducted is made in light of the *jus in bello* criteria. We shall briefly explore the meaning of both.[35]

Jus ad Bellum

85. Why and when recourse to war is permissible.

86. *a) Just Cause:* War is permissible only to confront "a real and certain danger," i.e., to protect innocent life, to preserve conditions necessary for decent human existence, and to secure basic human rights. As both Pope Pius XII and Pope John XXIII made clear, if war of retribution was ever justifiable, the risks of modern war negate such a claim today.

87. *b) Competent Authority:* In the Catholic tradition the right to use force has always been joined to the common good; war must be declared by those with responsibility for public order, not by private groups or individuals.

88. The requirement that a decision to go to war must be made by competent authority is particularly important in a democratic society. It needs detailed treatment here since it involves a broad spectrum of related issues. Some of the bitterest divisions of society in our own nation's history, for example, have been provoked over the question of whether or not a president of the United States has acted constitutionally and legally in involving our country in a *de facto* war, even if—indeed, especially if—war was never formally declared. Equally perplexing problems of conscience can be raised for individuals expected or legally required to go to war even though our duly elected representatives in Congress have, in fact, voted for war.

89. The criterion of competent authority is of further importance in a day when revolutionary war has become commonplace. Historically, the just-war tradition has been open to a "just revolution" position, recognizing that an oppressive government may lose its claim to legitimacy. Insufficient analytical attention has been given to the moral issues of revolutionary warfare. The mere possession of sufficient weaponry, for example, does not legitimize the initiation of war by "insurgents" against an established government, any more

---

[35] For an analysis of the content and relationship of these principles cf.: R. Potter, "The Moral Logic of War," *McCormick Quarterly* 23 (1970):203-33; J. Childress, "Just War Criteria," in T. Shannon, ed., *War or Peace: The Search for New Answers* (N.Y.: 1980).

than the government's systematic oppression of its people can be carried out under the doctrine of "national security."

90. While the legitimacy of revolution in some circumstances cannot be denied, just-war teachings must be applied as rigorously to revolutionary-counterrevolutionary conflicts as to others. The issue of who constitutes competent authority and how such authority is exercised is essential.

91. When we consider in this letter the issues of conscientious objection (C.O.) and selective conscientious objection (S.C.O.), the issue of competent authority will arise again.

92. *c) Comparative Justice:* Questions concerning the *means* of waging war today, particularly in view of the destructive potential of weapons, have tended to override questions concerning the comparative justice of the positions of respective adversaries or enemies. In essence: which side is sufficiently "right" in a dispute, and are the values at stake critical enough to override the presumption against war? The question in its most basic form is this: do the rights and values involved justify killing? For whatever the means used, war, by definition, involves violence, destruction, suffering, and death.

93. The category of comparative justice is designed to emphasize the presumption against war which stands at the beginning of just-war teaching. In a world of sovereign states recognizing neither a common moral authority nor a central political authority, comparative justice stresses that no state should act on the basis that it has "absolute justice" on its side. Every party to a conflict should acknowledge the limits of its "just cause" and the consequent requirement to use *only* limited means in pursuit of its objectives. Far from legitimizing a crusade mentality, comparative justice is designed to relativize absolute claims and to restrain the use of force even in a "justified" conflict.[36]

94. Given techniques of propaganda and the ease with which nations and individuals either assume or delude themselves into believing that God or right is clearly on their side, the test of comparative justice may be extremely difficult to apply. Clearly, however, this is not the case in every instance of war. Blatant aggression from without

---

[36] James T. Johnson, *Ideology, Reason and the Limitation of War*, cited; W. O'Brien, *The Conduct of Just and Limited War*, cited, pp. 13-30; W. Vanderpol, *La doctrine scolastique du droit de guerre*, p. 387ff; J. C. Murray, "Theology and Modern Warfare," in W. J. Nagel, ed., *Morality and Modern Warfare*, p. 80ff.

and subversion from within are often enough readily identifiable by all reasonably fair-minded people.

95.   d) Right Intention: Right intention is related to just cause—war can be legitimately intended only for the reasons set forth above as a just cause. During the conflict, right intention means pursuit of peace and reconciliation, including avoiding unnecessarily destructive acts or imposing unreasonable conditions (e.g., unconditional surrender).

96.   e) Last Resort: For resort to war to be justified, all peaceful alternatives must have been exhausted. There are formidable problems in this requirement. No international organization currently in existence has exercised sufficient internationally recognized authority to be able either to mediate effectively in most cases or to prevent conflict by the intervention of United Nations or other peacekeeping forces. Furthermore, there is a tendency for nations or peoples which perceive conflict between or among other nations as advantageous to themselves to attempt to prevent a peaceful settlement rather than advance it.

97.   We regret the apparent unwillingness of some to see in the United Nations organization the potential for world order which exists and to encourage its development. Pope Paul VI called the United Nations the last hope for peace. The loss of this hope cannot be allowed to happen. Pope John Paul II is again instructive on this point:

> I wish above all to repeat my confidence in you, the leaders and members of the International Organizations, and in you, the international officials! In the course of the last ten years, your organizations have too often been the object of attempts at manipulation on the part of nations wishing to exploit such bodies. However it remains true that the present multiplicity of violent clashes, divisions and blocks on which bilateral relations founder, offer the great International Organizations the opportunity to engage upon the qualitative change in their activities, even to reform on certain points their own structures in order to take into account new realities and to enjoy effective power.[37]

98.   f) Probability of Success: This is a difficult criterion to apply, but its purpose is to prevent irrational resort to force or hopeless resistance when the outcome of either will clearly be disproportionate or futile. The determination includes a recognition that at times defense of key values, even against great odds, may be a "proportionate" witness.

---

[37] John Paul II, "World Day of Peace Message 1983," #11.

99.   g) Proportionality: In terms of the *jus ad bellum* criteria, proportionality means that the damage to be inflicted and the costs incurred by war must be proportionate to the good expected by taking up arms. Nor should judgments concerning proportionality be limited to the temporal order without regard to a spiritual dimension in terms of "damage," "cost," and "the good expected." In today's interdependent world even a local conflict can affect people everywhere; this is particularly the case when the nuclear powers are involved. Hence a nation cannot justly go to war today without considering the effect of its action on others and on the international community.

100.   This principle of proportionality applies throughout the conduct of the war as well as to the decision to begin warfare. During the Vietnam war our bishops' conference ultimately concluded that the conflict had reached such a level of devastation to the adversary and damage to our own society that continuing it could not be justified.[38]

Jus in Bello

101.   Even when the stringent conditions which justify resort to war are met, the conduct of war (i.e., strategy, tactics, and individual actions) remains subject to continuous scrutiny in light of two principles which have special significance today precisely because of the destructive capability of modern technological warfare. These principles are proportionality and discrimination. In discussing them here, we shall apply them to the question of *jus ad bellum* as well as *jus in bello*; for today it becomes increasingly difficult to make a decision to use any kind of armed force, however limited initially in intention and in the destructive power of the weapons employed, without facing at least the possibility of escalation to broader, or even total, war and to the use of weapons of horrendous destructive potential. This is especially the case when adversaries are "superpowers," as the council clearly envisioned:

> Indeed, if the kind of weapons now stocked in the arsenals of the great powers were to be employed to the fullest, the result would be the almost complete reciprocal slaughter of one side by the other, not to speak of the widespread devastation that would follow in the world and the deadly after-effects resulting from the use of such weapons.[39]

---

[38] National Conference of Catholic Bishops, *Resolution on Southeast Asia* (Washington, D.C.: 1971).

[39] *Pastoral Constitution*, #80.

102.   It should not be thought, of course, that massive slaughter and destruction would result only from the extensive use of nuclear weapons. We recall with horror the carpet and incendiary bombings of World War II, the deaths of hundreds of thousands in various regions of the world through "conventional" arms, the unspeakable use of gas and other forms of chemical warfare, the destruction of homes and of crops, the utter suffering war has wrought during the centuries before and the decades since the use of the "atom bomb." Nevertheless, every honest person must recognize that, especially given the proliferation of modern scientific weapons, we now face possibilities which are appalling to contemplate. Today, as never before, we must ask not merely what *will* happen, but what *may* happen, especially if major powers embark on war. Pope John Paul II has repeatedly pleaded that world leaders confront this reality:

> [I]n view of the difference between classical warfare and nuclear or bac-
> teriological war—a difference so to speak of nature—and in view of the
> scandal of the arms race seen against the background of the needs of the
> Third World, this right [of defense], which is very real in principle, only
> underlines the urgency of world society to equip itself with effective means
> of negotiation. In this way the nuclear terror that haunts our time can
> encourage us to enrich our common heritage with a very simple discovery
> that is within our reach, namely that war is the most barbarous and least
> effective way of resolving conflicts.[40]

103.   The Pontifical Academy of Sciences reaffirmed the Holy Father's theme, in its November 1981 "Statement on the Consequences of Nuclear War." Then, in a meeting convoked by the Pontifical Academy, representatives of national academies of science from throughout the world issued a "Declaration on the Prevention of Nuclear War" which specified the meaning of Pope John Paul II's statement that modern warfare differs by nature from previous forms of war. The scientists said:

> Throughout its history humanity has been confronted with war, but since
> 1945 the nature of warfare has changed so profoundly that the future of
> the human race, of generations yet unborn, is imperiled. . . . For the first
> time it is possible to cause damage on such a catastrophic scale as to wipe
> out a large part of civilization and to endanger its very survival. The large-
> scale use of such weapons could trigger major and irreversible ecological
> and genetic changes whose limits cannot be predicted.[41]

And earlier, with such thoughts plainly in mind, the council had

---

[40] John Paul II, "World Day of Peace Message 1982," #12, cited.

[41] "Declaration on Prevention of Nuclear War" (Sept. 24, 1982).

made its own "the condemnation of total war already pronounced by recent popes."[42] This condemnation is demanded by the principles of proportionality and discrimination. Response to aggression must not exceed the nature of the aggression. To destroy civilization as we know it by waging a "total war" as today it *could* be waged would be a monstrously disproportionate response to aggression on the part of any nation.

104. Moreover, the lives of innocent persons may never be taken directly, regardless of the purpose alleged for doing so. To wage truly "total" war is by definition to take huge numbers of innocent lives. Just response to aggression must be discriminate; it must be directed against unjust aggressors, not against innocent people caught up in a war not of their making. The council therefore issued its memorable declaration:

> Any act of war aimed indiscriminately at the destruction of entire cities or of extensive areas along with their population is a crime against God and man himself. It merits unequivocal and unhesitating condemnation.[43]

105. When confronting choices among specific military options, the question asked by proportionality is: once we take into account not only the military advantages that will be achieved by using this means but also all the harms reasonably expected to follow from using it, can its use still be justified? We know, of course, that no end can justify means evil in themselves, such as the executing of hostages or the targeting of non-combatants. Nonetheless, even if the means adopted is not evil in itself, it is necessary to take into account the probable harms that will result from using it and the justice of accepting those harms. It is of utmost importance, in assessing harms and the justice of accepting them, to think about the poor and the helpless, for they are usually the ones who have the least to gain and the most to lose when war's violence touches their lives.

106. In terms of the arms race, if the *real* end in view is legitimate defense against unjust aggression, and the means to this end are not evil in themselves, we must still examine the question of proportionality concerning attendant evils. Do the exorbitant costs, the general climate of insecurity generated, the possibility of accidental detonation of highly destructive weapons, the danger of error and miscalculation that could provoke retaliation and war—do such evils or others attendant upon and indirectly deriving from the arms race

---

[42] *Pastoral Constitution*, #80.

[43] Ibid.

make the arms race itself a disproportionate response to aggression? Pope John Paul II is very clear in his insistence that the exercise of the right and duty of a people to protect their existence and freedom is contingent on the use of proportionate means.[44]

107. Finally, another set of questions concerns the interpretation of the principle of discrimination. The principle prohibits directly intended attacks on non-combatants and non-military targets. It raises a series of questions about the term "intentional," the category of "non-combatant," and the meaning of "military."

108. These questions merit the debate occurring with increasing frequency today. We encourage such debate, for concise and definitive answers still appear to be wanting. Mobilization of forces in modern war includes not only the military, but to a significant degree the political, economic, and social sectors. It is not always easy to determine who is directly involved in a "war effort" or to what degree. Plainly, though, not even by the broadest definition can one rationally consider combatants entire classes of human beings such as schoolchildren, hospital patients, the elderly, the ill, the average industrial worker producing goods not directly related to military purposes, farmers, and many others. They may never be directly attacked.

109. Direct attacks on military targets involve similar complexities. Which targets are "military" ones and which are not? To what degree, for instance, does the use (by either revolutionaries or regular military forces) of a village or housing in a civilian populated area invite attack? What of a munitions factory in the heart of a city? Who is directly responsible for the deaths of noncombatants should the attack be carried out? To revert to the question raised earlier, how many deaths of non-combatants are "tolerable" as a result of indirect attacks—attacks directed against combat forces and military targets, which nevertheless kill non-combatants at the same time?

110. These two principles, in all their complexity, must be applied to the range of weapons—conventional, nuclear, biological, and chemical—with which nations are armed today.

4. THE VALUE OF NON-VIOLENCE

111. Moved by the example of Jesus' life and by his teaching, some Christians have from the earliest days of the Church committed

---

[44] John Paul II, "World Day of Peace Message 1982," #12, cited.

themselves to a non-violent lifestyle.[45] Some understood the gospel of Jesus to prohibit all killing. Some affirmed the use of prayer and other spiritual methods as means of responding to enmity and hostility.
112. In the middle of the second century, St. Justin proclaimed to his pagan readers that Isaiah's prophecy about turning swords into ploughshares and spears into sickles had been fulfilled as a consequence of Christ's coming:

> And we who delighted in war, in the slaughter of one another, and in every other kind of iniquity have in every part of the world converted our weapons into implements of peace—our swords into ploughshares, our spears into farmers' tools—and we cultivate piety, justice, brotherly charity, faith and hope, which we derive from the Father through the crucified Savior . . .[46]

113. Writing in the third century, St. Cyprian of Carthage struck a similar note when he indicated that the Christians of his day did not fight against their enemies. He himself regarded their conduct as proper:

> They do not even fight against those who are attacking since it is not granted to the innocent to kill even the aggressor, but promptly to deliver up their souls and blood that, since so much malice and cruelty are rampant in the world, they may more quickly withdraw from the malicious and the cruel.[47]

114. Some of the early Christian opposition to military service was a response to the idolatrous practices which prevailed in the Roman army. Another powerful motive was the fact that army service involved preparation for fighting and killing. We see this in the case of St. Martin of Tours during the fourth century, who renounced his soldierly profession with the explanation: "Hitherto I have served you as a soldier. Allow me now to become a soldier of God . . . I am a soldier of Christ. It is not lawful for me to fight."[48]

---

[45] Representative authors in the tradition of Christian pacifism and non-violence include: R. Bainton, *Christian Attitudes Toward War and Peace* (Abington: 1960), chs. 4, 5, 10; J. Yoder, *The Politics of Jesus* (Grand Rapids: 1972), *Nevertheless: Varieties of Religious Pacifism* (Scottsdale: 1971); T. Merton, *Faith and Violence: Christian Teaching and Christian Practice* (Notre Dame: 1968); G. Zahn, *War, Conscience and Dissent* (New York: 1967); E. Egan, "The Beatitudes: Works of Mercy and Pacifism," in T. Shannon, ed., *War or Peace: The Search for New Answers* (New York: 1980), pp. 169-187; J. Fahey, "The Catholic Church and the Arms Race," *Worldview* 22 (1979):38-41; J. Douglass, *The Nonviolent Cross: A Theology of Revolution and Peace* (New York: 1966).

[46] Justin, *Dialogue with Trypho*, ch. 110; cf. also *The First Apology*, chs. 14, 39.

[47] Cyprian, *Collected Letters*; Letters to Cornelius.

[48] Sulpicius Severus, *The Life of Martin*, 4.3.

115.   In the centuries between the fourth century and our own day, the theme of Christian non-violence and Christian pacifism has echoed and re-echoed, sometimes more strongly, sometimes more faintly. One of the great non-violent figures in those centuries was St. Francis of Assisi. Besides making personal efforts on behalf of reconciliation and peace, Francis stipulated that laypersons who became members of his Third Order were not "to take up lethal weapons, or bear them about, against anybody."

116.   The vision of Christian non-violence is not passive about injustice and the defense of the rights of others; it rather affirms and exemplifies what it means to resist injustice through non-violent methods.

117.   In the twentieth century, prescinding from the non-Christian witness of a Mahatma Ghandi and its worldwide impact, the non-violent witness of such figures as Dorothy Day and Martin Luther King has had a profound impact upon the life of the Church in the United States. The witness of numerous Christians who had preceded them over the centuries was affirmed in a remarkable way at the Second Vatican Council.

118.   Two of the passages which were included in the final version of the *Pastoral Constitution* gave particular encouragement for Catholics in all walks of life to assess their attitudes toward war and military service in the light of Christian pacifism. In paragraph 79 the council fathers called upon governments to enact laws protecting the rights of those who adopted the position of conscientious objection to all war: "Moreover, it seems right that laws make humane provisions for the case of those who for reasons of conscience refuse to bear arms, provided, however, that they accept some other form of service to the human community."[49] This was the first time a call for legal protection of conscientious objection had appeared in a document of such prominence. In addition to its own profound meaning this statement took on even more significance in the light of the praise that the council fathers had given in the preceding section "to those who renounce the use of violence and the vindication of their rights."[50] In *Human Life in Our Day* (1968) we called for legislative provision to recognize selective conscientious objectors as well.[51]

---

[49] *Pastoral Constitution*, #79.

[50] Ibid., #78.

[51] United States Catholic Conference, *Human Life in Our Day* (Washington, D.C.: 1968), p. 44.

119. As Catholic bishops it is incumbent upon us to stress to our own community and to the wider society the significance of this support for a pacifist option for individuals in the teaching of Vatican II and the reaffirmation that the popes have given to nonviolent witness since the time of the council.

120. In the development of a theology of peace and the growth of the Christian pacifist position among Catholics, these words of the *Pastoral Constitution* have special significance: "All these factors force us to undertake a completely fresh reappraisal of war."[52] The council fathers had reference to "the development of armaments by modern science (which) has immeasurably magified the horrors and wickedness of war."[53] While the just-war teaching has clearly been in possession for the past 1,500 years of Catholic thought, the "new moment" in which we find ourselves sees the just-war teaching and non-violence as distinct but interdependent methods of evaluating warfare. They diverge on some specific conclusions, but they share a common presumption against the use of force as a means of settling disputes.

121. Both find their roots in the Christian theological tradition; each contributes to the full moral vision we need in pursuit of a human peace. We believe the two perspectives support and complement one another, each preserving the other from distortion. Finally, in an age of technological warfare, analysis from the viewpoint of non-violence and analysis from the viewpoint of the just-war teaching often converge and agree in their opposition to methods of warfare which are in fact indistinguishable from total warfare.

---

[52] *Pastoral Constitution*, #80.

[53] Ibid.

II

War and Peace in the
Modern World:
Problems and Principles

122. Both the just-war teaching and non-violence are confronted with a unique challenge by nuclear warfare. This must be the starting point of any further moral reflection: nuclear weapons particularly and nuclear warfare as it is planned today, raise new moral questions. No previously conceived moral position escapes the fundamental confrontation posed by contemporary nuclear strategy. Many have noted the similarity of the statements made by eminent scientists and Vatican II's observation that we are forced today "to undertake a completely fresh reappraisal of war." The task before us is not simply to repeat what we have said before; it is first to consider anew whether and how our religious-moral tradition can assess, direct, contain, and, we hope, help to eliminate the threat posed to the human family by the nuclear arsenals of the world. Pope John Paul II captured the essence of the problem during his pilgrimage to Hiroshima:

> In the past it was possible to destroy a village, a town, a region, even a country. Now it is the whole planet that has come under threat.[54]

123. The Holy Father's observation illustrates why the moral problem is also a religious question of the most profound significance. In the nuclear arsenals of the United States or the Soviet Union alone, there exists a capacity to do something no other age could imagine: we can threaten the entire planet.[55] For people of faith this means we read the Book of Genesis with a new awareness; the moral issue at stake in nuclear war involves the meaning of sin in its most graphic dimensions. Every sinful act is a confrontation of the creature and

---

[54] John Paul II, "Address to Scientists and Scholars," #4, cited, p. 621.

[55] Cf. "Declaration on Prevention of Nuclear War."

the creator. Today the destructive potential of the nuclear powers threatens the human person, the civilization we have slowly constructed, and even the created order itself.

124.   We live today, therefore, in the midst of a cosmic drama; we possess a power which should never be used, but which might be used if we do not reverse our direction. We live with nuclear weapons knowing we cannot afford to make one serious mistake. This fact dramatizes the precariousness of our position, politically, morally, and spiritually.

125.   A prominent "sign of the times" today is a sharply increased awareness of the danger of the nuclear arms race. Such awareness has produced a public discussion about nuclear policy here and in other countries which is unprecedented in its scope and depth. What has been accepted for years with almost no question is now being subjected to the sharpest criticism. What previously had been defined as a safe and stable system of deterrence is today viewed with political and moral skepticism. Many forces are at work in this new evaluation, and we believe one of the crucial elements is the gospel vision of peace which guides our work in this pastoral letter. The nuclear age has been the theater of our existence for almost four decades; today it is being evaluated with a new perspective. For many the leaven of the gospel and the light of the Holy Spirit create the decisive dimension of this new perspective.

A. The New Moment

126.   At the center of the new evaluation of the nuclear arms race is a recognition of two elements: the destructive potential of nuclear weapons, and the stringent choices which the nuclear age poses for both politics and morals.

127.   The fateful passage into the nuclear age as a military reality began with the bombing of Nagasaki and Hiroshima, events described by Pope Paul VI as a "butchery of untold magnitude."[56] Since then, in spite of efforts at control and plans for disarmament (e.g., the Baruch Plan of 1946), the nuclear arsenals have escalated, particularly in the two superpowers. The qualitative superiority of these two states, however, should not overshadow the fact that four other countries

---

[56] Paul VI, "World Day of Peace Message 1976," in *Documents*, p. 198.

possess nuclear capacity and a score of states are only steps away from becoming "nuclear nations."

128.   This nuclear escalation has been opposed sporadically and selectively but never effectively. The race has continued in spite of carefully expressed doubts by analysts and other citizens and in the face of forcefully expressed opposition by public rallies. Today the opposition to the arms race is no longer selective or sporadic, it is widespread and sustained. The danger and destructiveness of nuclear weapons are understood and resisted with new urgency and intensity. There is in the public debate today an endorsement of the position submitted by the Holy See at the United Nations in 1976: the arms race is to be condemned as a danger, an act of aggression against the poor, and a folly which does not provide the security it promises.[57]

129.   Papal teaching has consistently addressed the folly and danger of the arms race; but the new perception of it which is now held by the general public is due in large measure to the work of scientists and physicians who have described for citizens the concrete human consequences of a nuclear war.[58]

130.   In a striking demonstration of his personal and pastoral concern for preventing nuclear war, Pope John Paul II commissioned a study by the Pontifical Academy of Sciences which reinforced the findings of other scientific bodies. The Holy Father had the study transmitted by personal representative to the leaders of the United States, the Soviet Union, the United Kingdom, and France, and to the president of the General Assembly of the United Nations. One of its conclusions is especially pertinent to the public debate in the United States:

> Recent talk about winning or even surviving a nuclear war must reflect a failure to appreciate a medical reality: Any nuclear war would inevitably cause death, disease and suffering of pandemonic proportions and without the possibility of effective medical intervention. That reality leads to the same conclusion physicians have reached for life-threatening epidemics throughout history. Prevention is essential for control.[59]

131.   This medical conclusion has a moral corollary. Traditionally, the Church's moral teaching sought first to prevent war and then to

---

[57] "Statement of the Holy See to the United Nations" (1976), in *The Church and the Arms Race*; Pax Christi-USA (New York: 1976), pp. 23-24.

[58] R. Adams and S. Cullen, *The Final Epidemic: Physicians and Scientists on Nuclear War* (Chicago: 1981).

[59] Pontifical Academy of Sciences, "Statement on the Consequences of the Use of Nuclear Weapons," in *Documents*, p. 241.

limit its consequences if it occurred. Today the possibilities for placing political and moral limits on nuclear war are so minimal that the moral task, like the medical, is prevention: as a people, we must refuse to legitimate the idea of nuclear war. Such a refusal will require not only new ideas and new vision, but what the gospel calls conversion of the heart.

132. To say "no" to nuclear war is both a necessary and a complex task. We are moral teachers in a tradition which has always been prepared to relate moral principles to concrete problems. Particularly in this letter we could not be content with simply restating general moral principles or repeating well-known requirements about the ethics of war. We have had to examine, with the assistance of a broad spectrum of advisors of varying persuasions, the nature of existing and proposed weapons systems, the doctrines which govern their use, and the consequences of using them. We have consulted people who engage their lives in protest against the existing nuclear strategy of the United States, and we have consulted others who have held or do hold responsibility for this strategy. It has been a sobering and perplexing experience. In light of the evidence which witnesses presented and in light of our study, reflection, and consultation, we must reject nuclear war. But we feel obliged to relate our judgment to the specific elements which comprise the nuclear problem.

133. Though certain that the dangerous and delicate nuclear relationship the superpowers now maintain should not exist, we understand how it came to exist. In a world of sovereign states, devoid of central authority and possessing the knowledge to produce nuclear weapons, many choices were made, some clearly objectionable, others well-intended with mixed results, which brought the world to its present dangerous situation.

134. We see with increasing clarity the political folly of a system which threatens mutual suicide, the psychological damage this does to ordinary people, especially the young, the economic distortion of priorities—billions readily spent for destructive instruments while pitched battles are waged daily in our legislatures over much smaller amounts for the homeless, the hungry, and the helpless here and abroad. But it is much less clear how we translate a "no" to nuclear war into the personal and public choices which can move us in a new direction, toward a national policy and an international system which more adequately reflect the values and vision of the kingdom of God.

135. These tensions in our assessment of the politics and strategy of the nuclear age reflect the conflicting elements of the nuclear dilemma and the balance of terror which it has produced. We have

said earlier in this letter that the fact of war reflects the existence of sin in the world. The nuclear threat and the danger it poses to human life and civilization exemplify in a qualitatively new way the perennial struggle of the political community to contain the use of force, particularly among states.

136.   Precisely because of the destructive nature of nuclear weapons, strategies have been developed which previous generations would have found unintelligible. Today military preparations are undertaken on a vast and sophisticated scale, but the declared purpose is not to use the weapons produced. Threats are made which would be suicidal to implement. The key to security is no longer only military secrets, for in some instances security may best be served by informing one's adversary publicly what weapons one has and what plans exist for their use. The presumption of the nation-state system, that sovereignty implies an ability to protect a nation's territory and population, is precisely the presumption denied by the nuclear capacities of both superpowers. In a sense each is at the mercy of the other's perception of what strategy is "rational," what kind of damage is "unacceptable," how "convincing" one side's threat is to the other.

137.   The political paradox of deterrence has also strained our moral conception. May a nation threaten what it may never do? May it possess what it may never use? Who is involved in the threat each superpower makes: government officials? or military personnel? or the citizenry in whose defense the threat is made?

138.   In brief, the danger of the situation is clear; but how to prevent the use of nuclear weapons, how to assess deterrence, and how to delineate moral responsibility in the nuclear age are less clearly seen or stated. Reflecting the complexity of the nuclear problem, our arguments in this pastoral must be detailed and nuanced; but our "no" to nuclear war must, in the end, be definitive and decisive.

B. Religious Leadership and the Public Debate

139.   Because prevention of nuclear war appears, from several perspectives, to be not only the surest but only way to limit its destructive potential, we see our role as moral teachers precisely in terms of helping to form public opinion with a clear determination to resist resort to nuclear war as an instrument of national policy. If "prevention is the only cure," then there are diverse tasks to be performed in preventing what should never occur. As bishops we see

a specific task defined for us in Pope John Paul II's "World Day of Peace Message 1982":

> Peace cannot be built by the power of rulers alone. Peace can be firmly constructed only if it corresponds to the resolute determination of all people of good will. Rulers must be supported and enlightened by a public opinion that encourages them or, where necessary, expresses disapproval.[60]

140. The pope's appeal to form public opinion is not an abstract task. Especially in a democracy, public opinion can passively acquiesce in policies and strategies or it can, through a series of measures, indicate the limits beyond which a government should not proceed. The "new moment" which exists in the public debate about nuclear weapons provides a creative opportunity and a moral imperative to examine the relationship between public opinion and public policy. We believe it is necessary, for the sake of prevention, to build a barrier against the concept of nuclear war as a viable strategy for defense. There should be a clear public resistance to the rhetoric of "winnable" nuclear wars, or unrealistic expectations of "surviving" nuclear exchanges, and strategies of "protracted nuclear war." We oppose such rhetoric.

141. We seek to encourage a public attitude which sets stringent limits on the kind of actions our own government and other governments will take on nuclear policy. We believe religious leaders have a task in concert with public officials, analysts, private organizations, and the media to set the limits beyond which our military policy should not move in word or action. Charting a moral course in a complex public policy debate involves several steps. We will address four questions, offering our reflections on them as an invitation to a public moral dialogue:

1) the use of nuclear weapons;
2) the policy of deterrence in principle and in practice;
3) specific steps to reduce the danger of war;
4) long-term measures of policy and diplomacy.

C. The Use of Nuclear Weapons

142. Establishing moral guildelines in the nuclear debate means

---

[60] John Paul II, "World Day of Peace Message 1982," #6, cited, p. 476.

addressing first the question of the use of nuclear weapons. That question has several dimensions.

143. It is clear that those in the Church who interpret the gospel teaching as forbidding all use of violence would oppose any use of nuclear weapons under any conditions. In a sense the existence of these weapons simply confirms and reinforces one of the initial insights of the non-violent position, namely, that Christians should not use lethal force since the hope of using it selectively and restrictively is so often an illusion. Nuclear weapons seem to prove this point in a way heretofore unknown.

144. For the tradition which acknowledges some legitimate use of force, some important elements of contemporary nuclear strategies move beyond the limits of moral justification. A justifiable use of force must be both discriminatory and proportionate. Certain aspects of both U.S. and Soviet strategies fail both tests as we shall discuss below. The technical literature and the personal testimony of public officials who have been closely associated with U.S. nuclear strategy have both convinced us of the overwhelming probability that major nuclear exchange would have no limits.[61]

145. On the more complicated issue of "limited" nuclear war, we are aware of the extensive literature and discussion which this topic

---

[61] The following quotations are from public officials who have served at the highest policy levels in recent administrations of our government: "It is time to recognize that no one has ever succeeded in advancing any persuasive reason to believe that any use of nuclear weapons, even on the smallest scale, could reliably be expected to remain limited." M. Bundy, G. F. Kennan, R. S. McNamara and G. Smith, "Nuclear Weapons and the Atlantic Alliance," *Foreign Affairs* 60 (1982):757.

"From my experience in combat there is no way that [nuclear escalation] . . . can be controlled because of the lack of information, the pressure of time and the deadly results that are taking place on both sides of the battle line." Gen. A. S. Collins, Jr. (former deputy commander in chief of U.S. Army in Europe), "Theatre Nuclear Warfare: The Battlefield," in J. F. Reichart and S. R. Sturn, eds., *American Defense Policy*, 5th ed., (Baltimore: 1982), pp. 359-60.

"None of this potential flexibility changes my view that a full-scale thermonuclear exchange would be an unprecedented disaster for the Soviet Union as well as for the United States. Nor is it at all clear that an initial use of nuclear weapons—however selectively they might be targeted—could be kept from escalating to a full-scale thermonuclear exchange, especially if command-and-control centers were brought under attack. The odds are high, whether weapons were used against tactical or strategic targets, that control would be lost on both sides and the exchange would become unconstrained." Harold Brown, *Department of Defense Annual Report FY 1979* (Washington, D.C.: 1978).

Cf. also: *The Effects of Nuclear War* (Washington, D.C.: 1979, U.S. Government Printing Office).

has generated.[62] As a general statement, it seems to us that public officials would be unable to refute the following conclusion of the study made by the Pontifical Academy of Sciences:

Even a nuclear attack directed only at military facilities would be devastating to the country as a whole. This is because military facilities are widespread rather than concentrated at only a few points. Thus, many nuclear weapons would be exploded.

Furthermore, the spread of radiation due to the natural winds and atmospheric mixing would kill vast numbers of people and contaminate large areas. The medical facilities of any nation would be inadequate to care for the survivors. An objective examination of the medical situation that would follow a nuclear war leads to but one conclusion: prevention is our only recourse.[63]

Moral Principles and Policy Choices

146. In light of these perspectives we address three questions more explicitly: (1) counter population warfare; (2) initiation of nuclear war; and (3) limited nuclear war.

1. Counter Population Warfare

147. Under no circumstances may nuclear weapons or other instruments of mass slaughter be used for the purpose of destroying population centers or other predominantly civilian targets. Popes have repeatedly condemned "total war" which implies such use. For example, as early as 1954 Pope Pius XII condemned nuclear warfare "when it entirely escapes the control of man," and results in "the pure and simple annihilation of all human life within the radius of action."[64] The condemnation was repeated by the Second Vatican Council:

Any act of war aimed indiscriminately at the destruction of entire cities or of extensive areas along with their population is a crime against God and man itself. It merits unequivocal and unhesitating condemnation.[65]

---

62 For example, cf.: H. A. Kissinger, *Nuclear Weapons and Foreign Policy* (New York: 1957), *The Necessity for Choice* (New York: 1960); R. Osgood and R. Tucker, *Force, Order and Justice* (Baltimore: 1967); R. Aron, *The Great Debate: Theories of Nuclear Strategy* (New York: 1965); D. Ball, *Can Nuclear War Be Controlled?* Adelphi Paper #161 (London: 1981); M. Howard, "On Fighting a Nuclear War," *International Security* 5 (1981):3-17.

63 "Statement on the Consequences of the Use of Nuclear Weapons," cited, p. 243.

64 Pius XII, "Address to the VIII Congress of the World Medical Association," in *Documents*, p. 131.

65 *Pastoral Constitution*, #80.

148.   Retaliatory action whether nuclear or conventional which
would indiscriminately take many wholly innocent lives, lives of
people who are in no way responsible for reckless actions of their
government, must also be condemned. This condemnation, in our
judgment, applies even to the retaliatory use of weapons striking
enemy cities after our own have already been struck. No Christian
can rightfully carry out orders or policies deliberately aimed at killing
non-combatants.[66]

149.   We make this judgment at the beginning of our treatment of
nuclear strategy precisely because the defense of the principle of non-
combatant immunity is so important for an ethic of war and because
the nuclear age has posed such extreme problems for the principle.
Later in this letter we shall discuss specific aspects of U.S. policy in
light of this principle and in light of recent U.S. policy statements stressing
the determination not to target directly or strike directly against civilian
populations. Our concern about protecting the moral value of noncombatant immunity, however, requires that we make a clear reassertion of
the principle our first word on this matter.

2. The Initiation of Nuclear War

150.   We do not perceive any situation in which the deliberate
initiation of nuclear warfare, on however restricted a scale, can be
morally justified. Non-nuclear attacks by another state must be resisted by other than nuclear means. Therefore, a serious moral obligation exists to develop non-nuclear defensive strategies as rapidly
as possible.

151.   A serious debate is under way on this issue.[67] It is cast in
political terms, but it has a significant moral dimension. Some have
argued that at the very beginning of a war nuclear weapons might
be used, only against military targets, perhaps in limited numbers.
Indeed it has long been American and NATO policy that nuclear
weapons, especially so-called tactical nuclear weapons, would likely
be used if NATO forces in Europe seemed in danger of losing a
conflict that until then had been restricted to conventional weapons.
Large numbers of tactical nuclear weapons are now deployed in
Europe by the NATO forces and about as many by the Soviet Union.
Some are substantially smaller than the bomb used on Hiroshima,

---

[66] Ibid.

[67] M. Bundy, et al., "Nuclear Weapons," cited; K. Kaiser, G. Leber, A. Mertes, F. J.
Schulze, "Nuclear Weapons and the Preservation of Peace," *Foreign Affairs* 60 (1982):1157-
70; cf. other responses to Bundy article in the same issue of *Foreign Affairs*.

some are larger. Such weapons, if employed in great numbers, would totally devastate the densely populated countries of Western and Central Europe.

152. Whether under conditions of war in Europe, parts of Asia or the Middle East, or the exchange of strategic weapons directly between the United States and the Soviet Union, the difficulties of limiting the use of nuclear weapons are immense. A number of expert witnesses advise us that commanders operating under conditions of battle probably would not be able to exercise strict control; the number of weapons used would rapidly increase, the targets would be expanded beyond the military, and the level of civilian casualties would rise enormously.[68] No one can be certain that this escalation would not occur, even in the face of political efforts to keep such an exchange "limited." The chances of keeping use limited seem remote, and the consequences of escalation to mass destruction would be appalling. Former public officials have testified that it is improbable that any nuclear war could actually be kept limited. Their testimony and the consequences involved in this problem lead us to conclude that the danger of escalation is so great that it would be morally unjustifiable to initiate nuclear war in any form. The danger is rooted not only in the technology of our weapons systems but in the weakness and sinfulness of human communities. We find the moral responsibility of beginning nuclear war not justified by rational political objectives.

153. This judgment affirms that the willingness to initiate nuclear war entails a distinct, weighty moral responsibility; it involves transgressing a fragile barrier—political, psychological, and moral—which has been constructed since 1945. We express repeatedly in this letter our extreme skepticism about the prospects for controlling a nuclear exchange, however limited the first use might be. Precisely because of this skepticism, we judge resort to nuclear weapons to counter a conventional attack to be morally unjustifiable.[69] Consequently we seek to reinforce the barrier against any use of nuclear weapons. Our support of a "no first use" policy must be seen in this light.

154. At the same time we recognize the responsibility the United States has had and continues to have in assisting allied nations in their defense against either a conventional or a nuclear attack. Es-

---

[68] Testimony given to the National Conference of Catholic Bishops Committee during preparation of this pastoral letter. The testimony is reflected in the quotes found in note 61.

[69] Our conclusions and judgments in this area although based on careful study and reflection of the application of moral principles do not have, of course, the same force as the principles themselves and therefore allow for different opinions, as the Summary makes clear.

pecially in the European theater, the deterrence of a *nuclear* attack may require nuclear weapons for a time, even though their possession and deployment must be subject to rigid restrictions.

155. The need to defend against a conventional attack in Europe imposes the political and moral burden of developing adequate, alternative modes of defense to present reliance on nuclear weapons. Even with the best coordinated effort—hardly likely in view of contemporary political division on this question—development of an alternative defense position will still take time.

156. In the interim, deterrence against a conventional attack relies upon two factors: the not inconsiderable conventional forces at the disposal of NATO and the recognition by a potential attacker that the outbreak of large scale conventional war could escalate to the nuclear level through accident or miscalculation by either side. We are aware that NATO's refusal to adopt a "no first use" pledge is to some extent linked to the deterrent effect of this inherent ambiguity. Nonetheless, in light of the probable effects of initiating nuclear war, we urge NATO to move rapidly toward the adoption of a "no first use" policy, but doing so in tandem with development of an adequate alternative defense posture.

3. Limited Nuclear War

157. It would be possible to agree with our first two conclusions and still not be sure about retaliatory use of nuclear weapons in what is called a "limited exchange." The issue at stake is the *real* as opposed to the *theoretical* possibility of a "limited nuclear exchange."

158. We recognize that the policy debate on this question is inconclusive and that all participants are left with hypothetical projections about probable reactions in a nuclear exchange. While not trying to adjudicate the technical debate, we are aware of it and wish to raise a series of questions which challenge the actual meaning of "limited" in this discussion.

—Would leaders have sufficient information to know what is happening in a nuclear exchange?

—Would they be able under the conditions of stress, time pressures, and fragmentary information to make the extraordinarily precise decision needed to keep the exchange limited if this were technically possible?

—Would military commanders be able, in the midst of the destruction and confusion of a nuclear exchange, to maintain a policy of "discriminate targeting"? Can this be done in modern warfare, waged across great distances by aircraft and missiles?

—Given the accidents we know about in peacetime conditions, what assurances are there that computer errors could be avoided in the midst of a nuclear exchange?

—Would not the casualties, even in a war defined as limited by strategists, still run in the millions?

—How "limited" would be the long-term effects of radiation, famine, social fragmentation, and economic dislocation?

159. Unless these questions can be answered satisfactorily, we will continue to be highly skeptical about the real meaning of "limited." One of the criteria of the just-war tradition is a reasonable hope of success in bringing about justice and peace. We must ask whether such a reasonable hope can exist once nuclear weapons have been exchanged. The burden of proof remains on those who assert that meaningful limitation is possible.

160. A nuclear response to either conventional or nuclear attack can cause destruction which goes far beyond "legitimate defense." Such use of nuclear weapons would not be justified.

161. In the face of this frightening and highly speculative debate on a matter involving millions of human lives, we believe the most effective contribution or moral judgment is to introduce perspectives by which we can assess the empirical debate. Moral perspective should be sensitive not only to the quantitative dimensions of a question but to its psychological, human, and religious characteristics as well. The issue of limited war is not simply the size of weapons contemplated or the strategies projected. The debate should include the psychological and political significance of crossing the boundary from the conventional to the nuclear arena in any form. To cross this divide is to enter a world where we have no experience of control, much testimony against its possibility, and therefore no moral justification for submitting the human community to this risk.[70] We therefore express our view that the first imperative is to prevent any use of nuclear weapons and our hope that leaders will resist the notion that nuclear conflict can be limited, contained, or won in any traditional sense.

---

[70] Undoubtedly aware of the long and detailed technical debate on limited war, Pope John Paul II highlighted the unacceptable moral risk of crossing the threshold to nuclear war in his "Angelus Message" of December 13, 1981: "I have, in fact, the deep conviction that, in the light of a nuclear war's effects, which can be scientifically foreseen as certain, the only choice that is morally and humanly valid is represented by the reduction of nuclear armaments, while waiting for their future complete elimination, carried out simultaneously by all the parties, by means of explicit agreements and with the commitment of accepting effective controls." In *Documents*, p. 240.

836   *The Challenge of Peace*

D. Deterrence in Principle and Practice

162.   The moral challenge posed by nuclear weapons is not exhausted by an analysis of their possible uses. Much of the political and moral debate of the nuclear age has concerned the strategy of deterrence. Deterrence is at the heart of the U.S.-Soviet relationship, currently the most dangerous dimension of the nuclear arms race.

1. THE CONCEPT AND DEVELOPMENT OF DETERRENCE POLICY

163.   The concept of deterrence existed in military strategy long before the nuclear age, but it has taken on a new meaning and significance since 1945. Essentially, deterrence means "dissuasion of a potential adversary from initiating an attack or conflict, often by the threat of unacceptable retaliatory damage."[71] In the nuclear age, deterrence has become the centerpiece of both U.S. and Soviet policy. Both superpowers have for many years now been able to promise a retaliatory response which can inflict "unacceptable damage." A situation of stable deterrence depends on the ability of each side to deploy its retaliatory forces in ways that are not vulnerable to an attack (i.e., protected against a "first strike"); preserving stability requires a willingness by both sides to refrain from deploying weapons which appear to have a first strike capability.

164.   This general definition of deterrence does not explain either the elements of a deterrence strategy or the evolution of deterrence policy since 1945. A detailed description of either of these subjects would require an extensive essay, using materials which can be found in abundance in the technical literature on the subject of deterrence.[72] Particularly significant is the relationship between "declaratory policy" (the public explanation of our strategic intentions and capabilities) and "action policy" (the actual planning and targeting policies to be followed in a nuclear attack).

---

[71] W. H. Kincade and J. D. Porro, *Negotiating Security: An Arms Control Reader* (Washington, D.C.: 1979).

[72] Several surveys are available, for example cf.: J. H. Kahin, *Security in the Nuclear Age: Developing U.S. Strategic Policy* (Washington, D.C.: 1975); M. Mandelbaum, *The Nuclear Question: The United States and Nuclear Weapons 1946-1976* (Cambridge, England: 1979); B. Brodie, "Development of Nuclear Strategy," *International Security* 2 (1978):65-83.

165. The evolution of deterrence strategy has passed through several stages of declaratory policy. Using the U.S. case as an example, there is a significant difference between "massive retaliation" and "flexible response," and between "mutual assured destruction" and "countervailing strategy." It is also possible to distinguish between "counterforce" and "countervalue" targeting policies; and to contrast a posture of "minimum deterrence" with "extended deterrence." These terms are well known in the technical debate on nuclear policy; they are less well known and sometimes loosely used in the wider public debate. It is important to recognize that there has been substantial continuity in U.S. action policy in spite of real changes in declaratory policy.[73]

166. The recognition of these different elements in the deterrent and the evolution of policy means that moral assessment of deterrence requires a series of distinct judgments. They include: an analysis of the *factual character* of the deterrent (e.g., what is involved in targeting doctrine); analysis of the *historical development* of the policy (e.g., wnether changes have occurred which are significant for moral analysis of the policy): the relationship of deterrence policy and other aspects of *U.S.-Soviet affairs*; and determination of the key *moral questions* involved in deterrence policy.

2. THE MORAL ASSESSMENT OF DETERRENCE

167. The distinctively new dimensions of nuclear deterrence were recognized by policymakers and strategists only after much reflection. Similarly, the moral challenge posed by nuclear deterrence was grasped only after careful deliberation. The moral and political paradox posed by deterrence was concisely stated by Vatican II:

> Undoubtedly, armaments are not amassed merely for use in wartime. Since the defensive strength of any nation is thought to depend on its capacity for immediate retaliation, the stockpiling of arms which grows from year to year serves, in a way hitherto unthought of, as a deterrent to potential attackers. Many people look upon this as the most effective way known at the present time for maintaining some sort of peace among nations. Whatever one may think of this form of deterrent, people are convinced that the arms race, which quite a few countries have entered, is no infallible way of maintaining real peace and that the resulting so-called balance of power is no sure genuine path to achieving it. Rather than eliminate the causes of war, the arms race serves only to aggravate the position. As

---

[73] The relationship of these two levels of policy is the burden of an article by D. Ball, "U.S. Strategic Forces: How Would They Be Used?" *International Security* 7 (1982/83):31-60

long as extravagent sums of money are poured into the development of new weapons, it is impossible to devote adequate aid in tackling the misery which prevails at the present day in the world. Instead of eradicating international conflict once and for all, the contagion is spreading to other parts of the world. New approaches, based on reformed attitudes, will have to be chosen in order to remove this stumbling block, to free the earth from its pressing anxieties, and give back to the world a genuine peace.[74]

168.   Without making a specific moral judgment on deterrence, the council clearly designated the elements of the arms race: the tension between "peace of a sort" preserved by deterrence and "genuine peace" required for a stable international life; the contradiction between what is spent for destructive capacity and what is needed for constructive development.

169.   In the post-conciliar assessment of war and peace, and specifically of deterrence, different parties to the political-moral debate within the Church and in civil society have focused on one aspect or another of the problem. For some, the fact that nuclear weapons have not been used since 1945 means that deterrence has worked, and this fact satisfies the demands of both the political and the moral order. Others contest this assessment by highlighting the risk of failure involved in continued reliance on deterrence and pointing out how politically and morally catastrophic even a single failure would be. Still others note that the absence of nuclear war is not necessarily proof that the policy of deterrence has prevented it. Indeed, some would find in the policy of deterrence the driving force in the superpower arms race. Still other observers, many of them Catholic moralists, have stressed that deterrence may not morally include the intention of deliberately attacking civilian populations or non-combatants.

170.   The statements of the NCCB/USCC over the past several years have both reflected and contributed to the wider moral debate on deterrence. In the NCCB pastoral letter, *To Live In Christ Jesus* (1976), we focused on the moral limits of declaratory policy while calling for stronger measures of arms control.[75] In 1979 John Cardinal Krol, speaking for the USCC in support of SALT II ratification, brought into focus the other element of the deterrence problem: the actual use of nuclear weapons may have been prevented (a moral good), but the risk of failure and the physical harm and moral evil

---

[74] *Pastoral Constitution*, #81.

[75] United States Catholic Conference, *To Live in Christ Jesus* (Washington, D.C.: 1976), p. 34.

resulting from possible nuclear war remained. "This explains," Cardinal Krol stated, "the Catholic dissatisfaction with nuclear deterrence and the urgency of the Catholic demand that the nuclear arms race be reversed. It is of the utmost importance that negotiations proceed to meaningful and continuing reductions in nuclear stockpiles, and eventually to the phasing out altogether of nuclear deterrence and the threat of mutual-assured destruction."[76]

171. These two texts, along with the conciliar statement, have influenced much of Catholic opinion expressed recently on the nuclear question.

172. In June 1982, Pope John Paul II provided new impetus and insight to the moral analysis with his statement to the United Nations Second Special Session on Disarmament. The pope first situated the problem of deterrence within the context of world politics. No power, he observes, will admit to wishing to start a war, but each distrusts others and considers it necessary to mount a strong defense against attack. He then discusses the notion of deterrence:

> Many even think that such preparations constitute the way—even the only way—to safeguard peace in some fashion or at least to impede to the utmost in an efficacious way the outbreak of wars, especially major conflicts which might lead to the ultimate holocaust of humanity and the destruction of the civilization that man has constructed so laboriously over the centuries.
>
> In this approach one can see the "philosophy of peace" which was proclaimed in the ancient Roman principle: *Si vis pacem, para bellum.* Put in modern terms, this "philosophy" has the label of "deterrence" and one can find it in various guises of the search for a "balance of forces" which sometimes has been called, and not without reason, the "balance of terror."[77]

173. Having offered this analysis of the general concept of deterrence, the Holy Father introduces his considerations on disarmament, especially, but not only, nuclear disarmament. Pope John Paul II makes this statement about the morality of deterrence:

> In current conditions "deterrence" based on balance, certainly not as an end in itself but as a step on the way toward a progressive disarmament, may still be judged morally acceptable. Nonetheless in order to ensure peace, it is indispensable not to be satisfied with this minimum which is always susceptible to the real danger of explosion.[78]

---

76 John Cardinal Krol, "Testimony on Salt II," *Origins* (1979):197.

77 John Paul II, "Message U.N. Special Session 1982," #3.

78 Ibid., #8.

174.   In Pope John Paul II's assessment we perceive two dimensions
of the contemporary dilemma of deterrence. One dimension is the
danger of nuclear war, with its human and moral costs. The possession
of nuclear weapons, the continuing quantitative growth of the arms
race, and the danger of nuclear proliferation all point to the grave
danger of basing "peace of a sort" on deterrence. The other dimension
is the independence and freedom of nations and entire peoples, including the need to protect smaller nations from threats to their
independence and integrity. Deterrence reflects the radical distrust
which marks international politics, a condition identified as a major
problem by Pope John XIII in *Peace on Earth* and reaffirmed by
Pope Paul VI and Pope John Paul II. Thus a balance of forces,
preventing either side from achieving superiority, can be seen as a
means of safeguarding both dimensions.
175.   The moral duty today is to prevent nuclear war from ever
occurring *and* to protect and preserve those key values of justice,
freedom and independence which are necessary for personal dignity
and national integrity. In reference to these issues, Pope John Paul II
judges that deterrence may still be judged morally acceptable, "certainly not as an end in itself but as a step on the way toward a
progressive disarmament."
176.   On more than one occasion the Holy Father has demonstrated
his awareness of the fragility and complexity of the deterrence relationship among nations. Speaking to UNESCO in June 1980, he
said:

> Up to the present, we are told that nuclear arms are a force of dissuasion
> which have prevented the eruption of a major war. And that is probably
> true. Still, we must ask if it will always be this way.[79]

In a more recent and more specific assessment Pope John
Paul II told an international meeting of scientists on August 23, 1982:

> You can more easily ascertain that the logic of nuclear deterrence cannot
> be considered a final goal or an appropriate and secure means for safe-
> guarding international peace.[80]

177.   Relating Pope John Paul's general statements to the specific
policies of the U.S. deterrent requires both judgments of fact and an
application of moral principles. In preparing this letter we have tried,

---

[79] John Paul II, "Address to UNESCO, 1980," #21.

[80] John Paul II, "Letter to International Seminar on the World Implications of a Nuclear
Conflict," August 23, 1982, text in *NC News Documentary*, August 24, 1982.

through a number of sources, to determine as precisely as possible the factual character of U.S. deterrence strategy. Two questions have particularly concerned us: 1) the targeting doctrine and strategic plans for the use of the deterrent, particularly their impact on civilian casualties; and 2) the relationship of deterrence strategy and nuclear war-fighting capability to the likelihood that war will in fact be prevented.

Moral Principles and Policy Choices

178. Targeting doctrine raises significant moral questions because it is a significant determinant of what would occur if nuclear weapons were ever to be used. Although we acknowledge the need for deterrent, not all forms of deterrence are morally acceptable. There are moral limits to deterrence policy as well as to policy regarding use. Specifically, it is not morally acceptable to intend to kill the innocent as part of a strategy of deterring nuclear war. The question of whether U.S. policy involves an intention to strike civilian centers (directly targeting civilian populations) has been one of our factual concerns. *179.* This complex question has always produced a variety of responses, official and unofficial in character. The NCCB Committee has received a series of statements of clarification of policy from U.S. government officials.[81] Essentially these statements declare that it is not U.S. strategic policy to target the Soviet civilian population as such or to use nuclear weapons deliberately for the purpose of destroying population centers. These statements respond, in principle at least, to one moral criterion for assessing deterrence policy: the immunity of non-combatants from direct attack either by conventional or nuclear weapons.

---

[81]Particularly helpful was the letter of January 15, 1983, of Mr. William Clark, national security adviser, to Cardinal Bernardin. Mr. Clark stated: "For moral, political and military reasons, the United States does not target the Soviet civilian population as such. There is no deliberately opaque meaning conveyed in the last two words. We do not threaten the existence of Soviet civilization by threatening Soviet cities. Rather, we hold at risk the war-making capability of the Soviet Union—its armed forces, and the industrial capacity to sustain war. It would be irresponsible for us to issue policy statements which might suggest to the Soviets that it would be to their advantage to establish privileged sanctuaries within heavily populated areas, thus inducing them to locate much of their war-fighting capability within those urban sanctuaries." A reaffirmation of the administration's policy is also found in Secretary Weinberger's *Annual Report to the Congress* (Caspar Weinberger, *Annual Report to the Congress*, February 1, 1983, p. 55): "The Reagan Administration's policy is that under no circumstances may such weapons be used deliberately for the purpose of destroying populations." Also the letter of Mr. Weinberger to Bishop O'Connor of February 9, 1983, has a similar statement.

180. These statements do not address or resolve another very troublesome moral problem, namely, that an attack on military targets or militarily significant industrial targets could involve "indirect" (i.e., unintended) but massive civilian casualties. We are advised, for example, that the United States strategic nuclear targeting plan (SIOP—Single Integrated Operational Plan) has identified 60 "military" targets within the city of Moscow alone, and that 40,000 "military" targets for nuclear weapons have been identified in the whole of the Soviet Union.[82] It is important to recognize that Soviet policy is subject to the same moral judgment; attacks on several "industrial targets" or politically significant targets in the United States could produce massive civilian casualties. The number of civilians who would necessarily be killed by such strikes is horrendous.[83] This problem is unavoidable because of the way modern military facilities and production centers are so thoroughly interspersed with civilian living and working areas. It is aggravated if one side deliberately positions military targets in the midst of a civilian population. In our consultations, administration officials readily admitted that, while they hoped any nuclear exchange could be kept limited, they were prepared to retaliate in a massive way if necessary. They also agreed that once any substantial numbers of weapons were used, the civilian casualty levels would quickly become truly catastrophic, and that even with attacks limited to "military" targets, the number of deaths in a substantial exchange would be almost indistinguishable from what might occur if civilian centers had been deliberately and directly struck. These possibilities pose a different moral question and are to be judged by a different moral criterion: the principle of proportionality.

181. While any judgment of proportionality is always open to differing evaluations, there are actions which can be decisively judged to be disproportionate. A narrow adherence exclusively to the principle of noncombatant immunity as a criterion for policy is an inadequate moral posture for it ignores some evil and unacceptable consequences. Hence, we cannot be satisfied that the assertion of an intention not to strike civilians directly, or even the most honest effort to implement that intention, by itself constitutes a "moral policy" for the use of nuclear weapons.

---

[82] S. Zuckerman, *Nuclear Illusion and Reality* (New York: 1982); D. Ball, cited, p. 36; T. Powers, "Choosing a Strategy for World War III," *The Atlantic Monthly*, November 1982, pp. 82-110.

[83] Cf. the comments in Pontifical Academy of Sciences "Statement on the Consequences of the Use of Nuclear Weapons," cited.

182. The location of industrial or militarily significant economic targets within heavily populated areas or in those areas affected by radioactive fallout could well involve such massive civilian casualties that, in our judgment, such a strike would be deemed morally disproportionate, even though not intentionally indiscriminate.

183. The problem is not simply one of producing highly accurate weapons that might minimize civilian casualties in any single explosion, but one of increasing the likelihood of escalation at a level where many, even "discriminating," weapons would cumulatively kill very large numbers of civilians. Those civilian deaths would occur both immediately and from the long-term effects of social and economic devastation.

184. A second issue of concern to us is the relationship of deterrence doctrine to war-fighting strategies. We are aware of the argument that war-fighting capabilities enhance the credibility of the deterrent, particularly the strategy of extended deterrence. But the development of such capabilities raises other strategic and moral questions. The relationship of war-fighting capabilities and targeting doctrine exemplifies the difficult choices in this area of policy. Targeting civilian populations would violate the principle of discrimination—one of the central moral principles of a Christian ethic of war. But "counterforce targeting," while preferable from the perspective of protecting civilians, is often joined with a declaratory policy which conveys the notion that nuclear war is subject to precise rational and moral limits. We have already expressed our severe doubts about such a concept. Furthermore, a purely counterforce strategy may seem to threaten the viability of other nations' retaliatory forces, making deterrence unstable in a crisis and war more likely.

185. While we welcome any effort to protect civilian populations, we do not want to legitimize or encourage moves which extend deterrence beyond the specific objective of preventing the use of nuclear weapons or other actions which could lead directly to a nuclear exchange.

186. These considerations of concrete elements of nuclear deterrence policy, made in light of John Paul II's evaluation, but applying it through our own prudential judgments, lead us to a strictly conditioned moral acceptance of nuclear deterrence. We cannot consider it adequate as a long-term basis for peace.

187. This strictly conditioned judgment yields *criteria* for morally assessing the elements of deterrence strategy. Clearly, these criteria demonstrate that we cannot approve of every weapons system, strategic doctrine, or policy initiative advanced in the name of strengthening deterrence. On the contrary, these criteria require continual public scrutiny of what our government proposes to do with the deterrent.

188.   On the basis of these criteria we wish now to make some specific evaluations:

1) If nuclear deterrence exists only to prevent the *use* of nuclear weapons by others, then proposals to go beyond this to planning for prolonged periods of repeated nuclear strikes and counter-strikes, or "prevailing" in nuclear war, are not acceptable. They encourage notions that nuclear war can be engaged in with tolerable human and moral consequences. Rather, we must continually say "no" to the idea of nuclear war.

2) If nuclear deterrence is our goal, "sufficiency" to deter is an adequate strategy; the quest for nuclear superiority must be rejected.

3) Nuclear deterrence should be used as a step on the way toward progressive disarmanent. Each proposed addition to our strategic system or change in strategic doctrine must be assessed precisely in light of whether it will render steps toward "progressive disarmament" more or less likely.

189.   Moreover, these criteria provide us with the means to make some judgments and recommendations about the present direction of U.S. strategic policy. Progress toward a world freed of dependence on nuclear deterrence must be carefully carried out. But it must not be delayed. There is an urgent moral and political responsibility to use the "peace of a sort" we have as a framework to move toward authentic peace through nuclear arms control, reductions, and disarmament. Of primary importance in this process is the need to prevent the development and deployment of destabilizing weapons systems on either side; a second requirement is to insure that the more sophisticated command and control systems do not become mere hair triggers for automatic launch on warning; a third is the need to prevent the proliferation of nuclear weapons in the international system.

190.   In light of these general judgments *we oppose* some specific proposals in respect to our present deterrence posture:

1) The addition of weapons which are likely to be vulnerable to attack, yet also possess a "prompt hard-target kill" capability that threatens to make the other side's retaliatory forces vulnerable. Such weapons may seem to be useful primarily in a first strike;[84] we resist

---

[84] Several experts in strategic theory would place both the MX missile and Pershing II missiles in this category.

such weapons for this reason and we oppose Soviet deployment of such weapons which generate fear of a first strike against U.S. forces.

2) The willingness to foster strategic planning which seeks a nuclear war-fighting capability that goes beyond the limited function of deterrence outlined in this letter.

3) Proposals which have the effect of lowering the nuclear threshold and blurring the difference between nuclear and conventional weapons.

191.   In support of the concept of "sufficiency" as an adequate deterrent, and in light of the present size and composition of both the U.S. and Soviet strategic arsenals, *we recommend*:

1) Support for immediate, bilateral, verifiable agreements to halt the testing, production, and deployment of new nuclear weapons systems.[85]

2) Support for negotiated bilateral deep cuts in the arsenals of both superpowers, particularly those weapons systems which have destabilizing characteristics; U.S. proposals like those for START (Strategic Arms Reduction Talks) and INF (Intermediate-range Nuclear Forces) negotiations in Geneva are said to be designed to achieve deep cuts;[86] our hope is that they will be pursued in a manner which will realize these goals.

3) Support for early and successful conclusion of negotiations of a comprehensive test ban treaty.

4) Removal by all parties of short-range nuclear weapons which multiply dangers disproportionate to their deterrent value.

5) Removal by all parties of nuclear weapons from areas where they are likely to be overrun in the early stages of war, thus forcing rapid and uncontrollable decisions on their use.

6) Strengthening of command and control over nuclear weapons to prevent inadvertent and unauthorized use.

192.   These judgments are meant to exemplify how a lack of unequivocal condemnation of deterrence is meant only to be an attempt to acknowledge the role attributed to deterrence, but not to support its extension beyond the limited purpose discussed above. Some have

---

[85] In each of the successive drafts of this letter we have tried to state a central moral imperative: that the arms race should be stopped and disarmament begun. The implementation of this imperative is open to a wide variety of approaches. Hence we have chosen our own language in this paragraph, not wanting either to be identified with one specific political initiative or to have our words used against specific political measures.

[86] Cf. President Reagan's "Speech to the National Press Club" (November 18, 1981) and "Address at Eureka College" (May 9, 1982), Department of State, *Current Policy* #346 and #387.

urged us to condemn all aspects of nuclear deterrence. This urging has been based on a variety of reasons, but has emphasized particularly the high and terrible risks that either deliberate use or accidental detonation of nuclear weapons could quickly escalate to something utterly disproportionate to any acceptable moral purpose. That determination requires highly technical judgments about hypothetical events. Although reasons exist which move some to condemn reliance on nuclear weapons for deterrence, we have not reached this conclusion for the reasons outlined in this letter.

193. Nevertheless, there must be no misunderstanding of our profound skepticism about the moral acceptability of any use of nuclear weapons. It is obvious that the use of any weapons which violate the principle of discrimination merits unequivocal condemnation. We are told that some weapons are designed for purely "counterforce" use against military forces and targets. The moral issue, however, is not resolved by the design of weapons or the planned intention for use; there are also consequences which must be assessed. It would be a perverted political policy or moral casuistry which tried to justify using a weapon which "indirectly" or "unintentionally" killed a million innocent people because they happened to live near a "militarily significant target."

194. Even the "indirect effects" of initiating nuclear war are sufficient to make it an unjustifiable moral risk in any form. It is not sufficient, for example, to contend that "our" side has plans for "limited" or "discriminate" use. Modern warfare is not readily contained by good intentions or technological designs. The psychological climate of the world is such that mention of the term "nuclear" generates uneasiness. Many contend that the use of one tactical nuclear weapon could produce panic, with completely unpredictable consequences. It is precisely this mix of political, psychological, and technological uncertainty which has moved us in this letter to reinforce with moral prohibitions and prescriptions the prevailing political barrier against resort to nuclear weapons. Our support for enhanced command and control facilities, for major reductions in strategic and tactical nuclear forces, and for a "no first use" policy (as set forth in this letter) is meant to be seen as a complement to our desire to draw a moral line against nuclear war.

195. Any claim by any government that it is pursuing a morally acceptable policy of deterrence must be scrutinized with the greatest care. We are prepared and eager to participate in our country in the ongoing public debate on moral grounds.

196. The need to rethink the deterrence policy of our nation, to make the revisions necessary to reduce the possibility of nuclear war, and to move toward a more stable system of national and international security will demand a substantial intellectual, political, and moral effort. It also will require, we believe, the willingness to open ourselves to the providential care, power and word of God, which call us to recognize our common humanity and the bonds of mutual responsibility which exist in the international community in spite of political differences and nuclear arsenals.

197. Indeed, we do acknowledge that there are many strong voices within our own episcopal ranks and within the wider Catholic community in the United States which challenge the strategy of deterrence as an adequate response to the arms race today. They highlight the historical evidence that deterrence has not, in fact, set in motion substantial processes of disarmament.

198. Moreover, these voices rightly raise the concern that even the conditional acceptance of nuclear deterrence as laid out in a letter such as this might be inappropriately used by some to reinforce the policy of arms buildup. In its stead, they call us to raise a prophetic challenge to the community of faith—a challenge which goes beyond nuclear deterrence, toward more resolute steps to actual bilateral disarmament and peacemaking. We recognize the intellectual ground on which the argument is built and the religious sensibility which gives it its strong force.

199. The dangers of the nuclear age and the enormous difficulties we face in moving toward a more adequate system of global security, stability and justice require steps beyond our present conceptions of security and defense policy. In the following section we propose a series of steps aimed at a more adequate policy for preserving peace in a nuclear world.

III

The Promotion of
Peace: Proposals and
Policies

200.   In a world which is not yet the fulfillment of God's kingdom, a world where both personal actions and social forces manifest the continuing influence of sin and disorder among us, consistent attention must be paid to preventing and limiting the violence of war. But this task, addressed extensively in the previous section of this letter, does not exhaust Catholic teaching on war and peace. A complementary theme, reflected in the Scriptures and the theology of the Church and significantly developed by papal teaching in this century, is the building of peace as the way to prevent war. This traditional theme was vividly reasserted by Pope John Paul in his homily at Coventry Cathedral:

> Peace is not just the absence of war. It involves mutual respect and confidence between peoples and nations. It involves collaboration and binding agreements. Like a cathedral, peace must be constructed patiently and with unshakable faith.[87]

201.   This positive conception of peacemaking profoundly influences many people in our time. At the beginning of this letter we affirmed the need for a more fully developed theology of peace. The basis of such a theology is found in the papal teaching of this century. In this section of our pastoral we wish to illustrate how the positive vision of peace contained in Catholic teaching provides direction for policy and personal choices.

A. Specific Steps to Reduce the Danger of War

202.   The dangers of modern war are specific and visible; our

---

[87] John Paul II, "Homily at Bagington Airport," Coventry, #2, *Origins* 12 (1982):55.

teaching must be equally specific about the needs of peace. Effective arms control leading to mutual disarmament, ratification of pending treaties,[88] development of nonviolent alternatives, are but some of the recommendations we would place before the Catholic community and all men and women of good will. These should be part of a foreign policy which recognizes and respects the claims of citizens of every nation to the same inalienable rights we treasure, and seeks to ensure an international security based on the awareness that the creator has provided this world and all its resources for the sustenance and benefit of the entire human family. The truth that the globe is inhabited by a single family in which all have the same basic needs and all have a right to the goods of the earth is a fundamental principle of Catholic teaching which we believe to be of increasing importance today. In an interdependent world all need to affirm their common nature and destiny; such a perspective should inform our policy vision and negotiating posture in pursuit of peace today.

1. ACCELERATED WORKS FOR ARMS CONTROL, REDUCTION AND DISARMAMENT

203.   Despite serious efforts, starting with the Baruch plans and continuing through SALT I and SALT II, the results have been far too limited and partial to be commensurate with the risks of nuclear war. Yet efforts for negotiated control and reduction of arms must continue. In his 1982 address to the United Nations, Pope John Paul II left no doubt about the importance of these efforts:

> Today once again before you all I reaffirm my confidence in the power of true negotiations to arrive at just and equitable solutions.[89]

204.   In this same spirit, we urge negotiations to halt the testing, production, and deployment of new nuclear weapons systems. Not only should steps be taken to end development and deployment, but the numbers of existing weapons must be reduced in a manner which lessens the danger of war.

205.   Arms control and disarmament must be a process of verifiable agreements especially between two superpowers. While we do not advocate a policy of unilateral disarmament, we believe the urgent

---

[88] The two treaties are the Threshold Test Ban Treaty signed July 3, 1974, and the Treaty on Nuclear Explosions for Peaceful Purposes (P.N.E.) signed May 28, 1976.

[89] John Paul II, "Message to U.N. Special Session 1982," #8.

need for control of the arms race requires a willingness for each side to take some first steps. The United States has already taken a number of important independent initiatives to reduce some of the gravest dangers and to encourage a constructive Soviet response; additional initiatives are encouraged. By independent initiatives we mean carefully chosen limited steps which the United States could take for a defined period of time, seeking to elicit a comparable step from the Soviet Union. If an appropriate response is not forthcoming, the United States would no longer be bound by steps taken. Our country has previously taken calculated risks in favor of freedom and of human values; these have included independent steps taken to reduce some of the gravest dangers of nuclear war.[90] Certain risks are required today to help free the world from bondage to nuclear deterrence and the risk of nuclear war. Both sides, for example, have an interest in avoiding deployment of destabilizing weapons systems.

206.   There is some history of successful independent initiatives which have beneficially influenced the arms race without a formal public agreement. In 1963 President Kennedy announced that the United States would unilaterally forgo further nuclear testing; the next month Soviet Premier Nikita Khrushchev proposed a limited test ban which eventually became the basis of the U.S.-Soviet partial test ban treaty. Subsequently, both superpowers removed about 10,000 troops from Central Europe and each announced a cut in production of nuclear material for weapons.

207.   a) Negotiation on arms control agreements in isolation, without persistent and parallel efforts to reduce the political tensions which motivate the buildup of armaments, will not suffice. The United States should therefore have a continuing policy of maximum political engagement with governments of potential adversaries, providing for repeated, systematic discussion and negotiation of areas of friction. This policy should be carried out by a system of periodic, carefully prepared meetings at several levels of government, including summit meetings at regular intervals. Such channels of discussion are too important to be regarded by either of the major powers as a concession or an event made dependent on daily shifts in international developments.

208.   b) The Nuclear Non-Proliferation Treaty of 1968 (NPT) acknowledged that the spread of nuclear weapons to hitherto non-nuclear states (horizontal proliferation) could hardly be prevented in the long run in the absence of serious efforts by the nuclear states to control

---

[90] Mr. Weinberger's letter to Bishop O'Connor specifies actions taken on command and control facilities designed to reduce the chance of unauthorized firing of nuclear weapons.

and reduce their own nuclear arsenals (vertical proliferation). Article VI of the NPT pledged the superpowers to serious efforts to control and to reduce their own nuclear arsenals; unfortunately, this promise has not been kept. Moreoever, the multinational controls envisaged in the treaty seem to have been gradually relaxed by the states exporting fissionable materials for the production of energy. If these tendencies are not constrained, the treaty may eventually lose its symbolic and practical effectiveness. For this reason the United States should, in concert with other nuclear exporting states, seriously reexamine its policies and programs and make clear its determination to uphold the spirit as well as the letter of the treaty.

2. CONTINUED INSISTENCE ON EFFORTS TO MINIMIZE THE RISK OF ANY WAR

209. While it is right and proper that priority be given to reducing and ultimately eliminating the likelihood of nuclear war, this does not of itself remove the threat of other forms of warfare. Indeed, negotiated reduction in nuclear weapons available to the superpowers could conceivably increase the danger of non-nuclear wars.

210. a) Because of this we strongly support negotiations aimed at reducing and limiting conventional forces and at building confidence between possible adversaries, especially in regions of potential military confrontations. We urge that prohibitions outlawing the production and use of chemical and biological weapons be reaffirmed and observed. Arms control negotiations must take account of the possibility that conventional conflict could trigger the nuclear confrontation the world must avoid.

211. b) Unfortunately, as is the case with nuclear proliferation, we are witnessing a relaxation of restraints in the international commerce in conventional arms. Sales of increasingly sophisticated military aircraft, missiles, tanks, anti-tank weapons, anti-personnel bombs, and other systems by the major supplying countries (especially the Soviet Union, the United States, France, and Great Britain) have reached unprecedented levels.

212. Pope John Paul II took specific note of the problem in his U.N. address:

The production and sale of conventional weapons throughout the world is a truly alarming and evidently growing phenomenon . . . . Moreover the traffic in these weapons seems to be developing at an increasing rate and seems to be directed most of all toward developing countries.[91]

213.   It is a tragic fact that U.S. arms sales policies in the last decade have contributed significantly to the trend the Holy Father deplores. We call for a reversal of this course. The United States should renew earlier efforts to develop multilateral controls on arms exports, and should in this case also be willing to take carefully chosen independent initiatives to restrain the arms trade. Such steps would be particularly appropriate where the receiving government faces charges of gross and systematic human rights violations.[92]

214.   c) Nations must accept a limited view of those interests justifying military force. True self-defense may include the protection of weaker states, but does not include seizing the possessions of others, or the domination of other states or peoples. We should remember the caution of Pope John Paul II: "In alleging the threat of a potential enemy, is it really not rather the intention to keep for itself a means of threat, in order to get the upper hand with the aid of one's own arsenal of destruction?"[93] Central to a moral theory of force is the principle that it must be a last resort taken only when *all* other means of redress have been exhausted. Equally important in the age of modern warfare is the recognition that the justifiable reasons for using force have been restricted to instances of self-defense or defense of others under attack.

3. THE RELATIONSHIP OF NUCLEAR AND CONVENTIONAL DEFENSES

215.   The strong position we have taken against the use of nuclear weapons, and particularly the stand against the initiation of nuclear war in any form, calls for further clarification of our view of the requirements for conventional defense.

216.   Nuclear threats have often come to take the place of efforts to deter or defend against non-nuclear attack with weapons that are themselves non-nuclear, particularly in the NATO-Warsaw Pact confrontation. Many analysts conclude that, in the absence of nuclear

---

[91] Ibid. Cf. United States Catholic Conference, *At Issue #2: Arms Export Policies—Ethical Choices* (Washington, D.C.: 1978) for suggestions about controlling the conventional arms trade.

[92] The International Security Act of 1976 provides for such human rights review.

[93] John Paul II, "Address to the United Nations General Assembly," *Origins* 9 (1979):268.

deterrent threats, more troops and conventional (non-nuclear) weapons would be required to protect our allies. Rejection of some forms of nuclear deterrence could therefore conceivably require a willingness to pay higher costs to develop conventional forces. Leaders and peoples of other nations might also have to accept higher costs for their own defense, particularly in Western Europe, if the threat to use nuclear weapons first were withdrawn. We cannot judge the strength of these arguments in particular cases. It may well be that some strengthening of conventional defense would be a proportionate price to pay, if this will reduce the possibility of a nuclear war. We acknowledge this reluctantly, aware as we are of the vast amount of scarce resources expended annually on instruments of defense in a world filled with other urgent, unmet human needs.

217. It is not for us to settle the technical debate about policy and budgets. From the perspective of a developing theology of peace, however, we feel obliged to contribute a moral dimension to the discussion. We hope that a significant reduction in numbers of conventional arms and weaponry would go hand in hand with diminishing reliance on nuclear deterrence. The history of recent wars (even so-called "minor" or "limited" wars) has shown that conventional war can also become indiscriminate in conduct and disproportionate to any valid purpose. We do not want in any way to give encouragement to a notion of "making the world safe for conventional war," which introduces its own horrors.

218. Hence, we believe that any program directed at reducing reliance on nuclear weapons is not likely to succeed unless it includes measures to reduce tensions, and to work for the balanced reduction of conventional forces. We believe that important possibilities exist which, if energetically pursued, would ensure against building up conventional forces as a concomitant of reductions in nuclear weapons. Examples are to be found in the ongoing negotiations for mutual balanced force reductions, the prospects for which are certainly not dim and would be enhanced by agreements on strategic weapons, and in the confidence-building measures still envisaged under the Helsinki agreement and review conference.

219. We must re-emphasize with all our being, nonetheless, that it is not only nuclear war that must be prevented, but war itself. Therefore, with Pope John Paul II we declare:

Today, the scale and the horror of modern warfare—whether nuclear or not—makes it totally unacceptable as a means of settling differences between nations. War should belong to the tragic past, to history; it should find no place on humanity's agenda for the future.[94]

Reason and experience tell us that a continuing upward spiral, even in conventional arms, coupled with an unbridled increase in armed forces, instead of securing true peace will almost certainly be provocative of war.

4. CIVIL DEFENSE

220. Attention must be given to existing programs for civil defense against nuclear attack, including blast and fall-out shelters and relocation plans. It is unclear in the public mind whether these are intended to offer significant protection against at least some forms of nuclear attack or are being put into place to enhance the credibility of the strategic deterrent forces by demonstrating an ability to survive attack. This confusion has led to public skepticism and even ridicule of the program and casts doubt on the credibility of the government. An independent commission of scientists, engineers, and weapons experts is needed to examine if these or any other plans offer a realistic prospect of survival for the nation's population or its cherished values, which a nuclear war would presumably be fought to preserve.

5. EFFORTS TO DEVELOP NON-VIOLENT MEANS OF CONFLICT RESOLUTION

221. We affirm a nation's right to defend itself, its citizens, and its values. Security is the right of all, but that right, like everything else, must be subject to divine law and the limits defined by that law. We must find means of defending peoples that do not depend upon the threat of annihilation. Immoral means can never be justified by the end sought; no objective, however worthy of good in itself, can justify sinful acts or policies. Though our primary concern through this statement is war and the nuclear threat, these principles apply as well to all forms of violence, including insurgency, counter-insurgency, "destabilization," and the like.

222. a) The Second Vatican Council praised "those who renounce the use of violence in the vindication of their rights and who resort to methods of defense which are otherwise available to weaker parties, provided that this can be done without injury to the rights and duties

---

[94] John Paul II, "Homily at Bagington Airport," Coventry, 2; cited, p. 55.

of others or of the community itself."[95] To make such renunciation effective and still defend what must be defended, the arts of diplomacy, negotiation, and compromise must be developed and fully exercised. Non-violent means of resistance to evil deserve much more study and consideration than they have thus far received. There have been significant instances in which people have successfully resisted oppression without recourse to arms.[96] Non-violence is not the way of the weak, the cowardly, or the impatient. Such movements have seldom gained headlines, even though they have left their mark on history. The heroic Danes who would not turn Jews over to the Nazis and the Norwegians who would not teach Nazi prop°ganda in schools serve as inspiring examples in the history of non-violence.

223.   Non-violent resistance, like war, can take many forms depending upon the demands of a given situation. There is, for instance, organized popular defense instituted by government as part of its contingency planning. Citizens would be trained in the techniques of peaceable non-compliance and non-cooperation as a means of hindering an invading force or non-democratic government from imposing its will. Effective non-violent resistance requires the united will of a people and may demand as much patience and sacrifice from those who practice it as is now demanded by war and preparation for war. It may not always succeed. Nevertheless, before the possibility is dismissed as impractical or unrealistic, we urge that it be measured against the almost certain effects of a major war.

224.   b) Non-violent resistance offers a common ground of agreement for those individuals who choose the option of Christian pacifism even to the point of accepting the need to die rather than to kill, and those who choose the option of lethal force allowed by the theology of just war. Non-violent resistance makes clear that both are able to be committed to the same objective: defense of their country.

225.   c) Popular defense would go beyond conflict resolution and compromise to a basic synthesis of beliefs and values. In its practice, the objective is not only to avoid causing harm or injury to another creature, but, more positively, to seek the good of the other. Blunting the aggression of an adversary or oppressor would not be enough. The goal is winning the other over, making the adversary a friend.

---

[95] Pastoral Constitution, #78.

[96] G. Sharp, The Politics of Nonviolent Action (Boston: 1973); R. Fisher and W. Ury, Getting to Yes: Negotiating Agreement Without Giving In (Boston: 1981).

226. It is useful to point out that these principles are thoroughly compatible with—and to some extent derived from—Christian teachings and must be part of any Christian theology of peace. Spiritual writers have helped trace the theory of non-violence to its roots in scripture and tradition and have illustrated its practice and success in their studies of the church fathers and the age of martyrs. Christ's own teachings and example provide a model way of life incorporating the truth, and a refusal to return evil for evil.

227. Non-violent popular defense does not insure that lives would not be lost. Nevertheless, once we recognize that the almost certain consequences of existing policies and strategies of war carry with them a very real threat to the future existence of humankind itself, practical reason as well as spiritual faith demand that it be given serious consideration as an alternative course of action.

228. d) Once again we declare that the only true defense for the world's population is the rejection of nuclear war and the conventional wars which could escalate into nuclear war. With Pope John Paul II, we call upon educational and research institutes to take a lead in conducting peace studies: "Scientific studies on war, its nature, causes, means, objectives and risks have much to teach us on the conditions for peace . . ."[97] To achieve this end, we urge that funds equivalent to a designated percentage (even one-tenth of one percent) of current budgetary allotments for military purposes be set aside to support such peace research.

229. In 1981, the Commission on Proposals for the National Academy of Peace and Conflict Resolution recommended the establishment of the U.S. Academy of Peace, a recommendation nearly as old as this country's constitution. The commission found that "peace is a legitimate field of learning that encompasses rigorous, interdisciplinary research, education, and training directed toward peacemaking expertise."[98] We endorse the commission's recommendation and urge all citizens to support training in conflict resolution, non-violent resistance, and programs devoted to service to peace and education for peace. Such an academy would not only provide a center for peace studies and activities, but also be a tangible evidence of our nation's sincerity in its often professed commitment to international peace and the abolition of war. We urge universities, particularly Catholic

---

[97] John Paul II, "World Day of Peace Message 1982," #7, cited, p. 476.

[98] *To Establish the United States Academy of Peace: Report of the Commission on Proposals for the National Academy of Peace and Conflict Resolution* (Washington, D.C.: 1981), pp. 119-20.

universities, in our country to develop programs for rigorous, interdisciplinary research, education and training directed toward peacemaking expertise.

230. We, too, must be prepared to do our part to achieve these ends. We encourage churches and educational institutions, from primary schools to colleges and institutes of higher learning, to undertake similar programs at their own initiative. Every effort must be made to understand and evaluate the arms race, to encourage truly transnational perspectives on disarmament, and to explore new forms of international cooperation and exchange. No greater challenge or higher priority can be imagined than the development and perfection of a theology of peace suited to a civilization poised on the brink of self-destruction. It is our prayerful hope that this document will prove to be a starting point and inspiration for that endeavor.

6. THE ROLE OF CONSCIENCE

231. A dominant characteristic of the Second Vatican Council's evaluation of modern warfare was the stress it placed on the requirement for proper formation of conscience. Moral principles are effective restraints on power only when policies reflect them and individuals practice them. The relationship of the authority of the state and the conscience of the individual on matters of war and peace takes a new urgency in the face of the destructive nature of modern war.

232. a) In this connection we reiterate the position we took in 1980. Catholic teaching does not question the right in principle of a government to require military service of its citizens provided the government shows it is necessary. A citizen may not casually disregard his country's conscientious decision to call its citizens to acts of "legitimate defense." Moreover, the role of Christian citizens in the armed forces is a service to the common good and an exercise of the virtue of patriotism, so long as they fulfill this role within defined moral norms.[99]

233. b) At the same time, no state may demand blind obedience. Our 1980 statement urged the government to present convincing reasons for draft registration, and opposed reinstitution of conscription itself except in the case of a national defense emergency. Moreover, it reiterated our support for conscientious objection in general and for selective conscientious objection to participation in a partic-

---

[99] United States Catholic Conference, *Statement on Registration and Conscription for Military Service* (Washington, D.C.: 1980). Cf. also *Human Life in Our Day*, cited, pp. 42-45.

ular war, either because of the ends being pursued or the means being used. We called selective conscientious objection a moral conclusion which can be validly derived from the classical teaching of just-war principles. We continue to insist upon respect for and legislative protection of the rights of both classes of conscientious objectors. We also approve requiring alternative service to the community—not related to military needs—by such persons.

B. Shaping a Peaceful World

234. Preventing nuclear war is a moral imperative; but the avoidance of war, nuclear or conventional, is not a sufficient conception of international relations today. Nor does it exhaust the content of Catholic teaching. Both the political needs and the moral challenge of our time require a positive conception of peace, based on a vision of a just world order. Pope Paul VI summarized classical Catholic teaching in his encyclical, *The Development of Peoples*: "Peace cannot be limited to a mere absence of war, the result of an ever precarious balance of forces. No, peace is something built up day after day, in the pursuit of an order intended by God, which implies a more perfect form of justice among men and women."[100]

1. WORLD ORDER IN CATHOLIC TEACHING

235. This positive conception of peace sees it as the fruit of order; order, in turn, is shaped by the values of justice, truth, freedom and love. The basis of this teaching is found in sacred scripture, St. Augustine and St. Thomas. It has found contemporary expression and development in papal teaching of this century. The popes of the nuclear age, from Pius XII through John Paul II have affirmed pursuit of international order as the way to banish the scourge of war from human affairs.[101]

236. The fundamental premise of world order in Catholic teaching is a theological truth: the unity of the human family—rooted in

---

[100] Paul VI, *The Development of Peoples* (1967), #76.

[101] Cf. V. Yzermans, ed., *Major Addresses of Pius XII*, 2 vols. (St. Paul: 1961) and J. Gremillion, *The Gospel of Peace and Justice*, cited.

common creation, destined for the kingdom, and united by moral bonds of rights and duties. This basic truth about the unity of the human family pervades the entire teaching on war and peace: for the pacifist position it is one of the reasons why life cannot be taken, while for the just-war position, even in a justified conflict bonds of responsibility remain in spite of the conflict.

237. Catholic teaching recognizes that in modern history, at least since the Peace of Westphalia (1648) the international community has been governed by nation-states. Catholic moral theology, as expressed for example in chapters 2 and 3 of *Peace on Earth*, accords a real but relative moral value to sovereign states. The value is real because of the functions states fulfill as sources of order and authority in the political community; it is relative because boundaries of the sovereign state do not dissolve the deeper relationships of responsibility existing in the human community. Just as within nations the moral fabric of society is described in Catholic teaching in terms of reciprocal rights and duties—between individuals, and then between the individual and the state—so in the international community *Peace on Earth* defines the rights and duties which exist among states.[102]

238. In the past twenty years Catholic teaching has become increasingly specific about the content of these international rights and duties. In 1963, *Peace on Earth* sketched the political and legal order among states. In 1966, *The Development of Peoples* elaborated on order of economic rights and duties. In 1979, Pope John Paul II articulated the human rights basis of international relations in his "Address to the United Nations General Assembly."

239. These documents and others which build upon them, outlined a moral order of international relations, i.e., how the international community *should* be organized. At the same time this teaching has been sensitive to the actual pattern of relations prevailing among states. While not ignoring present geopolitical realities, one of the primary functions of Catholic teaching on world order has been to point the way toward a more integrated international system.

240. In analyzing this path toward world order, the category increasingly used in Catholic moral teaching (and, more recently, in the social sciences also) is the interdependence of the world today. The theological principle of unity has always affirmed a human interdependence; but today this bond is complemented by the growing

---

[102] Cf. John XXIII, *Peace on Earth* (1963), esp. #80-145.

political and economic interdependence of the world, manifested in a whole range of international issues.[103]

241.   An important element missing from world order today is a properly constituted political authority with the capacity to shape our material interdependence in the direction of moral interdependence. Pope John XXIII stated the case in the following way:

> Today the universal common good poses problems of world-wide dimensions, which cannot be adequately tackled or solved except by the efforts of public authority endowed with a wideness of powers, structure and means of the same proportions: that is, of public authority which is in a position to operate in an effective manner on a world-wide basis. The moral order itself, therefore, demands that such a form of public authority be established.[104]

242.   Just as the nation-state was a step in the evolution of government at a time when expanding trade and new weapons technologies made the feudal system inadequate to manage conflicts and provide security, so we are now entering an era of new, global interdependencies requiring global systems of governance to manage the resulting conflicts and ensure our common security. Major global problems such as worldwide inflation, trade and payments deficits, competition over scarce resources, hunger, widespread unemployment, global environmental dangers, the growing power of transnational corporations, and the threat of international financial collapse, as well as the danger of world war resulting from these growing tensions—cannot be remedied by a single nation-state approach. They shall require the concerted effort of the whole world community. As we shall indicate below, the United Nations should be particularly considered in this effort.

243.   In the nuclear age, it is in the regulation of interstate conflicts and ultimately the replacement of military by negotiated solutions that the supreme importance and necessity of a moral as well as a political concept of the international common good can be grasped. The absence of adequate structures for addressing these issues places even greater responsiblity on the policies of individual states. By a mix of political vision and moral wisdom, states are called to interpret the national interest in light of the larger global interest.

---

[103] A sampling of the policy problems and possibilities posed by interdependence can be found in: R. O. Keohane and J. S. Nye, Jr., *Power and Interdependence* (Boston: 1977); S. Hoffmann, *Primacy or World Order* (New York: 1978); The Overseas Development Council, *The U.S. and World Development* 1979; 1980; 1982 (Washington, D.C.).

[104] John XXIII, *Peace on Earth* (1963), #137.

244. We are living in a global age with problems and conflicts on a global scale. Either we shall learn to resolve these problems together, or we shall destroy one another. Mutual security and survival require a new vision of the world as one interdependent planet. We have rights and duties not only within our diverse national communities but within the larger world community.

2. THE SUPERPOWERS IN A DISORDERED WORLD

245. No relationship more dramatically demonstrates the fragile nature of order in international affairs today than that of the United States and the Soviet Union. These two sovereign states have avoided open war, nuclear or conventional, but they are divided by philosophy, ideology and competing ambitions. Their competition is global in scope and involves everything from comparing nuclear arsenals to printed propaganda. Both have been criticized in international meetings because of their policies in the nuclear arms race.[105]

246. In our 1980 pastoral letter on Marxism, we sought to portray the significant differences between Christian teaching and Marxism; at the same time we addressed the need for states with different political systems to live together in an interdependent world:

> The Church recognizes the depth and dimensions of the ideological differences that divide the human race, but the urgent practical need for cooperative efforts in the human interest overrules these differences. Hence Catholic teaching seeks to avoid exacerbating the ideological opposition and to focus upon the problems requiring common efforts across the ideological divide: keeping the peace and empowering the poor.[106]

247. We believe this passage reflects the teaching of *Peace on Earth*, the continuing call for dialogue of Pope Paul VI and the 1979 address of Pope John Paul II at the United Nations. We continue to stress this theme even while we recognize the difficulty of realizing its objectives.

248. The difficulties are particularly severe on the issue of the arms race. For most Americans, the danger of war is commonly defined primarily in terms of the threat of Soviet military expansionism and the consequent need to deter or defend against a Soviet military threat. Many assume that the existence of this threat is

---

[105] This has particularly been the case in the two U.N. Special Sessions on Disarmament, 1979, 1982.

[106] United States Catholic Conference, *Marxist Communism* (Washington, D.C.: 1980), p. 19.

permanent and that nothing can be done about it except to build and maintain overwhelming or at least countervailing military power.[107]
249.   The fact of a Soviet threat, as well as the existence of a Soviet imperial drive for hegemony, at least in regions of major strategic interest, cannot be denied. The history of the Cold War has produced varying interpretations of which side caused which conflict, but whatever the details of history illustrate, the plain fact is that the memories of Soviet policies in Eastern Europe and recent events in Afghanistan and Poland have left their mark in the American political debate. Many peoples are forcibly kept under communist domination despite their manifest wishes to be free. Soviet power is very great. Whether the Soviet Union's pursuit of military might is motivated primarily by defensive or aggressive aims might be debated, but the effect is nevertheless to leave profoundly insecure those who must live in the shadow of that might.
250.   Americans need have no illusions about the Soviet system of repression and the lack of respect in that system for human rights, or about Soviet covert operations and pro-revolutionary activities. To be sure, our own system is not without flaws. Our government has sometimes supported repressive governments in the name of pre-serving freedom, has carried out repugnant covert operations of its own, and remains imperfect in its domestic record of ensuring equal rights for all. At the same time, there is a difference. NATO is an

---

[107] The debate on U.S.-Soviet relations is extensive; recent examples of it are found in: A. Ulam, "U.S.-Soviet Relations: Unhappy Coexistence," *America and the World, 1978; Foreign Affairs* 57 (1979):556-71; W. G. Hyland, "U.S.-Soviet Relations: The Long Road Back," *America and the World, 1981; Foreign Affairs* 60 (1982):525-50; R. Legvold, "Containment Without Confrontation," *Foreign Policy* 40 (1980):74-98; S. Hoffmann, "Muscle and Brains," *Foreign Policy* 37 (1979-80):3-27; P. Hassner, "Moscow and The Western Alliance," *Problems of Communism* 30 (1981):37-54; S. Bialer, "The Harsh Decade: Soviet Policies in the 1980s," *Foreign Affairs* 59 (1981):999-1020; G. Kennan, *The Nuclear Delusion: Soviet-American Relations in the Atomic Age* (New York: 1982); N. Podhoretz, *The Present Danger* (New York: 1980); P. Nitze, "Strategy in the 1980s," *Foreign Affairs* 59 (1980):82-101; R. Strode and C. Gray, "The Imperial Dimension of Soviet Military Power," *Problems of Communism* 30 (1981):1-15; International Institute for Strategic Studies, *Prospects of Soviet Power in the 1980s*, Parts I and II, Adelphi Papers #151 and 152 (London: 1979); S. S. Kaplan, ed., *Diplomacy of Power: Soviet Armed Forces as a Political Instrument* (Washington, D.C.: 1981); R. Barnet, *The Giants: Russia and America* (New York: 1977); M. McGwire, *Soviet Military Requirements*, The Brookings Institution (Washington, D.C.: 1982); R. Tucker, "The Purposes of American Power," *Foreign Affairs* 59 (1980/81):241-74; A. Geyer, *The Idea of Disarmament: Rethinking the Unthinkable* (Washington, D.C.: 1982). For a review of Soviet adherence to treaties cf.: "The SALT Syndrome Charges and Facts: Analysis of an 'Anti-SALT Documentary,'" report prepared by U.S. government agencies (State, Defense, CIA, ACDA and NSC), reprinted in *The Defense Monitor* 10, #8A, Center for Defense Information.

alliance of democratic countries which have freely chosen their association; the Warsaw Pact is not.

251. To pretend that as a nation we have lived up to all our own ideals would be patently dishonest. To pretend that all evils in the world have been or are now being perpetrated by dictatorial regimes would be both dishonest and absurd. But having said this, and admitting our own faults, it is imperative that we confront reality. The facts simply do not support the invidious comparisons made at times, even in our own society, between our way of life, in which most basic human rights are at least recognized even if they are not always adequately supported, and those totalitarian and tyrannical regimes in which such rights are either denied or systematically suppressed. Insofar as this is true, however, it makes the promotion of human rights in our foreign policy, as well as our domestic policy, all the more important. It is the acid test of our commitment to our democratic values. In this light, any attempts to justify, for reasons of state, support for regimes that continue to violate human rights is all the more morally reprehensible in its hypocrisy.

252. A glory of the United States is the range of political freedoms its system permits us. We, as bishops, as Catholics, as citizens, exercise those freedoms in writing this letter, with its share of criticisms of our government. We have true freedom of religion, freedom of speech, and access to a free press. We could not exercise the same freedoms in contemporary Eastern Europe or in the Soviet Union. Free people must always pay a proportionate price and run some risks—responsibly—to preserve their freedom.

253. It is one thing to recognize that the people of the world do not want war. It is quite another thing to attribute the same good motives to regimes or political systems that have consistently demonstrated precisely the opposite in their behavior. There are political philosophies with understandings of morality so radically different from ours, that even negotiations proceed from different premises, although identical terminology may be used by both sides. This is no reason for not negotiating. It is a very good reason for not negotiating blindly or naively.

254. In this regard, Pope John Paul II offers some sober reminders concerning dialogue and peace:

> [O]ne must mention the tactical and deliberate lie, which misuses language, which has recourse to the most sophisticated techniques of propaganda, which deceives and distorts dialogue and incites to aggression . . . while certain parties are fostered by ideologies which, in spite of their declarations, are opposed to the dignity of the human person, ideologies which

see in struggle the motive force of history, that see in force the source of rights, that see in the discernment of the enemy the ABC of politics, dialogue is fixed and sterile. Or, if it still exists, it is a superficial and falsified reality. It becomes very difficult, not to say impossible, therefore. There follows almost a complete lack of communication between countries and blocs. Even the international institutions are paralyzed. And the setback to dialogue then runs the risk of serving the arms race. However, even in what can be considered as an impasse to the extent that individuals support such ideologies, the attempt to have a lucid dialogue seems still necessary in order to unblock the situation and to work for the possible establishment of peace on particular points. This is to be done by counting upon common sense, on the possibilities of danger for everyone and on the just aspirations to which the peoples themselves largely adhere.[108]

255.   The cold realism of this text, combined with the conviction that political dialogue and negotiations must be pursued, in spite of obstacles, provides solid guidance for U.S.-Soviet relations. Acknowledging all the differences between the two philosophies and political systems, the irreducible truth is that objective mutual interests do exist between the superpowers. Proof of this concrete if limited convergence of interest can be found in some vitally important agreements on nuclear weapons which have already been negotiated in the areas of nuclear testing and nuclear explosions in space as well as the SALT I agreements. *256.*   The fact that the Soviet union now possesses a huge arsenal of strategic weapons as threatening to us as ours may appear to them does not exclude the possibility of success in such negotiations. The conviction of many European observers that a *modus vivendi* (often summarized as "detente") is a practical possibility in political, economic, and scientific areas should not be lightly dismissed in our country. *257.*   Sensible and successful diplomacy, however, will demand that we avoid the trap of a form of anti-Sovietism which fails to grasp the central danger of a superpower rivalry in which both the U.S. and the U.S.S.R. are the players, and fails to recognize the common interest both states have in never using nuclear weapons. Some of those dangers and common interests would exist in any world where two great powers, even relatively benign ones, competed for power, influence, and security. The diplomatic requirement for addressing the U.S.-Soviet relationship is not romantic idealism about Soviet intentions and capabilities but solid realism which recognizes that everyone will lose in a nuclear exchange. *258.*   As bishops we are concerned with issues which go beyond diplomatic requirements. It is of some value to keep raising in the realm

---

[108] John Paul II, "World Day of Peace Message 1983," #7.

of the political debate truths which ground our involvement in the affairs of nations and peoples. Diplomatic dialogue usually sees the other as a potential or real adversary. Soviet behavior in some cases merits the adjective reprehensible, but the Soviet people and their leaders are human beings created in the image and likeness of God. To believe we are condemned in the future only to what has been the past of U.S.-Soviet relations is to underestimate both our human potential for creative diplomacy and God's action in our midst which can open the way to changes we could barely imagine. We do not intend to foster illusory ideas that the road ahead in superpower relations will be devoid of tension or that peace will be easily achieved. But we do warn against that "hardness of heart" which can close us or others to the changes needed to make the future different from the past.

3. INTERDEPENDENCE: FROM FACT TO POLICY

259. While the nuclear arms race focuses attention on the U.S.-Soviet relationship, it is neither politically wise nor morally justifiable to ignore the broader international context in which that relationship exists. Public attention, riveted on the big powers, often misses the plight of scores of countries and millions of people simply trying to survive. The interdependence of the world means a set of interrelated human questions. Important as keeping the peace in the nuclear age is, it does not solve or dissolve the other major problems of the day. Among these problems the pre-eminent issue is the continuing chasm in living standards between the industrialized world (East and West) and the developing world. To quote Pope John Paul II:

> So widespread is the phenomenon that it brings into question the financial, monetary, production and commercial mechanisms that, resting on various political pressures, support the world economy. These are proving incapable either of remedying the unjust social situations inherited from the past or of dealing with the urgent challenges and ethical demands of the present.[109]

260. The East-West competition, central as it is to world order and important as it is in the foreign policy debate, does not address this moral question which rivals the nuclear issue in its human significance. While the problem of the developing nations would itself require a pastoral letter, Catholic teaching has maintained an analysis of the problem which should be identified here. The analysis acknowledges internal causes of poverty, but also concentrates on the way the larger

---

[109]John Paul II, "The Redeemer of Man," #16, *Origins* 8 (1980):635.

international economic structures affect the poor nations. These particularly involve trade, monetary, investment and aid policies.

261.   Neither of the superpowers is conspicuous in these areas for initiatives designed to address "the absolute poverty" in which millions live today.[110]

262.   From our perspective and experience as bishops, we believe there is a much greater potential for response to these questions in the minds and hearts of Americans than has been reflected in U.S. policy. As pastors who often appeal to our congregations for funds destined for international programs, we find good will and great generosity the prevailing characteristics. The spirit of generosity which shaped the Marshall Plan is still alive in the American public.

263.   We must discover how to translate this personal sense of generosity and compassion into support for policies which would respond to papal teaching in international economic issues. It is precisely the need to expand our conception of international charity and relief to an understanding of the need for social justice in terms of trade, aid and monetary issues which was reflected in Pope John Paul II's call to American Catholics in Yankee Stadium:

> Within the framework of your national institutions and in cooperation with all your compatriots, you will also want to seek out the structural reasons which foster or cause the different forms of poverty in the world and in your own country, so that you can apply the proper remedies. You will not allow yourselves to be intimidated or discouraged by over-simplified explanations which are more ideological than scientific—explanations which try to account for a complex evil by some single cause. But neither will you recoil before the reforms—even profound ones—of attitudes and structures that may prove necessary in order to recreate over and over again the conditions needed by the disadvantaged if they are to have a fresh chance in the hard struggle of life. The poor of the United States and of the world are your brothers and sisters in Christ.[111]

264.   The Pope's words highlight an intellectual, moral, and political challenge for the United States. Intellectually, there is a need to rethink the meaning of national interest in an interdependent world. Morally, there is a need to build upon the spirit of generosity present in the U.S. public, directing it toward a more systematic response to the major issues affecting the poor of the world. Politically, there is

---

[110] The phrase and its description are found in R. S. McNamara, *Report to the Board of Governors of the World Bank* 1978; cf. also 1979; 1980 (Washington, D.C.).

[111] John Paul II, "Homily at Yankee Stadium," #4, *Origins* 9 (1979):311.

a need for U.S. policies which promote the profound structural reforms called for by recent papal teaching.

265. Precisely in the name of international order papal teaching has, by word and deed, sought to promote multilateral forms of cooperation toward the developing world. The U.S. capacity for leadership in multilateral institutions is very great. We urge much more vigorous and creative response to the needs of the developing countries by the United States in these institutions.

266. The significant role the United States could play is evident in the daily agenda facing these institutions. Proposals addressing the relationship of the industrialized and developing countries on a broad spectrum of issues, all in need of "profound reforms," are regularly discussed in the United Nations and other international organizations. Without U.S. participation, significant reform and substantial change in the direction of addressing the needs of the poor will not occur. Meeting these needs is an essential element for a peaceful world.

267. Papal teaching of the last four decades has not only supported international institutions in principle, it has supported the United Nations specifically. Pope Paul VI said to the U.N. General Assembly:

> The edifice which you have constructed must never fail; it must be perfected and made equal to the needs which world history will present. You mark a stage in the development of mankind for which retreat must never be admitted, but from which it is necessary that advance be made.[112]

268. It is entirely necessary to examine the United Nations carefully, to recognize its limitations and propose changes where needed. Nevertheless, in light of the continuing endorsement found in papal teaching, we urge that the United States adopt a stronger supportive leadership role with respect to the United Nations. The growing interdependence of the nations and peoples of the world, coupled with the extra-governmental presence of multinational corporations, requires new structures of cooperation. As one of the founders of and major financial contributors to the United Nations, the United States can, and should, assume a more positive and creative role in its life today.

269. It is in the context of the United Nations that the impact of the arms race on the prospects for economic development is highlighted. The numerous U.N. studies on the relationship of development and disarmament support the judgment of Vatican II cited earlier in this letter: "The arms race is one of the greatest curses on the human

---

[112] Paul VI, "Address to the General Assembly of the United Nations" (1965), #2.

race and the harm it inflicts upon the poor is more than can be endured."[113]

270.   We are aware that the precise relationship between disarmament and development is neither easily demonstrated nor easily reoriented. But the fact of a massive distortion of resources in the face of crying human need creates a moral question. In an interdependent world, the security of one nation is related to the security of all. When we consider how and what we pay for defense today, we need a broader view than the equation of arms with security.[114] The threats to the security and stability of an interdependent world are not all contained in missiles and bombers.

271.   If the arms race in all its dimensions is not reversed, resources will not be available for the human needs so evident in many parts of the globe and in our own country as well. But we also know that making resources available is a first step; policies of wise use would also have to follow. Part of the process of thinking about the economics of disarmament includes the possibilities of conversion of defense industries to other purposes. Many say the possibilities are great if the political will is present. We say the political will to reorient resources to human needs and redirect industrial, scientific, and technological capacity to meet those needs is part of the challenge of the nuclear age. Those whose livelihood is dependent upon industries which can be reoriented should rightfully expect assistance in making the transition to new forms of employment. The economic dimension of the arms race is broader than we can assess here, but these issues we have raised are among the primary questions before the nation.[115]

272.   An interdependent world requires an understanding that key policy questions today involve mutuality of interest. If the monetary and trading systems are not governed by sensitivity to mutual needs, they can be destroyed. If the protection of human rights and the promotion of human needs are left as orphans in the diplomatic arena, the stability we seek in increased armaments will eventually

---

[113] *Pastoral Constitution*, #81.

[114] Cf. Hoffman, cited; Independent Commission on Disarmament and Security Issues, *Common Security* (New York: 1982).

[115] For an analysis of the policy problems of reallocating resources, cf: Bruce M. Russett, *The Prisoners of Insecurity* (San Francisco: 1983). Cf.: *Common Security*, cited; Russett, cited; *U.N. Report on Disarmament and Development* (New York: 1982); United Nations, *The Relationship Between Disarmament and Development: A Summary*, Fact Sheet #21 (New York: 1982).

be threatened by rights denied and needs unmet in vast sectors of the globe. If future planning about conservation of and access to resources is relegated to a pure struggle of power, we shall simply guarantee conflict in the future.

273.   The moral challenge of interdependence concerns shaping the relationships and rules of practice which will support our common need for security, welfare, and safety. The challenge tests our idea of human community, our policy analysis, and our political will. The need to prevent nuclear war is absolutely crucial, but even if this is achieved, there is much more to be done.

IV

The Pastoral
Challenge and Response

A. The Church: A Community of Conscience,
Prayer and Penance

274.   Pope John Paul II, in his first encyclical, recalled with gratitude the teaching of Pius XII on the Church. He then went on to say:

> Membership in that body has for its source a particular call, united with the saving action of grace. Therefore, if we wish to keep in mind this community of the People of God, which is so vast and so extremely differentiated, we must see first and foremost Christ saying in a way to each member of the community: "Follow Me." It is the community of the disciples, each of whom in a different way—at times very consciously and ˙consistently, at other times not very consciously and very consistently—is following Christ. This shows also the deeply "personal" aspect and dimension of this society.[116]

275.   In the following pages we should like to spell out some of the implications of being a community of Jesus' disciples in a time when our nation is so heavily armed with nuclear weapons and is engaged in a continuing development of new weapons together with strategies for their use.

276.   It is clear today, perhaps more than in previous generations, that convinced Christians are a minority in nearly every country of the world—including nominally Christian and Catholic nations. In our own country we are coming to a fuller awareness that a response

---

[116] John Paul II, "The Redeemer of Man," #21, cited, p. 641. Much of the following reflects the content of A. Dulles, *A Church to Believe in: Discipleship and the Dynamics of Freedom* (New York: 1982), ch. 1.

to the call of Jesus is both personal and demanding. As believers we can identify rather easily with the early Church as a company of witnesses engaged in a difficult mission. To be disciples of Jesus requires that we continually go beyond where we now are. To obey the call of Jesus means separating ourselves from all attachments and affiliation that could prevent us from hearing and following our authentic vocation. To set out on the road to discipleship is to dispose oneself for a share in the cross (cf. Jn. 16:20). To be a Christian, according to the New Testament, is not simply to believe with one's mind, but also to become a doer of the word, a wayfarer with and a witness to Jesus. This means, of course, that we never expect complete success within history and that we must regard as normal even the path of persecution and the possibility of martyrdom.

277.   We readily recognize that we live in a world that is becoming increasingly estranged from Christian values. In order to remain a Christian, one must take a resolute stand against many commonly accepted axioms of the world. To become true disciples, we must undergo a demanding course of induction into the adult Christian community. We must continually equip ourselves to profess the full faith of the Church in an increasingly secularized society. We must develop a sense of solidarity, cemented by relationships with mature and exemplary Christians who represent Christ and his way of life.

278.   All of these comments about the meaning of being a disciple or a follower of Jesus today are especially relevant to the quest for genuine peace in our time.

B. Elements of a Pastoral Response

279.   We recommend and endorse for the faithful some practical programs to meet the challenge to their faith in this area of grave concern.

1. EDUCATIONAL PROGRAMS AND FORMATION OF CONSCIENCE

280.   Since war, especially the threat of nuclear war, is one of the central problems of our day, how we seek to solve it could determine the mode, and even the possibility, of life on earth. God made human beings stewards of the earth; we cannot escape this responsibility. Therefore we urge every diocese and parish to implement balanced

and objective educational programs to help people at all age levels to understand better the issues of war and peace. Development and implementation of such programs must receive a high priority during the next several years. They must teach the full impact of our Christian faith. To accomplish this, this pastoral letter in its entirety, including its complexity, should be used as a guide and a framework for such programs, as they lead people to make moral decisions about the problems of war and peace, keeping in mind that the applications of principles in this pastoral letter do not carry the same moral authority as our statements of universal moral principles and formal Church teaching.

281.   In developing educational programs, we must keep in mind that questions of war and peace have a profoundly moral dimension which responsible Christians cannot ignore. They are questions of life and death. True, they also have a political dimension because they are embedded in public policy. But the fact that they are also political is no excuse for denying the Church's obligation to provide its members with the help they need in forming their consciences. We must learn together how to make correct and responsible moral judgments. We reject, therefore, criticism of the Church's concern with these issues on the ground that it "should not become involved in politics." We are called to move from discussion to witness and action.

282.   At the same time, we recognize that the Church's teaching authority does not carry the same force when it deals with technical solutions involving particular means as it does when it speaks of principles or ends. People may agree in abhorring an injustice, for instance, yet sincerely disagree as to what practical approach will achieve justice. Religious groups are as entitled as others to their opinion in such cases, but they should not claim that their opinions are the only ones that people of good will may hold.

283.   The Church's educational programs must explain clearly those principles or teachings about which there is little question. Those teachings, which seek to make explicit the gospel call to peace and the tradition of the Church, should then be applied to concrete situations. They must indicate what the possible legitimate options are and what the consequences of those options may be. While this approach should be self-evident, it needs to be emphasized. Some people who have entered the public debate on nuclear warfare, at all points on the spectrum of opinion, appear not to understand or accept some of the clear teachings of the Church as contained in papal or conciliar documents. For example, some would place almost no limits on the use of nuclear weapons if they are needed for "self-defense.' Some on the other side of the debate insist on conclusions which may be legitimate options but cannot be made obligatory on the basis of actual Church teaching.

2. TRUE PEACE CALLS FOR "REVERENCE FOR LIFE"

284.　All of the values we are promoting in this letter rest ultimately in the disarmament of the human heart and the conversion of the human spirit to God who alone can give authentic peace. Indeed, to have peace in our world, we must first have peace within ourselves. As Pope John Paul II reminded us in his 1982 World Day of Peace message, world peace will always elude us until peace becomes a reality for each of us personally. "It springs from the dynamism of free wills guided by reason towards the common good that is to be attained in truth, justice and love."[117] Interior peace becomes possible only when we have a conversion of spirit. We cannot have peace with hate in our hearts.

285.　No society can live in peace with itself, or with the world, without a full awareness of the worth and dignity of every human person, and of the sacredness of all human life (Jas. 4:1-2). When we accept violence in any form as commonplace, our sensitivities become dulled. When we accept violence, war itself can be taken for granted. Violence has many faces: oppression of the poor, deprivation of basic human rights, economic exploitation, sexual exploitation and pornography, neglect or abuse of the aged and the helpless, and innumerable other acts of inhumanity. Abortion in particular blunts a sense of the sacredness of human life. In a society where the innocent unborn are killed wantonly, how can we expect people to feel righteous revulsion at the act or threat of killing noncombatants in war?

286.　We are well aware of the differences involved in the taking of human life in warfare and the taking of human life through abortion. As we have discussed throughout this document, even justifiable defense against aggression may result in the indirect or unintended loss of innocent human lives. This is tragic, but may conceivably be proportionate to the values defended. Nothing, however, can justify direct attack on innocent human life, in or out of warfare. Abortion is precisely such an attack.

---

[117] John Paul II, "World Day of Peace Message 1982," #4, cited, p. 475.

287.   We know that millions of men and women of good will, of all religious persuasions, join us in our commitment to try to reduce the horrors of war, and particularly to assure that nuclear weapons will never again be used, by any nation, anywhere, for any reason. Millions join us in our "no" to nuclear war, in the certainty that nuclear war would inevitably result in the killing of millions of innocent human beings, directly or indirectly. Yet many part ways with us in our efforts to reduce the horror of abortion and our "no" to war on innocent human life in the womb, killed not indirectly, but directly.

288.   We must ask how long a nation willing to extend a constitutional guarantee to the "right" to kill defenseless human beings by abortion is likely to refrain from adopting strategic warfare policies deliberately designed to kill millions of defenseless human beings, if adopting them should come to seem "expedient." Since 1973, approximately 15 million abortions have been performed in the United States, symptoms of a kind of disease of the human spirit. And we now find ourselves seriously discussing the pros and cons of such questions as infanticide, euthanasia, and the involvement of physicians in carrying out the death penalty. Those who would celebrate such a national disaster can only have blinded themselves to its reality.

289.   Pope Paul VI was resolutely clear: *If you wish peace, defend life.*[118] We plead with all who would work to end the scourge of war to begin by defending life at its most defenseless, the life of the unborn.

3. PRAYER

290.   A conversion of our hearts and minds will make it possible for us to enter into a closer communion with our Lord. We nourish that communion by personal and communal prayer, for it is in prayer that we encounter Jesus, who is our peace, and learn from him the way to peace.

291.   In prayer we are renewed in faith and confirmed in our hope in God's promise.

292.   The Lord's promise is that he is in our midst when we gather in prayer. Strengthened by this conviction, we beseech the risen Christ to fill the world with his peace. We call upon Mary, the first disciple and the Queen of Peace, to intercede for us and for the people of our

---

[118] Paul VI, "World Day of Peace Message 1977."

time that we may walk in the way of peace. In this context, we encouage devotion to Our Lady of Peace.

293.   As believers, we understand peace as a gift of God. This belief prompts us to pray constantly, personally and communally, particularly through the reading of scripture and devotion to the rosary, especially in the family. Through these means and others, we seek the wisdom to begin the search for peace and the courage to sustain us as instruments of Christ's peace in the world.

294.   The practice of contemplative prayer is especially valuable for advancing harmony and peace in the world. For this prayer rises, by divine grace, where there is total disarmament of the heart and unfolds in an experience of love which is the moving force of peace. Contemplation fosters a vision of the human family as united and interdependent in the mystery of God's love for all people. This silent, interior prayer bridges temporarily the "already" and "not yet," this world and God's kingdom of peace.

295.   The Mass in particular is a unique means of seeking God's help to create the conditions essential for true peace in ourselves and in the world. In the eucharist we encounter the risen Lord, who gave us his peace. He shares with us the grace of the redemption, which helps us to preserve and nourish this precious gift. Nowhere is the Church's urgent plea for peace more evident in the liturgy than in the Communion Rite. After beginning this rite of the Mass with the Lord's Prayer, praying for reconciliation now and in the kingdom to come, the community asks God to "grant us peace in our day," not just at some time in the distance future. Even before we are exhorted "to offer each other the sign of peace," the priest continues the Church's prayer for peace, recalling the Lord Jesus Christ's own legacy of peace:

> Lord Jesus Christ, you said to your apostles: I leave you peace, my peace I give you. Look not on our sins, but on the faith of your Church, and grant us the peace and unity of your kingdom.

Therefore we encourage every Catholic to make the sign of peace at Mass an authentic sign of our reconciliation with God and with one another. This sign of peace is also a visible expression of our commitment to work for peace as a Christian community. We approach the table of the Lord only after having dedicated ourselves as a Christian community to peace and reconciliation. As an added sign of commitment, we suggest that there always be a petition for peace in the general intercessions at every eucharistic celebration.

296.   We implore other Christians and everyone of good will to join us in this continuing prayer for peace, as we beseech God for

peace within ourselves, in our families and community, in our nation, and in the world.

4. PENANCE

297. Prayer by itself is incomplete without penance. Penance directs us toward our goal of putting on the attitudes of Jesus himself. Because we are all capable of violence, we are never totally conformed to Christ and are always in need of conversion. The twentieth century alone provides adequate evidence of our violence as individuals and as a nation. Thus, there is continual need for acts of penance and conversion. The worship of the Church, particularly through the sacrament of reconciliation and communal penance services, offers us multiple ways to make reparation for the violence in our own lives and in our world.

298. As a tangible sign of our need and desire to do penance we, for the cause of peace, commit ourselves to fast and abstinence on each Friday of the year. We call upon our people voluntarily to do penance on Friday by eating less food and by abstaining from meat. This return to a traditional practice of penance, once well observed in the U.S. Church, should be accompanied by works of charity and service toward our neighbors. Every Friday should be a day significantly devoted to prayer, penance, and almsgiving for peace.

299. It is to such forms of penance and conversion that the Scriptures summon us. In the words of the prophet Isaiah:

> Is not the sort of fast that pleases me, to break unjust fetters and undo the thongs of the yoke, to let the oppressed go free and break every yoke, to share your bread with the hungry, and shelter the homeless poor, to clothe the person you see to be naked and not turn from your own kin? Then will your light shine like the dawn and your wound be quickly healed over. If you do away with the yoke, the clenched fist, the wicked word, if you give your bread to the hungry and relief to the oppressed, your light will rise in the darkness, and your shadows become like noon (Is. 58:6-8; 10).

300. The present nuclear arms race has distracted us from the words of the prophets, has turned us from peace-making, and has focused our attention on a nuclear buildup leading to annihilation. We are called to turn back from this evil of total destruction and turn instead in prayer and penance toward God, toward our neighbor, and toward the building of a peaceful world:

> I set before you life or death, a blessing or a curse. Choose life then, so that you and your descendants may live in the love of Yahweh your God, obeying His voice, clinging to Him; for in this your life consists, and on

this depends your long stay in the land which Yahweh swore to your fathers
Abraham, Isacc and Jacob, He would give them (Dt. 30:19–20).

C. Challenge and Hope

301.   The arms race presents questions of conscience we may not
evade. As American Catholics, we are called to express our loyalty
to the deepest values we cherish: peace, justice and security for the
entire human family. National goals and policies must be measured
against that standard.

302.   We speak here in a specific way to the Catholic community.
After the passage of nearly four decades and a concomitant growth
in our understanding of the ever growing horror of nuclear war, we
must shape the climate of opinion which will make it possible for
our country to express profound sorrow over the atomic bombing in
1945. Without that sorrow, there is no possibility of finding a way
to repudiate future use of nuclear weapons or of conventional weapons
in such military actions as would not fulfill just-war criteria.

303.   **To Priests, Deacons, Religious and Pastoral Ministers:**
We recognize the unique role in the Church which belongs to priests
and deacons by reason of the sacrament of holy orders and their
unique responsibility in the community of believers. We also recognize the valued and indispensable role of men and women religious.
To all of them and to all other pastoral ministers we stress that the
cultivation of the gospel vision of peace as a way of life for believers
and as a leaven in society should be a major objective. As bishops,
we are aware each day of our dependence upon your efforts. We are
aware, too, that this letter and the new obligations it could present
to the faithful may create difficulties for you in dealing with those
you serve. We have confidence in your capacity and ability to convert
these difficulties into an opportunity to give a fuller witness to our
Lord and his message. This letter will be known by the faithful only
as well as you know it, preach and teach it, and use it creatively.

304.   **To Educators:** We have outlined in this letter Catholic teaching on war and peace, but this framework will become a living
message only through your work in the Catholic community. To teach
the ways of peace is not "to weaken the nation's will" but to be
concerned for the nation's soul. We address theologians in a particular
way, because we know that we have only begun the journey toward
a theology of peace; without your specific contributions this des-

perately needed dimension of our faith will not be realized. Through your help we may provide new vision and wisdom for church and state.

305. We are confident that all the models of Catholic education which have served the Church and our country so well in so many ways will creatively rise to the challenge of peace.

306. **To Parents:** Your role, in our eyes, is unsurpassed by any other; the foundation of society is the family. We are conscious of the continuing sacrifices you make in the efforts to nurture the full human and spiritual growth of your children. Children hear the gospel message first from your lips. Parents who consciously discuss issues of justice in the home and who strive to help children solve conflicts through non-violent methods enable their children to grow up as peacemakers. We pledge our continuing pastoral support in the common objective we share of building a peaceful world for the future of children everywhere.

307. **To Youth:** Pope John Paul II singles you out in every country where he visits as the hope of the future; we agree with him. We call you to choose your future work and professions carefully. How you spend the rest of your lives will determine, in large part, whether there will any longer be a world as we know it. We ask you to study carefully the teachings of the Church and the demands of the gospel about war and peace. We encourage you to seek careful guidance as you reach conscientious decisions about your civic responsibilities in this age of nuclear military forces.

308. We speak to you, however, as people of faith. We share with you our deepest conviction that in the midst of the dangers and complexities of our time God is with us, working through us and sustaining us all in our efforts of building a world of peace with justice for each person.

309. **To Men and Women in Military Service:** Millions of you are Catholics serving in the armed forces. We recognize that you carry special responsibilities for the issues we have considered in this letter. Our perspective on your profession is that of Vatican II: "All those who enter the military service in loyalty to their country should look upon themselves as the custodians of the security and freedom of their fellow-countrymen; and where they carry out their duty properly, they are contributing to the maintenance of peace."[119]

---

[119] *Pastoral Constitution,* #79.

310. It is surely not our intention in writing this letter to create problems for Catholics in the armed forces. Every profession, however, has its specific moral questions and it is clear that the teaching on war and peace developed in this letter poses a special challenge and opportunity to those in the military profession. Our pastoral contact with Catholics in military service, either through our direct experience or through our priests, impresses us with the demanding moral standards we already see observed and the commitment to Catholic faith we find. We are convinced that the challenges of this letter will be faced conscientiously. The purpose of defense policy is to defend the peace; military professionals should understand their vocation this way. We believe they do, and we support this view.

311. We remind all in authority and in the chain of command that their training and field manuals have long prohibited, and still do prohibit, certain actions in the conduct of war, especially those actions which inflict harm on innocent civilians. The question is not whether certain measures are unlawful or forbidden in warfare, but which measures: to refuse to take such actions is not an act of cowardice or treason but one of courage and patriotism.

312. We address particularly those involved in the exercise of authority over others. We are aware of your responsibilities and impressed by the standard of personal and professional duty you uphold. We feel, therefore, that we can urge you to do everything you can to assure that every peaceful alternative is exhausted before war is even remotely considered. In developing battle plans and weapons systems, we urge you to try to ensure that these are designed to reduce violence, destruction, suffering, and death to a minimum, keeping in mind especially non-combatants and other innocent persons.

313. Those who train individuals for military duties must remember that the citizen does not lose his or her basic human rights by entrance into military service. No one, for whatever reason, can justly treat a military person with less dignity and respect than that demanded for and deserved by every human person. One of the most difficult problems of war involves defending a free society without destroying the values that give it meaning and validity. Dehumanization of a nation's military personnel by dulling their sensibilities and generating hatred toward adversaries in an effort to increase their fighting effectiveness robs them of basic human rights and freedoms, degrading them as persons.

314. Attention must be given to the effects on military personnel themselves of the use of even legitimate means of conducting war. While attacking legitimate targets and wounding or killing opposed combat forces may be morally justified, what happens to military persons required to carry out these actions? Are they treated merely as instruments of war, insensitive as the weapons they use? With what moral or emotional experiences do they return from war and attempt to resume normal civilian lives? How does their experience affect society? How are they treated by society?

315. It is not only basic human rights of adversaries that must be respected, but those of our own forces as well. We re-emphasize, therefore, the obligation of responsible authorities to ensure appropriate training and education of combat forces and to provide appropriate support for those who have experienced combat. It is unconscionable to deprive those veterans of combat whose lives have been severely disrupted or traumatized by their combat experiences of proper psychological and other appropriate treatment and support.

316. Finally, we are grateful for the sacrifice so many in military service must make today and for the service offered in the past by veterans. We urge that those sacrifices be mitigated so far as possible by the provision of appropriate living and working conditions and adequate financial recompense. Military persons and their families must be provided continuing opportunity for full spiritual growth, the exercise of their religious faith, and a dignified mode of life.

317. We especially commend and encourage our priests in military service. In addition to the message already addressed to all priests and religious, we stress the special obligations and opportunities you face in direct pastoral service to the men and women of the armed forces. To complement a teaching document of this scope, we shall need the sensitive and wise pastoral guidance only you can provide. We promise our support in facing this challenge.

318. **To Men and Women in Defense Industries:** You also face specific questions, because the defense industry is directly involved in the development and production of the weapons of mass destruction which have concerned us in this letter. We do not presume or pretend that clear answers exist to many of the personal, professional and financial choices facing you in your varying responsibilities. In this letter we have ruled out certain uses of nuclear weapons, while also expressing conditional moral acceptance for deterrence. All Catholics, at every level of defense industries, can and should use the moral principles of this letter to form their consciences. We realize that different judgments of conscience will face different people, and we recognize the possibility of diverse concrete judgments being made in this complex area. We seek as moral teachers and pastors to be available to all who confront these questions of personal and vocational choice. Those who in conscience decide that they should no longer be associated with defense activities should find support in the Catholic community. Those who remain in these industries or earn a profit from the weapons industry should find in the Church guidance and support for the ongoing evaluation of their work.

319. **To Men and Women of Science:** At Hiroshima Pope John Paul said: "Criticism of science and technology is sometimes so severe that it comes close to condemning science itself. On the contrary, science and technology are a wonderful product of a God-given human creativity, since they have provided us with wonderful possibilities and we all gratefully benefit from them. But we know that this potential is not a neutral one: it can be used either for man's progress or for his degradation."[120] We appreciate the efforts of scientists, some of whom first unlocked the secret of atomic power and others of whom have developed it in diverse ways, to turn the enormous power of science to the cause of peace.

320. Modern history is not lacking scientists who have looked back with deep remorse on the development of weapons to which they contributed, sometimes with the highest motivation, even believing that they were creating weapons that would render all other weapons obsolete and convince the world of the unthinkableness of war. Such efforts have ever proved illusory. Surely, equivalent dedication of scientific minds to reverse current trends, and to pursue concepts as bold and adventuresome in favor of peace as those which in the past have magnified the risks of war, could result in dramatic benefits for all of humanity. We particularly note in this regard the extensive efforts of public education undertaken by physicians and scientists on the medical consequences of nuclear war.

321. We do not, however, wish to limit our remarks to the physical sciences alone. Nor do we limit our remarks to physical scientists. In his address at the United Nations University in Hiroshima, Pope John Paul II warned about misuse of "the social sciences and the human behavioral sciences when they are utilized to manipulate people, to crush their mind, souls, dignity and freedom . . ."[121] The positive role of social science in overcoming the dangers of the nuclear age is evident in this letter. We have been dependent upon the research and analysis of social scientists in our effort to apply the moral principles of the Catholic tradition to the concrete problems of our

---

[120] John Paul II, "Address to Scientists and Scholars," #3, cited, p. 621.

[121] Ibid.

day. We encourage social scientists to continue this work of relating moral wisdom and political reality. We are in continuing need of your insights.

322.   **To Men and Women of the Media:** We have directly felt our dependence upon you in writing this letter; all the problems we have confronted have been analyzed daily in the media. As we have grappled with these issues, we have experienced some of the responsibility you bear for interpreting them. On the quality of your efforts depends in great measure the opportunity the general public will have for understanding this letter.

323.   **To Public Officials:** Vatican II spoke forcefully of "the difficult yet noble art of politics."[122] No public issue is more difficult than avoiding war; no public task more noble than building a secure peace. Public officials in a democracy must both lead and listen; they are ultimately dependent upon a popular consensus to sustain policy. We urge you to lead with courage and to listen to the public debate with sensitivity.

324.   Leadership in a nuclear world means examining with great care and objectivity every potential initiative toward world peace, regardless of how unpromising it might at first appear. One specific initiative which might be taken now would be the establishment of a task force including the public sector, industry, labor, economists and scientists with the mandate to consider the problems and challenges posed by nuclear disarmament to our economic well-being and industrial output. Listening includes being particularly attentive to the consciences of those who sincerely believe that they may not morally support warfare in general, a given war, or the exercise of a particular role within the armed forces. Public officials might well serve all of our fellow citizens by proposing and supporting legislation designed to give maximum protection to this precious freedom, true freedom of conscience.

325.   In response to public officials who both lead and listen, we urge citizens to respect the vocation of public service. It is a role easily maligned but not easily fulfilled. Neither justice nor peace can be achieved with stability in the absence of courageous and creative public servants.

326.   **To Catholics as Citizens:** All papal teaching on peace has stressed the crucial role of public opinion. Pope John Paul II specified the tasks before us: "There is no justification for not raising the

---

[122] *Pastoral Constitution*, #75.

question of the responsibility of each nation and each individual in the face of possible wars and of the nuclear threat."[123] In a democracy, the responsibility of the nation and that of its citizens coincide. Nuclear weapons pose especially acute questions of conscience for American Catholics. As citizens we wish to affirm our loyalty to our country and its ideals, yet we are also citizens of the world who must be faithful to the universal principles proclaimed by the Church. While some other countries also possess nuclear weapons, we may not forget that the United States was the first to build and to use them. Like the Soviet Union, this country now possesses so many weapons as to imperil the continuation of civilization. Americans share responsibility for the current situation, and cannot evade responsibility for trying to resolve it.

327. The virtue of patriotism means that as citizens we respect and honor our country, but our very love and loyalty make us examine carefully and regularly its role in world affairs, asking that it live up to its full potential as an agent of peace with justice for all people.

> Citizens must cultivate a generous and loyal spirit of patriotism, but without being narrow-minded. This means that they will always direct their attention to the good of the whole human family, united by the different ties which bind together races, people, and nations.[124]

328. In a pluralistic democracy like the United States, the Church has a unique opportunity, precisely because of the strong constitutional protection of both religious freedom and freedom of speech and the press, to help call attention to the moral dimensions of public issues. In a previous pastoral letter, *Human Life In Our Day*, we said: "In our democratic system, the fundamental right of political dissent cannot be denied, nor is rational debate on public policy decisions of government in the light of moral and political principles to be discouraged. It is the duty of the governed to analyze responsibly the concrete issues of public policy."[125] In fulfilling this role, the Church helps to create a community of conscience in the wider civil community. It does this in the first instance by teaching clearly within the Church the moral principles which bind and shape the Catholic conscience. The Church also fulfills a teaching role, however, in striving to share the moral wisdom of the Catholic tradition with the larger society.

---

[123] John Paul II, "Address at Hiroshima," #2, *Origins* 10 (1981):620.

[124] *Pastoral Constitution*, #75.

[125] *Human Life in Our Day*, cited, p. 41.

329.   In the wider public discussion, we look forward in a special way to cooperating with all other Christians with whom we share common traditions. We also treasure cooperative efforts with Jewish and Islamic communities, which possess a long and abiding concern for peace as a religious and human value. Finally, we reaffirm our desire to participate in a common public effort with all men and women of good will who seek to reverse the arms race and secure the peace of the world.

Conclusion

330.   As we close this lengthy letter, we try to answer two key questions as directly as we can.

331.   Why do we address these matters fraught with such complexity, controversy and passion? We speak as pastors, not politicians. We are teachers, not technicians. We cannot avoid our responsibility to lift up the moral dimensions of the choices before our world and nation. The nuclear age is an era of moral as well as physical danger. We are the first generation since Genesis with the power to virtually destroy God's creation. We cannot remain silent in the face of such danger. Why do we address these issues? We are simply trying to live up to the call of Jesus to be peacemakers in our own time and situation.

332.   What are we saying? Fundamentally, we are saying that the decisions about nuclear weapons are among the most pressing moral questions of our age. While these decisions have obvious military and political aspects, they involve fundamental moral choices. In simple terms, we are saying that good ends (defending one's country, protecting freedom, etc.) cannot justify immoral means (the use of weapons which kill indiscriminately and threaten whole societies). We fear that our world and nation are headed in the wrong direction. More weapons with greater destructive potential are produced every day. More and more nations are seeking to become nuclear powers. In our quest for more and more security, we fear we are actually becoming less and less secure.

333.   In the words of our Holy Father, we need a "moral about-face." The whole world must summon the moral courage and technical means to say "no" to nuclear conflict; "no" to weapons of mass destruction; "no" to an arms race which robs the poor and the vulnerable; and "no" to the moral danger of a nuclear age which places before humankind indefensible choices of constant terror or surrender. Peacemaking is not an optional commitment. It is a requirement of our faith. We are called to be peacemakers, not by some movement of the moment, but by our Lord Jesus. The content and context of our peacemaking is set, not by some political agenda or ideological program, but by the teaching of his Church.

334.   Thus far in this pastoral letter we have made suggestions we hope will be helpful in the present world crisis. Looking ahead to the long and productive future of humanity for which we all hope, we feel that a more all-inclusive and final solution is needed. We speak here of the truly effective international authority for which Pope John XXIII ardently longed in *Peace on Earth,*[126] and of which Pope Paul VI spoke to the United Nations on his visit there in 1965.[127] The hope for such a structure is not unrealistic, because the point has been reached where public opinion sees clearly that, with the massive weaponry of the present, war is no longer viable. There *is* a substitute for war. There is negotiation under the supervision of a global body realistically fashioned to do its job. It must be given the equipment to keep constant surveillance on the entire earth. Present technology makes this possible. It must have the authority, freely conferred upon it by all the nations, to investigate what seems to be preparations for war by any one of them. It must be empowered by all the nations to enforce its commands on every nation. It must be so constituted as to pose no threat to any nation's sovereignty. Obviously the creation of such a sophisticated instrumentality is a gigantic task, but is it hoping for too much to believe that the genius of humanity, aided by the grace and guidance of God, is able to accomplish it? To create it may take decades of unrelenting daily toil by the world's best minds and most devoted hearts, but it shall never come into existence unless we make a beginning now.

335.   As we come to the end of our pastoral letter we boldly propose the beginning of this work. The evil of the proliferation of nuclear arms becomes more evident every day to all people. No one is exempt from their danger. If ridding the world of the weapons of war could be done easily, the whole human race would do it gladly tomorrow. Shall we shrink from the task because it is hard?

336.   We turn to our own government and we beg it to propose to the United Nations that it begin this work immediately; that it

---

[126] John XXIII, *Peace on Earth* (1963), #137.

[127] Paul VI, "Address to the General Assembly of the United Nations," (1965), #2.

create an international task force for peace; that this task force, with membership open to every nation, meet daily through the years ahead with one sole agenda: the creation of a world that will one day be safe from war. Freed from the bondage of war that holds it captive in its threat, the world will at last be able to address its problems and to make genuine human progress, so that every day there may be more freedom, more food, and more opportunity for every human being who walks the face of the earth.

337. Let us have the courage to believe in the bright future and in a God who wills it for us—not a perfect world, but a better one. The perfect world, we Christians believe, is beyond the horizon, in an endless eternity where God will be all in all. But a better world is here for human hands and hearts and minds to make.

338. For the community of faith the risen Christ is the beginning and end of all things. For all things were created through him and all things will return to the Father through him.

339. It is our belief in the risen Christ which sustains us in confronting the awesome challenge of the nuclear arms race. Present in the beginning as the word of the Father, present in history as the word incarnate, and with us today in his word, sacraments, and spirit, he is the reason for our hope and faith. Respecting our freedom, he does not solve our problems but sustains us as we take responsibility for his work of creation and try to shape it in the ways of the kingdom. We believe his grace will never fail us. We offer this letter to the Church and to all who can draw strength and wisdom from it in the conviction that we must not fail him. We must subordinate the power of the nuclear age to human control and direct it to human benefit. As we do this we are conscious of God's continuing work among us, which will one day issue forth in the beautiful final kingdom prophesied by the seer of the Book of Revelation:

> Then I saw a new heaven and a new earth; for the first heaven and the first earth had passed away and the sea was no more. And I saw the holy city, new Jerusalem, coming down out of heaven from God, prepared as a bride adorned for her husband; and I heard a great voice from the throne saying, "Behold, the dwelling of God is with men. He will dwell with them, and they shall be his people, and God himself will be with them, he will wipe away every tear from their eyes, and death shall be no more, neither shall there be mourning nor crying nor pain any more, for the former things have passed away." And he who sat upon the throne said, "Behold, I make all things new" (Rv. 21:1-5).

179. Enlarging the Dialogue on a Consistent Ethic of Life, March 11, 1984.

The so-called life issues of abortion, capital punishment, euthanasia, hunger, and war—each a single aspect of human rights in general—have been the subject of intense and often bitter debate among Americans in the generation since World War II. In the course of the debate on these topics deep differences have arisen, and that within the Catholic community of the United States, as well as within the broader national society. In an effort to establish a linkage between these individual issues that is based on general moral principles relating to life itself, there has evolved what has been called the 'seamless garment' approach. In the William Wade Lecture at Saint Louis University in March, 1984, Joseph Cardinal Bernardin, Archbishop of Chicago, sought to advance that approach by showing how each single life issue has relation to the whole. Source: *Origins,* 13 (April 5, 1984), 705-709.

I first wish to express my appreciation to St. Louis University for the invitation to deliver the 1984 Wade Lecture. The William Wade lecture series is a fitting way to celebrate Father Wade's life as a priest, a philosopher and a teacher. His interest in the moral issues confronting today's church and society was an inspiration to all who knew him. I hope that my participation in this series will help to keep alive his memory and his ideals.

Three months ago I gave a lecture at Fordham University honoring another Jesuit educator, Father Robert Gannon, and I addressed the topic of a consistent ethic of life. That lecture has generated a substantial discussion both inside and outside the church on the linkage of life issues, issues which I am convinced constitute a "seamless garment." This afternoon I would like to extend the discussion by expanding upon the idea of a consistent ethic of life.

The setting of a Catholic university is one deliberately chosen for these lectures. My purpose is to foster the kind of sustained intellectual analysis and debate which the Jesuit tradition has cultivated throughout its history. The discussion must go beyond the university, but it will not occur without the involvement of Catholic universities. I seek to call attention to the resources in the Catholic tradition for shaping a viable public ethic. I hope to engage others in the church and in the wider civil society in an examination of the challenges to human life which surround us today and the potential of a consistent ethic of life. The Fordham lecture has catalyzed a vigorous debate; I seek to enlarge it, not to end it.

I will address three topics today: 1) the case for a consistent ethic of life; 2) the distinct levels of the problem; and 3) the contribution of a consisent ethic to the church and society generally.

I. The Logic of the Seamless Garment

The invitation extended to me for both the Gannon Lecture at Fordham and the Wade Lecture today asked that I address some aspect of the bishops' pastoral, "The Challenge of Peace: God's Promise and Our Response." While I would gladly have spent each lecture on the question of war and peace, I decided that it was equally necessary to show how the pastoral is rooted in a wider moral vision. Understanding that vision can enhance the way we address specific questions like the arms race.

When I set forth the argument about this wider moral vision—a consistent ethic of life—it evoked favorable comments, often from individuals and groups who had supported the peace pastoral but found themselves at odds with other positions the Catholic Church has taken on issues touching human life. At the same time, the Fordham address also generated letters from people who fear that the case for a consistent ethic will smother the Catholic opposition to abortion or will weaken our stance against the arms race.

Precisely in response to these concerns, I wish to state the essence of the case for a consistent ethic of life, specifying why it is needed and what is actually being advocated in a call for such an ethic. There are, in my view, two reasons why we need to espouse a consistent ethic of life: 1) the dimensions of the threats to life today; and 2) the value of our moral vision.

The threat to human life posed by nuclear war is so tangible that it has captured the attention of the nation. Public opinion polls rank it as one of the leading issues in the 1984 election campaign; popular movements like the nuclear freeze and professional organizations of physicians and scientists have shaped the nuclear question in terms which engage citizens and experts alike. The church is part of the process which has raised the nuclear issue to a new standing in our public life. I submit that the church should be a leader in the dialogue which shows that the nuclear question itself is part of the larger cultural, political, moral drama. Pope John Paul II regularly situates his examination of the nuclear issue in the framework of the broader problem of technology, politics and ethics.

When this broader canvas is analyzed, the concern for a

specific issue does not recede, but the meaning of multiple threats to life today—the full dimension of the problems of politics and technology—becomes vividly clear. The case being made here is not a condemnation of either politics or technology, but a recognition with the pope that on a range of key issues "it is only through a conscious choice and through a deliberate policy that humanity can be saved." That quote from the Holy Father has unique relevance to nuclear war, but it can be used creatively to address other threats to life.

The range of application is all too evident: Nuclear war threatens life on a previously unimaginable scale; abortion takes life daily on a horrendous scale; public executions are fast becoming weekly events in the most advanced technological society in history; and euthanasia is now openly discussed and even advocated. Each of these assaults on life has its own meaning and morality; they cannot be collapsed into one problem, but they must be confronted as pieces of a larger pattern.

The reason I have placed such stress on the idea of a consistent ethic of life from the beginning of my term as chairman of the pro-life committee of the National Conference of Catholic Bishops is twofold; I am persuaded by the interrelatedness of these diverse problems, and I am convinced that the Catholic moral vision has the scope, the strength and the subtlety to address this wide range of issues in an effective fashion. It is precisely the potential of our moral vision that is often not recognized even within the community of the church. The case for a consistent ethic of life—one which stands for the protection of the right to life and the promotion of the rights which enhance life from womb to tomb—manifests the positive potential of the Catholic moral and social tradition. It is both a complex and a demanding tradition; it joins the humanity of the unborn infant and the humanity of the hungry; it calls for positive legal action to prevent the killing of the unborn or the aged and positive societal action to provide shelter for the homeless and education for the illiterate. The potential of the moral and social vision is appreciated in a new way when the systemic vision of Catholic ethics is seen as the background for the specific positions we take on a range of issues.

In response to those who fear otherwise, I contend that the systemic vision of a consistent ethic of life will not erode our crucial public opposition to the direction of the arms race; neither will it smother our persistent and necessary public opposition to abortion. The systemic vision is rooted in the conviction that our opposition to these distinct problems has a common foundation and that both church and society are served by making it evident. A consistent ethic of life does not equate the problem of taking life (e.g., through abortion and in war) with the problem of promoting human dignity (through humane programs of nutrition, health care and housing). But a consistent ethic identifies both the protection of life and its promotion as moral questions. It argues for a continuum of life which must be sustained in the face of diverse and distinct threats.

A consistent ethic does not say everyone in the church must do all things, but it does say that as individuals and groups pursue one issue, whether it is opposing abortion or capital punishment, the way we oppose one threat should be related to support for a systemic vision of life. It is not necessary or possible for every person to engage in each issue, but it is both possible and necessary for the church as a whole to cultivate a conscious explicit connection among the several issues. And it is very necessary for preserving a systemic vision that individuals and groups who seek to witness to life at one point of the spectrum of life not be seen as insensitive to or even opposed to other moral claims on the overall spectrum of life. Consistency does rule out contradictory moral positions about the unique value of human life. No one is called to do everything, but each of us can do something. And we can strive not to stand against each other when the protection and the promotion of life are at stake.

II. Levels of the Question

A consistent ethic of life should honor the complexity of the multiple issues it must address. It is necessary to distinguish several levels of the question. Without attempting to be comprehensive, allow me to explore four distinct dimensions of a consistent ethic.

First, at the level of general moral principles, it is possible to identify a single principle with diverse applications. In the Fordham address I used the prohibition against direct attacks on innocent life. This principle is both central to the Catholic moral vision and systematically related to a range of specific moral issues. It prohibits direct attacks on unborn life in the womb, direct attacks on civilians in warfare and the direct killing of patients in nursing homes. Each of these topics has a constituency in society concerned with the morality of abortion, war and care of the aged and dying. A consistent ethic of life encourages the specific concerns of each constituency, but also calls them to see the interrelatedness of their efforts. The need to defend the integrity of the moral principle in the full range of its application is a responsibility of each distinct constituency. If the principle is eroded in the public mind, all lose.

A second level of a consistent ethic stresses the distinction among cases rather than their similarities. We need different moral principles to apply to diverse cases. The classical distinction between ordinary and extraordinary means has applicability in the care of the dying but no relevance in the case of warfare. Not all moral principles have relevance across the whole range of life issues. Moreover, sometimes a systemic vision of the life issues requires a combination of moral insights to provide direction on one issue. At Fordham I cited the classical teaching on capital punishment which gives the state the right to take life in defense of key social values. But I also pointed out how a concern for promoting a public attitude of respect for life has led the bishops of the United States to oppose the exercise of that right.

Some of the responses I have received on the Fordham address correctly say that abortion and captial punishment are not identical issues. The principle which protects innocent life distinguishes the unborn child from the convicted murderer. Other letters stress that while nuclear war is a threat to life, abortion involves the actual taking of life, here and now. I accept both of these distinctions, of course, but I also find compelling the need to relate the cases while keeping them in distinct categories. Abortion is taking of life in ever growing numbers in our society. Those concerned about it, I believe, will find their case enhanced by taking note of the rapidly expanding use of public execution. In a similar way, those who are particularly concerned about these executions, even if the accused has taken another life, should recognize the elementary truth that a society which can be indifferent to the innocent life of an unborn child will not be easily stirred to concern for a convicted criminal. There is, I maintain, a political and psychological linkage among the life issues—from war to welfare concerns—which we ignore at our own peril: a systemic vision of life seeks to expand the moral imagination of a society, not partition it into airtight categories.

A third level of the question before us involves how we relate a commitment to principles to our public witness of life. As I have said, no one can do everything. There are limits to both competency and energy; both point to the wisdom of setting priorities and defining distinct functions. The church, however, must be credible across a wide range of issues; the very scope of our moral vision requires a commitment to a multiplicity of questions. In this way the teaching of the church will sustain a variety of individual commitments. Neither the Fordham address nor this one is intended to constrain wise and vigorous efforts to protect and promote life through specific, precise forms of action. Both addresses do seek to cultivate a dialogue within the church and in the wider society among individuals and groups which draw on common principles (e.g., the prohibition against killing the innocent), but seem convinced that they do not share common ground. The appeal here is not for anyone to do everything, but to recognize points of interdependence which should be stressed, not denied.

A fourth level, one where dialogue is sorely needed, is the relationship between moral principles and concrete political choices. The moral questions of abortion, the arms race, the fate of social programs for the poor and the role of human rights in foreign policy are public moral issues. The arena in which they are ultimately decided is not the academy or the church, but the political process. A consistent ethic of life seeks to present coherent linkage among a diverse set of issues. It can and should be used to test party platforms, public policies and political candidates. The church legitimately fulfills a public role by articulating a framework for political choices, by relating that framework to specific issues and by calling for systematic moral analysis of all areas of public policy.

This is the role our bishops' conference has sought to fulfill by publishing a statement on political responsibility during each of the presidential and congressional election years in the past decade. The purpose is surely not to tell citizens how to vote, but to help shape the public debate and form personal conscience so that every citizen will vote thoughtfully and responsibly. Our statement on political responsibility has always been, like our respect life program, a multi-issue approach to public morality. The fact that this statement sets forth a spectrum of issues of current concern to the church and society should not be understood as implying that all issues are qualitatively equal from a moral perspective. As I indicated earlier, each of the life issues—while related to all the others—is distinct and calls for its own specific moral analysis. Both the statement and the respect life program have direct relevance to the political order, but they are applied concretely by the choice of citizens. This is as it should be. In the political order the church is primarily a teacher; it possesses a carefully cultivated tradition of moral analysis of personal and public issues. It makes that tradition available in a special manner for the community of the church, but it offers it also to all who find meaning and guidance in its moral teaching.

III. A Pastoral and Public Contribution

The moral teaching of the church has both pastoral and public significance. Pastorally, a consistent ethic of life is a contribution to the witness of the church's defense of the human person. Publicly, a consistent ethic fills a void in our public policy debate today.

Pastorally, I submit that a church standing forth on the entire range of issues which the logic of our moral vision bids us to confront will be a church in the style of both Vatican II's *Gaudium et Spes* and in the style of Pope John Paul II's consistent witness to life. The pastoral life of the church should not be guided by a simplistic criterion of relevance. But the capacity of faith to shed light on the concrete questions of personal and public life today is one way in which the value of the Gospel is assessed. Certainly the serious, sustained interest manifested throughout American society in the bishops' letter on war and peace provides a unique pastoral opportunity for the church. Demonstrating how the teaching on war and peace is supported by a wider concern for all of life may bring others to see for the first time what our tradition has affirmed for a very long time: the linkage among the life issues.

The public value of a consistent ethic of life is connected directly to its pastoral role. In the public arena we should always speak and act like a church. But the unique public possibility for a consistent ethic is provided precisely by the unstructured character of the public debate on the life questions. Each of the issues I have identified today—abortion, war, hunger and human rights, euthanasia and capital punishment—is treated as a separate, self-contained topic in our public life. Each is distinct, but an ad hoc approach to each one fails to illustrate how our choices in one area can affect our decisions in other areas. There must be a public attitude of respect for all of life if public actions are to respect it in concrete cases.

The pastoral on war and peace speaks of a "new moment" in the nuclear age. The pastoral has been widely studied and applauded because it caught the spirit of the new moment and spoke with moral substance to the issues of the new moment. I am convinced there is an open moment before us on the agenda of life issues. It is a significant opportunity for the church to demonstrate the strength of a sustained moral vision. I submit that a clear witness to a consistent ethic of life will allow us to grasp the opportunity of this open moment and serve both the sacredness of every human life and the God of life who is the origin and support of our common humanity.

180. What We Have Seen and Heard, Black Bishops' Pastoral Letter on Evangelization, September 9, 1984.

"From the earliest period of the church's history in our land, we have been the hands and arms that helped build the church from Baltimore to Bardstown, from New Orleans to Los Angeles, from St. Augustine to St. Louis." Rarely has an official pronouncement of American Catholic churchmen been more suffused with historical memories than is true of this pastoral letter. Moreover, with the exception of the native American Indians, never has the history of a segment of the Catholic community of the United States contained a sadder story than that of the black Catholics. The neglect, the discrimination, and the indifference with which they have been treated account in good measure for the fact that today of the more than 28,000,000 American blacks only about 1,300,000 are Catholics. Yet the black bishops do not dwell here on the negative aspects of their racial history. Instead they acknowledge the improved situation of their people, outline in detail the principal instruments for their evangelization, while candidly admitting the distance that has yet to be traversed before blacks in general, and black Catholics in particular, may be said to have achieved true justice and their rightful recognition within the national community. Source: *Origins,* 14 (October 18, 1984), 273-287.

Introduction

Within the history of every Christian community there comes the time when it reaches adulthood. This maturity brings with it the duty, the privilege and the joy to share with others the rich experience of the "word of life." Always conscious of the need to hear the word and ever ready to listen to its proclamation, the mature Christian community feels the irresistible urge to speak that word:

"This is what we proclaim to you: what was from the beginning, what we have heard, what we have seen with our eyes, what we have looked upon and our hands have touched—we speak the word of life. (This life became visible; we have seen and bear witness to it, and we proclaim to you the eternal life that was present to the Father and became visible to us.) What we have seen and heard we proclaim in turn to you so that you may share life with us. This fellowship of ours is with the Father and with his Son, Jesus Christ. Indeed, our purpose in writing you this is that our joy may be complete" (1 Jn. 1:1-4).

We, the 10 black bishops of the United States, chosen from among you to serve the people of God, are a significant sign among many other signs that the black Catholic community in the American church has now come of age. We write to you as brothers that "you may share life with us." We write also to all those who by their faith make up the people of God in the United States that "our joy may be complete." And what is this joy? It is that joy that the Ethiopian eunuch, the treasurer of the African queen, expressed in the Book of Acts when he was baptized by the deacon, Philip: He "went on his way rejoicing" (Acts 8:39). We rejoice because, like this African court official, we, the descendants of Africans brought to these shores, are now called to share our faith and to demonstrate our witness to our risen Lord.

We write to you, black brothers and sisters, because each one of us is called to a special task. The Holy Spirit now calls us all to the work of evangelization. As he did for Peter, the Lord Jesus has prayed for us that our faith might not fail (Lk. 22:32), and with Paul we all are compelled to confess: "Yet preaching the Gospel is not the subject of a boast; I am under compulsion and have no choice. I am ruined if I do not preach it!" (1 Cor. 9:16).

Evangelization is both a call and a response. It is the call of Jesus reverberating down the centuries: "Go into the whole world and proclaim the good news to all creation" (Mk. 16:15). The response is, "Conduct yourselves, then, in a way worthy of the Gospel of Christ" (Phil. 1:27). Evangelization means not only preaching but witnessing; not only conversion but renewal; not only entry into the community but the building up of the community; not only hearing the word but sharing it. Evangelization, said Pope Paul VI, "is a question not only of preaching the Gospel in ever wider geographic areas or to ever greater numbers of people, but also of affecting and as it were upsetting, through the power of the Gospel, mankind's criteria of judgment, determining values, points of interest, lines of thought, sources of inspiration and models of life, which are in contrast with the word of God and plan of salvation."[1]

Pope Paul VI issued that call to the peoples of Africa when he said to them at Kampala in Uganda, "You are now missionaries to yourselves." And Pope Paul also laid out for all sons and daughters of Africa the nature of the response, "You must now give your gifts of blackness to the whole church."[2]

We believe that these solemn words of our Holy Father Paul VI were addressed not only to Africans today but also to us, the children of the Africans of yesterday. We believe that the Holy Father has laid a challenge before us to share the gift of our blackness with the church in the United States. This is a challenge to be evangelizers, and so we want to write about this gift, which is also a challenge. First, we shall write about the gifts we share, gifts rooted in our African heritage. Then we will write about the obstacles to evangelization that we must still seek to overcome.

GRATEFUL REMEMBRANCE FOR OUR OWN EVANGELIZATION
(*CF. "EVANGELII NUNTIANDI,"* 59, 68-69, 71.)

Before we go on, however, we must at the beginning remember those who brought us to new birth within the faith. When we as black Catholics speak of missionaries, we shall never forget the devoted service that many white priests, vowed religious and laypersons gave to us as a people and still give to us daily. We shall remember and never forget that this ministry was often given at great personal sacrifice and hardship. The same holds true today.

We remember especially that those of us who have grown up in the faith owe this faith to the black men and women who have gone before us strong in the faith and steadfast in their personal conviction. If we have reached adulthood in the fullness

---

[1]Pope Paul VI, "On Evangelization in the Modern World," 19.

[2]The actual words of Pope Paul VI are the following: If you are able to avoid the possible dangers of religious pluralism, the danger of making your Christian profession into a kind of local folklore, or into exclusivist racism, or into egoistic tribalism or arbitrary separatism, then you will be able to remain sincerely African even in your own interpretation of the Christian life; you will be able to formulate Catholicism in terms congenial to your own culture; you will be capable of bringing to the Catholic Church the precious and original contribution of 'negritude,' which she needs particularly in this historic hour." "To the Heart of Africa" (Address to the Bishops of the African Continent at the Closing Session of a Symposium Held in Kampala, Uganda), The Pope Speaks, vol. 14 (1969), p. 219.

of the age of Christ, it is most of all thanks to our fathers and mothers and all our ancestors who kept alive an unflagging commitment to Christ and to his church throughout bitter days of slavery and the troubled times of racial segregation. Their faith was passed on to us despite the peculiar structures of racism and bondage that marred the Catholic Church in America in an earlier time.

I. The Gifts We Share

BLACK CULTURE AND VALUES: INFORMED BY FAITH (*CF. "EVANGELII NUNTIANDI,"* 62-64.)

There is a richness in our black experience that we must share with the entire people of God. These are gifts that are part of an African past. For we have heard with black ears and we have seen with black eyes and we have understood with an African heart. We thank God for the gifts of our Catholic faith, and we give thanks for the gifts of our blackness. In all humility we turn to the whole church that it might share our gifts so that "our joy may be complete."

To be Catholic is to be universal. To be universal is not to be uniform. It does mean, however, that the gifts of individuals and of particular groups become the common heritage shared by all. Just as we lay claim to the gift of blackness, so we share these gifts within the black community at large and within the church. This will be our part in the building up of the whole church. This will also be our way of enriching ourselves. "For it is in giving that we receive."[3] Finally, it is our way to witness to our brothers and sisters within the black community that the Catholic Church is both one and also home to us all.

SCRIPTURE (*CF. "EVANGELII NUNTIANDI,"* 42-43.)

African-American spirituality is based on the sacred scriptures. In the dark days of slavery, reading was forbidden, but for our ancestors the Bible was never a closed book. The stories were told and retold in sermons, spirituals and shouts, proverbs and turns of phrase borrowed freely from the Bible. The Bible was not for our ancestors a mere record of the wonderful works of God in a bygone age; it was a present record of what was soon to come. God will lead his people from the bondage of Egypt. God will preserve

---

[3]From the prayer attributed to St. Francis of Assisi.

his children in the midst of the fiery furnace. God's power will make the dry bones scattered on the plain snap together, and he will breathe life into them. Above all, the birth and death, the suffering and the sorrow, the burial and the resurrection tell how the story will end for all who are faithful, no matter what the present tragedy is.

For black people the story is our story; the Bible promise is our hope. Thus when the word of scripture is proclaimed in the black community, it is not a new message but a new challenge. Scripture is part of our roots; the Bible has sunk deep into our tradition; and the good news of the Gospel has been enmeshed in our past of oppression and pain. Still the message was heard, and we learned to celebrate in the midst of sorrow, to hope in the depths of despair and to fight for freedom in the face of all obstacles. The time has now come to take this precious heritage and to go and "tell it on the mountain."

OUR GIFT OF FREEDOM
(*CF. "EVANGELII NUNTIANDI,"* 30-39.)

The good news of the Gospel is the message of liberation. "You will know the truth," said Jesus, "and the truth will set you free" (Jn. 8:32). Recently our Holy Father, Pope John Paul II, spoke at length on the relation between truth and freedom:

"Jesus himself links 'liberation' with knowledge of the truth: 'You will know the truth, and the truth will make you free' (Jn. 8:32). In this affirmation is the deep meaning of freedom that Christ gives man as a consequence coming from knowledge of the truth. It is question of a spritual process of maturing, by means of which man becomes a representative and spokesman of 'righteousness and holiness'(Eph. 4:24) at the different levels of personal, individual and social life. But this truth is not mere truth of a scientific or historical nature; it is Christ himself—the word incarnate of the Father—who can say of himself, 'I am the way, the truth, the life'(Jn. 14:6). For this reason, Jesus, although aware of what was in store for him, repeatedly and forcefully, with firmness and with decision, opposed 'non-truth' in his earthly life.

"This service of truth, participation in the prophetic service of Christ, is a task of the church, which tries to carry it out in the different historical contexts. It is necessary to call clearly by name injustice, the exploitation of man by man, the exploitation of man by the state or by the mechanisms of systems and regimes. It is necessary to call by name all social injustice, all discrimination, all violence inflicted on man with regard to his body, his spirit, his conscience, his dignity as a person, his life."[4]

Black people know what freedom is because we remember the dehumanizing force of slavery, racist prejudice and oppression. No one can understand so well the meaning of the proclamation that Christ has set us free than those who have experienced the denial of freedom. For us, therefore, freedom is a cherished gift. For its preservation, no sacrifice is too great.

Hence, freedom brings responsibility. It must never be abused, equated with license or taken for granted. Freedom is God's gift, and we are accountable to him for our loss of it. And we are accountable for the gift of freedom in the lives of others. We oppose all oppression and all injustice, for unless all are free, none are free. Moreover, oppression by some means freedom's destruction for both the oppressor and the oppressed, and liberation liberates the oppressor and the oppressed.

Our African-American ancestors knew the liberating hand of God. Even before emancipation they knew the inner spiritual freedom that comes from Jesus. Even under slavery they found ways to celebrate that spiritual freedom which God alone can give. They left us the lesson that without spiritual freedom we cannot fight for that broader freedom which is the right of all who are brothers and sisters in Christ. This is the gift we have to share with the whole church. This is the responsibility that freedom brings: to teach to others its value and work to see that its benefits are denied to none.

THE GIFT OF RECONCILIATION
(*CF. "EVANGELII NUNTIANDI,"* 2, 30-31, 61-64.)

The gospel message is a message that liberates us from hate and calls us to forgiveness and reconciliation. As a people we must be deeply committed to reconciliation. This is a value coming from our African heritage and deepened by our belief in the gospel teaching. When in recent years we rejected "token integration" for "self-determination," it was not to choose confrontation in place of cooperation, but to insist on collaboration with mutual respect for the dignity and unique gifts of all. Reconciliation can never mean unilateral elevation and another's subordination, unilateral giving and another's constant receiving, unilateral flexibility and another's resistance. True reconciliation arises only where there is mutu-

---

[4]Pope John Paul II, "Be Witnesses to Christ, the Truth!" *You Are the Future, You Are the Hope: To the Young People of the World, John Paul II* (Daughters of St. Paul, 1979), p. 105.

ally perceived equality. This is what is meant by justice.

Without justice, any meaningful reconciliation is impossible. Justice safeguards the rights and delineates the responsibility of all. A people must safeguard their own cultural identity and their own cultural values. Likewise they must respect the cultural values of others. For this reason sincere reconciliation builds on mutual recognition and mutual respect. On this foundation can be erected an authentic Christian love.

"But now in Christ Jesus you who once were far off have been brought near through the blood of Christ. It is he who is our peace, and who made the two of us one by breaking down the barrier of hostility that kept us apart" (Eph. 2:13-14).

We seek justice, then, because we seek reconciliation, and we seek reconciliation because by the blood of Christ we are made one. The desire for reconciliation is for us a most precious gift, for reconciliation is the fruit of liberation. Our contribution to the building up of the church in America and in the world is to be an agent of change for both.

Finally, as we speak of reconciliation, let us note that as members of a truly universal church our efforts must never be limited to the black community in this country alone. Our minds and hearts turn toward the church of the poor in the Third World, especially those "who hunger and thirst for justice" in Africa, Asia and Latin America. We turn also to the members of the "church of silence" and to the various minority groups in the East and in the West.

We shall remind ourselves and our compatriots that we are called to be "instruments of peace." This peace is the fruit of justice. We must be a part of those movements for justice that seek to reduce bombs and increase bread, to replace bullets with the printing of books. We must work with all who strive to make available the fruits of creation to all God's children everywhere. It was in chains that our parents were brought to these shores and in violence were we maintained in bondage. Let us who are the children of pain be now a bridge of reconciliation. Let us who are the offspring of violence become the channels of compassion. Let us, the sons and daughters of bondage, be the bringers of peace.

OUR SPIRITUALITY AND ITS GIFTS
(*CF. "EVANGELII NUNTIANDI,"* 61-64.)

Black Americans are a people rich with spiritual gifts. Some aspects of this spirituality have already been mentioned. It is fitting, however, to present briefly the major characteristics of what

can be termed "black spirituality." As members of a church universal both in time and place, we have no difficulty with this term. All
peoples and all cultures have been molded by the Holy Spirit, and
the Holy Spirit has distributed his gifts in the language, culture and
traditions of each.

Black spirituality has four major characteristics; It is contemplative. It is holistic. It is joyful. It is communitarian.

The Contemplative Dimension

Black spirituality is contemplative. By this we mean that
prayer is spontaneous and pervasive in the black tradition. Every
place is a place for prayer because God's presence is heard and felt
in every place. Black spirituality senses the awe of God's transcendence and the vital intimacy of his closeness. God's power breaks
into the "sin-sick world" of everyday. The sense of God's presence
and power taught our ancestors that no one can run from him and
no one need hide from him.

Black spirituality has taught us what it means to "let go"
and "to lean on God." In an age of competition and control we have
learned to surrender to God's love and to let him work his power
through us. In an age of technology and human engineering our
spiritual heritage has never let us forget that God takes us each by
the hand and leads us in ways we might not understand. It is this
sense of God's power in us that calls us to work for evangelization
in the modern world.

Holistic

Black spirituality, in contrast with much of Western tradition, is holistic. Like the biblical tradition, there is no dualism.
Divisions between intellect and emotion, spirit and body, action
and contemplation, individual and community, sacred and secular
are foreign to us. In keeping with our African heritage, we are not
ashamed of our emotions. For us, the religious experience is an
experience of the whole human being—both the feelings and the
intellect, the heart as well as the head. Moreover, we find foreign
any notion that the body is evil. We find our own holistic spiritual
approach to be in accord with the scriptures and the logic of the
incarnation.

In sharing this approach we contribute greatly to evangelization in our day. St. Paul wrote Timothy, "Everything God
created is good; nothing is to be rejected when it is received with
thanksgiving" (1 Tm. 4:4). The material world need not lead us

away from God, but can and should bring us closer to him.

We dare to suggest that black spirituality in its holistic approach also presents a solution to one of the problems of our time: the progressive dehumanization brought about by a technocratic society. Not only is it possible to counteract the dehumanizing forces in our world and our work, but we can restore the human. We can put back the human factor by rediscovering that "the world is charged with the grandeur of God"[5] and that "the whole world is in his hands." We affirm that the advances in technology, when understood with God's presence in all things, will be a powerful force for the coming of the kingdom and the human progress of all people.

The Gift of Joy

Joy is a hallmark of black spirituality. Joy is first of all celebration. Celebration is movement and song, rhythm and feeling, color and sensation, exultation and thanksgiving. We celebrate the presence and the proclamation of the word.

This joy is a sign of our faith and especially our hope. It is never an escape from reality, however harsh it may be. Indeed this joy is often present even in the midst of deep anguish and bitter tears.

"You will weep and mourn while the world rejoices; you will grieve for a time, but your grief will be turned into joy" (Jn. 16:20).

This joy is a result of our conviction that "in the time of trouble, he will lead me." This joy comes from the teaching and wisdom of mothers and fathers in the faith that, looking at Jesus, we must burst forth into song so that all might hear, "He's sweet I know..."

This gift of joy is something we must share. If the message of evangelization is the "good news" about Jesus, we must react with joy. If we do indeed feel a profound joy, we shall know that we have heard and that we have understood; and we are thus enabled to share our good news.

One who is joyful is impelled to love and cannot hate. A joyful person seeks to reconcile and will not cause division. A joyful person is troubled by the sight of another's sadness. A joyful person seeks to console, strives to encourage and brings to all true peace.

---

[5]"God's Grandeur," *The Poems of Gerard Manley Hopkins,* 4th ed., W.H. Gardner and N.H. MacKenzie, eds. (Oxford University Press, 1970), p. 66.

Such is the gift so clearly needed in our time. Such is the gift that Jesus passed on to us on the evening he died. "All this I tell you that my joy may be yours and your joy may be complete" (Jn. 15:11).

Community (Cf. "Evangelii Nuntiandi," 60.)

In African culture the "I" takes its meaning in the "we." In other words, individual identity is to be found within the context of the community. Even today black Christianity is eminently a social reality. The sense of community is a major component of black spirituality.

This communal dimension of our spirituality is a gift we also need to share. In the world in which we live, a high value is placed on competition. Hence, so many of us become "losers" so that others might prevail as "winners." And again so many place personal profit and personal advancement before the good of the community and the benefit of the whole.

The communal dimension of black spirituality permeates our experience of liturgy and worship. Worship must be shared. Worship is always a celebration of community. No one stands in prayer alone. One prays and acts within and for the community. Each one supports, encourages and enriches the other and is in turn enriched, encouraged and supported.

Community, however, means social concern and social justice. Black spirituality never excludes concern for human suffering and other people's concerns. "As often as you did it for one of my least brothers, you did it for me" (Mt. 25:40) are the words of Christ that cut through any supposed tension between secular concerns and the sacred or between prayerful pursuits and the profane. Ours is a spiritual heritage that always embraces the total human person.

THE FAMILY (*CF. "EVANGELII NUNTIANDI,"* 71.)

The heart of the human community is the family. In our society today traditional family values are openly questioned and rejected. For many reasons the black family has been especially assailed, despite the importance that families still have in the black cultural and spiritual tradition.

For us the family has always meant "the extended family"—the grandparents, the uncles and aunts, the godparents, all those related by kinship or strong friendship. This rich notion of family was not only part of an African tradition but also was our own African-American experience. Child care became the responsibility of many persons, for necessity demanded that many share the labor, distribute the burden and, yes, even the joy.

In practice, the extended family often goes beyond kinship and marital relationship to include persons who, having no family of their own, have been accepted into the wider family circle. These family members feel a deep responsibility for one another in both ordinary times of daily life and in the extraordinary moments of need or crisis.

It is for this reason that, despite the erosion of family life among us, we as a people continue to have a strong sense of family bonds. In its Christian setting this family sense enhances the role of godparents and other relatives who must often shoulder the responsibility for passing on the faith and strengthening the religious values of the young. Moreover, there is more than one priestly or religious vocation among us that was nurtured by the support and encouragement of some adult in the extended family. Not infrequently young blacks in the seminary or religious-formation house have been informally adopted by a sponsor or have been welcomed into the circle of a second family.

This sense of family in our own African-American tradition can easily be translated into a richer sense of church as a great and all-embracing family. In our parishes we should truly look upon ourselves as brothers and sisters to one another. The elders among us should be a living resource for the young, for they have much to tell and teach. Our celebrations should be the affirmation of our kinship and our common bond. The words of the third Eucharistic Prayer, "Father, hear the prayers of the family you have gathered here before you," are not a pious fiction but a sacred reality that defines the meaning of the Catholic community. In a word, evangelization for black Catholics is a celebration of the family, a renewal of the family and a call to welcome new members into the family of God.

The Role of Black Men (Cf. "Evangelii Nuntiandi," 73,76.)

Central to any discussion of the black family today is the question of the black man as husband, father, co-provider and co-protector. For many historical reasons the black man has been forced to bear the crushing blows of racial hate and economic repression. Too often barred from access to decent employment, too often stripped of his dignity and manhood and too often forced into a stereotype that was a caricature of his manhood, the black male finds himself depreciated and relegated to the margins of family life and influence. Not the least of the evil fruits of racial segregation has been the artificially fashioned rivalry between black women and men.

It is important, we believe, to encourage a re-evaluation of the fundamental vocation to fatherhood that black men must have in the context of the black family. In our cultural heritage the father provides the courage and wisdom to help maintain the family and to ensure its growth. We challenge black men of today to assert their spiritual strength and to demonstrate their sense of responsibility and ethnic pride. We call upon black men to become what their fathers were—even when an evil institution sought to destroy their individuality and their initiative—that is, models of virtue for their children and partners in love and nurturing with their wives. Without a father no family life can be fully complete. Let the black father find his model in the fatherhood of God, who by his providence nourishes us, who by his wisdom guides us and who by his love cherishes us and makes us all one and holy in his family of grace.

The Role of Women (Cf. "Evangelii Nuntiandi," 73, 76.)

The civil rights movement of the 1960s that we as a people initiated and in which we suffered raised the consciousness of many people to the reality of social inequities and social injustice. In many ways our struggle served as a pattern and a model for others who were made aware of their own plight. Within the last decade we all have become more conscious of the social inequities that women as a group have suffered and continued to suffer in our society. In a very special way these inequities weigh most heavily on black women and women of other racial minorities.

On the other hand, black women have had and continue to have a place within the black community that is unique. In traditional black society women have had to assume responsibilities within the family and within the community out of necessity. As a result, black women historically have been not only sources of strength, they also have been examples of courage and resolution. This strength and courage are for us all a source of power and a powerful gift that we as a people can share with the larger society.

The role of black women within the context of black history, however, has not been a subordinate role to black men, but a complementary role. Women like Sojourner Truth, Harriet Tubman and Mary McLeod Bethune were heirs of an African tradition.

If this is true of the African-American tradition, it is even more so for us who are the heirs of a black Catholic tradition. Before there were black Catholic priests in the United States, there were black women religious. The challenge of evangelization within the black Catholic community was taken up by four black women in the hostile environment of Baltimore, under the leadership of Elizabeth Lange. The church gave approval to her work when the Oblate Sisters of Providence were officially recognized as a religious congregation in 1831. Evangelization among the blacks of New Orleans was also the task assumed by Henriette Delille, who in the face of crushing opposition founded the Sisters of the Holy Family in 1842. These two black congregations of religious women were joined by a third in our own century when Mother Theodore Williams helped establish the Franciscan Handmaids of the Most Pure Heart of Mary in 1916 in Savannah, Ga.

These black women religious leaders and the sisters whom they formed were not only witnesses of faith; they were also a sign of the faith of many black Catholic families who, even in the dark days of slavery, gave not only support, but even their daughters and sisters in the service of the Gospel.

Within the black Catholic community today, black women continue to witness in various non-ordained ministries, both as religious and lay. This ministry is to be found on the parochial and the diocesan level. It is a ministry in schools and in the social apostolate. Needless to say, this potential for service within our own community needs to be more fully recognized and utilized by the Catholic Church in the United States. Black women can and should be considered as collaborators in the work of evangelization. The words of the pastoral commission of the Congregation for the Evangelization of Peoples are eminently true of women in the black Catholic community: "Givers of life, consecrated by nature to its service, it is for women to give to evangelization a living and realistic face before the world."[6]

Abortion and Black Values (Cf. "Evangelii Nuntiandi,' 65.)

Today the black family is assailed on all sides. Much has been said by others about the economic plight of the black family.

---

[6]Pastoral Commission of the Congregation for the Evangelization of Peoples, *The Role of Women in Evangelization, Vatican II: More Postconciliar Documents,* Austin Flannery, O.P., gen. ed. (Northport, N.Y., 1982), p. 327.

We would like to add a word regarding the moral aspect of this plight.

The acceptance of abortion by many as a common procedure and even as a right is a reality not only in our American society as a whole, but also within the black community. And yet life, and especially new life within the mother, has always been a value to Africans and to African-Americans. Historically, even children conceived outside of marriage were cherished and given a place in the extended family. Black cultural tradition has always valued life and the mystery of its transmission and growth. Children have always been for us a sign of hope. The loss of this perspective is a cultural and spiritual impoverishment for us as a people.

From our point of view as Catholics and as black people, we see the efforts made "to provide" low-cost abortions as another form of subjugation. Indeed there are those who would even characterize it as a form of genocide. As a people of faith, it is our task to fight for the right to life of all our children and in all the circumstances of their existence. It is our duty to reassert the gift of our traditional African-American values of family and children to our own people and to our society as a whole. It is equally our duty, however, to show practical concern and honest compassion for the many mothers-to-be who are too often encouraged to seek an abortion by the conventional wisdom of our society today.

Finally, we add this unfortunate observation: If society truly valued our children and our mothers—mothers who have already made a choice for life—they would have day-care centers, jobs, good schools and all else that a just society should offer to its people. Sadly we observe that if abortion were abolished tomorrow, the same disastrous ills would plague our black mothers and children.

ECUMENISM (*CF. "EVANGELII NUNTIANDI,"* 39, 65-68, 77-79, 80.)

There exists a reality which is called "the black church." It crosses denominational boundaries and is without a formal structure. Yet it is a reality cherished by many black Christians, who feel at ease joining in prayer and in Christian action with one another. This black church is a result of our common experience and history—it has made it possible for many blacks to understand and appreciate each other.

This does not mean that black people, and especially black Catholics, are indifferent to the distinctions of various denominations. Black Catholics as well as all black Christians are loyal to their respective faith communities. Black Catholics most particularly, whether by birth or conversion in later life, insist upon total loyalty to all that is Catholic. A deep abiding love of the Catholic Church is a characteristic of black Catholicism.

Nevertheless, because we as a people have been a deeply religious people, we as black Catholics are in a special position to serve as a bridge with our brothers and sisters of other Christian traditions. We wish to encourage our black Catholics to deepen their awareness and understanding of the whole black church, inasmuch as the majority of black Christians in this country are separated from Catholic unity.

It is to this end that Pope Paul VI called us when he stated: "As Catholics our best ecumenical efforts are directed both to removing the causes of separation that still remain, as well as to giving adequate expression to the communion which already exists among all Christians. We are sustained and encouraged in this task because so many of the most significant elements and endowments 'that are Christ's gifts to his church are the common source of our strength.'" [7]

And, in reference to the wealth of spiritual joy and expression in the black church, these words spoken by Pope John Paul II in New York would seem especially appropriate for us: "I wish to greet in you the rich variety of your nation, where people of different ethnic origins and creeds can live, work and prosper together in mutual respect." [8]

Finally, the following words of Pope John Paul II would seem appropriate for our relationships with our Moslem and Jewish brothers and sisters:

"Does it not sometimes happen that the firm belief of the followers of the non-Christian religions—a belief that is also an effect of the Spirit of truth operating outside the visible confines of the mystical body—can make Christians ashamed at being often themselves so disposed to doubt concerning the truths revealed by

---

[7]Pope Paul VI, "Message to the World Council of Churches General Assembly at Nairobi," *Doing the Truth in Charity: Statements of Pope Paul VI, John Paul I, John Paul II, and the Secretariat for Promoting Christian Unity, 1964-1980* (Paulist Press, 1982), p. 291.

[8]Pope John Paul II, "The Ideal of Liberty, a Moving Force," *U.S.A.: The Message of Justice, Peace and Love* (Daughters of St. Paul, 1979), p. 96.

God and proclaimed by the church and so prone to relax moral principles and open the way to ethical permissiveness." [9]

II. The Call of God to His People

PERSPECTIVE (CF. "EVANGELII NUNTIANDI," 61-62.)

If the story of America is told with honesty and clarity, we must all recognize the role that blacks have played in the growth of this country. At every turning point of American history, we come face to face with the black man and black woman. What is true of our national history is even truer of American Catholic history.

Just as the church in our history was planted by the efforts of the Spaniards, the French and the English, so did it take root among Indians, black slaves and the various racial mixtures of them all. Blacks—whether Spanish-speaking, French-speaking or English-speaking—built the churches, tilled church lands and labored with those who labored in spreading the Gospel. From the earliest period of the church's history in our land, we have been the hands and arms that helped build the church from Baltimore to Bardstown, from New Orleans to Los Angeles, from St. Augustine to St. Louis. Too often neglected and too much betrayed, our faith was witnessed by black voices and black tongues—such as Jean-Baptiste Point du Sable, Pierre Toussaint, Elizabeth Lange, Henriette Delille and Augustus Tolton.

The historical roots of black America and those of Catholic America are intimately intertwined. Now is the time for us who are black Americans and black Catholics to reclaim our roots and to shoulder the responsibilities of being both black and Catholic.

The responsibility is both to our own people and to our own church. To the former, we owe the witness of our faith in Christ and in his body, the church. To the latter, we owe this witness of faith as well as the unstinting labor to denounce racism as a sin and to work for justice and inner renewal.

It is to this responsibility that we now address ourselves in this second half of our pastoral letter. We do so by setting forth the opportunities and challenges that lie before us as a people and as a church.

BLACK INITIATIVE
(CF. "EVANGELII NUNTIANDI," 62-63.)

We call upon our black Catholic sisters and brothers to

---

[9]Pope John Paul II, *Redemptor Hominis,* 6.

shoulder the responsibility laid upon us by our baptism into the body of Christ. This responsibility is to proclaim our faith and to take an active part in building up the church. The Second Vatican Council in its Decree on the Missionary Activity of the Church stated:

"The church has not been truly established and is not yet fully alive, nor is it a perfect sign of Christ among men, unless there exists a laity worthy of the name working along with the hierarchy. . . .

"Their main duty. . . is the witness which they are bound to bear to Christ by their life and works in the home, in their social group and in their own professional circle. . . . They must give expression to this newness of life in the social and cultural framework of their own homeland, according to their own national traditions. They must heal it and preserve it. . . . Let them also spread the faith of Christ among those with whom they live . . . . This obligation is all the more urgent, because very many men can hear of the Gospel and recognize Christ only by means of the laity who are their neighbors."[10]

The black community in the United States for a long time has been a component of the missionary enterprise of the American church. In this sense these words from the Decree on Missionary Activity are perfectly valid for the American black community. We are conscious of the debt of gratitude we owe to those who have served among us as home missionaries.

Yet we are also aware that we, like other African-Americans, are also descendants of slaves and freedmen. Like them we are victims of oppression and racism, and like them we are fighters for the same freedom and dignity. We likewise speak with the same accents and sing the same songs, and we are heirs of the same cultural achievements. Thus we have a privileged position to gain access to the hearts and minds of the African-American community. Hence, we have the solemn responsibility to take the lead in the church's work within the black community.

On the other hand, we are in a position to counter the assumption which many have advanced that to become a Catholic is to abandon one's racial heritage and one's people! The Catholic Church is not a "white church" nor a "Euro-American church." It is essentially universal and hence Catholic. The black presence within the American Catholic Church is a precious witness to the universal character of Catholicism.

---

[10] *Ad Gentes* (Decree on the Missionary Activity of the Church), 21.

The church, however, must preserve its multicultural identity. As Paul VI wrote, "Evangelization loses much of its force and effectiveness if it does not take into consideration the actual people to whom it is addressed, if it does not use their language, their signs and symbols, if it does not answer the questions they ask and if it does not have an impact on their concrete life."[11]

In our response to the invitation to evangelize, we as black Catholics have before us several opportunities to assure the universal aspect of the American church. We can do so by permitting the Catholic Church in this country to reflect the richness of African-American history and its heritage. This is our gift to the church in the United States; this is our contribution to the building up of the universal church.

AUTHORIZATION AND ENCOURAGEMENT
(*CF. "EVANGELII NUNTIANDI,"* 66-73.)

Since African-American members of the American church are to assume the responsibility to which the church and our racial heritage call us, black leaders in the church—clergy, religious and lay—need encouragement and the authorization to use their competencies and to develop their expertise. Unhappily we must acknowledge that the major hindrance to the full development of black leadership within the church is still the fact of racism. The American Catholic bishops wrote in the pastoral letter on racism:

'The church...must be constantly attentive to the Lord's voice as he calls on his people daily not to harden their hearts (Ps. 94:8). We urge that on all levels the Catholic Church in the United States examine its conscience regarding attitudes and behavior toward blacks, Hispanics, native Americans and Asians. We urge consideration of the evil of racism as it exists in the local church and reflection upon the means of combating it. We urge scrupulous attention at every level to ensure that minority representation goes beyond mere tokenism and involves authentic sharing in the responsibility and decision making."[12]

These words have not had the full impact on the American church that was originally hoped. Blacks and other minorities still remain absent from many aspects of Catholic life and are only meagerly represented on the decision-making level. Inner-city

---

[11]"On Evangelization in the Modern World," 63.

[12]National Conference of Catholic Bishops, "Brothers and Sisters to Us: A Pastoral Letter on Racism," *Quest for Justice,* J. Brian Benestad and Francis J. Butler, co-eds. (U.S. Catholic Conference, 1981), p. 382.

schools continue to disappear, and black vocational recruitment lacks sufficient support. In spite of the fact that Catholic schools are a principal instrument of evangelization, active evangelization is not always a high priority.

This racism, at once subtle and masked, still festers within our church as within our society. It is this racism that in our minds remains the major impediment to evangelization within our community. Some little progress has been made, but success is not yet attained. This stain of racism on the American church continues to be a source of pain and disappointment to all, both black and white, who love it and desire it to be the bride of Christ "without stain or wrinkle" (Eph. 5:27). This stain of racism, which is so alien to the Spirit of Christ, is a scandal to many, but for us it must be the opportunity to work for the church's renewal as part of our task of evangelization. To "profess the truth in love" (Eph. 4:15) to our brothers and sisters within the faith remains for black Catholics the first step in proclaiming the gospel message. We, like St. John the Baptist, proclaim a baptism of repentance for the forgiveness of sins, and we call on the American church to produce the fruit of repentance and not presume to tell themselves we have Abraham for our father, for we all belong to the family of God (cf. Lk. 3:1-9).

Our demand for recognition, our demand for leadership roles in the task of evangelization, is not a call for separatism but a pledge of our commitment to the church and to share in her witnessing to the love of Christ. For the Christ we proclaim is he who prayed on the night before he died "that all may be one as you, Father, are in me, and I in you; I pray that they may be (one) in us, that the world may believe that you sent me" (Jn. 17:21).

OPPORTUNITIES FOR EVANGELIZATION

There exist numerous opportunities for evangelization within the black community. It is not our intention to enumerate all of these. We do propose, however, to point out those that in our opinion are the most important and the most essential. For some of these the black community can and must seize the initiative. For others we need the cooperation and the encouragement of the entire American church.

Vocations to the Priesthood and Religious Life

From apostolic times, the local church called forth its ministers from within itself for the sake of evangelization. Paul and Barnabas evangelized the communities of Iconium, Lystra and

Derbe. "In each church they installed presbyters and, with prayer and fasting, commended them to the Lord in whom they had put their faith" (Acts 14:23). This became the established practice: to plant the new church and draw from it the clergy and the teachers to continue the work of evangelization and nurture the growing congregation with pastoral care. In this way were the early churches of Africa evangelized in Egypt, Nubia, Ethiopia and North Africa.

Unfortunately, later missionaries did not always carry out this traditional practice. For too long the way to a fully indigenous clergy and religious was blocked by an attitude that was paternalistic and racist. It was especially through the efforts of the Holy See that the earlier practice was resumed. Beginning with Pope Benedict XV in 1919, with the encyclical *Maximum Illud,* and continuing on until the Second Vatican Council, the highest authority within the church has called in season and out of season for the creation of an indigenous clergy. This was to be done as soon as possible as part of the actual process of evangelization:

"It is not enough for the Christian people to be present and organized in a given nation. Nor is it enough for them to carry out an apostolate of good example. They are organized and present for the purpose of announcing Christ to their non-Christian fellow citizens by word and deed, and of aiding them toward the full reception of Christ.

"Now, if the church is to be planted and the Christian community is to grow, various ministries are needed. These are raised up by divine vocation from the midst of the faithful and are to be carefully fostered and cultivated by all."[13]

If in the history of the American church many black men and women found their vocations to the religious life and priesthood blocked by racist attitudes, this is no longer tolerable. It is now the responsibility and the duty of the black Catholic community to encourage young men and women to follow Christ in the priesthood and in the consecrated life.

The duty lies especially with all those who have contact with youth. We call first upon the black family to set before the eyes of the young the value of service to Christ in ministry of others, both at the altar and in the manifold areas of evangelization. Black parents will do this by passing on to their children the truths of the Catholic religion and the spiritual values of our African-American heritage. When a child shows signs of a priestly or religious

---

[13]*Ad Gentes,* 15.

vocation, the parents will respect and even encourage this sign of God's call.

We call upon teachers and educators and all those who work with youth in the black community to be aware of this vocation when it appears among black youth. Let them not underestimate their influence for good regarding the young. Let them never belittle or discourage the manifestation of the Spirit. Moreover, let them encourage those more mature men and women who, touched by grace, follow a religious vocation as a second career.

Most particularly we remind our black sisters and brothers who have already answered God's call that they especially have the task to foster black vocations. All young people crave role models. Black sisters, brothers and priests must be such models for black youth today. Let them take care to be always a positive influence. If in their own lives of service they have had to struggle because of racial discrimination, let them now be beacons of hope for those who follow after. Even if in their own lives they have experienced the contradictions of a racist society, let them show forth the joy that comes to those who leave all to follow the crucified king.

In this matter of vocations, so crucial to the cause of evangelization in the black community, we need the collaboration of the entire American church. In fact, we suggest that the recruitment of minority youth for the priesthood and religious life must have the highest priority. More precisely, let diocesan vocation directors collaborate with leaders in the black Catholic community in strategic planning for the recruitment of black young men for the diocesan priesthood. The same planning and collaborative effort should be part of the vocational planning of the many religious congregations and seminaries. Care should be taken to know and understand the attitudes and concerns of black young people in order to show how ministry would be relevant to their lives and experience. Above all, it is necessary for those engaged in recruitment programs, whether for the diocesan clergy or for religious life, to go where black young people are found. It means visits to innercity schools and the use of vocational materials that portray blacks, Hispanics, Asians and other racial or ethnic groups.

Regretfully, experience has shown that once inside a seminary, a novitiate or a house of formation many minority students face a period of cultural and social alienation. Here again, collaborative effort is needed between seminary and formation leaders on the one hand and the minority community on the other. In the case of black students this means helping the student to maintain contact with the black community and to renew contact with black

culture, black history and black theological studies. The National Conference of Catholic Bishops called for this in 1981:
"Students who come from diverse racial and cultural backgrounds should participate in programs and adopt a pattern of life geared to ready them for pastoral responsibility among their respective peoples and to intensify their own sense of ethnic identity. . . .

"Seminarians from various ethnic groups need to maintain and develop their identity with both family and community. This will require a special sensitivity on the part of those responsible for administration and formation."[14]

Not only blacks, but all who would work in and with the black community must understand the history, values, culture and ethos of the black community. The American bishops call for this in the same document.

"The seminary should include in its program of studies courses presenting the history and the development of the cultural heritage of black, Hispanic and native Americans, and other cultural and ethnic groups within the United States. Moreover, opportunities for intercultural contacts should be offered to enable future ministers to become more aware, through workshops, seminars and special sessions, of the positive values offered by other cultures . . . . Such an experience is imperative for those whose ministry, because of the ethnic population of their region, will bring them into contact with large numbers of certain racial and cultural groups. . . .

"The seminary course in church history should also include a treatment of the church's relationship to these various ethnic groups to give an insight into present difficulties facing the church in her ministry to minority groups in the United States today."[15]

Finally, we believe it important that black men and women be encouraged to follow the Spirit in every sector of the church. This will include the strictly contemplative orders as well. It is our profound conviction that the Holy Spirit is working among us as a people and will continue to work to bring forth fruits of holiness and prayer.

---

[14]National Conference of Catholic Bishops, *The Program of Priestly Formation*, 3rd ed., nos. 531, 534, 535.

[15]*Ibid.*, 531, 533.

Permanent Deacons

It is a sign of the times that the Second Vatican Council in its wisdom called for the restoration of the permanent order of deacons. In the black community this unique calling is of special importance because it provides an opportunity for men of competence who have had an experience of life much broader than that of many priests and religious. Even after ordination, many permanent deacons continue to pursue their occupation in the workaday world and in family life. This gives them access to opportunities for evangelization in places where a priest or religious might find entry difficult. This is particularly true for black deacons in the black community, where many of the clergy are not black. The permanent diaconate provides an opportunity to utilize those men who are natural leaders. Furthermore, it makes use of an institution that is familiar to most blacks, since deacons are part of the congregation in many black Christian communities.

The permanent diaconate sacramentalizes this reality which is already present and gives it a prestige which cannot but redound to the advantage of the church in proclaiming the good news to the whole community. Incorporated into the hierarchy through the sacrament of orders and yet part of the community in whose life he shares, the black deacon has a role of mediator which is truly unique.

Every effort should be made to recruit qualified candidates for the office of deacon from within every black parish. All members of the parish community should be involved. Pastors should actively strive to identify and recruit likely candidates. Those who feel the desire to serve in this way should prayerfully and assiduously pursue their call. All members of the parish can make an invaluable contribution by searching out candidates and giving them encouragement and support.

What we have said regarding the formation of black priests and religious applies to that of deacons as well. If anything, it is even more important. The deacon is called for service not only in the parish, but also at times in the diocese at large. This service demands the acquisition of those skills necessary for effective ministry. The black deacon especially must synthesize in his life and in his understanding not only faith, but also his cultural and racial heritage. We call upon those responsible for the deacon's training and formation to prepare him for this unique task.

The Laity (Cf. "Evangelii Nuntiandi," 24, 38, 41, 54.)

The work of evangelization is not confined to the clergy and the religious alone. It is also the responsibility of the laity. "Incorporated into Christ's mystical body through baptism and strengthened by the power of the Holy Spirit through confirmation, they are assigned to the apostolate by the Lord himself."[16]

Within the tradition of the black community, laypersons in the black church have always had important roles. Within the history of the black Catholic community, at a time when the black clergy were few, many laypersons provided leadership. We need only mention Daniel Rudd and the black lay Catholic congresses in the 19th century and Thomas Wyatt Turner and the Federated Colored Catholics in the period prior to the Second World War.

The role of the laity needs to be better understood by both the clergy and the laity themselves. In many instances this will require study and reflection, and in some cases a change in attitude. Such understanding, moreover, is only a beginning; for if the laity are to exercise their special form of evangelization, that which is understood in theory must lead to practical plans for action and even structural change.

It is the responsibility of the clergy to facilitate, inspire and coordinate the work of the whole Christian community. This entails calling upon lay women and lay men to join in the work of spreading the good news and authorizing and encouraging them to do so. It also means involving them in the formulation and execution of all programs leading to the building up the body of Christ, which is the church.

Lay people in turn must become more aware of their responsibilities and their opportunities for furthering the mission of the church. They must not passively wait for directives or even an invitation from the clergy. As the Second Vatican Council has pointed out:

"Certain forms of the apostolate of the laity are given explicit recognition by the hierarchy, though in various ways....

"Thus, making various dispositions of the apostolate according to circumstances, the hierarchy joins some particular form of it more closely with its own apostolic function. Yet the proper nature and individuality of each apostolate must be pre-

---

[16]*Apostolicam Actuositatem* (Decree on the Apostolate of the Laity), 3.

served, and the laity must not be deprived of the possibility of acting on their own accord."[17]

Adulthood in Christ, to which all the laity are called, means seizing the opportunity for initiative and creativity in place of complaining about what cannot be done.

Above all let there be no strife or conflict among us as a community and a people. How important it is to recognize and to respect each other's gifts! The pressures of the present age and the pressures of a minority status inevitably lead at times to self-doubt and even self-disdain. But there is always the love of Christ, which calls us beyond ourselves and even beyond our local concerns and rivalries.

"Each of us has received God's favor in the measure in which Christ bestows it. . . . It is he who gave apostles, prophets, evangelists, pastors and teachers in roles of service for the faithful to build up the body of Christ, till we become one in the faith and in the knowledge of God's Son, and form that perfect man who is Christ come to full stature" (Eph. 4:7, 11-13).

Youth (Cf. "Evangelii Nuntiandi," 72.)

Our youth are the present and the future of the church in the black community. If they must be the subject of evangelization in a special way, they should also be taught that they too have a unique opportunity to evangelize their peers.

Black youth are especially vulnerable in our modern society. Today's youth in the black community undergo many pressures. Especially in our urban areas—where disillusionment and despair, desires and drugs, passion and poverty entrap the young—adults and mature youths dedicated to Christ are needed to counsel, to inspire and to motivate those whom Jesus loved and placed first in his kingdom. These youths in turn will be the heralds of the kingdom to other young people in our urban areas today.

Programs for youth—such as retreats, camps, recreational facilities, youth centers and vacation schools—need to be tailored for the black community following the guidelines for youth ministry set up by the local church. Black Catholics who commit themselves to a vigorous youth ministry are to be commended and supported on the parish and diocesan level.

---

[17] *Ibid.,* 24.

Rite of Christian Initiation of Adults (Cf. "Evangelii Nuntiandi," 17-18, 23, 47.)

The newly restored Rite of Christian Initiation of Adults, creatively adapted to the life and culture of the black community, will serve as a powerful instrument of evangelization among our people. The careful and thorough preparation of the catechumens; the appeal to the whole person, both head and heart (so character-istic of black spirituality); the graduated liturgical stages of involvement by the whole Christian community—all these are features of the new rite which recommend it to us as especially useful for the work of evangelization.

We strongly urge that those among us competent to do so undertake as soon as possible the study needed to adapt the rite to the black situation. We appeal to the appropriate authorities of the church to encourage this endeavor.

Catholic Education (Cf. "Evangelii Nuntiandi," 40.)

Even prior to emancipation, blacks in the United States clamored for educational opportunities. Families uprooted themselves, necessities were sacrificed, extra toil was assumed in order that the children would receive an education and, where possible, an even better one was expected for each succeeding child. Today many parents, very often single parents, make similar sacrifices; for black people believe that the key to a better life is the school.

Black Catholics have placed their hope in Catholic schools with even greater zeal. The first Black Lay Catholic Congress in 1889 wrote:

"The education of a people being the great and fundamental means of elevating it to the higher planes to which all Christian civilization tends, we pledge ourselves to aid in establishing, wherever we are to be found, Catholic schools, embracing the primary and higher branches of knowledge, as in them and through them alone can we expect to reach the large masses of colored children now growing up in this country without a semblance of Christian education."[18]

Today the Catholic school still represents for many in the black community, especially in the urban areas, an opportunity for quality education and character development. It also repre-

---

[18]"Proceedings of the First Colored Catholic Congress Held in Washington, D.C., Jan. 1, 2 and 3, 1889," *Three Catholic Afro-American Congresses,* reprint ed. (New York, 1978), pp. 68-69.

sents—and this is not less important—a sign of stability in an environment of chaos and flux. It should be a source of legitimate pride that our schools are sought after by many who are not Catholic as well as Catholics because of the religious and moral values considered as part of a quality education.

The Catholic school has been and remains one of the chief vehicles of evangelization within the black community. We cannot overemphasize the tremendous importance of parochial schools for the black community. We even dare to suggest that the efforts made to support them and to ensure their continuation are a touchstone of the local church's sincerity in the evangelization of the black community.

We are aware of the economic reality, but we are equally aware of the gospel injunction to teach all peoples (cf. Mt. 28:19). Cost effectiveness can never be the sole criterion for decisions regarding the continuation of a Catholic school in the black community. For this reason we express our profound admiration and deep gratitude to our fellow bishops, religious communities and laypersons, along with other church leaders, who with a true evangelical spirit have done so much to maintain Catholic schools in our neighborhoods. We remind those who must make decisions concerning these schools to consult with the people of the community, inviting them to participate during the entire process when any decision concerning the existence of a particular school is to be made.

On the other hand, Catholic schools in our neighborhoods should be the concern of the entire black community. As an important agent for evangelization they must be the concern even of those who have no children in the schools. By the same token, these schools must be thoroughly Catholic in identity and teaching. This does not mean coercing students to join the Catholic Church, but rather to expose all the students to the religious values and teaching that make these schools unique. In a particular way this means that faculty, administration, staff and students will by their manner of life bear witness to gospel values. In this way not a few—as experience has shown—will freely choose to investigate the Catholic faith and seek fellowship within the Catholic community.

Support should also be given to Catholic and public institutions of higher learning as well as the traditional black colleges which have particularly close ties with the black community. Their excellence in scholarship and their continued growth should be a constant concern for black Catholics. Xavier University in New

Orleans, the only black Catholic university in the United States, should hold a place of pride for us. Similarly, Newman centers on public campuses, which have the means of addressing the spiritual needs of our people, deserve our special attention.

Finally, we address an invitation to black youth and black adults to consider well the profession of teaching on all levels of Catholic education in our community. Theirs is a wonderful opportunity to spread the kingdom in the black community.

"When a man is wise to his own advantage, the fruits of his knowledge are seen in his own person; when a man is wise to his peoples' advantage, the fruits of his knowledge are enduring" (Sir. 37:21-22).

Liturgy (Cf. "Evangelii Nuntiandi," 17, 23, 42-43, 47.)

The celebration of the sacred mysteries is that moment when the church is most fully actualized and most clearly revealed. No treatment of evangelization would be complete without a discussion of the role of liturgy in this regard.

In the African-American tradition the communal experience of worship has always had a central position. In our heritage the moment of celebration has always been a time for praise and thanksgiving, and the affirmation of ourselves as God's children. It is a moment of profound expression, not a flight from reality (as some have suggested), but an experience of God's power and love.

From the standpoint of evangelization in the black community, the liturgy of the Catholic Church has always demonstrated a way of drawing many to the faith and also of nourishing and deepening the faith of those who already believe. We believe that the liturgy of the Catholic Church can be an even more intense expression of the spiritual vitality of those who are of African origin, just as it has been for other ethnic and cultural groups:

"The church has no wish to impose a rigid uniformity in matters which do not involve the faith or the good of the whole community. Rather she respects and fosters the spiritual adornments and gifts of the various races and peoples."[19]

Through the liturgy, black people will come to realize that the Catholic Church is a homeland for black believers just as she is for people of other cultural and ethnic traditions. In recent years remarkable progress has been made in our country by many talented black experts to adapt the liturgy to the needs and the

---

[19] *Sacrosanctum Concilium* (Constitution on the Sacred Liturgy), 37.

genius of the African-American community. In order that this work can be carried on more fully within the Catholic tradition and at the same time be enriched by our own cultural heritage, we wish to recall the essential qualities that should be found in a liturgical celebration within the black Catholic community. It should be authentically black. It should be truly Catholic. And it should be well prepared and well executed.

Authentically Black: The liturgy is simultaneously a ritualization of the divine reality which transcends all human limitations and also an expression of what is most intimate and personal in the participants. What is expressed is the mystery of Christ, which transcends all cultures. The way, however, in which this mystery is expressed is mediated by the culture and traditions of the participants. All people should be able to recognize themselves when Christ is presented, and all should be able to experience their own fulfillment when these mysteries are celebrated. Hence, we can legitimately speak of an African-American cultural idiom or style in music, in preaching, in bodily expression, in artistic furnishings and vestments, and even in tempo. It is for this reason that we encourage those in pastoral ministry to introduce the African-American cultural idiom into the expression of the Roman liturgy.

It is not our purpose at this time to detail all the characteristics this African-American cultural idiom may have nor to suggest the limits of cultural authenticity. It is important that from our own community there arise competent liturgical scholars and artists who will mutually contribute to a black Catholic liturgical critique.

We do wish to remind our fellow black Catholics, however, that the African-American cultural heritage is vast and rich. The cultural idiom of American black people has never been uniform, but has varied according to region and ethos. African, Haitian, Latin and West Indian cultural expressions also continue to this day to nurture the black American cultural expression. For this reason, and authentic black Catholic liturgy need never be confined to a narrowly based concept of what is truly black. There is a splendid opportunity for the vast richness of African-American culture to be expressed in our liturgy. It is this opportunity, thanks to the norms established in the revised Roman liturgy, which enables our work of evangelization to be filled with such promise for the future.

Truly Catholic: The liturgy not only expresses the worship of a given Catholic community, it also expresses the unity of the Catholic Church. Black Catholic liturgy should express not only our African-American cultural heritage, but also our Catholic faith and unity. In this way, unlike some other Christian communities in the black community, our worship is not confined to preaching the word alone, but also includes the sacrament as celebration.

For this reason neither the preaching nor the music nor any other ritual action has exclusive domain at liturgical celebration. If one or the other prevails, the evangelical dimension as well as the prayerful experience of the liturgy suffers.

"Evangelization thus exercises its full capacity when it achieves the most intimate relationship, or better still, a permanent and unbroken intercommunication, between the word and the sacraments. In a certain sense it is a mistake to make a contrast between evangelization and sacramentalization. . . . The role of evangelization is precisely to educate people in the faith in such a way as to lead each individual Christian to live the sacraments as true sacraments of faith—and not to receive them passively or reluctantly."[20]

Both the liturgical preaching and the music should invite the worshiping community to a more profound participation in the total sacramental experience. Neither preaching nor music should overwhelm the liturgical worship and prevent it from exhibiting a balanced unified action.

Proper Preparation and Excellence in Execution: We wish to commend those who have tirelessly presented workshops and conferences on black liturgical expression. We urge the continued training of liturgists and musicians from the black Catholic community. We likewise wish to commend those who have generously given their talents as musicians and artists for the enhancement of our liturgical worship. We wish to encourage black artists, composers, musicians and vocalists to continue to dedicate their skills in God's service. Finally, we urge men and women steeped in the African-American tradition and culture to collaborate with our liturgical worship in our community. It is especially in this regard that we can use our rich gifts of blackness for the whole church.

In the liturgy, preparation begins with prayerful reflection and is completed and perfected by an execution that culminates in total prayer. We urge that this prayerful preparation and prayerful performance and execution be the result of a collaborative effort of many gifted people each Sunday in our parishes.

---

[20]"On Evangelization in the Modern World," 47.

The Social Apostolate (Cf. "Evangelii Nuntiandi," 8-12, 29-39.)

The proclamation of the good news by Jesus began with the proclamation of justice and compassion in the context of social reform:

"When the book of the prophet Isaiah was handed him, he unrolled the scroll and found the passage where it was written: 'The spirit of the Lord is upon me; therefore he has anointed me. He has sent me to bring glad tidings to the poor, to proclaim liberty to captives, recovery of sight to the blind and release to prisoners, to announce a year of favor from the Lord'" (Lk. 4:17-19).

For us the causes of justice and social concern are an essential part of evangelization. Our own history has taught us that preaching to the poor and to those who suffer injustice without concern for their plight and the systemic cause of their plight is to trivialize the Gospel and mock the cross. To preach to the powerful without denouncing oppression is to promise Easter without Calvary, forgiveness without conversion and healing without cleansing the wound.

Our concern for social justice, moreover, goes beyond denouncing injustice in the world around us. It brings us to the examination of our own hearts and intentions. It reminds us that it was the despised and rejected Samaritan who had the compassion to bind up the wounds of the other and to provide a lesson for the chosen (cf. Lk. 10:29-37). As black people in a powerful nation we must have concern for those who hunger and thirst for justice everywhere in the present world. We must not forget that in a world of suffering even compassion may still be selective. Let us not ignore those whom others tend to forget. It should be our concern to remind others of the plight of Haitian refugees, the hunger of drought-ridden Africans, the forgotten blacks in a war-torn Namibia and the many other forgotten minorities and ill-starred majorities in the world of the downtrodden and deprived. Political expediency and diplomatic advantages should not be bought with the human rights of others.

As a people we must have the courage to speak out and even contribute our efforts and money on behalf of any people or any segment of the human family that the powerful may seek to neglect or forget as a matter of policy. Be assured that we too must render an account for what the Lord has given us (cf. Ps. 116:12). When we share our talents and our possessions with the forgotten ones of this world, we share Christ. This in not the prelude to evangelization, it is the essence of evangelization itself.

Conclusion

(Cf. "Evangelii Nuntiandi," 3-5, 41-46, 68-69, 70-73, 78-79.)

We write this letter to you, our brothers and sisters, strong in the faith and in the knowledge that what has been begun in you will be brought to perfection in the day of our Lord Jesus Christ. We urge you to study and discuss the points laid before you in this, our pastoral letter. We ask that you heed the opportunities that are ours today. Let us not deprive the church of the rich gifts that God has granted us.

For this reason we write to you, brothers and sisters, in the many parishes across our country. We urge the black people of these parishes to take to heart our words of encouragement to spread the message of Christ to our own and to those of all ethnic and racial groups. We ask pastors, co-pastors, pastoral assistants, classroom teachers and directors of religious education—indeed all who are staff and board members in the parish and in the diocese—to speak the good news clearly in the idiom and expression of our people. Let it be the responsibility of every parish council and every parish team to ponder the meaning of black evangelization and the burden of this pastoral letter in each respective community.

We write to those among us who are writers and poets, teachers and musicans, social scientists and theologians, philosophers and artists, academics and scholars—to all those who are the specialists whom we need to write the commentaries, edit the texts, lay out the critiques, analyze the possibilities, draw up the study guides and gather the bibliographies—to make our efforts for black evangelization bear fruit in practical planning and innovative, imaginative proposals.

We turn to those of you who are lay leaders in the black Catholic community. In a particular way it will be your ministry to help implement the actions called for in this letter—some on the dioscesan level, others on the national level. We address the National Association of Black Catholic Administrators, the National Office for Black Catholics and the National Black Lay Catholic Caucus. You, and those whom you represent, will be the key to unlock the doors of opportunities for a wider field of evangelization in our community.

We ask especially our brothers and sisters in the priesthood, the diaconate and the religious life, and our sisters in the consecrated life, as well as our seminarians, to aid us by your ministry to make actual in a concrete way what we have sought to set forth in guidelines and suggested proposals. We ask for your experience as black men and women of God, for your zealous support and for your broad vision to give us counsel and to facilitate our common task in the service of our own people.

We look to those who are responsible on the diocesan level for the various offices and departments of education and evangelization, administrators, teachers, directors; we turn to seminary teachers and staff as well as leaders of formation; we ask all to study the proposals gathered here and to take to heart the concerns of the church among the black members of Christ's body as set forth above.

Finally, we ask you, brothers in the episcopacy, upon whom weigh the cares of all the churches and to whom the seamless robe of Christ's unity has been entrusted—we ask you, our brother bishops, to look carefully at the needs of those black Catholics who reside within your care. Without your guidance and support the wealth of black giftedness risks being lost, the abundance of our opportunities risks being squandered.

Last of all, we turn to Mary, the mother of God and the mother of the African-American community. She is the poor woman and the bearer of the word, the first to believe and the first to proclaim the word. We entrust to her powerful intercession this work within the black community.

May our Heavenly Father perfect us, his church, in faith and love, that we might be always and everywhere faithful witnesses to the power of the resurrection of our Lord Jesus Christ, through whom be all the honor and the glory in the Holy Spirit, now and forever. Amen.

181. Mario M. Cuomo, Religious Belief and Public Morality, September 13, 1984.

The national political campaign of 1984 projected religious belief into the debates with more insistence and vehemence than had been seen in any campaign since the presidential candidacy of John F. Kennedy in 1960. It took various forms and revealed widespread differences on the part of the electorate, but on no single aspect did religious belief arouse greater heat—and bitterness—than the debate over abortion. The position taken by the Governor of New York, a practising Catholic, namely, personal opposition to abortion coupled with a belief that as a public official he had the duty to refrain from urging his personal view on Americans who differed with him, demonstrated a stance at variance with that of the American bishops. Governor Cuomo set forth his opinions in an address at the University of Notre Dame that attracted national attention both during and after the election. Source: *Origins,* 14 (September 27, 1984), 235-240.

I would like to begin by drawing your attention to the title of this lecture: "Religious Belief and Public Morality: A Catholic Governor's Perspective." I was not invited to speak on church and state generally. Certainly not Mondale vs. Reagan. The subject assigned is difficult enough. I will not try to do more than I've been asked.

It's not easy to stay contained. Certainly, although everybody talks about a wall of separation between church and state, I've seen religious leaders scale that wall with all the dexterity of Olympic athletes. In fact, I've seen so many candidates in churches and synagogues that I think we should change election day from Tuesdays to Saturdays and Sundays.

I am honored by this invitation, but the record shows that I am not the first governor of New York to appear at an event involving Notre Dame. One of my great predecessors, Al Smith, went to the Army-Notre Dame football game each time it was played in New York.

His fellow Catholics expected Smith to sit with Notre Dame; protocol required him to sit with Army because it was the home team. Protocol prevailed. But not without Smith noting the dual demands on his affections. "I'll take my seat with Army," he said, "but I commend my soul to Notre Dame!"

Today I'm happy to have no such problem: Both my seat and my soul are with Notre Dame. And as long as Father McBrien doesn't invite me back to sit with him at the Notre Dame-St. John's basketball game, I'm confident my loyalties will remain undivided.

In a sense, it's a question of loyalty that Father McBrien has asked me here today to discuss. Specifically, must politics and religion in America divide our loyalties? Does the "separation between church and state" imply separation between religion and politics? Between morality and government? Are these different propositions? Even more specifically, what is the relationship of my Catholicism to my politics? Where does the one end and other begin? Or are the two divided at all? And if they're not, should they be?

Hard questions.

No wonder most of us in public life—at least until

recently—preferred to stay away from them, heeding the biblical advice that if "hounded and pursued in one city," we should flee to another.

Now, however, I think that it is too late to flee. The questions are all around us, and answers are coming from every quarter. Some of them have been simplistic, most of them fragmentary and a few, spoken with a purely political intent, demagogic.

There has been confusion and compounding of confusion, a blurring of the issue, entangling it in personalities and election strategies instead of clarifying it for Catholics, as well as others.

Today I would like to try to help correct that.

I can offer you no final truths, complete and unchallengeable. But it's possible this one effort will provoke other efforts— both in support and contradiction of my position—that will help all of us understand our differences and perhaps even discover some basic agreement.

In the end, I'm convinced we will all benefit if suspicion is replaced by discussion, innuendo by dialogue; if the emphasis in our debate turns from a search for talismanic criteria and neat but simplistic answers to an honest—more intelligent—attempt at describing the role religion has in our public affairs and the limits placed on that role.

And if we do it right—if we're not afraid of the truth even when the truth is complex—this debate, by clarification, can bring relief to untold numbers of confused—even anguished—Catholics, as well as to many others who want only to make our already great democracy even stronger than it is.

I believe the recent discussion in my own state has already produced some clearer definition. In early summer an impression was created in some quarters that official church spokespeople would ask Catholics to vote for or against candidates on the basis of their political position on the abortion issue. I was one of those given that impression. Thanks to the dialogue that ensued over the summer—only partially reported by the media—we learned that the impression was not accurate.

Confusion had presented an opportunity for clarification, and we seized it. Now all of us are saying one thing—in chorus— reiterating the statement of the National Conference of Catholic Bishops that they will not "take position for or against political candidates" and that their stand on specific issues would not be perceived "as an expression of political partisanship."

Of course the bishops will teach—they must—more and

more vigorously and more and more extensively. But they have said they will not use the power of their position, and the great respect it receives from all Catholics, to give an imprimatur to individual politicians or parties.

Not that they couldn't if they wished to—some religious leaders do; some are doing it at this very moment.

Not that it would be a sin if they did—God doesn't insist on political neutrality. But because it is the judgment of the bishops, and most of us Catholic lay people, that it is not wise for prelates and politicians to be tied too closely together.

I think that getting this consensus was an extraordinarily useful achievement.

Now, with some trepidation, I take up your gracious invitation to continue the dialogue in the hope that it will lead to still further clarification.

Let me begin this part of the effort by underscoring the obvious. I do not speak as a theologian; I do not have that competence. I do not speak as philosopher; to suggest that I could would be to set a new record for false pride. I don't presume to speak as a "good" person except in the ontological sense of that word. My principal credential is that I serve in a position that forces me to wrestle with the problems you've come here to study and debate.

I am by training a lawyer and by practice a politician. Both professions make me suspect in many quarters, including among some of my own coreligionists. Maybe there's no better illustration of the public perception of how politicians unite their faith and their profession than the story they tell in New York about "Fish-hooks" McCarthy, a famous Democratic leader on the Lower East Side and right-hand man to Al Smith.

"Fishhooks," the story goes, was devout. So devout that every morning on his way to Tammany Hall to do his political work, he stopped into St. James Church on Oliver Street in downtown Manhattan, fell on his knees and whispered the same simple prayer: "Oh, Lord, give me health and strength. We'll steal the rest."

"Fishhooks" notwithstanding, I speak here as a politician. And also as a Catholic, a lay person baptized and raised in the pre-Vatican II church, educated in Catholic schools, attached to the church first by birth, then by choice, now by love. An old-fashioned Catholic who sins, regrets, struggles, worries, gets confused and most of the time feels better after confession.

The Catholic Church is my spiritual home. My heart is there and my hope.

There is, of course, more to being a Catholic than a sense of spiritual and emotional resonance. Catholicism is a religion of the head as well as the heart, and to be a Catholic is to say "I believe" to the essential core of dogmas that distinguishes our faith.

The acceptance of this faith requires a lifelong struggle to undertand it more fully and to live it more truly, to translate truth into experience, to practice as well as to believe.

That's not easy: Applying religious belief to everyday life often presents challenges.

It's always been that way. It certainly is today. The America of the late 20th century is a consumer society, filled with endless distractions, where faith is more often dismissed than challenged, where the ethnic and other loyalties that once fastened us to our religions seem to be weakening.

In addition to all the weaknesses, dilemmas and temptations that impede every pilgrim's progress, the Catholic who holds political office in a pluralistic democracy—who is elected to serve Jews and Moslems, atheists and Protestants, as well as Catholics— bears special responsibility. He or she undertakes to help create conditions under which all can live with a maximum of dignity and with a reasonable degree of freedom; where everyone who chooses may hold beliefs different from specifically Catholic ones— sometimes contradictory to them; where the laws protect people's rights to divorce, to use birth control and even to choose abortion.

In fact, Catholic public officials take an oath to preserve the Constitution that guarantees this freedom. And they do so gladly. Not because they love what others do with their freedom, but because they realize that in guaranteeing freedom for all, they guarantee our right to be Catholics: our right to pray, to use the sacraments, to refuse birth control devices, to reject abortion, not to divorce and remarry if we believe it to be wrong.

The Catholic public official lives the political truth most Catholics through most of American history have accepted and insisted on: the truth that to assure our freedom we must allow others the same freedom, even if occasionally it produces conduct by them which we would hold to be sinful.

I protect my right to be a Catholic by preserving your right to believe as a Jew, a Protestant or non-believer, or as anything else you choose.

We know that the price of seeking to force our beliefs on

others is that they might some day force theirs on us.

This freedom is the fundamental strength of our unique experiment in government. In the complex interplay of forces and considerations that go into the making of our laws and politics, its preservation must be a pervasive and dominant concern.

But insistence on freedom is easier to accept as a general proposition than in its applications to specific situations. There are other valid general principles firmly embedded in our Constitution which, operating at the same time, create interesting and occasionally troubling problems. Thus the same amendment of the Constitution that forbids the establishment of a state church affirms my legal right to argue that my religious belief would serve well as an article of our universal public morality. I may use the prescribed processes of government—the legislative and executive and judicial processes—to convince my fellow citizens—Jews and Protestants and Buddhists and nonbelievers—that what I propose is as beneficial for them as I believe it is for me; that it is not just parochial or narrowly sectarian but fulfills a human desire for order, peace, justice, kindness, love, any of the values most of us agree are desirable even apart from their specific religious base or context.

I am free to argue for a governmental policy for a nuclear freeze, not just to avoid sin but because I think my democracy should regard it as a desirable goal.

I can, if I wish, argue that the state should not fund the use of contraceptive devices, not because the pope demands it, but because I think that the whole community—for the good of the whole community—should not sever sex from an openness to the creation of life.

And surely I can, if so inclined, demand some kind of law against abortion, not because my bishops say it is wrong, but because I think that the whole community, regardless of its religious beliefs, should agree on the importance of protecting life—including life in the womb, which is at the very least potentially human and should not be extinguished casually.

No law prevents us from advocating any of these things: I am free to do so.

So are the bishops. And so is Rev. Falwell.

In fact, the Constitution guarantees my right to try. And theirs. And his.

But should I? Is it helpful? Is it essential to human dignity? Does it promote harmony and understanding? Or does it divide us so fundamentally that it threatens our ability to function as a pluralistic community?

When should I argue to make my religious value your morality? My rule of conduct your limitation?

What are the rules and policies that should influence the exercise of this right to argue and promote?

I believe I have a salvific mission as a Catholic. Does that mean I am in conscience required to do everything I can as governor to translate all my religious values into the laws and regulations of the state of New York or the United States? Or be branded a hypocrite if I don't?

As a Catholic, I respect the teaching authority of the bishops.

But must I agree with everything in the bishops' pastoral letter on peace and fight to include it in party platforms?

And will I have to do the same for the forthcoming pastoral on economics even if I am an unrepentant supply-sider?

Must I, having heard the pope renew the church's ban on birth control devices, veto the funding of contraceptive programs for non-Catholics or dissenting Catholics in my state?

I accept the Church's teaching on abortion. Must I insist you do? By law? By denying you Medicaid funding? By a constitutional amendment? If so, which one? Would that be the best way to avoid abortions or to prevent them?

These are only some of the questions for Catholics. People with other religious beliefs face similar problems.

Let me try some answers.

Almost all Americans accept some religious values as a part of our public life. We are a religious people, many of us descended from ancestors who came here expressly to live their religious faith free from coercion or repression. But we are also a people of many religions, with no established church, who hold different beliefs on many matters.

Our public morality, then—moral standards we maintain for everyone, not just the ones we insist on in our private lives—depends on a consensus view of right and wrong. The values derived from religious belief will not—and should not—be accepted as part of the public morality unless they are shared by the pluralistic community at large, by consensus.

That values happen to be religious values does not deny them acceptability as a part of this consensus. But it does not require their acceptability, either.

The agnostics who joined the civil rights struggle were not deterred because that crusade's values had been nurtured and sustained in black Christian churches. Those on the political left are not perturbed today by the religious bias of the clergy and lay people who join them in the protest against the arms race and hunger and exploitation.

The arguments start when religious values are used to support positions which would impose on other people restrictions they find unacceptable. Some people do object to Catholic demands for an end to abortion, seeing it as a violation of the separation of church and state. And some others, while they have no compunction about invoking the authority of the Catholic bishops in regard to birth control and abortion, might reject out of hand their teaching on war and peace and social policy.

Ultimately, therefore, the question whether or not we admit religious values into our public affairs is too broad to yield a single answer. Yes, we create our public morality through consensus, and in this country that consensus reflects to some extent religious values of a great majority of Americans. But no, all religiously based values don't have an *a priori* place in our public morality.

The community must decide if what is being proposed would be better left to private discretion than public policy; whether it restricts freedoms and if so to what end, to whose benefit; whether it will produce a good or bad result; whether overall it will help the community or merely divide it.

The right answers to these questions can be elusive. Some of the wrong answers, on the other hand, are quite clear. For example, there are those who say there is a simple answer to all these questions; they say that by history and practice of our people we were intended to be—and should be—a Christian country in law.

But where would that leave the non-believers? And whose Christianity would be law, yours or mine?

This "Christian-nation" argument should concern—even frighten—two groups: non-Christians and thinking Christians.

I believe it does.

I think it's already apparent that a good part of this nation understands—if only instinctively—that anything which seems to suggest that God favors a political party or the establishment of a state church is wrong and dangerous.

Way down deep the American people are afraid of an entangling relationship between formal religions—or whole bodies of religious belief—and government. Apart from constitutional law and religious doctrine, there is a sense that tells us it's wrong to presume to speak for God or to claim God's sanction of our particular legislation and his rejection of all other positions. Most of us are offended when we see religion being trivialized by its appearance in political throwaway pamphlets.

The American people need no course in philosophy or political science or church history to know that God should not be made into a celestial party chairman.

To most of us, the manipulative invoking of religion to advance a politician or a party is frightening and divisive. The American people will tolerate religious leaders taking positions for or against candidates, although I think the Catholic bishops are right in avoiding that position. But the American people are leery about large religious organizations, powerful churches or synagogue groups engaging in such activities—again, not as a matter of law or doctrine, but because our innate wisdom and democratic instinct teach us these things are dangerous.

Today there are a number of issues involving life and death that raise questions of public morality. They are also questions of concern to most religions. Pick up a newspaper and you are almost certain to find a bitter controversy over any one of them: Baby Jane Doe, the right to die, artificial insemination, embryos *in vitro*, abortion, birth control—not to mention nuclear war and the shadow it throws across all existence.

Some of these issues touch the most intimate recesses of our lives, our roles as someone's mother or child or husband; some affect women in a unique way. But they are also public questions, for all of us.

Put aside what God expects—assume if you like there is no God—then the greatest thing still left to us is life. Even a radically secular world must struggle with the questions of when life begins, under what circumstances it can be ended, when it must be protected, by what authority; it too must decide what protection to extend to the helpless and the dying, to the aged and the unborn, to life in all its phases.

As a Catholic I have accepted certain answers as the right ones for myself and my family and because I have, they have influenced me in special ways, as Matilda's husband, as a father of five children, as a son who stood next to his own father's deathbed trying to decide if the tubes and needles no longer served a purpose.

As a governor, however, I am involved in defining policies that determine other people's rights in these same areas of life and death. Abortion is one of these issues, and while it is one issue among many, it is one of the most controversial and affects me in a special way as a Catholic public official.

So let me spend some time considering it.

I should start, I believe, by noting that the Catholic Church's actions with respect to the interplay of religious values and public policy make clear that there is no inflexible moral principle which determines what our political conduct should be. For example, on divorce and birth control, without changing its moral teaching the church abides the civil law as it now stands, thereby accepting—without making much of a point of it—that in our pluralistic society we are not required to insist that all our religious values be the law of the land.

Abortion is treated differently.

Of course there are differences both in degree and quality between abortion and some of the other religious positions the church takes: Abortion is a "matter of life and death," and degree counts. But the differences in approach reveal a truth, I think, that is not well enough perceived by Catholics and therefore still further complicates the process for us. That is, while we always owe our bishops' words respectful attention and careful consideration, the question whether to engage the political system in a struggle to have it adopt certain articles of our belief as part of public morality is not a matter of doctrine: It is a matter of prudential political judgment.

Recently Michael Novak put it succinctly: "Religious judgment and political judgment are both needed," he wrote. "But they are not identical."

My church and my conscience require me to believe certain things about divorce, birth control and abortion. My church does not order me—under pain of sin or expulsion—to pursue my salvific mission according to a precisely defined political plan.

As a Catholic I accept the church's teaching authority. While in the past some Catholic theologians may appear to have disagreed on the morality of some abortions (it wasn't, I think, until 1869 that excommunication was attached to all abortions without distinction), and while some theologians still do, I accept the bishops' position that abortion is to be avoided.

As Catholics my wife and I were enjoined never to use abortion to destroy the life we created, and we never have. We thought church doctrine was clear on this, and—more than that— both of us felt it in full agreement with what our hearts and our consciences told us. For me, life or fetal life in the womb should be protected, even if five of nine justices of the Supreme Court and my neighbor disagree with me. A fetus is different from an appendix or a set of tonsils. At the very least, even if the argument is made by some scientists or some theologians that in the early stages of fetal development we can't discern human life, the full potential of human life is indisputably there. That—to my less subtle mind—by itself should demand respect, caution, indeed—reverence.

But not everyone in our society agrees with me and Matilda.

And those who don't—those who endorse legalized abortions—aren't a ruthless, callous alliance of anti-Christians determined to overthrow our moral standards. In many cases the proponents of legal abortion are the very people who have worked with Catholics to realize the goals of social justice set out in papal encyclicals: the American Lutheran Church, the Central Conference of American Rabbis, the Presbyterian Church in the United States, B'nai B'rith Women, the Women of the Episcopal Church. These are just a few of the religious organizations that don't share the church's position on abortion.

Certainly we should not be forced to mold Catholic morality to conform to disagreement by non-Catholics however sincere or severe their disagreement. Our bishops should be teachers, not pollsters. They should not change what we Catholics believe in order to ease our consciences or please our friends or protect the church from criticism.

But if the breadth, intensity and sincerity of opposition to church teaching shouldn't be allowed to shape our Catholic morality, it can't help but determine our ability—our realistic, political ability—to translate our Catholic morality into civil law, a law not for the believers who don't need it but for the disbelievers who reject it.

And it is here, in our attempt to find a political answer to abortion—an answer beyond our private observance of Catholic morality—that we encounter controversy within and without the church over how and in what degree to press the case that our morality should be everybody else's, and to what effect.

I repeat, there is no church teaching that mandates the best political course for making our belief everyone's rule, for spreading this part of our Catholicism. There is neither an encyclical nor a catechism that spells out a political strategy for achieving legislative goals.

And so the Catholic trying to make moral and prudent judgments in the political realm must discern which, if any, of the actions one could take would be best.

This latitude of judgment is not something new in the church, not a development that has arisen only with the abortion issue. Take, for example, the question of slavery. It has been argued that the failure to endorse a legal ban on abortions is equivalent to refusing to support the cause of abolition before the Civil War. This analogy has been advanced by the bishops of my own state.

But the truth of the matter is, few if any Catholic bishops spoke for abolition in the years before the Civil War. It wasn't, I believe, that the bishops endorsed the idea of some humans owning and exploiting other humans; Pope Gregory XVI in 1839 had condemned the slave trade. Instead it was a practical political judgment that the bishops made. They weren't hypocrites; they were realists. At the time Catholics were a small minority, mostly immigrants despised by much of the population, often vilified and the object of sporadic violence. In the face of a public controversy that aroused tremendous passions and threatened to break the country apart, the bishops made a pragmatic decision. They believed their opinion would not change people's minds. Moreover they knew that there were Southern Catholics, even some priests, who owned slaves. They concluded that under the circumstances arguing for a constitutional amendment against slavery would do more harm than good, so they were silent, as they have been generally in recent years on the question of birth control. And as the church has been on even more controversial issues in the past, even ones that dealt with life and death.

What is relevant to this discussion is that the bishops were making judgments about translating Catholic teachings into public policy, not about the moral validity of the teachings. In so doing they grappled with the unique political complexities of their time. The decision they made to remain silent on a constitutional amendment to abolish slavery or on the repeal of the Fugitive Slave Law wasn't a mark of their moral indifference; it was a measured attempt to balance moral truths against political realities. Their decision reflected their sense of complexity, not their diffidence. As history reveals, Lincoln behaved with similar discretion.

The parallel I want to draw here is not between or among what we Catholics believe to be moral wrongs. It is in the Catholic response to those wrongs. Church teaching on slavery and abortion is clear. But in the application of those teachings—the exact way we translate them into action, the specific laws we propose, the exact legal sanctions we seek—there was and is not one, clear, absolute route that the church says, as a matter of doctrine, we must follow.

The bishops' pastoral letter "The Challenge of Peace" speaks directly to this point. "We recognize," the bishops wrote, "that the church's teaching authority does not carry the same force when it deals with technical solutions involving particular means as it does when it speaks of principles or ends. People may agree in abhorring an injustice, for instance, yet sincerely disagree as to what practical approach will achieve justice. Religious groups are as entitled as others to their opinion in such cases, but they should not claim that their opinions are the only ones that people of good will may hold."

With regard to abortion, the American bishops have had to weigh Catholic moral teaching against the fact of a pluralistic country where our view is in the minority, acknowledging that what is ideally desirable isn't always feasible, that there can be different political approaches to abortion besides unyielding adherence to an absolute prohibition.

This is in the American Catholic tradition of political realism. In supporting or opposing specific legislation, the church in this country has never retreated into a moral fundamentalism that will settle for nothing less than total acceptance of its views.

Indeed, the bishops have already confronted the fact that an absolute ban on abortion doesn't have the support necessary to be placed in our Constitution. In 1981 they put aside earlier efforts to describe a law they could accept and get passed, and supported the Hatch Amendment instead.

Some Catholics felt the bishops had gone too far with that action, some not far enough. Such judgments were not a rejection of the bishop's teaching authority: The bishops even disagreed among themselves. Catholics are allowed to disagree on these technical political questions without having to confess.

Respectfully and after careful consideration of the position and arguments of the bishops, I have concluded that the approach of a constitutional amendment is not the best way for us to seek to deal with abortion.

I believe that legal interdicting of abortion by either the federal government or the individual states is not a plausible possibility and even if it could be obtained, it wouldn't work. Given present attitudes, it would be Prohibition revisited, legislating what couldn't be enforced and in the process creating a disrespect for law in general. And as much as I admire the bishops' hope that a constitutional amendment against abortion would be the basis for a full, new bill of rights for mothers and children, I disagree that this would be the result.

I believe that, more likely, a constitutional prohibition would allow people to ignore the causes of many abortions instead of addressing them, much the way the death penalty is used to escape dealing more fundamentally and more rationally with the problem of violent crime.

Other legal options that have been proposed are, in my view, equally ineffective. The Hatch Amendment, by returning the question of abortion to the states, would have given us a checkerboard of permissive and restrictive jurisdictions. In some cases people might have been forced to go elsewhere to have abortions, and that might have eased a few consciences, but it wouldn't have done what the church wants to do—it wouldn't have created a deepseated respect for life. Abortions would have gone on, millions of them.

Nor would a denial of Medicaid funding for abortion achieve our objectives. Given *Roe* vs. *Wade,* it would be nothing more than an attempt to do indirectly what the law says cannot be done directly; worse, it would do it in a way that would burden only the already disadvantaged. Removing funding from the Medicaid program would not prevent the rich and middle classes from having abortions. It would not even assure that the disadvantaged wouldn't have them; it would only impose financial burdens on poor women who want abortions.

Apart from that unevenness, there is a more basic question. Medicaid is designed to deal with health and medical needs. But the arguments for the cutoff of Medicaid abortion funds are not related to those needs. They are moral arguments. If we assume health and medical needs exist, our personal view of morality ought not to be considered a relevant basis for discrimination.

We must keep in mind always that we are a nation of laws—when we like those laws and when we don't.

The supreme Court has established a woman's constitutional right to abortion. The Congress has decided the federal government should not provide federal funding in the Medicaid program for abortion. That, of course, does not bind states in the allocation of their own state funds. Under the law, the individual states need not follow the federal lead, and in New York I believe we cannot follow that lead. The equal protection clause in New York's Constitution has been interpreted by the courts as a standard of fairness that would preclude us from denying only the poor—indirectly, by a cutoff of funds—the practical use of the constitutional right given by *Roe* vs. *Wade*.

In the end, even if after a long and divisive struggle we were able to remove all Medicaid funding for abortion and restore the law to what it was—if we could put most abortions out of our sight, return them to the backrooms where they were performed for so long—I don't believe our responsibility as Catholics would be any closer to being fulfilled than it is now, with abortion guaranteed by law as a woman's right.

The hard truth is that abortion isn't a failure of government. No agency or department of government forces women to have abortions, but abortion goes on. Catholics, the statistics show, support the right to abortion in equal proportion to the rest of the population. Despite the teaching in our homes and schools and pulpits, despite the sermons and pleadings of parents and priests and prelates, despite all the effort at defining our opposition to the sin of abortion, collectively we Catholics apparently believe—and perhaps act—little differently from those who don't share our commitment.

Are we asking government to make criminal what we believe to be sinful because we ourselves can't stop committing the sin?

The failure here is not Caesar's. This failure is our failure, the failure of the entire people of God.

Nobody has expressed this better than a bishop in my own state, Joseph Sullivan, a man who works with the poor in New York City, is resolutely opposed to abortion and argues, with his fellow bishops, for a change of law. "The major problem the church has is internal," the bishop said last month in reference to abortion. "How do we teach? As much as I think we're responsible for advocating public-policy issues, our primary responsibility is to teach our own people. We haven't done that. We're asking politicians to do what we haven't done effectively ourselves."

I agree with the bishop. I think our moral and social mission as Catholics must begin with the wisdom contained in the words "Physician, heal thyself." Unless we Catholics educate ourselves better to the values that define—and can ennoble—our lives, following those teachings better than we do now, unless we set an example that is clear and compelling, then we will never convince this society to change the civil laws to protect what we preach is precious human life.

Better than any law or rule or threat of punishment would be the moving strength of our own good example, demonstrating our lack of hypocrisy, proving the beauty and worth of our instruction.

We must work to find ways to avoid abortions without otherwise violating our faith. We should provide funds and opportunity for young women to bring their child to term, knowing both of them will be taken care of if that is necessary; we should teach our young men better than we do now their responsibilities in creating and caring for human life.

It is this duty of the church to teach through its practice of love that Pope John Paul II has proclaimed so magnificently to all peoples. "The church," he wrote in *Redemptor Hominis* (1979), "which has no weapons at her disposal apart from those of the Spirit, of the word and of love, cannot renounce her proclamation of 'the word. . . in season and out of season.' For this reason she does not cease to implore. . . everybody in the name of God and in the name of man: Do not kill! Do not prepare destruction and extermination for each other! Think of your brothers and sisters who are suffering hunger and misery! Respect each one's dignity and freedom!"

The weapons of the word and of love are already available to us: We need no statute to provide them.

I am not implying that we should stand by and pretend indifference to whether a woman takes a pregnancy to its conclusion or aborts it. I believe we should in all cases try to teach a respect for life. And I believe with regard to abortion that, despite *Roe* vs. *Wade,* we can, in practical ways. Here, in fact, it seems to me that all of us can agree.

Without lessening their insistence on a woman's right to an abortion, the people who call themselves "pro-choice" can support the development of government programs that present an impoverished mother with the full range of support she needs to bear and raise her children, to have a real choice. Without dropping their campaign to ban abortion, those who gather under the banner of "pro-life" can join in developing and enacting a legislative bill of rights for mothers and children, as the bishops have already proposed.

While we argue over abortion, the U.S. infant-mortality rate places us 16th among the nations of the world. Thousands of infants die each year because of inadequate medical care. Some are born with birth defects that, with proper treatment, could be prevented. Some are stunted in their physical and mental growth because of improper nutrition.

If we want to prove our regard for life in the womb, for the helpless infant—if we care about women having real choices in their lives and not being driven to abortions by a sense of helplessness and despair about the future of their child—then there is work enough for all of us. Lifetimes of it.

In New York, we have put in place a number of programs to begin this work, assisting women in giving birth to healthy babies. This year we doubled Medicaid funding to private-care physicians for prenatal and delivery services.

The state already spends $20 million a year for prenatal care in outpatient clinics and for inpatient hospital care.

One program in particular we believe holds a great deal of promise. It's called "New Avenues to Dignity," and it seeks to provide a teen-age mother with the special service she needs to continue with her education, to train for a job, to become capable of standing on her own, to provide for herself and the child she is bringing into the world.

My dissent, then, from the contention that we can have effective and enforceable legal prohibitions on abortion is by no means an argument for religious quietism, for accepting the world's wrongs because that is our fate as "the poor banished children of Eve."

Let me make another point.

Abortion has a unique significance but not a pre-emptive significance.

Apart from the question of the efficacy of using legal weapons to make people stop having abortions, we know our Christian responsibility doesn't end with any one law or amendment, that it doesn't end with abortion. Because it involves life and death, abortion will always be a central concern of Catholics. But so will nuclear weapons, and hunger and homelessness and joblessness, all the forces diminishing human life and threatening to destroy it. The "seamless garment" that Cardinal Bernardin has spoken of is a challenge to all Catholics in public office, conservatives as well as liberals.

We cannot justify our aspiration to goodness simply on the basis of the vigor of our demand for an elusive and questionable civil law declaring what we already know, that abortion is wrong.

Approval or rejection of legal restrictions on abortion should not be the exclusive litmus test of Catholic loyalty. We should understand that whether abortion is outlawed or not, our work has barely begun: the work of creating a society where the right to life doesn't end at the moment of birth; where an infant isn't helped into a world that doesn't care if it's fed properly, housed decently, educated adequately; where the blind or retarded child isn't condemned to exist rather than empowered to live.

The bishops stated this duty clearly in 1974 in their statement to the Senate subcommittee considering a proposed amendment to restrict abortions. They maintained such an amendment could not be seen as an end in itself. "We do not see a constitutional amendment as the final product of our commitment or of our legislative activity," they said. "It is instead the constitutional base on which to provide support and assistance to pregnant women and their unborn children. This would include nutritional, prenatal, childbirth and postnatal care for the mother, and also nutritional pediatric care for the child through the first year of life. . . . We believe that all of these should be available as a matter of right to all pregnant women and their children."

The bishops reaffirmed that view in 1976, in 1980 and again this year when the U.S. Catholic Conference asked Catholics to judge candidates on a wide range of issues—on abortion, yes; but also on food policy, the arms race, human rights, education, social justice and military expenditures.

The bishops have been consistently "pro-life" in the full meaning of that term, and I respect them for that.

The problems created by the matter of abortion are complex and confounding. Nothing is clearer to me than my inadequacy to find compelling solutions to all of their moral, legal and social implications. I—and many others like me—are eager for enlightenment, eager to learn new and better ways to manifest respect for the deep reverence for life that is our religion and our instinct. I hope that this public attempt to describe the problems as I understand them will give impetus to the dialogue in the Catholic community and beyond, a dialogue which could show me a better wisdom than I've been able to find so far.

It would be tragic if we let that dialogue become a prolonged, divisive argument that destroys or impairs our ability to practice any part of the morality given us in the Sermon on the Mount, to touch, heal and affirm the human life that surrounds us.

We Catholic citizens of the richest, most powerful nation that has ever existed are like the stewards made responsible over a great household: From those to whom so much has been given, much shall be required. It is worth repeating that ours is not a faith that encourages its believers to stand apart from the world, seeking their salvation alone, separate from the salvation of those around them.

We speak of ourselves as a body. We come together in

worship as companions, in the ancient sense of that word, those who break bread together and who are obliged by the commitment we share to help one another, everywhere, in all we do and in the process to help the whole human family. We see our mission to be "the completion of the work of creation."

This is difficult work today. It presents us with many hard choices.

The Catholic Church has come of age in America. The ghetto walls are gone, our religion no longer a badge of irredeemable foreignness. This newfound status is both an opportunity and a temptation. If we choose, we can give in to the temptation to become more and more assimilated into a larger, blander culture, abandoning the practice of the specific values that made us different, worshiping whatever gods the marketplace has to sell while we seek to rationalize our own laxity by urging the political system to legislate on others a morality we no longer practice ourselves.

Or we can remember where we come from, the journey of two millennia, clinging to our personal faith, to its insistence on constancy and service and on hope. We can live and practice the morality Christ gave us, maintaining his truth in this world, struggling to embody his love, practicing it especially where that love is most needed, among the poor and the weak and the dispossessed, not just by trying to make laws for others to live by, but by living the laws already written for us by God, in our hearts and our minds.

We can be fully Catholic: proudly, totally at ease with ourselves, a people in the world, transforming it, a light to this nation, appealing to the best in our people, not the worst, persuading not coercing, leading people to truth by love, and still, all the while, respecting and enjoying our unique pluralistic democracy. And we can do it even as politicians.

182. Religion and Politics. Statement of James W. Malone, October 14, 1984.

"I have observed that when ministers of religion leave the duties of their profession to take a busy part in political matters, they generally fall into contempt, and sometimes even bring discredit to the cause in whose service they are engaged." [Annabelle M. Melville, *John Carroll of Baltimore. Founder of the American Catholic Hierarchy.* New York: Charles Scribner's Sons. 1955. p. 45]. That statement of 1776 by the churchman who was to become the first Catholic bishop of the United States set the tone, so to speak, for Catholic clerical involvement in American politics. With a few exceptions, e.g., the active role played in Republican Party affairs by John Ireland, Archbishop of Saint Paul, the position taken by Carroll has been maintained. While urging the Catholic faithful in their capacity as citizens to participation in politics, the bishops have been insistent that the Church should remain aloof from a show of partisanship. Such was the principal point made by the President of the National Conference of Catholic Bishops several weeks before the close of the presidential campaign of 1984. Source: *Origins,* 14 (October 25, 1984), 289-291.

The Administrative Board of the U.S. Catholic Conference, meeting September 11-13, asked that I issue a statement reaffirming the conference's position on the question of religion and politics. I am pleased to do so, since our pluralistic society should welcome discussion of the moral dimensions of public policy and thoughtful examination of the relationship of religious bodies to the political order.

As a nation we are constitutionally committed to the separation of church and state, but not to the separation of religious and moral values from public life. The genius of the American political tradition lies in preserving religious freedom for all—but not at the price of excluding religious and moral content from discussion of domestic and foreign policy.

The question therefore is not whether we should discuss the relationship of religion, morality and politics, but how to discuss the relationship. While responsibility for the quality and character of this discussion rests with all citizens, it rests especially with religious leaders, political leaders and the media.

The Catholic conference's statement on political responsibility last March, its testimony to the platform committees of the two major parties in June and August, and my own statement of August 9th express the views of the Catholic bishops concerning the church's engagement in the political process. I repeat here a basic principle of these documents: We do not take positions for or against particular parties or individual candidates.

Bishops are teachers in the Catholic Church entrusted with the responsibility of communicating the content of Catholic moral teaching and illustrating its relevance to social and political isssues. We do not seek the formation of a voting block nor do we pre-empt the right and duty of individuals to decide conscientiously whom they will support for public office. Rather, having stated our positions, we encourage members of our own church and all citizens to examine the positions of candidates on issues and decide who will best contribute to the common good of society.

The content of Catholic teaching leads us to take positions on many public issues; we are not a one-issue church. Many of our positions are reflected in the statement on political responsibility and our platform testimony.

As I said August 9th, these concerns range from protecting human life from the attack of abortion to safeguarding human life from the devastation of nuclear war; they extend to the enhancement of life through promoting human rights and satisfying human needs like nutrition, education, housing and health care, especially for the poor. We emphasize that the needs of the poor must be adequately addressed if we are to be considered a just and compassionate society. Attention to the least among us is the test of our moral vision, and it should be applied to candidates at every level of our government.

Our platform testimony points out that, in speaking of human dignity and the sanctity of life, we give special emphasis to two issues today. They are the prevention of nuclear war and the protection of unborn human life.

These issues pertaining to the sanctity of human life itself are and cannot help but be matters of public morality. Evident in the case of war and peace this is no less true in the case of abortion, where the human right to life of the unborn and society's interest in protecting it necessarily makes this a matter of public, not merely private, morality.

On questions such as these, we realize that citizens and public officials may agree with our moral arguments while disagreeing with us and among themselves on the most effective legal and policy remedies. The search for political and public-policy solutions to such problems as war and peace and abortion may well be long and difficult, but a prudential judgment that political solutions are not now feasible does not justify failure to undertake the effort.

Whether the issue be the control, reduction and elimination of nuclear arms or the legal protection of the unborn, the task is to work for the feasibility of what may now be deemed unfeasible. The pursuit of complex objectives like these ought not to be set aside because the goals may not be immediately reachable. In debating such matters there is much room for dialogue about what constitutes effective, workable responses; but the debate should not be about whether a response in the political order is needed.

None of these issues will be resolved quickly. All will

extend far beyond the present political campaign. The discussion of religion and politics will also be pursued long after the campaign. Let us conduct our immediate dialogue with reason and civility, so that the resources of religious and moral vision and the method of rational political debate will be sustained and enhanced in our public life.

183. John J. O'Connor. Human Lives, Human Rights, October 15, 1984.

Of all the controversial issues that have divided the American people in recent years none has been the subject of more bitter debate and heated demonstrations than that related to abortion. Nor does that topic show any indication of being less controversial in the time ahead. In spite of the clear teaching of the Catholic Church on the matter, an increasing number of American Catholics have been disposed to accept abortion. The complexity of the problem for Catholic politicians has been especially acute, as indicated in the address of Governor Cuomo (No 181). Probably no spokesman for the Church's stance has addressed the issue with more forceful expression and detailed consideration than the Archbishop of New York. If he marshalled every argument against abortion, he was no less at pains to suggest remedies and to give evidence of the instrumentalities that the Archdiocese of New York has provided for the care of women who might be tempted to have an abortion. He sought as well to refute the view that concentration on abortion was at variance with the more general approach known as the 'seamless garment' that is intended to embrace all pro-life issues, e.g., nuclear warfare, capital punishment, justice for ethnic and racial groups, hunger, etc. Source: *Origins,* 14 (October 25, 1984), 292-301.

Nowhere else has it been expressed more beautifully than in the 139th Psalm:

"For it was you who created my being, knit me together in my mother's womb. I thank you for the wonder of my being, for the wonders of all your creation."

And perhaps no one ever captured the magic and the mystery of those words and reflected them more faithfully in his own life than did our late beloved Cardinal Terence Cooke.

It would be as absurd as it would be sad and unkind were this man, of all men, ever referred to as representative of an "ecclesiastical powerhouse." Powerful he was indeed in his gentleness, powerful in his personal spirituality, powerful in his love for every human being, the blind, the lame, the halt, the aged, the unborn, the poor, the wealthy. And never was he more powerful than on his deathbed, filled with suffering and seemingly helpless, like Christ on the cross. It was from that real "powerhouse" of pain in his waning hours, while preparing for his rendezvous with death, that he spoke most powerfully of life:

"From the beginning of human life, from conception until death and at every moment between, it is the Lord Our God who gives us life, and we, who are his creatures, should cry out with joy and thanksgiving for this precious gift.

"The 'gift of life,' God's special gift, is no less beautiful when it is accompanied by illness or weakness, hunger or poverty, mental or physical handicaps, loneliness or old age. Indeed, at these times, human life gains extra splendor as it requires our special care, concern and reverence. It is in and through the weakest of human vessels that the Lord continues to reveal the power of his love."

It is with deep gratitude to Cardinal Cooke for his powerful witness to the sacredness of all human life and with a sense of great personal privilege that I have announced that as of this day the board of Flower Hospital has unanimously determined to change the name to the Terence Cardinal Cooke Health Care Center, and as of this day forward the hospital shall be so named.

It is not totally foreign to our reasons for accepting Flower Hospital's offer to co-sponsor my address today that prior to Cardinal Cooke's assuming responsibility for the hospital it performed some 800 abortions every year. None, of course, has been performed since.

I was motivated to give this address under such auspices also because of the magnificent work the hospital carries out today for the least of God's little ones. I wish every New Yorker, indeed every American, could see the dedication, the professionalism, the personal commitment, the overpowering love demonstrated by doctors, nurses, administrators and staff toward the helpless, the brain-damaged, the other severely handicapped of all ages. Flower Hospital, now Terence Cardinal Cooke Health Care Center, is a rich blessing in our midst, a magnificent memorial to the sacredness of all human life.

I felt it appropriate as well to accept the offer of co-sponsorship of this address from the Institute on Human Values in Medical Ethics, initiated with funding from the Alfred E. Smith Memorial Foundation, at the instance of Cardinal Cooke, and from friends of New York Medical College, to deal with the moral and ethical issues of contemporary medicine in ways that support the value and the inherent dignity of all human life. I am grateful especially to Dr. John Connolly, president, New York Medical College and to Dr. Samuel H. Rubin, director, Institute of Human Values in Medical Ethics, New York Medical College.

A Nation's Enduring Heartache

Let me start by telling you the story of the man who puzzled his daughter when he told her that the day he had his heart attack was the happiest day of his life. And then he explained why.

"It is very simple, my child," he said. "I have witnessed so much death and suffering and survived it all. At times I wondered if I had a heart at all. This heart attack reassured me that I indeed have one. For how can a man without a heart have a heart attack?"

The story is my favorite among the *Hasidic Tales of the Holocaust* told by Professor Yaffa Eliach of the Department of Judaic Studies at Brooklyn College

The pain of the heart attack was reassuring to the man because it proved to him that he had not been hardened by human suffering by the experiences he had survived. He still had a heart!

There is a great deal of pain in our country today. I am not happy about it, but I am encouraged by it. I am encouraged to believe that there is deep pain throughout the land in respect to a number of crucial problems. I believe, further, that this profound and pervasive anxiety is rooted in the reality that as a people we do have a heart—an enormous heart, a warm and generous heart, a heart that is experiencing a gnawing pain, an enduring heartache, if not an outright spiritual and emotional heart attack.

We know that we are doing so many things right as a nation, but we know too or we feel, a vague uneasiness and at times an acute anxiety that we are doing some things wrong—terribly wrong.

We know there is something wrong as we pass the bag ladies, the bag men in the streets. We know there is something wrong about gentrification that flushes lonely, elderly people out of homes and apartments with absolutely no place to go. We know there is something wrong when drugs control and destroy our neighborhoods, when we can't build prisons fast enough to meet the demand. We know there is something wrong when the most incredible pornography is defended as freedom of speech, when child abuse reaches horrifying proportions, when people are disenfranchised or exploited because of where they were born, or their sex or the color of their skin. We know there is something wrong in the sexual exploitation and violence that Father Bruce Ritter deals with every day right here in Manhattan and in the hopelessness of the burned-out buildings in cities all over the country.

We know there is something wrong in Central America, in the Middle East, in the north of Ireland, in Cambodia and in Poland, in much of the vast continent of Africa and elsewhere in the world. We know there is something wrong, something terrifyingly wrong, about the arms race and about the horrifying potential of nuclear weapons.

And all of this knowledge and more pains us, because we are basically a good people, a good and kind and merciful people. And the pain comes in knowing that we are doing some things terribly wrong and in either not truly wanting to right them or in not seeming to know how to right them. So, many of us—a great many of us—do what is very understandable: We try to forget the problems, to busy ourselves with a thousand legitimate preoccupations, to hope that someone else will solve the problems or that they will simply go away.

Like the bag people. We didn't put them on the streets. We don't want them on the streets. We can't understand why they are on the streets, we disbelieve how many are on the streets, we wish they would go away or someone would take them away. But in the meanwhile, particularly as we hustle to our own homes on bitter winter nights, we pass them by, and we know they are there, and the knowing pains us because we know simultaneously that somehow there has to be a better way.

I am deeply convinced that it is this same kind of uneasiness, this same kind of anxiety, this same kind of pain that we feel as a nation, knowing that we lose 4,000 lives every day through abortion. And that's a large part of the answer to the question people ask me all the time: Why is this front-page news all over the country? Why are people talking about it all over the world? No single statement by any one bishop—no series of statements by all the bishops combined—could have created the depth and the breadth and the intensity of feeling about this if it hadn't been there all along, stirring down inside us, gnawing at our hearts. You can't make an issue out of a non-issue. This one was there, long before a single bishop said a single word.

We know somehow, whatever our religious persuasion, that there is something wrong when 1.5 million unborn human lives are taken every year in our beloved country. We know that, whatever the reason, there must be a better way. We know that this magnificent country, with its incredible resources, its ability to put a man on the moon, the skill to transplant hearts, the heart to give our lives for the oppressed all over the world—this marvelous country must surely have a better answer to the violence of poverty than to inflict the violence of death on the innocent; it must surely have a better answer for the lonely, confused, frightened young woman, the teen-ager, the 10- or 11- or 12-year-old pregnant girl, than to destroy the new life within her. Our nation must surely have more to offer a bewildered family than the money to help pay for a daughter's abortion. Our society must, surely must, have more support for the woman torn with conflict over a pregnancy than to point her toward an abortion clinic.

Is this simply a religious perspective? Is my grief over abortion born merely of what I have been taught as a Catholic? I can't believe that. I know that millions of Jews, Protestants, Orthodox, Moslems, people of many other religious persuasions and people who profess no religious faith at all grieve as I do over this destruction of life.

Abortion: The Destruction of Life

Or is abortion not the destruction of life? Are we, in fact, not putting babies to death?

If we are not destroying human life, of course, then our concern, our anxiety, our pain over abortion virtually disappears. There is a dramatic difference between removing 4,000 pieces of tissue each day from the bodies of 4,000 women and taking the lives of 4,000 babies.

What is abortion then? Can we face that question honestly? Can we raise it without rancor, without accusation, without judgment or condemnation of anyone? Surely it is a crucial question. Surely it deserves an answer.

One of the very reasons I wanted to give this talk to an audience composed largely of medical people is that I believe that you in particular must ask and answer this question honestly. I turn to you and to your medical colleagues for what you and they have to say. I do not ask you or them to speak from religious beliefs. I do not ask you or them to determine at what point the unborn becomes a human person. I ask you and them to speak from your common-sense experience of human life and from the scientific evidence you observe.

I turn, for example, to Dr. Bernard Nathanson, the well-known Jewish obstetrician-gynecologist who identifies himself as an atheist. Dr. Nathanson's background is fascinating. By his own admission, he presided over 60,000 abortions in the first and largest abortion clinic in the Western world, the clinic he directed. He now calls those abortions 60,000 deaths. Here are his own words:

"Sometime ago—after a tenure of a year and a half—I resigned as director of the Center for Reproductive and Sexual Health. The center had performed 60,000 abortions .... I am deeply troubled by my own increasing certainty that I had in fact presided over 60,000 deaths.

"There is no longer serious doubt in my mind that human life exists within the womb from the very onset of pregnancy, despite the fact that the nature of the intrauterine life has been the subject of considerable dispute in the past.

"Electrocardiographic evidence of heart function has been established in embryos as early as six weeks. Electroencephalographic recordings of human brain activity have been noted in embryos at eight weeks. Our capacity to measure signs of life is daily becoming more sophisticated, and as time goes by, we will doubtless be able to isolate life signs at earlier stages in fetal development."

Dr. Nathanson now spends a large part of his life pleading against abortion, not because of a religious conversion, but because of the evidence yielded by ultrasound scanning, intrauterine surgery, *in vitro* fertilization and other advances in science and technology. Dr. Nathanson previously used the impersonal term *alpha* to describe what he now calls "the person in the womb." Scientific findings have convinced him beyond a shadow of a doubt that "prenatality is just another passage in our lives—lives which commence with fertilization and end with death."

Dr. Nathanson is far from alone. Indeed, the American Medical Association itself urged strict laws against abortion more than a century ago, simply because the scientific evidence said that human life begins at conception. In 1871 the AMA told its members that a fetus becomes animated long before quickening. Quoting from *Archbold's Criminal Practice and Pleadings,* it said this: "No other doctrine appears to be consonant with reason or physiology but that which admits the embryo to possess vitality from the very moment of conception." No statement by the AMA in more recent times has contradicted the position it took then.

In our own day, miracles of modern science confirm what we have known all along—that life exists in the womb. Reporting on an article by Dr. Mitchell S. Golbus called "Healing the Unborn," the 1983 Medical and Health Annual of the Encyclopedia Britannica says:

"Prenatal medicine is now beginning to be able to intervene, before birth, to alleviate and even cure conditions that previously would have severely compromised the fetus. This promises survival for thousands of threatened lives. . . . The concept that the fetus is a patient, an individual whose disorders are a proper subject for medical therapy, has been established."

But sadly all of our new knowledge seems to have taught us very little. A famous article in the journal called California Medicine, written in 1970, concedes that life is present before birth, but warns physicians that if they want people to think that abortion is morally acceptable, they'll have to come up with a brand new language. Semantic gymnastics, they call it.

This was surely the attitude Sir William Liley had in mind when he lamented the direction that too many in the medical world and society in general have taken. Sir William, of the faculty of the Postgraduate School of Obstetrics and Gynecology of the University of Auckland, listed a series of developments that gave us new insights into the miracle of life before birth, and then continued:

"For a generation which reputedly prefers scientific fact to barren philosophy, we might have thought this new information would engender a new respect for the welfare and appreciation of the importance of intrauterine life.

"Instead, around the world we find a systematic campaign clamoring for the destruction of the embryo and fetus as a cure-all for every social and personal problem. I, for one, find it a bitter irony that just when the embryo and fetus arrive on the medical scene there should be such sustained pressure to make him, or her, a social non-entity."

Some evidence, however, does seem to make a profound impression on many medical and lay people as well. That's what happened when Congressman Lawrence J. Hogan saw some startling pictures, as he told a congressional subcommittee on constitutional amendments.

"Until a few years ago, I really did not think much about abortion. It did not mean very much to me. I somehow equated it with birth control.

"My brother, Dr. William Hogan, who. . . is with me today and is an obstetrician, had been trying to discuss abortion with me, but I kept putting him off, saying that it was not a popular political issue.

"Finally, one day he came to my house and showed me some color pictures of what unborn babies look like. I saw what some people call a chemical reaction, sucking a thumb. I saw perfectly formed human babies just a few weeks from conception. I saw the pictures of the 21-week-old fetus, a little girl, who survived out of the womb. I saw other little babies who did not survive. Some were scalded red from saline solution which flushed them from the womb. I saw others torn apart from the machine, I could see a little foot and a little hand. I was stunned. I was shocked. And I was bitterly ashamed.

"I did not know what I really thought abortion was. I just did not think very much about it. But certainly I did not think we were killing babies. How could I have been so stupid?

"If we are not killing babies in abortion, what are we doing?"

When discarded fetuses are found in the trash, why are we horrified? Why do we rebel when our highest court tells us that the matter of when life begins is constitutionally irrelevant? In the light of all that we know and in the name of sheer common sense, is it not because we are profoundly convinced that the unborn child is human? What can we possibly say except that we are putting to death 4,000 human beings every day—1.5 million every year.

Isn't there something wrong with this? Where does it all stop?

I know there are those who sincerely believe that abortion is an evil, but that not to have an abortion might be even worse. I know it, and my heart goes out to them. I know there are women and parents and young girls who are frantic about a pregnancy. They don't know which way to turn or what to do. They're under enormous pressure. Who can condemn them? Who can fail to understand all they're going though? Their abortions are still tragic; their babies are still put to death. But they think they're doing the right thing. Do I condemn them for feeling that way? No, never. I would do anything I could to help them pick up the pieces of their lives after an abortion.

The same is true of families, of parents who might abhor the idea of abortion, but when their own daughter is pregnant believe that unless she has an abortion her life will be ruined. There can be no question of the grief they feel, the conflict that rips at their very hearts, the deep suffering they endure in coming to a decision that an abortion is the only way.

But is it? Is it the only way? Is it the best answer we can come up with after these many centuries of civilization? What does it do to the woman herself, the young girl, the family?

I wish there were time to read to you some of the letters I have received from women who have had abortions or from families that encouraged or urged or even pressured them to do so. I am speaking of women and of families of all religious persuasions and of none. Many suffer for years. My own heart aches for them. I try to respond to the best of my ability, to offer them whatever help I possibly can. But in some cases, I fear, the wound never seems to heal. In my view, the tragedy in every such case is at least doubled: An innocent baby has been deprived of life; a woman has been deprived of peace of mind and heart, sometimes for the rest of her life. Indeed, in every such case there are at least two victims, the baby and the woman herself. In many cases the fathers of the baby aborted, the families involved, suffer terribly as well.

It is inevitably the woman, however, who is confronted most immediately and intimately with the terrible conflicts that can accompany a pregnancy and with the anguish of decision. We have no sympathy with the man who judges a woman's dilemma glibly or who detaches himself from the reality of the conflict and the suffering involved. Nor can we respect the man who walks callously away from his own obligations when confronted with a woman's unplanned pregnancy. Such, of course, is not always the case. It can happen that the father of an unborn baby who is deliberately aborted can suffer deeply.

One of the most poignant stories I have ever read was by a former CBS correspondent. Writing in the Los Angeles Times in March of 1976, he describes his joy when his wife told him she was pregnant, and his shock and fury when she told him she had already talked with several friends, had a doctor's name and intended to have an abortion. Shouting and pleading followed, with his wife insisting it was her body and should be her decision alone. Finally, he drove her to the doctor's office and waited in the car.

He tells the story 20 years later. Why? Because suddenly and unexpectedly he passed the corner of the doctor's office and it all came flooding back, and he found himself wondering over and over what might have been. By the time he arrived at his meeting, the tears were flowing and wouldn't stop.

"Whatever sort of person the lost one might have been," he writes, "I feel even now that we had no right to take his/her life."

"Religion has nothing to do with my feelings. It is a gut response—still so strong that it overwhelmed me" some 20 years later:

"Even now I find myself wondering about my first child that never was, and I wonder too about others in my shoes. How many men share my haunting feelings about children who might have been, but were denied? Why are we, the fathers who never were, so reluctant to talk about such feelings? If it is all so painful for us, how much worse must it be for the women who nurture and then give up the very fact of life itself?"

A sad story? Of course it is, and there are countless stories like it. I know that your hearts go out, just as mine does, to all those whose lives have been so tragically touched. I do not repeat the story to rewaken bitter memories or to revive buried guilt. On the contrary, I believe as profoundly as I believe anything in this world that God wants nothing more than to forgive whatever mistakes we have made and pleads with us to let him do so.

A Plea to the Medical Profession

But what of the future? Can we do more? Of course we can, all of us. And here I appeal particularly to you in the medical profession. I ask boldly that you help in at least three ways.

First, very simply, I ask you to think about the Hippocratic Oath. Ask yourself with absolute honesty what abortion really is. Test what is done to the unborn against the Hippocratic Oath many of you once took. You remember how it used to go: "I will give no deadly medicine to anyone if asked, nor suggest any such counsel; and in like manner I will not give a pessary to a woman to produce an abortion." And you know that the words about abortion are now so frequently omitted. Why? Why?

Second, teach us what we must learn about taking care of the whole person—the entire family, physically and emotionally. Teach us far, far more than we have been willing to learn to date about the critical importance of decent housing, of security in our streets, of the destructiveness of drugs. Teach us that good medicine requires that people need jobs, and meaningful jobs, to be able to hold their heads high, to feed, to clothe, to educate their children. Teach us that poverty is dangerous to our health, that malnutrition in mothers breeds disabilities in children. Plead for daycare centers, increased numbers of facilities for the handicapped. Raise your voices precisely as medical professionals to plead for a just social order indispensable to effective medicine. Teach that abortion is what it is, without pretense, but help bring about circumstances which will help a pregnant woman recognize that there is a better way for her than to have her own child destroyed.

Teach us above all, however, that you of the medical profession recognize the absolutely crucial role you play in regard to the entire issue of abortion. The overwhelming number of the

4,000 abortions carried out every day are carried out by members of the medical profession. What enormous power is yours, what leadership for life you could provide! Do you consider abortion your responsibility, whether or not you personally have ever been involved in or would be involved in an abortion? As the Holy Father reminded us recently when he spoke to a group of anesthesiologists, the responsibility extends to everyone in the medical field. For whatever my personal opinion is worth, I am convinced that the medical profession could change the entire picture of abortion in America and the world. Such is your influence, your prestige. Such is our dependence on you as nurturers and guardians of human life.

And third, here is a request as direct as I can make it: If it's needed to save the life of an unborn child, give your medical services without cost. I do not know how many abortions are performed free of charge, but I would like to believe that you and your colleagues would be willing to deliver live—and free of charge where necessary—every baby that would otherwise be aborted. I am certain that many of you do this already, but I urge you to make it widely known that you want to go out of your way to help, at no cost to the pregnant girl or woman in need.

And I appeal to you, our hospital administrators, boards and staff to provide free of charge, when necessary, all the medical care required for both mother and child.

My appeal is extended to those in the legal profession as well, to assist women and families, without charge when necessary, to learn what federal or state or city funding may be available to them and to help them in adoption processes, should they choose this route.

The Commitment of the Archdiocese

I can assure all of you, as I appeal to you, and I can assure every single or married woman facing an unplanned pregnancy that the Archdiocese of New York will give you free, confidential help of highest quality. Here are just some of the services the archdiocese will provide, whatever your religious affiliation. It makes no difference whether you are Jewish, Protestant, Catholic, Orthodox, Moslem, of any other religion or of no religion at all, or single or married—and your confidentiality will be completely respected.

You will get help with medical care and you do not have to worry about bills. If you have medical insurance, you may be able to use this. If you choose adoption, the adopting family is responsible for your medical bills. If you wish to keep your baby, your social worker will help you get Medicaid. There is no fee for our services to you.

Our social workers will make arrangements to meet you close to your home. They travel widely throughout New York, New Jersey and Connecticut. If you live in another state, we will help you get service from another agency or arrange for you to come to New York whenever possible.

If you cannot live at home during your pregnanacy, other living arrangements can be made for you. The social worker we will provide you will suggest to you a variety of arrangements. You can choose the one best for you.

If you decide to keep your baby, your social worker will locate medical services, community resources, financial aid and support services to help you.

If you choose adoption, you will have a choice about the family with whom your baby is placed. Your social worker will give you profiles of approved couples on the waiting list. She will discuss these with you, but you make the selection. Let me say it simply and straightforwardly. The Archdiocese of New York is prepared to do everything in its power to help you and your unborn baby, to make absolutely certain that you need never feel that you must have an abortion.

A Plea to Those in Public Service

I have appealed to you members of the medical professions, to those of you in the legal profession and to those of you who may personally experience an unplanned pregnancy. May I now address all who hold or who seek public office and ask this: Commit yourself unconditionally to a just social order for all—to decent housing, to jobs, to the end of all discrimination, to the ultimate ending of the arms race. Do these things not for political gain, but out of respect for all human life. I've heard it said that those who plead for protection for the unborn are obsessed with a single issue. But what is that issue other than life itself? No one in public life would dare admit to being a racist or a warmonger. But suppose someone did? Would we be accused of obsession with a single issue if we challenged that position? And is any value that is threatened anywhere greater than life itself?

Why, then, is it argued that questioning a candidate about abortion is somehow unfair or unethical? Must a candidate or an office holder explicitly support abortion? Of course not! He or she is free to tell the world:

"I am not only personally opposed to abortion, but I intend to do everything I can within the law to bring about a change in the law. I do not believe in abortion on demand. I do not believe that the right to privacy overrides the right to life of an unborn child."

There's nothing unconstitutional about that. You have to uphold the law, the Constitution says. It does not say that you must agree with the law or that you cannot work to change the law.

What do we ask of a candidate or someone already in office? Nothing more than this: a statement opposing abortion on demand and a commitment to work for a modification of the permissive interpretations issued on the subject by the U.S. Supreme Court. It will simply not do to argue that "laws" won't work or that "we can't legislate morality." Nor will it do to argue, "I won't impose my morality on others." There is nothing personal or private in the morality that teaches that the taking of unborn life is wrong.

And so I plead with you above all for the most innocent, those who have no voice of their own to cry out for your protection. Your personal belief is not an issue with me nor are your politics. Whether you hold political office or aspire to such, whatever your party, my appeal is precisely the same. I speak to elect no candidate, to reject no candidate.

There are critical needs in our society. All must be addressed on a continuing basis. None will go away overnight regardless of who holds public office at whatever level. Some needs are so crucial that they require absolutely the best leadership this country can provide. It is neither my prerogative nor my desire to determine who those leaders are to be. But I am passionately convinced that no need is more crucial than to protect the right of the unborn. I can but pray that those who are chosen to lead us will do everything possible to protect those rights, for such, in my judgment, is the indispensable step in protecting the rights of all who cannot protect themselves—and one day that can be any one of us.

In a speech last April at Mount Saint Mary's College in Emmitsburg, Md., Speaker of the House Thomas P. O'Neill Jr. quoted the truly noble words of Senator Hubert Humphrey that could be read as an ominous warning as well: "The moral test of government is how it treats those who are in the dawn of life, the children; those who are in the twilight of life, the aged; and those who are in the shadows of life, the sick, the needy and handicapped."

Abortion and the Law

Since 1973 some of the finest legal scholars in the United States have argued that the Supreme Court decisions were not solidly based on the Constitution, and one Supreme Court justice who dissented from the majority called the abortion decision an act of "raw judicial power." In other words, the will of seven justices was imposed on an entire nation.

Given this reality, when charges are so loosely made that those who plead for a recovery of legal protection for the unborn are trying to impose their will on the majority, it is apparently forgotten that virtually every state in the union had some kind of protective law which was swept away by the Supreme Court. If we are going to argue that law must reflect a consensus, we must admit that there was a strong, national consensus against abortion on demand before the Supreme Court issued its decree that the unborn is "not a person whose life state law could legally protect."

There are those who argue that we cannot legislate morality and that the answer to abortion does not lie in the law. The reality is that we do legislate behavior every day. Our entire society is structured by law. We legislate against going through red lights, selling heroin, committing murder, burning down people's houses, stealing, child abuse, slavery and a thousand other acts that would deprive other people of their rights.

And this is precisely the key: Law is intended to protect us from one another regardless of private and personal moral or religious beliefs. The law does not ask me if I personally believe stealing to be moral or immoral. The law does not ask me if my religion encourages me to burn down houses. As far as the law is concerned, the distinction between private and public morality is quite clear. Basically, when I violate other people's rights, I am involved in a matter of public morality, subject to penalty under law.

Is it outlandish to think that laws against abortions might have some protective effect? It is obvious that law is not the entire answer to abortion. Nor is it the entire answer to theft, arson, child abuse or shooting police officers. Everybody knows that. But who would suggest that we repeal the laws against such crimes because the laws are so often broken?

Of course we need far more education, and speaking in this high school auditorium I call upon our school administrators and teachers to carry out this responsibility. Of course we need far more love and respect and reverence for human life. Of course those churches that believe abortion to be sinful have the obligation to teach their adherents.

The National Conference of Catholic Bishops testified before the Senate in 1981, "We have no intention of asking the government to take over our own task of teaching moral principles and forming consciences." The testimony went on to argue, however, that the law has a critical teaching function. On this basis too we would appeal to those in public life who could do so much to help achieve modifications in the current laws.

Every American is brought up, ideally, to respect the law. We know that some individual laws are good, some bad, some just, some unjust, but it's the concept of law that we respect. We know laws are necessary because we are all weak human beings, and while we may chafe under laws that are personally inconvenient to us, we know we must have laws or have chaos.

It is one of our proudest traditions that bad laws can be changed. There is no better example than the slave laws. And while many blacks still suffer in our country and are still far from enjoying all the human and civil rights due them by both moral and civil law, the reality is that if the 1857 Supreme Court decision in the famous Dred Scott case had been allowed to stand, they would still be legally slaves, non-citizens, forever unable to become citizens. In 1857, it was not enough for people of good will to call slavery wrong; it was absolutely essential that they call the law wrong and worked to change it.

We need only look at the mentality that has developed under current laws in recent years. An assistant district attorney argues in the case of the smothering of a newborn by her grandmother, "This is what you might call a two-minute abortion because the baby was unwanted." A Nobel Prize winner has suggested that parents should be given a period of three days after the birth of a baby to determine whether the baby should live or die. Physicians are asked to determine by amniocentesis and other means the sex of the unborn so that an abortion can be performed if the sex is not acceptable to the parents. We hear of trafficking in fetuses which are sold nationally and internationally for commercial purposes such as the manufacture of cosmetics. The judicial trend since 1973 has even allowed a court's ordering abortion for a mentally retarded or incompetent woman.

Why maintain laws against child abuse when abortion—the most violent form of child abuse in society—is protected as a right? Why have laws against racism when—as the 10 black

Roman Catholic bishops of the United States recently charged—liberal abortion policies amount to another form of subjugation of poor black people.

Deeply as we feel the pain of the individual and aware as we are that many, many women have abortions because that seems to them their only choice, we cannot, we must not, treat abortion as though it were a matter of concern only to an individual woman or man or family. We are already seeing cruel signs of what an abortion mentality can mean for all society.

Again we ask how safe will the retarded be, the handicapped, the aged, the wheelchaired, the incurably ill, when the so-called "quality of life" becomes the determinant of who is to live and who is to die? Who is to determine which life is "meaningful," which life is not? Who is to have a right to the world's resources, to food, to housing, to medical care? The prospects are frightening and far too realistic to be brushed aside as "scare tactics."

Father Hesburgh of Notre Dame phrases the issue well. "It is difficult to explain how a moral America, so brilliantly successful in confronting racial injustice in the '60s has the most permissive abortion law of any Western country, recognizing virtually no protection for unborn human beings."

So we must change the laws. This is one reason why I am encouraged by Governor Cuomo's calling for a task force to "take our highest aspirations and most noble pronouncements about life and seek to convert them into working laws and policies." I applaud such an objective vigorously as long as it is indeed pointed toward changing the current laws and as long as we forthrightly recognize that a task force can but recommend. We continue to look to our highest elected officials for leadership in bringing about those changes in current laws and policies so critically needed to protect every human life at every stage of its existence.

False Charges of Abortion Advocates: A Response

There is strong resistance by some to any change in the laws to make them less permissive or to reduce the possibility of "abortion on demand" (for that is the real issue). Some costly advertising campaigns are designed to discredit the "pro-life" movement.

Some pro-abortionists convey the impression that "masses" of women would die undergoing "back-alley" abortions if abortion were illegal. We are informed that this is not supported by figures issued by the U.S. government before 1973 nor following the 1979 cutoff of Medicaid funds for abortion.

Certainly rape is always a frightening possibility and a crime to be abhorred in every way. It is understandable that many would feel that an abortion should be justifiable if a woman or a young girl becomes pregnant through rape. We in no way minimize the horror and the trauma of rape.

Obviously, whether we are speaking of a thousand cases or one case, a woman's life, a family's future, can be virtually destroyed. But, as we have asked before, will violence against an unborn child compensate for the violence against the woman raped or will it in many cases simply increase her suffering? Is it at least possible that bearing a child, however conceived, and either rearing it or offering it for adoption to the hundreds of thousands of couples pleading to adopt, might bring, even out of the tragedy of rape, a rich fulfillment?

Permit me to read you just one of the letters I have received from women who have been raped:

"Twenty-two years ago I was raped. I had no home at this time. Some Sisters took me in when I became ill.

"I could not give my daughter what she needed when my own life was so hard, so I let her go (for adoption).

"Sixteen years later—without even knowing her name I found my daughter. My daughter and I are close friends. She is now married.

"I tell you all of this because no matter how life was conceived, we are to stand firm in being thankful for the gift of life no matter what tragedy is connected with it.

"Yes, it was a horrible experience to be raped. Yes, it was I who felt like the bad person. Yes, there was worry if my child would be healthy. Yes, I had no idea how I could take care of my baby. Yes, I was ashamed to be seen—so young and not married.

"Still, I suffered through this nightmare that deeply affected me rather than have an abortion because of my deep reverence for all living creatures created by God. I wasn't a Catholic at the time and yet I knew what the truth was and still is. If I had taken my child's life before she was born, there wouldn't be a daughter telling her friends that she is proud of me for being just me."

The charge that the "pro-life" movement considers abortion a political decision, rather than personal and medical, is equally misleading. Certainly the lives of its future citizens are of concern to the "body politic." Appropriate political activity is both a right and duty for every citizen.

It is precisely concern for the personal that prompts us to exercise our right and duty to use the political process to try to bring about legislation that protects the right of every person, including the unborn. This is a far cry from asking our politicians to tell us what is morally good for us. We have no more desire to see politicians determine what is moral and immoral than we have to see such abortion decisions forced upon medical doctors.

There are also the implications that the "pro-life" movement sees "birth control" and abortion as equal evils. These are, of course, grossly untrue. Abortion destroys life already conceived.

Again, while anything is possible and therefore some groups or individuals somewhere may be attempting to have all contraception declared illegal, this is not the intention of the "pro-life" movement, whatever may be proposed by individuals within the movement. And it is certainly not an intention approved by the bishops.

Nor is the "pro-life" movement dedicated, as some critics imply, to a world without sex and the legitimate joys it can bring to those who engage in sexual activity responsibly in marriage. The church teaches very explicitly that married couples need not intend to conceive a child to enjoy the sexual relations of marriage, and those of our acquaintance in the "pro-life" movement share this belief. They see the sexual as beautiful, sacred, meaningful, joyous. They would add what some others might deny—that it must also and always be responsible.

Much of the argument of pro-abortionists is based on the assumption that the right to be born is dependent on being wanted. How many unplanned children have been born to parents whose attitudes changed completely to total acceptance and love? How many unwanted children have made enormous contributions to the world as musicians, writers, doctors, entertainers, teachers, parents or in other capacities?

But beyond such questions lies an even more basic one: Who can claim the right to be wanted? Does the Constitution guarantee such a right? Could the Congress legislate that babies are to be wanted by parents or that a husband is to be wanted by his wife, a wife by her husband?

When we speak of equal employment opportunity we don't argue that employers must personally want to hire given individuals. The law requires only that individuals not be refused employment because of a characteristic unrelated to the nature of the job, such as color. Is anyone arguing seriously today that an employee has the right to be wanted? Hardly. But certainly an employee has a right to life!

Is an unborn baby to be denied such a right? Is an unborn

baby to be denied even the opportunity to have someone plead with a mother to let the baby live, wanted or not? Is the unwanted baby to be denied the opportunity given to millions of refugees who have been admitted into the United States?

Finally, we deeply regret any allegations that in arguing for the protection of the unborn or in questioning the positions held by others, any of our bishops have encouraged violence in any form or have invited attacks on property. First, such charges take the spotlight off the basic violence of the deaths of 4,000 unborn every day. Second, in any movement involving millions of people the possibilities of reprehensible activity on the part of a minority— particularly a very small minority—are obvious. Such activity is to be abhorred. It has no place in a true "pro-life" movement. We reject it completely. Violence is not the answer to violence.

Responsibility of Catholic Bishops

I come finally to the questions that have been raised about the involvement of the bishops of the United States in the matters at hand and the allegations of undue intervention in the political process, including even the charge that in a programed and conspiratorial fashion the bishops, or some of us, are trying to destroy the so-called wall between church and state; that the bishops are "perilously close" to threatening the tax-exempt status of their churches or, even more crudely, that the bishops are simply lusting for power.

What is actually going on? The bishops have been saying substantially the same thing about abortion for years. Likewise, for years the bishops have been challenging the state on a broad spectrum of laws and policies, economic, racial, social, military. Most recently the challenge was addressed to issues of war and peace, with the widely publicized formulation of the pastoral letter, "The Challenge of Peace: God's Promise and Our Response." While much was made in that letter of nuclear war, even more was made—and has been little noted—of the causes of war, injustice, oppression, economic and other forms of violence and exploitation and indignities against the human person. It was not by accident that the bishops included in that document on war and peace the following:

"No society can live in peace with itself or with the world without a full awarenss of the worth and dignity of every human person and of the sacredness of all human life. When we accept violence in any form as commonplace, our sensitivities become dulled.... Abortion in particular blunts a sense of the sacredness of human life. In a society where the innocent unborn are killed wantonly, how can we expect people to feel righteous revulsion at the act or threat of killing non-combatants in war?"

What would those who criticize our speaking out during an election campaign have us do? Were those holding or seeking public office expressing explicit support for racism, for drug abuse, for pornography, for rape, for nuclear war, would we be expected to remain silent? Or would we be damned for doing so? Obviously, no one in or seeking office is calling for any of these.

Are we to be silent then on the question of abortion, if we are convinced that it is the taking of human life? Why would we be free to indict racism—indeed be generally applauded for doing so—but damned for indicting abortion? Why would we not be "imposing morality" on others when we oppose rape, but "imposing our morality" on others when we oppose abortion? What a strange democracy it would be that would encourage bishops to cry out their convictions as long as these were popular, but to remain mute when so ordered!

In his speech previously mentioned, Speaker O'Neill referred to the letter on national economic policy being drafted by the Catholic bishops of the United States, predicting that it will have "a dramatic impact on public debate in our country." He cited critics who "say the church should stay out of economic issues...argue that religious concerns have no place in the marketplace...that the only thing that matters in the business world is personal drive and ambition; that the only thing that matters in the affairs of man is force of arms," and he replied, "I believe that we who share Christian values have a responsibility to put those values into action—whether those values are popular or not, whether they are fashionable or not, whether they are high in the polls or not."

As one who argued strongly on Labor Day of this year that the bishops have a long tradition of addressing economic issues and the right and the obligation to do so, I am personally grateful to Speaker O'Neill for his statement applauding efforts to put values into action, whether or not they are popular, fashionable or high in the polls. In the same address he stated that "we must protect those people who cannot protect themselves." I must assume that the Speaker would want to include all people, certainly those least able to protect themselves, the unborn, and would want to welcome the bishops into today's debate on this issue of critical public policy as well.

I am grateful too for a letter from Governor Cuomo to the

president of the National Conference of Catholic Bishops in 1983 in which he praised the bishops' pastoral letter on war and peace. As a member of the committee of bishops that formulated the pastoral letter I am proud of the governor's words:

"It would have been easy to compromise your position so as to offend no one. You chose instead to tend to your duties as shepherds, to teach the moral law as best you can. You can do no more."

"Our church has sometimes been accused of not having spoken out when it might have. Now you, our bishops, show the courage and moral judgment to meet this issue of nuclear holocaust with a collective expression of where the church in America stands."

The pastoral letter on war and peace, of course, made much of a fundamental principle of moral law that we can never, under any circumstances, for any reason, deliberately and intentionally attack the innocent. Since the pastoral explicitly referred both to innocent civilians who must be protected in war and to the innocent unborn who must be protected in their mothers' wombs, I must assume also that the governor would have intended to include our protection of the unborn in his praise of the pastoral letter. I know, of course, that the governor welcomes the bishops into the debate on the subject. He has said so loudly and clearly.

I feel an obligation as a citizen to address issues of critical moral import whenever opportunity is given me to do so within the framework of our political system. I have another obligation, however, that I can delegate to no one. The primary teacher of Catholic doctrine in any diocese is the bishop. As Archbishop of New York I have the responsibility of spelling out for our Catholic people with accuracy and clarity what the church officially teaches about all human life, the life of the unborn and abortion. I have simultaneously the obligation to try to dispel confusion about such teaching wherever it exists, however it has been generated, regardless of who may have generated it. It is easy to dismiss a bishop as narrow, rigid, ultraconservative, unfeeling, lacking in theological training or understanding, anti-feminist or guilty of a thousand other alleged charges for presenting this teaching exactly as it is, rather than some might like it to be.

Church Divided?

But let no one be mistaken about the unanimity of this teaching on the part of the bishops. Those who would seek divisiveness between or among bishops do not understand the principles on which we stand. Those who would seem to suggest, for example, that the "consistent ethic of life" approach so well articulated by my good and valued friend, Cardinal Joseph Bernardin, Archbishop of Chicago, differs in what it has to say about abortion from what some others of us are saying, including myself, simply do not understand Cardinal Bernardin, or me or our mutual unconditional commitment to the life of the unborn and to life at every stage of its existence.

Those who would try to derive comfort from the "consistent ethic of life" approach by interpreting it to suggest that an officeholder's or a candidate's position on abortion does not matter so long as positions on other life issues are acceptable, miss the point of Cardinal Bernardin's argument altogether. Indeed they distort the very essence of his argument.

So what does the church really teach? Catholics the world over recognize the authority of the Second Vatican Council. Its teaching is as clear and unambiguous as anything could possibly be:

"God, the Lord of life, has entrusted to human beings that noble mission of safeguarding life, and they must carry it out in a manner worthy of themselves. Life must be protected with the utmost care from the moment of conception: Abortion and infanticide are abominable crimes."

Pope Paul VI left no doubt. In his words:

"To attack human life under any pretext whatsoever and under whatever form... is to repudiate one of the essential values of our civilization. In the very depths of our consciences—as each one of us experiences—we affirm as an incontestable sacred principle respect for every form of human life, life that is awakening, life that asks only to develop, life that is drawing to a close, life especially that is weak, unprovided for, defenseless, at the mercy of others."

The bishops of the United States have been equally clear and unequivocal. In 1970 they stated:

"Our defense of human life is rooted in the biblical prohibition, 'Thou shall not kill'.... The life of the unborn child is a human life. The destruction of any human life is not a private matter, but the concern of every responsible citizen."

Pope John Paul II has stated forcefully:

"It is the task of the church to reaffirm that abortion is death; it is the killing of an innocent creature. Consequently, the church considers all legislation in favor of abortion as a very serious offense against primary human rights and the divine commandment, 'You shall not kill.'"

The declaration on abortion issued by the Vatican's Sacred Congregation of the Faith and promulgated by Pope Paul VI in 1974, declared:

"It must be clearly understood that whatever may be laid down by civil law in this matter (of abortion), one can never obey a law which is in itself immoral and such is the case of a law which would admit in principle the illicity of abortion. Nor can one take part in a propaganda campaign in favor of such a law or vote for it. Moreover, one may not collaborate in its application."

So speaks the church. What do I mean here by "the church"? I mean what the average individual means when he or she asks, "What does the Catholic Church teach?" Such a question is not intended to ask what occasional theologians may speculate, or what any group of individuals who form organizations has to say or what one finds in letters to the editor or on Op-Ed pages. Indeed it is sometimes these speculations and accusations and claims that lead people to ask, "What does the Catholic Church really teach?"

It has ever been the belief of the church and is no less so today that we must turn to the bishops, the teachers of the church, when we seek to discern the truths of our faith. The Second Vatican Council stated it simply and clearly, "By virtue of the Holy Spirit who has been given to them, bishops have been constituted true and authentic teachers of the faith."

Church teaching on abortion is quite clear, regardless of allegations that it has changed through the years. Speculations on such questions as when the soul enters the body have changed as scientific knowledge has accrued. Church penalties for abortions have changed. The teaching about the grave immorality of abortion itself has never changed.

We hear a great deal about opinion polls and are frequently told that Catholics seem to approve of abortion in about the same percentages that other people do. There are several things wrong with such statements. Polling results depend in part on the knowledge of the persons polled; ignorance concerning the real nature of abortion and many of the so-called facts surrounding abortion is appalling. Unfortunately, some ignorance and confusion even seem to be provoked.

The main issue, however, is that polling results depend primarily on the way the questions are asked. Who would be prepared to ask, for example, "Under what circumstances would you feel justified in putting your unborn baby to death?" The fact is, that in poll after poll, only 25 percent of those polled support abortion on demand. Much abortion advertising would have us believe that an overwhelming majority would favor it. Even were such the case, however, Catholic teaching on morality is simply not determined on the basis of polls.

I recognize the dilemma confronted by some Catholics in political life. I cannot resolve that dilemma for them. As I see it, their disagreement, if they do disagree, is not simply with me; it is with the teaching of the Catholic Church.

Conclusion

I beg leave to add one further plea—that all women and men of good will try to open their minds and hearts to at least the possibility that we are unjustifiably taking 4,000 innocent human lives each day, regardless of whatever convictions they may hold to the contrary. I plead for the understanding that it is not the national effort to protect the unborn that is divisive; it is the destruction of the unborn that is divisive. And I plead for honest and open dialogue toward the goal of saving human lives.

As Father Hesburgh of Notre Dame has observed, tragically, in essence we may never again come to an agreement in our land that all abortion should be declared illegal, and some may passionately believe that exception should be made in cases of rape, of incest or truly grave threat to the actual physical survival of the mother. Whatever we may believe about such exceptions, however, we know that they constitute a fraction of the abortions taking place, so that at the very least we can come to grips with what is the real and the frightening issue of the day: abortion on demand.

And so I come to the end of this long address—this personal pilgrimage, if you will—fearing I have said so little of what must yet be said and that I have said virtually nothing of what in the final analysis alone makes everything understandable—the indispensable power of love. Before leaving a recent visit to Flower Hospital, now the Terence Cardinal Cooke Health Care Center, I told the director of the hospital that I really need not give a speech at all. I need but ask the world to visit that hospital, to see not merely what doctors and nurses and staff are doing for their helpless patients, but what the helpless patients are doing for the doctors, the nurses and the staff.

The love those helpless ones generate in those who serve as their arms and legs and eyes and ears and tongues is more beautiful to behold than the most magnificent work of art in our own Metropolitan Museum. Except that such love is not a museum piece. It is vibrantly alive, pulsating through the corridors of that hospital and through the very being of those medical professionals and staff, women and men, literally giving their own lives every day that the least of God's little ones may not only live, but that in the depths of their beings, far removed from our sight and unfathomable by the most sophisticated techniques that science can devise, they, the helpless, may in turn love and teach us to love, who need so desperately to learn how.

And thus it can happen through the creative power of God's own mysterious love for each one of us, of whatever color, or creed, or background, or sex or personal beliefs—thus the miracle can happen in the strange design of that God who writes straight with crooked lines—that every child in this world, born or unborn, wanted or unwanted, with or without limbs or hearing or sight, nurtured lovingly or horrifyingly battered, abused and neglected, becomes not only what Mother Teresa of Calcutta calls something beautiful for God, but someone extraordinarily beautiful for every one of us, their brothers and sisters in the Lord.

184. Sidney Callahan. The Pastoral on Women: What Should the Bishops Say? May 18, 1985.

"In truth it must still be regretted that fundamental personal rights are not yet being universally honored. Such is the case of a woman who is denied the right and freedom to choose a husband, to embrace a state of life, or to acquire an education or cultural benefits equal to those recognized for men." [Walter M. Abbott, S.J. and Joseph Gallagher (Eds.), *The Documents of Vatican II.* New York: America Press. 1966. p. 228]. Since that conciliar statement of 1965 the issue of women's role in the Church has become ever more urgent and insistent, an issue as it is frequently said, that 'will not go away.' To state that the contribution of American Catholic women—both religious and lay—has been incalculable is obvious. Yet that contribution was not until very recently recognized as calling for an equal sharing in policy-making. The problem was highlighted for religious women by Sister Theresa Kane, R.S.M., President of the Leadership Conference of Women Religious, when on October 7, 1979, she addressed Pope John Paul II at the National Shrine of the Immaculate Conception in Washington. The National Conference of Catholic Bishops appointed a committee of its members to draw up a pastoral letter on this subject. Whether or not the pastoral will ultimately be agreed upon and published, remains to be seen. Meanwhile the need for discussion of the issue continues. The balanced judgment of a professional psychologist, wife, and mother will lend assistance toward that end regardless of the ultimate disposition of the proposed pastoral letter. Source: *America,* 152 (May 18, 1985), 404-406.

Can any all-male group have anything to say to women? How dare men speak when they belong to a body that has systematically excluded women from membership and denied them full participation in decision making? When the American bishops address a democratic society on the subject of women, they carry the heavy burden of their own suspect practice. Who will listen if the trumpet sounds from a rotting platform shakily supported on termite-ridden pillars?

Triumphant trumpet calls are definitely unsuitable in this case. Better there should be an apologetic opening that voices sincere regret that, once again, women and women's issues are being addressed by a body of men who have excluded women. However, as we can all see, in order for change to come about and more equal structures to be instituted in the future, those presently in power must act. Leaders, designated or elected, male or female, have to lead or be held irresponsible. If the bishops recognize their problematic position and are open to ongoing dialogue and reform, they can make a real contribution with a strong pastoral letter.

So what should they say after they say they are sorry? When discussing women the bishops face an array of issues, some of which are fairly simple and some of which are monstrously difficult. The easy matters to address have to do with Christianity's basic justice agenda as it is focused upon the needs of women. Here almost everyone agrees with the ideals, but getting anything actually done is another kettle of conundrums. Unfortunately, women are still being discriminated against, especially as society's commitment to affirmative action withers. Women need equal opportunity, equal pay for equal work, protection from sexual harassment on the job and from unfair insurance, health and Social Security provisions. Old women need care, and divorced, displaced homemakers need job training. Women of all ages need elementary protection from rape, wife-beating, sexual abuse and exploitation.

Beyond these familiar litanies of feminine needs is the desperate and growing injustice found in the feminization of poverty. Women are getting poorer, and more single women are raising children in increasingly stressful and deprived circumstances. The latest research on the negative effects of divorce upon children is ominous. When fewer adults socialize children, the children suffer from lowered I.Q. scores and lessened levels of moral development. Good preschool programs, however, have been shown to make a long-term difference in even the most deprived child's life. Recognizing this, the church could perhaps best help women and children at the same time, by concentrating on providing supportive networks and programs for single parents and preschool children. What the church did for the immigrants, it can do for our newly vulnerable women and preschool children.

In fact, all parental and family support programs will help relieve the stress working women experience. The pro-life stance of the church has to be buttressed with women-centered help, from sex education, to problem pregnancy alternatives, to health care and finally to child-care allowances. The economic pressure upon women with dependents is fierce, even when homelessness and food are not a problem. The point can be quickly made when it becomes clear that in the United States, women are more likely to be poor, more likely to be physically vulnerable, more likely to be solely responsible for dependents and thus more in need of help. The rising rates of female alcohol and drug abuse, anorexia and bulimia, abortion, crime and suicide, reflect the increasing strains and conflicts of women's lives.

Whatever happened to women's liberation? With questions of women's sexual roles, sexual identity, sexual functioning and reproduction, the bishops enter the mine fields and confront the hard cases. The sexual arena is an unmapped new terrain, with no sure pathways marked out by past generations. Never has a society been so medically and technologically advanced, while holding a democratic basically Christian commitment to the goodness of sexuality and women's social equality. The convergence of fertility control, the sexual revolution, the changing roles of women and the instability of marriage have produced a turbulent scene. In the midst of all this struggle there is no one feminine party line; women are disagreeing with women both within and outside the churches.

Women fought for and against the E.R.A. Women make up the ranks of activists working for the pro-choice and pro-life movements. Phyllis Schlafly and her troops prove that politically women can be hawks as well as peace activists. Even within the feminist movement, there are ideological conflicts between women; in the yet more specialized world of feminist theology, different feminist theologians clash with claims and counterclaims regarding Christianity or Judaism.

I think these controversies among women are a sign of our progress. At last we have conflicts of women, by women, for women. No longer can all women be lumped together in some undifferentiated mass that supposedly thinks and feels alike because of common sexual characteristics. To me, a "minority" most suffers from the group stereotype, mindlessly applied to all; with more social power, individual identities and differentiated agendas are recognized as the natural manifestations of unique selves. Thus quarrels among women reflect spirited independence and maturity.

Amid these controversies, I would of course like to have the Catholic bishops support the feminist synthesis that seems best to me. Those of us who keep writing do so in hopes of influencing the course of both the church and the women's movement. From where I stand I see all sorts of mistaken turnings both to the right and left of "the Catholic center," which has to hold when things fall apart.

One alarming mistake I find mostly among young women. I have been attacked by bright young women on avant-garde liberal college campuses who scorn the feminist movement and reject its ideals as passé. They never experienced the bad old days and so have little sense of the valiant struggles of the women who went before them. In low moments I sometimes think that we are in for another full-scale backlash, so that in 50 years women will be starting all over at square one. Maybe the bishops can help stave off that kind of disaster. Often the church reminds me of a turtle that keeps inching along in the right direction and eventually ends up ahead of the hares who have come and gone already.

Two other misguided manifestations of the women's movement may have helped turn off the young. Occasionally, the media feature rapier-wielding, swashbuckling feminists who have made it in some competitive male world by outtoughing all and sundry on their upward climb. These women take on the worst values of the male world as they find it and play to win with innovative aggressive power plays. Like some of the conniving queens of history, they prove that a Machiavellian is a Machiavellian, whatever the sex. Power can corrupt women, just as their more usual condition of powerlessness may deform them.

Another group of feminists is also on the wrong track, I am afraid. There exist some hyperfeminists who, like all true believers, seem to have lost their mother wit while distorting the mother tongue. These feminist groups maintain that women have special positive gifts and insights inherent in their sexual identity, just as males possess negative traits. Since women think and feel differently, developing the feminine will bring about world revolution, if not the millennium. Religion, ethics, science, history, medicine, family life—you name it—will be transformed when the power of woman-spirit is liberated in the land. Blowing with this wind, many of these feminists have spun right out of traditional historical religions and created forms of goddess worship and nature cults. A few of these groups are also radical separatists who reject all males and view partiarchy as the incarnation of all evil. They defend the faith by asserting that women are naturally nurturing, loving and lifegiving, while males are inherently destructive, oppressive and deadly.

Another disturbing element in the extremist feminist cults is the glorification of the unconscious at the expense of reason and conscious will. Women's intuitive nature is relied upon to make her moral judgments all but infallible, especially when it comes to abortion. Since men have oppressed women and "male" civilization has exalted reason, now women must trust their feelings and concentrate on their own needs. Free sexual expression either in heterosexual or lesbian forms is another necessity for feminine fulfillment and growth. Patriarchy's repressive control of feminine sexuality has to be overthrown.

In contrast to these true believers, I see women, and men, to be liberated by recognizing the relatively minor importance of sexual identity and sexual function. Men and women are at their best androgynous and differ very little. Essentially, the human brain is the primary sexual organ, and our beliefs, reasoned meanings and cultural conditioning shape most human behavior. The most essential aspects of the self may be beyond sexual identity and be like Yahweh, "I am who I am." Certainly, consciousness and reason are always more to be trusted than misty unproven unconscious forces, so subject to the latest psycholocical scheme, whether of the woolly Jungian variety, or whatever. I can see only that the problem with Western civilization has been that it has been too irrational and out of touch with reason. As for women, I know in every Bryn Mawr bluestocking bone in my body that no one does better by women than those who teach women how to think well.

Bishops need to think well too, of course. Perhaps this time out they will not be able to endorse women's ordination, revise the contraception and sterilization rulings, revoke mandatory celibacy or strike for democratic rights within the church. But they can further justice and avoid fashionable errors by asserting that "in

Christ there is neither male nor female." Sex is a most happy accident of nature, to be respected but not revered. Anatomy is not destiny, and Love and Truth are one.

185. Economic Justice for All. Pastoral Letter on Catholic Social Teaching and the United States Economy, November 18, 1986.

"In so far as you did this to one of the least of these brothers of mine, you did it to me." (*Matthew,* 25:40). With this mandate of Christ in mind the Church has ever concerned herself with the needs of the poor and oppressed. Through the centuries that concern has taken a variety of approaches, and though at times neglected it has never been entirely forgotten. For most of the 200 years since Catholicism was organized in 1790 in the United States, Catholics followed a paternalistic approach with institutions founded, most frequently by religious communities of men and women, for the care of the needy. For example, one sees that in the daughters of Saint Elizabeth Seton answering the call from Philadelphia to take charge of Saint Joseph's Orphanage in 1814. Thus social consciousness was implemented in the form of numerous institutions of charity. As industrialization played an increasingly important role in the lives of the working class social, theory supplemented social action in such statements as that of Cardinal Gibbons in defense of the Knights of Labor in 1887. Gradually Catholic social teaching evolved and produced such notable expressions as that of the Bishops' Program of Social Reconstruction of 1919. It is in that tradition that the *ad hoc* committee of Rembert G. Weakland, O.S.B., Archbishop of Milwaukee, and his fellow bishops launched one of the most exhaustive consultations on the state of the American economy and its relation to the moral and ethical teaching of the Church. As will be seen in this final draft, the paternalistic approach has given way to an emphasis on the means by which those in need may be heard and be made to share in working out remedies for the inequities in the socio-economic order.

Source: Washington: United States Catholic Conference, Inc. 1986.

CONTENTS

A Pastoral Message

ECONOMIC JUSTICE FOR ALL

Brothers and Sisters in Christ:

1.   We are believers called to follow Our Lord Jesus Christ and proclaim his Gospel in the midst of a complex and powerful economy. This reality poses both opportunities and responsibilities for Catholics in the United States. Our faith calls us to measure this economy, not only by what it produces, but also by how it touches human life and whether it protects or undermines the dignity of the human person. Economic decisions have human consequences and moral content; they help or hurt people, strengthen or weaken family life, advance or diminish the quality of justice in our land.

2.   This is why we have written *Economic Justice for All: A Pastoral Letter on Catholic Social Teaching and the U.S. Economy*. This letter is a personal invitation to Catholics to use the resources of our faith, the strength of our economy, and the opportunities of our democracy to shape a society that better protects the dignity and basic rights of our sisters and brothers, both in this land and around the world.

3.   The pastoral letter has been a work of careful inquiry, wide consultation, and prayerful discernment. The letter has been greatly enriched by this

979

process of listening and refinement. We offer this introductory pastoral message to Catholics in the United States seeking to live their faith in the marketplace—in homes, offices, factories, and schools; on farms and ranches; in boardrooms and union halls; in service agencies and legislative chambers. We seek to explain why we wrote the pastoral letter, to introduce its major themes, and to share our hopes for the dialogue and action it might generate.

Why We Write

4.   We write to share our teaching, to raise questions, to challenge one another to live our faith in the world. We write as heirs of the biblical prophets who summon us "to do the right, and to love goodness, and to walk humbly with your God" (Mi 6:8). We write as followers of Jesus who told us in the Sermon on the Mount: "Blessed are the poor in spirit. . . . Blessed are the meek. . . . Blessed are they who hunger and thirst for righteousness. . . . You are the salt of the earth. . . . You are the light of the world" (Mt 5:1-6,13-14). These words challenge us not only as believers but also as consumers, citizens, workers, and owners. In the parable of the Last Judgment, Jesus said, "For I was hungry and you gave me food, I was thirsty and you gave me drink. . . . As often as you did it for one of my least brothers, you did it for me" (Mt 25:35-40). The challenge for us is to discover in our own place and time what it means to be "poor in spirit" and "the salt of the earth" and what it means to serve "the least among us" and to "hunger and thirst for righteousness."

5.   Followers of Christ must avoid a tragic separation between faith and everyday life. They can neither shirk their earthly duties nor, as the Second Vatican

Council declared, "immerse [them]selves in earthly activities as if these latter were utterly foreign to religion, and religion were nothing more than the fulfillment of acts of worship and the observance of a few moral obligations" (*Pastoral Constitution on the Church in the Modern World*, no. 43).

6.   Economic life raises important social and moral questions for each of us and for society as a whole. Like family life, economic life is one of the chief areas where we live out our faith, love our neighbor, confront temptation, fulfill God's creative design, and achieve our holiness. Our economic activity in factory, field, office, or shop feeds our families—or feeds our anxieties. It exercises our talents—or wastes them. It raises our hopes—or crushes them. It brings us into cooperation with others—or sets us at odds. The Second Vatican Council instructs us "to preach the message of Christ in such a way that the light of the Gospel will shine on all activities of the faithful" (*Pastoral Constitution*, no. 43). In this case, we are trying to look at economic life through the eyes of faith, applying traditional church teaching to the U.S. economy.

7.   In our letter, we write as pastors, not public officials. We speak as moral teachers, not economic technicians. We seek not to make some political or ideological point but to lift up the human and ethical dimensions of economic life, aspects too often neglected in public discussion. We bring to this task a dual heritage of Catholic social teaching and traditional American values.

8.   As *Catholics*, we are heirs of a long tradition of thought and action on the moral dimensions of economic activity. The life and words of Jesus and the teaching of his Church call us to serve those in need and to work actively for social and economic justice. As a community of believers, we know that our faith is tested by the quality of justice among us, that we can best measure our life together by how the poor

and the vulnerable are treated. This is not a new concern for us. It is as old as the Hebrew prophets, as compelling as the Sermon on the Mount, and as current as the powerful voice of Pope John Paul II defending the dignity of the human person.

9.   As *Americans*, we are grateful for the gift of freedom and committed to the dream of "liberty and justice for all." This nation, blessed with extraordinary resources, has provided an unprecedented standard of living for millions of people. We are proud of the strength, productivity, and creativity of our economy, but we also remember those who have been left behind in our progress. We believe that we honor our history best by working for the day when all our sisters and brothers share adequately in the American dream.

10.   As bishops, in proclaiming the Gospel for these times we also manage institutions, balance budgets, meet payrolls. In this we see the human face of our economy. We feel the hurts and hopes of our people. We feel the pain of our sisters and brothers who are poor, unemployed, homeless, living on the edge. The poor and vulnerable are on our doorsteps, in our parishes, in our service agencies, and in our shelters. We see too much hunger and injustice, too much suffering and despair, both in our own country and around the world.

11.   As pastors, we also see the decency, generosity, and vulnerability of our people. We see the struggles of ordinary families to make ends meet and to provide a better future for their children. We know the desire of managers, professionals, and business people to shape what they do by what they believe. It is the faith, good will, and generosity of our people that gives us hope as we write this letter.

Principal Themes of the Pastoral Letter

12.   The pastoral letter is not a blueprint for the American economy. It does not embrace any particular theory of how the economy works, nor does it attempt to resolve the disputes between different schools of economic thought. Instead, our letter turns to Scripture and to the social teachings of the Church. There, we discover what our economic life must serve, what standards it must meet. Let us examine some of these basic moral principles.

13.   *Every economic decision and institution must be judged in light of whether it protects or undermines the dignity of the human person.* The pastoral letter begins with the human person. We believe the person is sacred—the clearest reflection of God among us. Human dignity comes from God, not from nationality, race, sex, economic status, or any human accomplishment. We judge any economic system by what it does *for* and *to* people and by how it permits all to *participate* in it. The economy should serve people, not the other way around.

14.   *Human dignity can be realized and protected only in community.* In our teaching, the human person is not only sacred but also social. How we organize our society—in economics and politics, in law and policy—directly affects human dignity and the capacity of individuals to grow in community. The obligation to "love our neighbor" has an individual dimension, but it also requires a broader social commitment to the common good. We have many partial ways to measure and debate the health of our economy: Gross National Product, per capita income, stock market prices, and so forth. The Christian vision of economic life looks beyond them all and asks, Does economic

life enhance or threaten our life together as a community?

15.   *All people have a right to participate in the economic life of society.* Basic justice demands that people be assured a minimum level of participation in the economy. It is wrong for a person or group to be excluded unfairly or to be unable to participate or contribute to the economy. For example, people who are both able and willing, but cannot get a job are deprived of the participation that is so vital to human development. For, it is through employment that most individuals and families meet their material needs, exercise their talents, and have an opportunity to contribute to the larger community. Such participation has a special significance in our tradition because we believe that it is a means by which we join in carrying forward God's creative activity.

16.   *All members of society have a special obligation to the poor and vulnerable.* From the Scriptures and church teaching, we learn that the justice of a society is tested by the treatment of the poor. The justice that was the sign of God's covenant with Israel was measured by how the poor and unprotected—the widow, the orphan, and the stranger—were treated. The kingdom that Jesus proclaimed in his word and ministry excludes no one. Throughout Israel's history and in early Christianity, the poor are agents of God's transforming power. "The Spirit of the Lord is upon me, therefore he has anointed me. He has sent me to bring glad tidings to the poor"(Lk 4:18). This was Jesus' first public utterance. Jesus takes the side of those most in need. In the Last Judgment, so dramatically described in St. Matthew's Gospel, we are told that we will be judged according to how we respond to the hungry, the thirsty, the naked, the stranger. As followers of Christ, we are challenged to make a fundamental "option for the poor"—to speak for the voiceless, to defend the defenseless, to assess life

styles, policies, and social institutions in terms of their impact on the poor. This "option for the poor" does not mean pitting one group against another, but rather, strengthening the whole community by assisting those who are most vulnerable. As Christians, we are called to respond to the needs of *all* our brothers and sisters, but those with the greatest needs require the greatest response.

17.   *Human rights are the minimum conditions for life in community.* In Catholic teaching, human rights include not only civil and political rights but also economic rights. As Pope John XXIII declared, "all people have a right to life, food, clothing, shelter, rest, medical care, education, and employment." This means that when people are without a chance to earn a living, and must go hungry and homeless, they are being denied basic rights. Society must ensure that these rights are protected. In this way, we will ensure that the minimum conditions of economic justice are met for all our sisters and brothers.

18.   *Society as a whole, acting through public and private institutions, has the moral responsibility to enhance human dignity and protect human rights.* In addition to the clear responsibility of private institutions, government has an essential responsibility in this area. This does not mean that government has the primary or exclusive role, but it does have a positive moral responsibility in safeguarding human rights and ensuring that the minimum conditions of human dignity are met for all. In a democracy, government is a means by which we can act together to protect what is important to us and to promote our common values.

19.   These six moral principles are not the only ones presented in the pastoral letter, but they give an overview of the moral vision that we are trying to share. This vision of economic life cannot exist in a vacuum; it must be translated into concrete measures. Our pastoral letter spells out some specific applications of

Catholic moral principles. We call for a new national commitment to full employment. We say it is a social and moral scandal that one of every seven Americans is poor, and we call for concerted efforts to eradicate poverty. The fulfillment of the basic needs of the poor is of the highest priority. We urge that all economic policies be evaluated in light of their impact on the life and stability of the family. We support measures to halt the loss of family farms and to resist the growing concentration in the ownership of agricultural resources. We specify ways in which the United States can do far more to relieve the plight of poor nations and assist in their development. We also reaffirm church teaching on the rights of workers, collective bargaining, private property, subsidiarity, and equal opportunity.

20.   We believe that the recommendations in our letter are reasonable and balanced. In analyzing the economy, we reject ideological extremes and start from the fact that ours is a "mixed" economy, the product of a long history of reform and adjustment. We know that some of our specific recommendations are controversial. As bishops, we do not claim to make these prudential judgments with the same kind of authority that marks our declarations of principle. But, we feel obliged to teach by example how Christians can undertake concrete analysis and make specific judgments on economic issues. The Church's teachings cannot be left at the level of appealing generalities.

21.   In the pastoral letter, we suggest that the time has come for a "New American Experiment"—to implement economic rights, to broaden the sharing of economic power, and to make economic decisions more accountable to the common good. This experiment can create new structures of economic partnership and participation within firms at the regional level, for the whole nation, and across borders.

22.   Of course, there are many aspects of the economy the letter does not touch, and there are basic questions it leaves to further exploration. There are also many specific points on which men and women of good will may disagree. We look for a fruitful exchange among differing viewpoints. We pray only that all will take to heart the urgency of our concerns; that together we will test our views by the Gospel and the Church's teaching; and that we will listen to other voices in a spirit of mutual respect and open dialogue.

A Call to Conversion and Action

23.   We should not be surprised if we find Catholic social teaching to be demanding. The Gospel is demanding. We are always in need of conversion, of a change of heart. We are richly blessed, and as St. Paul assures us, we are destined for glory. Yet, it is also true that we are sinners; that we are not always wise or loving or just; that, for all our amazing possibilities, we are incompletely born, wary of life, and hemmed in by fears and empty routines. We are unable to entrust ourselves fully to the living God, and so we seek substitute forms of security in material things, in power, in indifference, in popularity, in pleasure. The Scriptures warn us that these things can become forms of idolatry. We know that, at times, in order to remain truly a community of Jesus' disciples, we will have to say "no" to certain aspects in our culture, to certain trends and ways of acting that are opposed to a life of faith, love, and justice. Changes in our hearts lead naturally to a desire to change how we act. With what care, human kindness, and justice do I conduct myself at work? How will my economic decisions to buy, sell, invest, divest, hire, or fire serve human dignity and the common good? In what career can I

best exercise my talents so as to fill the world with the Spirit of Christ? How do my economic choices contribute to the strength of my family and community, to the values of my children, to a sensitivity to those in need? In this consumer society, how can I develop a healthy detachment from things and avoid the temptation to assess who I am by what I have? How do I strike a balance between labor and leisure that enlarges my capacity for friendships, for family life, for community? What government policies should I support to attain the well-being of all, especially the poor and vulnerable?

24.   The answers to such questions are not always clear—or easy to live out. But, conversion is a lifelong process. And, it is not undertaken alone. It occurs with the support of the whole believing community, through baptism, common prayer, and our daily efforts, large and small, on behalf of justice. As a Church, we must be people after God's own heart, bonded by the Spirit, sustaining one another in love, setting our hearts on God's kingdom, committing ourselves to solidarity with those who suffer, working for peace and justice, acting as a sign of Christ's love and justice in the world. The Church cannot redeem the world from the deadening effects of sin and injustice unless it is working to remove sin and injustice in its own life and institutions. All of us must help the Church to practice in its own life what it preaches to others about economic justice and cooperation.

25.   The challenge of this pastoral letter is not merely to think differently, but also to act differently. A renewal of economic life depends on the conscious choices and commitments of individual believers who practice their faith in the world. The road to holiness for most of us lies in our secular vocations. We need a spirituality that calls forth and supports lay initiative and witness not just in our churches but also in business, in the labor movement, in the professions, in

education, and in public life. Our faith is not just a weekend obligation, a mystery to be celebrated around the altar on Sunday. It is a pervasive reality to be practiced every day in homes, offices, factories, schools, and businesses across our land. We cannot separate what we believe from how we act in the marketplace and the broader community, for this is where we make our primary contribution to the pursuit of economic justice.

26. We ask each of you to read the pastoral letter, to study it, to pray about it, and match it with your own experience. We ask you to join with us in service to those in need. Let us reach out personally to the hungry and the homeless, to the poor and the powerless, and to the troubled and the vulnerable. In serving them, we serve Christ. Our service efforts cannot substitute for just and compassionate public policies, but they can help us practice what we preach about human life and human dignity.

27. The pursuit of economic justice takes believers into the public arena, testing the policies of government by the principles of our teaching. We ask you to become more informed and active citizens, using your voices and votes to speak for the voiceless, to defend the poor and the vulnerable and to advance the common good. We are called to shape a constituency of conscience, measuring every policy by how it touches the least, the lost, and the left-out among us. This letter calls us to conversion and common action, to new forms of stewardship, service, and citizenship.

28. The completion of a letter such as this is but the beginning of a long process of education, discussion, and action. By faith and baptism, we are fashioned into new creatures, filled with the Holy Spirit and with a love that compels us to seek out a new profound relationship with God, with the human family, and with all created things. Jesus has entered our

history as God's anointed son who announces the coming of God's kingdom, a kingdom of justice and peace and freedom. And, what Jesus proclaims, he embodies in his actions. His ministry reveals that the reign of God is something more powerful than evil, injustice, and the hardness of hearts. Through his crucifixion and resurrection, he reveals that God's love is ultimately victorious over all suffering, all horror, all meaninglessness, and even over the mystery of death. Thus, we proclaim words of hope and assurance to all who suffer and are in need.

29.   We believe that the Christian view of life, including economic life, can transform the lives of individuals, families, schools, and our whole culture. We believe that with your prayers, reflection, service, and action, our economy can be shaped so that human dignity prospers and the human person is served. This is the unfinished work of our nation. This is the challenge of our faith.

Chapter I

THE CHURCH AND THE FUTURE
OF THE U.S. ECONOMY

1. Every perspective on economic life that is human, moral, and Christian must be shaped by three questions: What does the economy do *for* people? What does it do *to* people? And how do people *participate* in it? The economy is a human reality: men and women working together to develop and care for the whole of God's creation. All this work must serve the material and spiritual well-being of people. It influences what people hope for themselves and their loved ones. It affects the way they act together in society. It influences their very faith in God.[1]

2. The Second Vatican Council declared that "the joys and hopes, the griefs and anxieties of the people of this age, especially those who are poor or in any way afflicted, these too are the joys and hopes, the griefs and anxieties of the followers of Christ."[2] There are many signs of hope in U.S. economic life today:

---

[1] Vatican Council II, *The Pastoral Constitution on the Church in the Modern World*, 33. [Note: This pastoral letter frequently refers to documents of the Second Vatican Council, papal encyclicals, and other official teachings of the Roman Catholic Church. Most of these texts have been published by the United States Catholic Conference Office of Publishing and Promotion Services; many are available in collections, though no single collection is comprehensive. See selected bibliography.]

[2] *Pastoral Constitution*, 1.

- Many fathers and mothers skillfully balance the arduous responsibilities of work and family life. There are parents who pursue a purposeful and modest way of life and by their example encourage their children to follow a similar path. A large number of women and men, drawing on their religious tradition, recognize the challenging vocation of family life and child rearing in a culture that emphasizes material display and self-gratification.
- Conscientious business people seek new and more equitable ways to organize resources and the workplace. They face hard choices over expanding or retrenching, shifting investments, hiring or firing.
- Young people choosing their life's work ask whether success and security are compatible with service to others.
- Workers whose labor may be toilsome or repetitive try daily to ennoble their work with a spirit of solidarity and friendship.
- New immigrants brave dislocations while hoping for the opportunities realized by the millions who came before them.

3. These signs of hope are not the whole story. There have been failures—some of them massive and ugly:

- Poor and homeless people sleep in community shelters and in our church basements; the hungry line up in soup lines.
- Unemployment gnaws at the self-respect of both middle-aged persons who have lost jobs and the young who cannot find them.
- Hardworking men and women wonder if the system of enterprise that helped them yesterday might destroy their jobs and their communities tomorrow.

- Families confront major new challenges: dwindling social supports for family stability; economic pressures that force both parents of young children to work outside the home; a driven pace of life among the successful that can sap love and commitment; lack of hope among those who have less or nothing at all. Very different kinds of families bear different burdens of our economic system.
- Farmers face the loss of their land and way of life; young people find it difficult to choose farming as a vocation; farming communities are threatened; migrant farmworkers break their backs in serf-like conditions for disgracefully low wages.

4.   *And beyond our own shores, the reality of 800 million people living in absolute poverty and 450 million malnourished or facing starvation casts an ominous shadow over all these hopes and problems at home.*

5.   Anyone who sees all this will understand our concern as pastors and bishops. People shape the economy and in turn are shaped by it. Economic arrangements can be sources of fulfillment, of hope, of community—or of frustration, isolation, and even despair. They teach virtues—or vices—and day by day help mold our characters. They affect the quality of people's lives; at the extreme even determining whether people live or die. Serious economic choices go beyond purely technical issues to fundamental questions of value and human purpose.[3] We believe that in facing these questions the Christian religious and moral tradition can make an important contribution.

---

[3] See ibid., 10, 42, 43; Congregation for the Doctrine of the Faith, *Instruction on Christian Freedom and Liberation*, (Washington, D.C.: USCC Office of Publishing and Promotion Services, 1986), 34-36.

A. The U.S. Economy Today: Memory and Hope

6. The United States is among the most economically powerful nations on earth. In its short history the U.S. economy has grown to provide an unprecedented standard of living for most of its people. The nation has created productive work for millions of immigrants and enabled them to broaden their freedoms, improve their families' quality of life, and contribute to the building of a great nation. Those who came to this country from other lands often understood their new lives in the light of biblical faith. They thought of themselves as entering a promised land of political freedom and economic opportunity. The United States *is* a land of vast natural resources and fertile soil. It *has* encouraged citizens to undertake bold ventures. Through hard work, self-sacrifice, and cooperation, families have flourished; towns, cities, and a powerful nation have been created.

7. But we should recall this history with sober humility. The American experiment in social, political, and economic life has involved serious conflict and suffering. Our nation was born in the face of injustice to native Americans, and its independence was paid for with the blood of revolution. Slavery stained the commercial life of the land through its first two hundred and fifty years and was ended only by a violent civil war. The establishment of women's suffrage, the protection of industrial workers, the elimination of child labor, the response to the Great Depression of the 1930s, and the civil rights movement of the 1960s all involved a sustained struggle to transform the political and economic institutions of the nation.

8. The U.S. value system emphasizes economic freedom. It also recognizes that the market is limited

by fundamental human rights. Some things are never to be bought or sold.[4] This conviction has prompted positive steps to modify the operation of the market when it harms vulnerable members of society. Labor unions help workers resist exploitation. Through their government, the people of the United States have provided support for education, access to food, unemployment compensation, security in old age, and protection of the environment. The market system contributes to the success of the U. S. economy, but so do many efforts to forge economic institutions and public policies that enable *all* to share in the riches of the nation. The country's economy has been built through a creative struggle; entrepreneurs, business people, workers, unions, consumers, and government have all played essential roles.

9.   The task of the United States today is as demanding as that faced by our forebears. Abraham Lincoln's words at Gettysburg are a reminder that complacency today would be a betrayal of our nation's history: "It is for us, the living, rather to be dedicated here to the unfinished work . . . they have thus far nobly advanced."[5] There is unfinished business in the American experiment in freedom and justice for all.

---

[4] See Pope John Paul II, *On Human Work* (1981), 14; and Pope Paul VI, *Octogesima Adveniens* (1971), 35. See also Arthur Okun, *Equality and Efficiency: The Big Tradeoff* (Washington, D.C.: The Brookings Institution, 1975), ch. 1; Michael Walzer, *Spheres of Justice: A Defense of Pluralism and Equality* (New York: Basic Books, 1983), ch. 4; Jon P. Gunnemann, "Capitalism and Commutative Justice," paper presented at the 1985 meeting of the Society of Christian Ethics.

[5] Abraham Lincoln, Address at Dedication of National Cemetery at Gettysburg, November 19, 1863.

B. Urgent Problems of Today

10.   The preeminent role of the United States in an increasingly interdependent global economy is a central sign of our times.[6] The United States is still the world's economic giant. Decisions made here have immediate effects in other countries; decisions made abroad have immediate consequences for steelworkers in Pittsburgh, oil company employees in Houston, and farmers in Iowa. U.S. economic growth is vitally dependent on resources from other countries and on their purchases of our goods and services. Many jobs in U.S. industry and agriculture depend on our ability to export manufactured goods and food.

11.   In some industries the mobility of capital and technology makes wages the main variable in the cost of production. Overseas competitors with the same technology but with wage rates as low as one-tenth of ours put enormous pressure on U.S. firms to cut wages, relocate abroad, or close. U.S. workers and their communities should not be expected to bear these burdens alone.

12.   All people on this globe share a common ecological environment that is under increasing pressure. Depletion of soil, water, and other natural resources endangers the future. Pollution of air and water threatens the delicate balance of the biosphere on which future generations will depend.[7] The resources of the earth have been created by God for the benefit of all, and we who are alive today hold them in trust. This is a challenge to develop a new ecological ethic that will help shape a future that is both just and sustainable.

---

[6] Pope John XXIII, *Peace on Earth* (1963), 130-131.
[7] Synod of Bishops, *Justice in the World* (1971), 8; Pope John Paul II, *Redeemer of Man* (1979), 15.

13.   In short, nations separated by geography, culture, and ideology are linked in a complex commercial, financial, technological, and environmental network. These links have two direct consequences. First, they create hope for a new form of community among all peoples, one built on dignity, solidarity, and justice. Second, this rising global awareness calls for greater attention to the stark inequities across countries in the standards of living and control of resources. We must not look at the welfare of U.S. citizens as the only good to be sought. Nor may we overlook the disparities of power in the relationships between this nation and the developing countries. The United States is the major supplier of food to other countries, a major source of arms sales to developing nations, and a powerful influence in multilateral institutions such as the International Monetary Fund, the World Bank, and the United Nations. What Americans see as a growing interdependence is regarded by many in the less developed countries as a pattern of domination and dependence.

14.   Within this larger international setting, there are also a number of challenges to the domestic economy that call for creativity and courage. The promise of the "American dream"—freedom for all persons to develop their God-given talents to the full—remains unfulfilled for millions in the United States today.

15.   Several areas of U.S. economic life demand special attention. Unemployment is the most basic. Despite the large number of new jobs the U.S. economy has generated in the past decade, approximately 8 million people seeking work in this country are unable to find it, and many more are so discouraged they have stopped looking.[8] Over the past two decades the nation has come to tolerate an increasing level of un-

---

[8] U.S. Department of Labor, Bureau of Labor Statistics, *The Employment Situation: August 1985* (September 1985), Table A-1.

employment. The 6 to 7 percent rate deemed acceptable today would have been intolerable twenty years ago. Among the unemployed are a disproportionate number of blacks, Hispanics, young people, or women who are the sole support of their families.[9] Some cities and states have many more unemployed persons than others as a result of economic forces that have little to do with people's desire to work. Unemployment is a tragedy no matter whom it strikes, but the tragedy is compounded by the unequal and unfair way it is distributed in our society.

16.   Harsh poverty plagues our country despite its great wealth. More than 33 million Americans are poor; by any reasonable standard another 20 to 30 million are needy. Poverty is increasing in the United States, not decreasing.[10] For a people who believe in "progress," this should be cause for alarm. These burdens fall most heavily on blacks, Hispanics, and Native Americans. Even more disturbing is the large increase in the number of women and children living in poverty. Today children are the largest single group among the poor. This tragic fact seriously threatens the nation's future. That so many people are poor in a nation as rich as ours is a social and moral scandal that we cannot ignore.

17.   Many working people and middle-class Americans live dangerously close to poverty. A rising number of families must rely on the wages of two or even three members just to get by. From 1968 to 1978 nearly a quarter of the U. S. population was in poverty part of the time and received welfare benefits in at least

---

[9] Ibid.

[10] U.S. Bureau of the Census, *Current Population Reports*, Series P-60, 145, *Money Income and Poverty Status of Families and Persons in the United States: 1983* (Washington, D.C.: U.S. Government Printing Office, 1984), 20.

one year.[11] The loss of a job, illness, or the breakup of a marriage may be all it takes to push people into poverty.

18.   The lack of a mutually supportive relation between family life and economic life is one of the most serious problems facing the United States today.[12] The economic and cultural strength of the nation is directly linked to the stability and health of its families.[13] When families thrive, spouses contribute to the common good through their work at home, in the community, and in their jobs; and children develop a sense of their own worth and of their responsibility to serve others. When families are weak or break down entirely, the dignity of parents and children is threatened. High cultural and economic costs are inflicted on society at large.

19.   The precarious economic situation of so many people and so many families calls for examination of U.S. economic arrangements. Christian conviction and the American promise of liberty and justice for all give the poor and the vulnerable a special claim on the nation's concern. They also challenge all members of the Church to help build a more just society.

20.   The investment of human creativity and material resources in the production of the weapons of war makes these economic problems even more difficult to solve. Defense Department expenditures in the United States are almost $300 billion per year. The rivalry and mutual fear between superpowers divert into projects that threaten death, minds, and money that could better human life. Developing countries engage in arms races they can ill afford, often with the encouragement of the superpowers. Some of the

---

[11] Greg H. Duncan, *Years of Poverty, Years of Plenty: The Changing Economic Fortunes of American Workers and Their Families* (Ann Arbor, Mich.: Institute for Social Research, University of Michigan, 1984).
[12] See Pope John Paul II, *Familiaris Consortio* (1981), 46.
[13] *Pastoral Constitution*, 47.

poorest countries of the world use scarce resources to buy planes, guns, and other weapons when they lack the food, education, and health care their people need. Defense policies must be evaluated and assessed in light of their real contribution to freedom, justice, and peace for the citizens of our own and other nations. We have developed a perspective on these multiple moral concerns in our 1983 pastoral letter, *The Challenge of Peace: God's Promise and Our Response*.[14] When weapons or strategies make questionable contributions to security, peace, and justice and will also be very expensive, spending priorities should be redirected to more pressing social needs.[15]

21.　　　　Many other social and economic challenges require careful analysis: the movement of many industries from the Snowbelt to the Sunbelt, the federal deficit and interest rates, corporate mergers and takeovers, the effects of new technologies such as robotics and information systems in U.S. industry, immigration policy, growing international traffic in drugs, and the trade imbalance. All of these issues do not provide a complete portrait of the economy. Rather they are symptoms of more fundamental currents shaping U.S. economic life today: the struggle to find meaning and value in human work, efforts to support individual freedom in the context of renewed social cooperation, the urgent need to create equitable forms of global interdependence in a world now marked by extreme inequality. These deeper currents are cultural and moral in content. They show that the long-range challenges facing the nation call for sustained reflection

---

[14] National Conference of Catholic Bishops, *The Challenge of Peace: God's Promise and Our Response* (Washington, D.C.: USCC Office of Publishing and Promotion Services, 1983).

[15] Cardinal Joseph L. Bernardin and Cardinal John J. O'Connor, Testimony before the House Foreign Relations Committee, June 26, 1984, *Origins* 14:10 (August 10, 1984): 157.

on the values that guide economic choices and are embodied in economic institutions. Such explicit reflection on the ethical content of economic choices and policies must become an integral part of the way Christians relate religious belief to the realities of everyday life. In this way, the "split between the faith which many profess and their daily lives,"[16] which Vatican II counted among the more serious errors of the modern age, will begin to be bridged.

C. The Need for Moral Vision

22.   Sustaining a common culture and a common commitment to moral values is not easy in our world. Modern economic life is based on a division of labor into specialized jobs and professions. Since the industrial revolution, people have had to define themselves and their work ever more narrowly to find a niche in the economy. The benefits of this are evident in the satisfaction many people derive from contributing their specialized skills to society. But the costs are social fragmentation, a decline in seeing how one's work serves the whole community, and an increased emphasis on personal goals and private interests.[17] This is vividly clear in discussions of economic justice. Here it is often difficult to find a common ground among people with different backgrounds and concerns. One of our chief hopes in writing this letter is to encourage and contribute to the development of this common ground.[18]

---

[16] *Pastoral Constitution*, 43.

[17] See, for example, Peter Berger, Brigitte Berger, and Hansfried Kellner, *The Homeless Mind: Modernization and Consciousness* (New York: Vintage, 1974).

[18] For a recent study of the importance and difficulty of achieving such a common language and vision see Robert N. Bellah, Richard

23.   Strengthening common moral vision is essential if the economy is to serve all people more fairly. Many middle-class Americans feel themselves in the grip of economic demands and cultural pressures that go far beyond the individual family's capacity to cope. Without constructive guidance in making decisions with serious moral implications, men and women who hold positions of responsibility in corporations or government find their duties exacting a heavy price. We want these reflections to help them contribute to a more just economy.

24.   The quality of the national discussion about our economic future will affect the poor most of all, in this country and throughout the world. The life and dignity of millions of men, women, and children hang in the balance. Decisions must be judged in light of what they do *for* the poor, what they do *to* the poor, and what they enable the poor to do *for themselves*. The fundamental moral criterion for all economic decisions, policies, and institutions is this: They must be at the service of *all people, especially the poor*.

25.   This letter is based on a long tradition of Catholic social thought, rooted in the Bible and developed over the past century by the popes and the Second Vatican Council in response to modern economic conditions. This tradition insists that human dignity, realized in community with others and with the whole of God's creation, is the norm against which every social institution must be measured.[19]

26.   This teaching has a rich history. It is also dynamic and growing.[20] Pope Paul VI insisted that all

Madsen, William M. Sullivan, Ann Swidler, and Stephen M. Tipton, *Habits of the Heart: Individualism and Commitment in American Life* (Berkeley, Calif.: University of California Press, 1985). See also Martin E. Marty, *The Public Church* (New York: Crossroads, 1981).

[19] Pope John XXIII, *Mater et Magistra* (1961), 219; *Pastoral Constitution*, 40.

[20] Congregation for the Doctrine of the Faith, *Instruction on Cer-*

Christian communities have the responsibility "to analyze with objectivity the situation which is proper to their own country, to shed on it the light of the Gospel's unalterable words and to draw principles of reflection, norms of judgment, and directives for action from the social teaching of the Church."[21] Therefore, we build on the past work of our own bishops' conference, including the 1919 Program of Social Reconstruction and other pastoral letters.[22] In addition many people from the Catholic, Protestant, and Jewish communities, in academic, business or political life, and from many different economic backgrounds have also provided guidance. We want to make the legacy of Christian social thought a living, growing resource that can inspire hope and help shape the future.

27.   We write, then, first of all to provide guidance for members of our own Church as they seek to form their consciences about economic matters. No one may claim the name Christian and be comfortable in the face of the hunger, homelessness, insecurity, and injustice found in this country and the world. At the same time, we want to add our voice to the public debate about the directions in which the U.S. economy should be moving. We seek the cooperation and support of those who do not share our faith or tradition.

tain Aspects of the Theology of Liberation (Washington, D.C.: USCC Office of Publishing and Promotion Services, 1984); Pope Paul VI, Octogesima Adveniens (1971), 42.

   [21] Octogesima Adveniens, 4.

   [22] Administrative Committee of the National Catholic War Council, Program of Social Reconstruction, February 12, 1919. Other notable statements on the economy by our predecessors are The Present Crisis, April 25, 1933; Statement on Church and Social Order, February 4, 1940; The Economy: Human Dimensions, November 20, 1975. These and numerous other statements of the U.S. Catholic episcopate can be found in Hugh J. Nolan, ed., Pastoral Letters of the United States Catholic Bishops, 4 vols. (Washington, D.C.: USCC Office of Publishing and Promotion Services, 1984).

The common bond of humanity that links all persons is the source of our belief that the country can attain a renewed public moral vision. The questions are basic and the answers are often elusive; they challenge us to serious and sustained attention to economic justice.

Chapter II

THE CHRISTIAN VISION OF ECONOMIC LIFE

28.   The basis for all that the Church believes about the moral dimensions of economic life is its vision of the transcendent worth—the sacredness—of human beings. *The dignity of the human person, realized in community with others, is the criterion against which all aspects of economic life must be measured.*[1] All human beings, therefore, are ends to be served by the institutions that make up the economy, not means to be exploited for more narrowly defined goals. Human personhood must be respected with a reverence that is religious. When we deal with each other, we should do so with the sense of awe that arises in the presence of something holy and sacred. For that is what human beings are: we are created in the image of God (Gn 1:27). Similarly, all economic institutions must support the bonds of community and solidarity that are essential to the dignity of persons. Wherever our economic arrangements fail to conform to the demands of human dignity lived in community, they must be questioned and transformed. These convictions have a biblical basis. They are also supported by a long tradition of theological and philosophical reflection and through the reasoned analysis of human experience by contemporary men and women.

---

[1] *Mater et Magistra,* 219-220. See *Pastoral Constitution,* 63.

29.   In presenting the Christian moral vision, we turn first to the Scriptures for guidance. Though our comments are necessarily selective, we hope that pastors and other church members will become personally engaged with the biblical texts. The Scriptures contain many passages that speak directly of economic life. We must also attend to the Bible's deeper vision of God, of the purpose of creation, and of the dignity of human life in society. Along with other churches and ecclesial communities who are "strengthened by the grace of Baptism and the hearing of God's Word," we strive to become faithful hearers and doers of the word.[2] We also claim the Hebrew Scriptures as common heritage with our Jewish brothers and sisters, and we join with them in the quest for an economic life worthy of the divine revelation we share.

A. Biblical Perspectives

30.   The fundamental conviction of our faith is that human life is fulfilled in the knowledge and love of the living God in communion with others. The Sacred Scriptures offer guidance so that men and women may enter into full communion with God and with each other, and witness to God's saving acts. We discover there a God who is creator of heaven and earth, and of the human family. Though our first parents reject the God who created them, God does not abandon them, but from Abraham and Sarah forms a people of promise. When this people is enslaved in an alien land, God delivers them and makes a covenant with them in which they are summoned to be faithful to the *torah* or sacred teaching. The focal points of Israel's faith—creation, covenant, and community—provide

---

[2] Vatican Council II, *Decree on Ecumenism,* 22-23.

a foundation for reflection on issues of economic and social justice.

1. Created in God's Image

31.   After the exile, when Israel combined its traditions into a written *torah*, it prefaced its history as a people with the story of the creation of all peoples and of the whole world by the same God who created them as a nation (Gn 1-11). God is the creator of heaven and earth (Gn 14:19-22; Is 40:28; 45:18); creation proclaims God's glory (Ps 89:6-12) and is "very good" (Gn 1:31). Fruitful harvests, bountiful flocks, a loving family are God's blessings on those who heed God's word. Such is the joyful refrain that echoes throughout the Bible. One legacy of this theology of creation is the conviction that no dimension of human life lies beyond God's care and concern. God is present to creation, and creative engagement with God's handiwork is itself reverence for God.

32.   At the summit of creation stands the creation of man and woman, made in God's image (Gn 1:26-27). *As such every human being possesses an inalienable dignity that stamps human existence prior to any division into races or nations and prior to human labor and human achievement (Gn 4-11).* Men and women are also to share in the creative activity of God. They are to be fruitful, to care for the earth (Gn 2:15), and to have "dominion" over it (Gn 1:28), which means they are "to govern the world in holiness and justice and to render judgment in integrity of heart" (Wis 9:3). Creation is a gift; women and men are to be faithful stewards in caring for the earth. They can justly consider that by their labor they are unfolding the Creator's work.[3]

---

[3] C. Westermann, *Creation* (Philadelphia: Fortress Press, 1974); and B. Vawter, *On Genesis: A New Reading* (Garden City, N.Y.: Doubleday, 1977). See also *Pastoral Constitution*, 34.

33.   The narratives of Genesis 1-11 also portray the origin of the strife and suffering that mar the world. Though created to enjoy intimacy with God and the fruits of the earth, Adam and Eve disrupted God's design by trying to live independently of God through a denial of their status as creatures. They turned away from God and gave to God's creation the obedience due to God alone. For this reason the prime sin in so much of the biblical tradition is idolatry: service of the creature rather than of the creator (Rom 1:25), and the attempt to overturn creation by making God in human likeness. The Bible castigates not only the worship of idols, but also manifestations of idolatry, such as the quest for unrestrained power and the desire for great wealth (Is 40:12-20; 44:1-20; Wis 13:1-14:31; Col 3:5, "the greed that is idolatry"). The sin of our first parents had other consequences as well. Alienation from God pits brother against brother (Gn 4:8-16), in a cycle of war and vengeance (Gn 4:22-23). Sin and evil abound, and the primeval history culminates with another assault on the heavens, this time ending in a babble of tongues scattered over the face of the earth (Gn 11:1-9). Sin simultaneously alienates human beings from God and shatters the solidarity of the human community. Yet this reign of sin is not the final word. The primeval history is followed by the call of Abraham, a man of faith, who was to be the bearer of the promise to many nations (Gn 12:1-4). Throughout the Bible we find this struggle between sin and repentance. God's judgment on evil is followed by God's seeking out a sinful people.

34.   The biblical vision of creation has provided one of the most enduring legacies of Church teaching. To stand before God as the creator is to respect God's creation, both the world of nature and of human history. *From the patristic period to the present, the Church has affirmed that misuse of the world's resources or appropriation of them by a minority of the world's population*

betrays the gift of creation since "whatever belongs to God belongs to all."[4]

2. A People of the Covenant

35.   When the people of Israel, our forerunners in faith, gathered in thanksgiving to renew their covenant (Jos 24:1-15), they recalled the gracious deeds of God (Dt 6:20-25; 26: 5-11). When they lived as aliens in a strange land and experienced oppression and slavery, they cried out. The Lord, the God of their ancestors, heard their cries, knew their afflictions, and came to deliver them (Ex 3:7-8). By leading them out of Egypt, God created a people that was to be the Lord's very own (Jer 24:7; Hos 2:25). They were to imitate God by treating the alien and the slave in their midst as God had treated them (Ex 22:20-22; Jer 34:8-14).

36.   In the midst of this saving history stands the covenant at Sinai (Ex 19-24). It begins with an account of what God has done for the people (Ex 19:1-6; cf. Jos 24:1-13) and includes from God's side a promise of steadfast love (*hesed*) and faithfulness (*'emeth*, Ex 34:5-7). The people are summoned to ratify this covenant by faithfully worshiping God alone and by directing their lives according to God's will, which was made explicit in Israel's great legal codes such as the Decalogue (Ex 20:1-17) and the Book of the Covenant (Ex 20:22-23:33). Far from being an arbitrary restriction on the life of the people, these codes made life in

---

[4] St. Cyprian, *On Works and Almsgiving*, 25, trans. R. J. Deferrari, *St. Cyprian: Treatises*, 36 (New York: Fathers of the Church, 1958), 251. Original text in Migne, *Patrologia Latina*, vol. 4, 620. On the Patristic teaching, see C. Avila, *Ownership: Early Christian Teaching* (Maryknoll, N.Y.: Orbis Books, 1983). Collection of original texts and translations.

community possible.[5] The specific laws of the covenant protect human life and property, demand respect
for parents and the spouses and children of one's
neighbor, and manifest a special concern for the vulnerable members of the community: widows, orphans, the poor, and strangers in the land. Laws such
as that for the Sabbath year when the land was left
fallow (Ex 23:11; Lv 25:1-7) and for the year of release
of debts (Dt 15:1-11) summoned people to respect the
land as God's gift and reminded Israel that as a people
freed by God from bondage they were to be concerned
for the poor and oppressed in their midst. Every fif-
tieth year a jubilee was to be proclaimed as a year of
"liberty throughout the land" and property was to be
restored to its original owners (Lv 25:8-17, cf. Is 61:1-
2; Lk 4:18-19).[6] The codes of Israel reflect the norms
of the covenant: reciprocal responsibility, mercy, and
truthfulness. They embody a life in freedom from
oppression: worship of the One God, rejection of idolatry, mutual respect among people, care and protection for every member of the social body. Being free
and being a co-responsible community are God's intentions for us.

37.   When the people turn away from the living
God to serve idols and no longer heed the commands
of the covenant, God sends prophets to recall his
saving deeds and to summon them to return to the
one who betrothed them "in right and in justice, in
love and in mercy" (Hos 2:21). The substance of

---

[5] T. Ogletree, The Use of the Bible in Christian Ethics (Philadelphia:
Fortress Press, 1983), 47-85.

[6] Though scholars debate whether the Jubilee was a historical
institution or an ideal, its images were continually evoked to stress
God's sovereignty over the land and God's concern for the poor
and the oppressed (e.g., Is 61:1-2; Lk 4:16-19). See R. North, So-
ciology of the Biblical Jubilee (Rome: Biblical Institute, 1954); S. Ringe,
Jesus, Liberation and the Biblical Jubilee: Images for Ethics and Christology
(Philadelphia: Fortress Press, 1985).

prophetic faith is proclaimed by Micah: "to do justice and to love kindness, and to walk humbly with your God" (Mi 6:8, RSV). Biblical faith in general, and prophetic faith especially, insist that fidelity to the covenant joins obedience to God with reverence and concern for the neighbor. The biblical terms which best summarize this double dimension of Israel's faith are *sedaqah*, justice (also translated as righteousness), and *mishpat* (right judgment or justice embodied in a concrete act or deed). The biblical understanding of justice gives a fundamental perspective to our reflections on social and economic justice.[7]

38.   God is described as a "God of justice" (Is 30:18) who loves justice (Is 61:8, cf. Pss 11:7; 33:5; 37:28; 99:4) and delights in it (Jer 9:23). God demands justice from the whole people (Dt 16:20) and executes justice for the needy (Ps 140:13). Central to the biblical presentation of justice is that the justice of a community is measured by its treatment of the powerless in society, most often described as the widow, the orphan, the poor, and the stranger (non-Israelite) in the land. The Law, the Prophets, and the Wisdom literature of the Old Testament all show deep concern for the proper treatment of such people.[8] What these groups of people have in common is their vulnerability and lack of power. They are often alone and have no protector or advocate. Therefore, it is God who hears their cries (Pss 109:21; 113:7), and the king who is God's anointed is commanded to have special concern for them.

---

[7] On justice, see J. R. Donahue, "Biblical Perspectives on Justice," in Haughey, ed., *The Faith That Does Justice* (New York: Paulist Press, 1977), 68-112; and S. C. Mott, *Biblical Ethics and Social Change* (New York: Oxford University Press, 1982).

[8] See Ex 22:20-26; Dt 15:1-11; Jb 29:12-17; Pss 69:34; 72:2, 4, 12-24; 82:3-4; Prv 14:21, 31; Is 3:14-15; 10:2; Jer 22:16; Zec 7:9-10.

39.　　　　　　　　Justice has many nuances.[9] Fundamentally, it suggests a sense of what is right or of what should happen. For example, paths are just when they bring you to your destination (Gn 24:48; Ps 23:3), and laws are just when they create harmony within the community, as Isaiah says: "Justice will bring about peace; right will produce calm and security" (Is 32:17). God is "just" by acting as God should, coming to the people's aid and summoning them to conversion when they stray. People are summoned to be "just," that is, to be in a proper relation to God, by observing God's laws which form them into a faithful community. Biblical justice is more comprehensive than subsequent philosophical definitions. It is not concerned with a strict definition of rights and duties, but with the rightness of the human condition before God and within society. Nor is justice opposed to love; rather, it is both a manifestation of love and a condition for love to grow.[10] Because God loves Israel, he rescues them from oppression and summons them to be a people that "does justice" and loves kindness. The quest for justice arises from loving gratitude for the saving acts of God and manifests itself in wholehearted love of God and neighbor.

40.　　　　　　　　These perspectives provide the foundation for a biblical vision of economic justice. Every human person is created as an image of God, and the denial of dignity to a person is a blot on this image. Creation is a gift to all men and women, not to be appropriated for the benefit of a few; its beauty is an object of joy and reverence. The same God who came to the aid of an oppressed people and formed them into a covenant community continues to hear the cries of the

---

[9] J. Pedersen, *Israel: Its Life and Culture*, vol. I-II (London: Oxford University Press, 1926), 337-340.

[10] J. Alfaro, *Theology of Justice in the World* (Rome: Pontifical Commission on Justice and Peace, 1973), 40-41; E. McDonagh, *The Making of Disciples* (Wilmington, Del.: Michael Glazier, 1982), 119.

oppressed and to create communities which are responsive to God's word. God's love and life are present when people can live in a community of faith and hope. These cardinal points of the faith of Israel also furnish the religious context for understanding the saving action of God in the life and teaching of Jesus.

3. The Reign of God and Justice

41.   Jesus enters human history as God's anointed son who announces the nearness of the reign of God (Mk 1:9-14). This proclamation summons us to acknowledge God as creator and covenant partner and challenges us to seek ways in which God's revelation of the dignity and destiny of all creation might become incarnate in history. It is not simply the promise of the future victory of God over sin and evil, but that this victory has already begun—in the life and teaching of Jesus.

42.   What Jesus proclaims by word, he enacts in his ministry. He resists temptations of power and prestige, follows his Father's will, and teaches us to pray that it be accomplished on earth. He warns against attempts to "lay up treasures on earth" (Mt 6:19) and exhorts his followers not to be anxious about material goods but rather to seek first God's reign and God's justice (Mt 6:25-33). His mighty works symbolize that the reign of God is more powerful than evil, sickness, and the hardness of the human heart. He offers God's loving mercy to sinners (Mk 2:17), takes up the cause of those who suffered religious and social discrimination (Lk 7:36-50; 15:1-2), and attacks the use of religion to avoid the demands of charity and justice (Mk 7:9-13; Mt 23:23).

43.   When asked what was the greatest commandment, Jesus quoted the age-old Jewish affirmation of faith that God alone is One and to be loved with the

whole heart, mind, and soul (Dt 6:4-5) and immediately adds: "You shall love your neighbor as yourself" (Lv 19:18, Mk 12:28-34). This dual command of love that is at the basis of all Christian morality is illustrated in the Gospel of Luke by the parable of a Samaritan who interrupts his journey to come to the aid of a dying man (Lk 10:29-37). Unlike the other wayfarers who look on the man and pass by, the Samaritan "was moved with compassion at the sight"; he stops, tends the wounded man, and takes him to a place of safety. In this parable compassion is the bridge between mere seeing and action; love is made real through effective action.[11]

44.   Near the end of his life, Jesus offers a vivid picture of the last judgment (Mt 25: 31-46). All the nations of the world will be assembled and will be divided into those blessed who are welcomed into God's kingdom or those cursed who are sent to eternal punishment. The blessed are those who fed the hungry, gave drink to the thirsty, welcomed the stranger, clothed the naked, and visited the sick and imprisoned; the cursed are those who neglected these works of mercy and love. Neither the blessed nor the cursed are astounded that they are judged by the Son of Man, nor that judgment is rendered according to works of charity. The shock comes when they find that in neglecting the poor, the outcast, and the oppressed, they were rejecting Jesus himself. Jesus who came as "Emmanuel" (God with us, Mt 1:23) and who promises to be with his people until the end of the age (Mt 28:20) is hidden in those most in need; to reject them is to reject God made manifest in history.

---

[11] Pope John Paul II has drawn on this parable to exhort us to have a "compassionate heart" to those in need in his Apostolic Letter "On the Christian Meaning of Human Suffering" (*Salvifici Doloris*) (Washington, D.C.: USCC Office of Publishing and Promotion Services, 1984), 34-39.

4. Called To Be Disciples in Community

45.   Jesus summoned his first followers to a change of heart and to take on the yoke of God's reign (Mk 1:14-15; Mt 11:29). They are to be the nucleus of that community which will continue the work of proclaiming and building God's kingdom through the centuries. As Jesus called the first disciples in the midst of their everyday occupations of fishing and tax collecting; so he again calls people in every age in the home, in the workplace, and in the marketplace.

46.   The Church is, as Pope John Paul II reminded us, "a community of disciples" in which "we must see first and foremost Christ saying to each member of the community: follow me."[12] To be a Christian is to join with others in responding to this personal call and in learning the meaning of Christ's life. It is to be sustained by that loving intimacy with the Father that Jesus experienced in his work, in his prayer, and in his suffering.

47.   Discipleship involves imitating the pattern of Jesus' life by openness to God's will in the service of others (Mk 10:42-45). Disciples are also called to follow him on the way of the cross, and to heed his call that those who lose their lives for the sake of the Gospel will save them (Mk 8:34-35). Jesus' death is an example of that greater love which lays down one's life for others (cf. Jn 15:12-18). It is a model for those who suffer persecution for the sake of justice (Mt 5:10). The death of Jesus was not the end of his power and presence, for he was raised up by the power of God. Nor did it mark the end of the disciples' union with him. After Jesus had appeared to them and when they received the gift of the Spirit (Acts 2:1-12), they became apostles of the good news to the ends of the earth. In the face of poverty and persecution they trans-

---

[12] *Redeemer of Man*, 21.

formed human lives and formed communities which became signs of the power and presence of God. Sharing in this same resurrection faith, contemporary followers of Christ can face the struggles and challenges that await those who bring the gospel vision to bear on our complex economic and social world.

5. Poverty, Riches, and the Challenge of Discipleship

48.   The pattern of Christian life as presented in the Gospel of Luke has special relevance today. In her *Magnificat*, Mary rejoices in a God who scatters the proud, brings down the mighty, and raises up the poor and lowly (Lk 1:51-53). The first public utterance of Jesus is "The Spirit of the Lord is upon me, because he has anointed me to preach the good news to the poor" (Lk 4:18 cf. Is 61:1-2). Jesus adds to the blessing on the poor a warning, "Woe to you who are rich, for you have received your consolation" (Lk 6:24). He warns his followers against greed and reliance on abundant possessions and underscores this by the parable of the man whose life is snatched away at the very moment he tries to secure his wealth (Lk 12:13-21). In Luke alone, Jesus tells the parable of the rich man who does not see the poor and suffering Lazarus at his gate (Lk 16:19-31). When the rich man finally "sees" Lazarus, it is from the place of torment and the opportunity for conversion has passed. Pope John Paul II has often recalled this parable to warn the prosperous not to be blind to the great poverty that exists beside great wealth.[13]

49.   Jesus, especially in Luke, lives as a poor man, like the prophets takes the side of the poor, and warns

---

[13] Address to Workers at Sao Paulo, 8, *Origins* 10:9 (July 31, 1980): 139; and Address at Yankee Stadium, *Origins* 9:19 (October 25, 1979): 311-312.

of the dangers of wealth.[14] The terms used for poor, while primarily describing lack of material goods, also suggest dependence and powerlessness. The poor are also an exiled and oppressed people whom God will rescue (Is 51:21-23) as well as a faithful remnant who take refuge in God (Zep 3:12-13). Throughout the Bible, material poverty is a misfortune and a cause of sadness. A constant biblical refrain is that the poor must be cared for and protected and that when they are exploited, God hears their cries (Prv 22:22-23). Conversely, even though the goods of the earth are to be enjoyed and people are to thank God for material blessings, wealth is a constant danger. The rich are wise in their own eyes (Prv 28:11), and are prone to apostasy and idolatry (Am 5:4-13; Is 2:6-8), as well as to violence and oppression (Jas 2:6-7).[15] Since they are neither blinded by wealth nor make it into an idol, the poor can be open to God's presence; throughout Israel's history and in early Christianity the poor are agents of God's transforming power.

50.   The poor are often related to the lowly (Mt 5:3,5) to whom God reveals what was hidden from the wise (Mt 11:25-30). When Jesus calls the poor "blessed," he is not praising their condition of poverty, but their openness to God. When he states that the reign of God is theirs, he voices God's special concern for them, and promises that they are to be the beneficiaries of God's mercy and justice. When he summons disciples to leave all and follow him, he

---

[14] J. Dupont and A. George, eds., *La pauvrete evangelique* (Paris: Cerf, 1971); M. Hengel, *Property and Riches in the Early Church* (Philadelphia: Fortress Press, 1974); L. Johnson, *Sharing Possessions: Mandate and Symbol of Faith* (Philadelphia: Fortress Press, 1981); D. L. Mealand, *Poverty and Expectation in the Gospels* (London: SPCK, 1980); W. Pilgrim, *Good News to the Poor: Wealth and Poverty in Luke-Acts* (Minneapolis: Augsburg, 1981); and W. Stegemann, *The Gospel and the Poor* (Philadelphia: Fortress Press, 1984).

[15] See Am 4:1-3; Jb 20:19; Sir 13:4-7; Jas 2:6; 5:1-6; Rv 18:11-19.

is calling them to share his own radical trust in the
Father and his freedom from care and anxiety (cf. Mt
6:25-34). The practice of evangelical poverty in the
Church has always been a living witness to the power
of that trust and to the joy that comes with that freedom.

51.   Early Christianity saw the poor as an object of
God's special love, but it neither canonized material
poverty nor accepted deprivation as an inevitable fact
of life. Though few early Christians possessed wealth
or power (1 Cor 1:26-28; Jas 2:5), their communities
had well-off members (Acts 16:14; 18:8). Jesus' concern
for the poor was continued in different forms in the
early Church. The early community at Jerusalem distributed its possessions so that "there was no needy
person among them," and held "all things in common"—a phrase that suggests not only shared material possessions, but more fundamentally, friendship
and mutual concern among all its members (Acts 4:32-
34; 2:44). While recognizing the dangers of wealth,
the early Church proposed the proper use of possessions to alleviate need and suffering, rather than universal dispossession. Beginning in the first century
and throughout history, Christian communities have
developed varied structures to support and sustain
the weak and powerless in societies that were often
brutally unconcerned about human suffering.

52.   Such perspectives provide a basis today for what
is called the "preferential option for the poor."[16]
Though in the Gospels and in the New Testament as
a whole the offer of salvation is extended to all peoples, Jesus takes the side of those most in need, physically and spiritually. The example of Jesus poses a
number of challenges to the contemporary Church.
It imposes a prophetic mandate to speak for those
who have no one to speak for them, to be a defender

---

[16] See paras. 85-91.

of the defenseless, who in biblical terms are the poor. It also demands a compassionate vision that enables the Church to see things from the side of the poor and powerless and to assess lifestyle, policies, and social institutions in terms of their impact on the poor. It summons the Church also to be an instrument in assisting people to experience the liberating power of God in their own lives so that they may respond to the Gospel in freedom and in dignity. Finally, and most radically, it calls for an emptying of self, both individually and corporately, that allows the Church to experience the power of God in the midst of poverty and powerlessness.

6. A Community of Hope

53.   The biblical vision of creation, covenant, and community, as well as the summons to discipleship, unfolds under the tension between promise and fulfillment. The whole Bible is spanned by the narratives of the first creation (Gn 1-3) and the vision of a restored creation at the end of history (Rv 21:1-4). Just as creation tells us that God's desire was one of wholeness and unity between God and the human family and within this family itself, the images of a new creation give hope that enmity and hatred will cease and justice and peace will reign (Is 11:4-6; 25:1-8). Human life unfolds "between the times," the time of the first creation and that of a restored creation (Rom 8:18-25). Although the ultimate realization of God's plan lies in the future, Christians in union with all people of good will are summoned to shape history in the image of God's creative design, and in response to the reign of God proclaimed and embodied by Jesus.

54.   A Christian is a member of a new community, "God's own people" (1 Pt 2:9-10), who, like the people of Exodus, owes its existence to the gracious gift of God and is summoned to respond to God's will made

manifest in the life and teaching of Jesus. A Christian walks in the newness of life (Rom 6:4), and is "a new creation; the old has passed away, the new has come" (2 Cor 5:17). This new creation in Christ proclaims that God's creative love is constantly at work, offers sinners forgiveness, and reconciles a broken world. Our action on behalf of justice in our world proceeds from the conviction that, despite the power of injustice and violence, life has been fundamentally changed by the entry of the Word made flesh into human history.

55.   Christian communities that commit themselves to solidarity with those suffering and to confrontation with those attitudes and ways of acting which institutionalize injustice, will themselves experience the power and presence of Christ. They will embody in their lives the values of the new creation while they labor under the old. The quest for economic and social justice will always combine hope and realism, and must be renewed by every generation. It involves diagnosing those situations that continue to alienate the world from God's creative love as well as presenting hopeful alternatives that arise from living in a renewed creation. This quest arises from faith and is sustained by hope as it seeks to speak to a broken world of God's justice and loving kindness.

7. A Living Tradition

56.   Our reflection on U.S. economic life today must be rooted in this biblical vision of the kingdom and discipleship, but it must also be shaped by the rich and complex tradition of Catholic life and thought. Throughout its history, the Christian community has listened to the words of Scripture and sought to enact them in the midst of daily life in very different historical and cultural contexts.

57. In the first centuries, when Christians were a minority in a hostile society, they cared for one an-

other through generous almsgiving. In the patristic era, the church fathers repeatedly stressed that the goods of the earth were created by God for the benefit of every person without exception, and that all have special duties toward those in need. The monasteries of the Middle Ages were centers of prayer, learning, and education. They contributed greatly to the cultural and economic life of the towns and cities that sprang up around them. In the twelfth century the new mendicant orders dedicated themselves to following Christ in poverty and to the proclamation of the good news to the poor.

58.   These same religious communities also nurtured some of the greatest theologians of the Church's tradition, thinkers who synthesized the call of Christ with the philosophical learning of Greek, Roman, Jewish, and Arab worlds. Thomas Aquinas and the other scholastics devoted rigorous intellectual energy to clarifying the meaning of both personal virtue and justice in society. In more recent centuries Christians began to build a large network of hospitals, orphanages, and schools, to serve the poor and society at large. And beginning with Leo XIII's *Rerum Novarum*, down to the writings and speeches of John Paul II, the popes have more systematically addressed the rapid change of modern society in a series of social encyclicals. These teachings of modern popes and of the Second Vatican Council are especially significant for efforts to respond to the problems facing society today.[17]

59.   We also have much to learn from the strong emphasis in Protestant traditions on the vocation of lay people in the world and from ecumenical efforts to develop an economic ethic that addresses newly emergent problems. And in a special way our fellow Catholics in developing countries have much to teach

---

[17] See Selected Bibliography.

us about the Christian response to an ever more interdependent world.

60.   Christians today are called by God to carry on this tradition through active love of neighbor, a love that responds to the special challenges of this moment in human history. The world is wounded by sin and injustice, in need of conversion and of the transformation that comes when persons enter more deeply into the mystery of the death and Resurrection of Christ. The concerns of this pastoral letter are not at all peripheral to the central mystery at the heart of the Church.[18] They are integral to the proclamation of the Gospel and part of the vocation of every Christian today.[19]

B. Ethical Norms for Economic Life

61.   These biblical and theological themes shape the overall Christian perspective on economic ethics. This perspective is also subscribed to by many who do not share Christian religious convictions. Human understanding and religious belief are complementary, not contradictory. For human beings are created in God's image, and their dignity is manifest in the ability to reason and understand, in their freedom to shape their own lives and the life of their communities, and in the capacity for love and friendship. In proposing ethical norms, therefore, we appeal both to Christians and to all in our pluralist society to show that respect and reverence owed to the dignity of every person. Intelligent reflection on the social and economic realities of today is also indispensable in the effort to

---

[18] Extraordinary Synod of Bishops (1985) *The Final Report*, II, A (Washington, D.C.: USCC Office of Publishing and Promotion Services, 1986).
[19] Pope Paul VI, *On Evangelization in the Modern World*, 31.

respond to economic circumstances never envisioned in biblical times. Therefore, we now want to propose an ethical framework that can guide economic life today in ways that are both faithful to the Gospel and shaped by human experience and reason.

62.   First we outline the *duties* all people have to each other and to the whole community: love of neighbor, the basic requirements of justice, and the special obligation to those who are poor or vulnerable. Corresponding to these duties are the *human rights* of every person; the obligation to protect the dignity of all demands respect for these rights. Finally these duties and rights entail several *priorities* that should guide the economic choices of individuals, communities, and the nation as a whole.

1. The Responsibilities of Social Living

63.   Human life is life in community. Catholic social teaching proposes several complementary perspectives that show how moral responsibilities and duties in the economic sphere are rooted in this call to community.

a. Love and Solidarity

64.   *The commandments to love God with all one's heart and to love one's neighbor as oneself are the heart and soul of Christian morality.* Jesus offers himself as the model of this all-inclusive love: ". . . love one another as I have loved you" (Jn 15:12). These commands point out the path toward true human fulfillment and happiness. They are not arbitrary restrictions on human freedom. Only active love of God and neighbor makes the fullness of community happen. Christians look forward in hope to a true communion among all persons with each other and with God. The Spirit of

Christ labors in history to build up the bonds of solidarity among all persons until that day on which their union is brought to perfection in the Kingdom of God.[20] Indeed Christian theological reflection on the very reality of God as a trinitarian unity of persons—Father, Son, and Holy Spirit—shows that being a person means being united to other persons in mutual love.[21]

65.   What the Bible and Christian tradition teach, human wisdom confirms. Centuries before Christ, the Greeks and Romans spoke of the human person as a "social animal" made for friendship, community, and public life. These insights show that human beings achieve self-realization not in isolation, but in interaction with others.[22]

66.   The virtues of citizenship are an expression of Christian love more crucial in today's interdependent world than ever before. These virtues grow out of a lively sense of one's dependence on the commonweal and obligations to it. This civic commitment must also guide the economic institutions of society. In the absence of a vital sense of citizenship among the businesses, corporations, labor unions, and other groups that shape economic life, society as a whole is endangered. Solidarity is another name for this social friendship and civic commitment that make human moral and economic life possible.

67.   The Christian tradition recognizes, of course, that the fullness of love and community will be achieved only when God's work in Christ comes to completion in the kingdom of God. This kingdom has been inaugurated among us, but God's redeeming and transforming work is not yet complete. Within history, knowledge of how to achieve the goal of social unity is limited. Human sin continues to wound the

---

[20] Ibid., 24.
[21] *Pastoral Constitution*, 32.
[22] Ibid., 25.

lives of both individuals and larger social bodies and places obstacles in the path toward greater social solidarity. If efforts to protect human dignity are to be effective, they must take these limits on knowledge and love into account. Nevertheless, sober realism should not be confused with resigned or cynical pessimism. It is a challenge to develop a courageous hope that can sustain efforts that will sometimes be arduous and protracted.

b. Justice and Participation

68.   Biblical justice is the goal we strive for. This rich biblical understanding portrays a just society as one marked by the fullness of love, compassion, holiness, and peace. On their path through history, however, sinful human beings need more specific guidance on how to move toward the realization of this great vision of God's Kingdom. This guidance is contained in the norms of basic or minimal justice. These norms state the *minimum* levels of mutual care and respect that all persons owe to each other in an imperfect world.[23] Catholic social teaching, like much philosophical reflection, distinguishes three dimensions of basic justice: commutative justice, distributive justice, and social justice.[24]

69.   *Commutative justice calls for fundamental fairness in all agreements and exchanges between individuals or private social groups.* It demands respect for the equal human dignity of all persons in economic transactions, contracts, or promises. For example, workers owe their employers diligent work in exchange for

---

[23] See para. 39.

[24] Josef Pieper, *The Four Cardinal Virtues* (Notre Dame, Ind.: University of Notre Dame Press, 1966), 43-116; David Hollenbach, "Modern Catholic Teachings concerning Justice," in John C. Haughey ed., *The Faith That Does Justice* (New York: Paulist Press, 1977), 207-231.

their wages. Employers are obligated to treat their employees as persons, paying them fair wages in exchange for the work done and establishing conditions and patterns of work that are truly human.[25]

70.　　　　　*Distributive justice requires that the allocation of income, wealth, and power in society be evaluated in light of its effects on persons whose basic material needs are unmet.* The Second Vatican Council stated: "The right to have a share of earthly goods sufficient for oneself and one's family belongs to everyone. The fathers and doctors of the Church held this view, teaching that we are obliged to come to the relief of the poor and to do so not merely out of our superfluous goods."[26] Minimum material resources are an absolute necessity for human life. If persons are to be recognized as members of the human community, then the community has an obligation to help fulfill these basic needs unless an absolute scarcity of resources makes this strictly impossible. No such scarcity exists in the United States today.

71.　　　　　Justice also has implications for the way the larger social, economic, and political institutions of society are organized. *Social justice implies that persons have an obligation to be active and productive participants in the life of society and that society has a duty to enable them to participate in this way.* This form of justice can also be called "contributive," for it stresses the duty of all who are able to help create the goods, services, and other nonmaterial or spiritual values necessary for the welfare of the whole community. In the words of Pius XI, "It is of the very essence of social justice to demand from each individual all that is necessary

---

[25] Jon P. Gunnemann, "Capitalism and Commutative Justice," presented at the 1985 meeting of the Society of Christian Ethics, forthcoming in *The Annual of the Society of Christian Ethics.*
[26] *Pastoral Constitution,* 69.

for the common good."²⁷ Productivity is essential if the community is to have the resources to serve the well-being of all. Productivity, however, cannot be measured solely by its output in goods and services. Patterns of production must also be measured in light of their impact on the fulfillment of basic needs, employment levels, patterns of discrimination, environmental quality, and sense of community.

72.   The meaning of social justice also includes a duty to organize economic and social institutions so that people can contribute to society in ways that respect their freedom and the dignity of their labor. Work should enable the working person to become "more a human being," more capable of acting intelligently, freely, and in ways that lead to self-realization.²⁸

73.   Economic conditions that leave large numbers of able people unemployed, underemployed, or employed in dehumanizing conditions fail to meet the converging demands of these three forms of basic justice. Work with adequate pay for all who seek it is the primary means for achieving basic justice in our society. Discrimination in job opportunities or income levels on the basis of race, sex, or other arbitrary standards can never be justified.²⁹ It is a scandal that such discrimination continues in the United States today. Where the effects of past discrimination persist, society has the obligation to take positive steps to overcome the legacy of injustice. Judiciously administered affirmative action programs in education and em-

---

²⁷ Pope Pius XI, *Divini Redemptoris*, 51. See John A. Ryan, *Distributive Justice*, third edition (New York: Macmillan, 1942), 188. The term "social justice" has been used in several different but related ways in the Catholic ethical tradition. See William Ferree, "The Act of Social Justice," *Philosophical Studies*, vol. 72 (Washington, D.C.: The Catholic University of America Press, 1943).

²⁸ *On Human Work*, 6, 9.

²⁹ *Pastoral Constitution*, 29.

ployment can be important expressions of the drive
for solidarity and participation that is at the heart of
true justice. Social harm calls for social relief.

74.   Basic justice also calls for the establishment of
a floor of material well-being on which all can stand.
This is a duty of the whole of society and it creates
particular obligations for those with greater resources.
This duty calls into question extreme inequalities of
income and consumption when so many lack basic
necessities. Catholic social teaching does not maintain
that a flat, arithmetical equality of income and wealth
is a demand of justice, but it does challenge economic
arrangements that leave large numbers of people impoverished. Further, it sees extreme inequality as a
threat to the solidarity of the human community, for
great disparities lead to deep social divisions and conflict.[30]

75.   This means that all of us must examine our way
of living in light of the needs of the poor. Christian
faith and the norms of justice impose distinct limits
on what we consume and how we view material goods.
The great wealth of the United States can easily blind
us to the poverty that exists in this nation and the
destitution of hundreds of millions of people in other
parts of the world. Americans are challenged today
as never before to develop the inner freedom to resist
the temptation constantly to seek more. Only in this
way will the nation avoid what Paul VI called "the
most evident form of moral underdevelopment,"
namely greed.[31]

76.   These duties call not only for individual charitable giving but also for a more systematic approach
by businesses, labor unions, and the many other
groups that shape economic life—as well as government. The concentration of privilege that exists today

---

[30] Ibid. See below, paras. 180-182.
[31] Pope Paul VI, *On the Development of Peoples* (1967), 19.

results far more from institutional relationships that distribute power and wealth inequitably than from differences in talent or lack of desire to work. These institutional patterns must be examined and revised if we are to meet the demands of basic justice. For example, a system of taxation based on assessment according to ability to pay[32] is a prime necessity for the fulfillment of these social obligations.

c. Overcoming Marginalization and Powerlessness

77.   These fundamental duties can be summarized this way: *Basic justice demands the establishment of minimum levels of participation in the life of the human community for all persons.* The ultimate injustice is for a person or group to be treated actively or abandoned passively as if they were nonmembers of the human race. To treat people this way is effectively to say that they simply do not count as human beings. This can take many forms, all of which can be described as varieties of marginalization, or exclusion from social life.[33] This exclusion can occur in the political sphere: restriction of free speech, concentration of power in the hands of a few, or outright repression by the state. It can also take economic forms that are equally harmful. Within the United States, individuals, families, and local communities fall victim to a downward cycle of poverty generated by economic forces they are powerless to influence. The poor, the disabled, and the unemployed too often are simply left behind. This pattern is even more severe beyond our borders in the least-developed countries. Whole nations are prevented from fully participating in the international economic order because they lack the power to change

---

[32] *Mater et Magistra*, 132.
[33] *Justice in the World*, 10, 16; and *Octogesima Adveniens*, 15.

their disadvantaged position. Many people within the less developed countries are excluded from sharing in the meager resources available in their homelands by unjust elites and unjust governments. These patterns of exclusion are created by free human beings. In this sense they can be called forms of social sin.[34] Acquiescence in them or failure to correct them when it is possible to do so is a sinful dereliction of Christian duty.

78.   Recent Catholic social thought regards the task of overcoming these patterns of exclusion and powerlessness as a most basic demand of justice. Stated positively, justice demands that social institutions be ordered in a way that guarantees all persons the ability to participate actively in the economic, political, and cultural life of society.[35] The level of participation may legitimately be greater for some persons than for others, but there is a basic level of access that must be made available for all. Such participation is an essential expression of the social nature of human beings and of their communitarian vocation.

2. Human Rights: The Minimum Conditions for Life in Community

79.   Catholic social teaching spells out the basic demands of justice in greater detail in the human rights of every person. These fundamental rights are prerequisites for a dignified life in community. The Bible vigorously affirms the sacredness of every person as

---

[34] *Pastoral Constitution*, 25; *Justice in the World*, 51; Pope John Paul II, *The Gift of the Redemption* Apostolic Exhortation on Reconciliation and Penance (Washington, D.C: USCC Office of Publishing and Promotion Services, 1984), 16; Congregation for the Doctrine of the Faith, *Instruction on Christian Freedom and Liberation*, 42, 74.

[35] In the words of the 1971 Synod of Bishops: "Participation constitutes a right which is to be applied in the economic and in the social and political field," *Justice in the World*, 18.

a creature formed in the image and likeness of God. The biblical emphasis on covenant and community also shows that human dignity can only be realized and protected in solidarity with others. In Catholic social thought, therefore, respect for human rights and a strong sense of both personal and community responsibility are linked, not opposed. Vatican II described the common good as "the sum of those conditions of social life which allow social groups and their individual members relatively thorough and ready access to their own fulfillment."[36] These conditions include the rights to fulfillment of material needs, a guarantee of fundamental freedoms, and the protection of relationships that are essential to participation in the life of society.[37] These rights are bestowed on human beings by God and grounded in the nature and dignity of human persons. They are not created by society. Indeed society has a duty to secure and protect them.[38]

80.   The full range of human rights has been systematically outlined by John XXIII in his encyclical *Peace on Earth*. His discussion echoes the United Nations Universal Declaration of Human Rights and implies that internationally accepted human rights standards are strongly supported by Catholic teaching. These rights include the civil and political rights to freedom of speech, worship, and assembly. A number of human rights also concern human welfare and are of a specifically economic nature. First among these are the rights to life, food, clothing, shelter, rest, medical care, and basic education. These are indispensable to the protection of human dignity. In order to ensure

---

[36] *Pastoral Constitution*, 26.

[37] Pope John Paul II, Address at the General Assembly of the United Nations (October 2, 1979), 13, 14.

[38] See Pope Pius XII, 1941 Pentecost Address, in V. Yzermans, *The Major Addresses of Pope Pius XII*, vol. I (St. Paul: North Central, 1961), 32-33.

these necessities, all persons have a right to earn a living, which for most people in our economy is through remunerative employment. All persons also have a right to security in the event of sickness, unemployment, and old age. Participation in the life of the community calls for the protection of this same right to employment, as well as the right to healthful working conditions, to wages, and other benefits sufficient to provide individuals and their families with a standard of living in keeping with human dignity, and to the possibility of property ownership.[39] These fundamental personal rights—civil and political as well as social and economic—state the minimum conditions for social institutions that respect human dignity, social solidarity, and justice. They are all essential to human dignity and to the integral development of both individuals and society, and are thus moral issues.[40] Any denial of these rights harms persons and wounds the human community. Their serious and sustained denial violates individuals and destroys solidarity among persons.

81.   Social and economic rights call for a mode of implementation different from that required to secure civil and political rights. Freedom of worship and of speech imply immunity from interference on the part of both other persons and the government. The rights

---

[39] *Peace on Earth*, 8-27. See *On Human Work*, 18-19. *Peace on Earth* and other modern papal statements refer explicitly to the "right to work" as one of the fundamental economic rights. Because of the ambiguous meaning of the phrase in the United States, and also because the ordinary way people earn their living in our society is through paid employment, the NCCB has affirmed previously that the protection of human dignity demands that the right to useful employment be secured for all who are able and willing to work. See NCCB, *The Economy: Human Dimensions* (November 20, 1975), 5, in NCCB, *Justice in the Marketplace*, 470. See also Congregation for the Doctrine of the Faith, *Instruction on Christian Freedom and Liberation*, 85.

[40] *The Development of Peoples*, 14.

to education, employment, and social security, for example, are empowerments that call for positive action by individuals and society at large.

82.   However, both kinds of rights call for positive action to create social and political institutions that enable all persons to become active members of society. Civil and political rights allow persons to participate freely in the public life of the community, for example, through free speech, assembly, and the vote. In democratic countries these rights have been secured through a long and vigorous history of creating the institutions of constitutional government. In seeking to secure the full range of social and economic rights today, a similar effort to shape new economic arrangements will be necessary.

83.   The first step in such an effort is the development of a new cultural consensus that the basic economic conditions of human welfare are essential to human dignity and are due persons by right. Second, the securing of these rights will make demands on *all* members of society, on all private sector institutions, and on government. A concerted effort on all levels in our society is needed to meet these basic demands of justice and solidarity. Indeed political democracy and a commitment to secure economic rights are mutually reinforcing.

84.   Securing economic rights for all will be an arduous task. There are a number of precedents in U.S. history, however, which show that the work has already begun.[41] The country needs a serious dialogue about the appropriate levels of private and public sector involvement that are needed to move forward. There is certainly room for diversity of opinion in the Church and in U.S. society on *how* to protect the hu-

---

[41] Martha H. Good, "Freedom from Want: The Failure of United States Courts to Protect Subsistence Rights," *Human Rights Quarterly* 6 (1984): 335-365.

man dignity and economic rights of all our brothers and sisters.[42] In our view, however, there can be no legitimate disagreement on the basic moral objectives.

3. Moral Priorities for the Nation

85.   *The common good demands justice for all, the protection of the human rights of all.*[43] Making cultural and economic institutions more supportive of the freedom, power, and security of individuals and families must be a central, long-range objective for the nation. Every person has a duty to contribute to building up the commonweal. All have a responsibility to develop their talents through education. Adults must contribute to society through their individual vocations and talents. Parents are called to guide their children to the maturity of Christian adulthood and responsible citizenship. Everyone has special duties toward the poor and the marginalized. Living up to these responsibilities, however, is often made difficult by the social and economic patterns of society. Schools and educational policies both public and private often serve the privileged exceedingly well, while the children of the poor are effectively abandoned as second-class citizens. Great stresses are created in family life by the way work is organized and scheduled, and by the social and cultural values communicated on TV. Many in the lower middle class are barely getting by and fear becoming victims of economic forces over which they have no control.

86.   *The obligation to provide justice for all means that the poor have the single most urgent economic claim on the conscience of the nation.* Poverty can take many forms, spiritual as well as material. All people face struggles of the spirit as they ask deep questions about their

---

[42] *Pastoral Constitution*, 43.
[43] *Mater et Magistra*, 65.

purpose in life. Many have serious problems in marriage and family life at some time in their lives, and all of us face the certain reality of sickness and death. The Gospel of Christ proclaims that God's love is stronger than all these forms of diminishment. Material deprivation, however, seriously compounds such sufferings of the spirit and heart. To see a loved one sick is bad enough, but to have no possibility of obtaining health care is worse. To face family problems, such as the death of a spouse or a divorce, can be devastating, but to have these lead to the loss of one's home and end with living on the streets is something no one should have to endure in a country as rich as ours. In developing countries these human problems are even more greatly intensified by extreme material deprivation. This form of human suffering can be reduced if our own country, so rich in resources, chooses to increase its assistance.

87.   As individuals and as a nation, therefore, we are called to make a fundamental "option for the poor."[44] The obligation to evaluate social and economic activity from the viewpoint of the poor and the powerless arises from the radical command to love one's neighbor as one's self. Those who are marginalized and whose rights are denied have privileged claims if society is to provide justice for *all*. This obligation is deeply rooted in Christian belief. As Paul VI stated:

---

[44] On the recent use of this term see: Congregation for the Doctrine of the Faith, *Instruction on Christian Freedom and Liberation*, 46-50, 66-68; *Evangelization in Latin America's Present and Future*, Final Document of the Third General Conference of the Latin American Episcopate (Puebla, Mexico, January 27-February 13, 1979), esp. part VI, ch. 1, "A Preferential Option for the Poor," in J. Eagleson and P. Scharper, eds., *Puebla and Beyond* (Maryknoll: Orbis Books, 1979), 264-267; Donal Dorr, *Option for the Poor: A Hundred Years of Vatican Social Teaching* (Dublin: Gill and Macmillan/Maryknoll, N.Y.: Orbis Books, 1983).

> In teaching us charity, the Gospel instructs us in the preferential respect due the poor and the special situation they have in society: the more fortunate should renounce some of their rights so as to place their goods more generously at the service of others.[45]

John Paul II has described this special obligation to the poor as "a call to have a special openness with the small and the weak, those that suffer and weep, those that are humiliated and left on the margin of society, so as to help them win their dignity as human persons and children of God."[46]

88.   The prime purpose of this special commitment to the poor is to enable them to become active participants in the life of society. It is to enable *all* persons to share in and contribute to the common good.[47] The "option for the poor," therefore, is not an adversarial slogan that pits one group or class against another. Rather it states that the deprivation and powerlessness of the poor wounds the whole community. The extent of their suffering is a measure of how far we are from being a true community of persons. These wounds will be healed only by greater solidarity with the poor and among the poor themselves.

89.   In summary, the norms of love, basic justice, and human rights imply that personal decisions, social policies, and economic institutions should be governed by several key priorities. These priorities do not specify everything that must be considered in economic decision making. They do indicate the most fundamental and urgent objectives.

90.   a. *The fulfillment of the basic needs of the poor is of the highest priority.* Personal decisions, policies of pri-

---

[45] *Octogesima Adveniens*, 23.

[46] Address to Bishops of Brazil, 6, 9, *Origins* 10:9 (July 31, 1980): 135.

[47] Pope John Paul II, Address to Workers at Sao Paulo, 4, *Origins*, 10:9 (July 31, 1980): 138; Congregation for the Doctrine of the Faith, *Instruction on Christian Freedom and Liberation*, 66-68.

vate and public bodies, and power relationships must all be evaluated by their effects on those who lack the minimum necessities of nutrition, housing, education, and health care. In particular, this principle recognizes that meeting fundamental human needs must come before the fulfillment of desires for luxury consumer goods, for profits not conducive to the common good, and for unnecessary military hardware.

91.   b. *Increasing active participation in economic life by those who are presently excluded or vulnerable is a high social priority.* The human dignity of all is realized when people gain the power to work together to improve their lives, strengthen their families, and contribute to society. Basic justice calls for more than providing help to the poor and other vulnerable members of society. It recognizes the priority of policies and programs that support family life and enhance economic participation through employment and widespread ownership of property. It challenges privileged economic power in favor of the well-being of all. It points to the need to improve the present situation of those unjustly discriminated against in the past. And it has very important implications for both the domestic and the international distribution of power.

92.   c. *The investment of wealth, talent, and human energy should be specially directed to benefit those who are poor or economically insecure.* Achieving a more just economy in the United States and the world depends in part on increasing economic resources and productivity. In addition, the ways these resources are invested and managed must be scrutinized in light of their effects on non-monetary values. Investment and management decisions have crucial moral dimensions: they create jobs or eliminate them; they can push vulnerable families over the edge into poverty or give them new hope for the future; they help or hinder the building of a more equitable society. Indeed

they can have either positive or negative influence on the fairness of the global economy. Therefore, this priority presents a strong moral challenge to policies that put large amounts of talent and capital into the production of luxury consumer goods and military technology while failing to invest sufficiently in education, health, the basic infrastructure of our society, and economic sectors that produce urgently needed jobs, goods, and services.

93.   d. *Economic and social policies as well as the organization of the work world should be continually evaluated in light of their impact on the strength and stability of family life.* The long-range future of this nation is intimately linked with the well-being of families, for the family is the most basic form of human community.[48] Efficiency and competition in the marketplace must be moderated by greater concern for the way work schedules and compensation support or threaten the bonds between spouses and between parents and children. Health, education, and social service programs should be scrutinized in light of how well they ensure both individual dignity and family integrity.

94.   These priorities are not policies. They are norms that should guide the economic choices of all and shape economic institutions. They can help the United States move forward to fulfill the duties of justice and protect economic rights. They were strongly affirmed as implications of Catholic social teaching by Pope John Paul II during his visit to Canada in 1984: "The needs of the poor take priority over the desires of the rich; the rights of workers over the maximization of profits; the preservation of the environment over uncontrolled industrial expansion; production to meet social needs over production for military purposes."[49]

---

[48] *Pastoral Constitution*, 47.
[49] Address on Christian Unity in a Technological Age (Toronto, September 14, 1984) in *Origins* 14:16 (October 4, 1984): 248.

There will undoubtedly be disputes about the concrete applications of these priorities in our complex world. We do not seek to foreclose discussion about them. However, we believe that an effort to move in the direction they indicate is urgently needed.

95.   The economic challenge of today has many parallels with the political challenge that confronted the founders of our nation. In order to create a new form of political democracy they were compelled to develop ways of thinking and political institutions that had never existed before. Their efforts were arduous and their goals imperfectly realized, but they launched an experiment in the protection of civil and political rights that has prospered through the efforts of those who came after them. *We believe the time has come for a similar experiment in securing economic rights: the creation of an order that guarantees the minimum conditions of human dignity in the economic sphere for every person.* By drawing on the resources of the Catholic moral-religious tradition, we hope to make a contribution through this letter to such a new "American Experiment": a new venture to secure economic justice for all.

C. Working for Greater Justice: Persons and Institutions

96.   The economy of this nation has been built by the labor of human hands and minds. Its future will be forged by the ways persons direct all this work toward greater justice. The economy is not a machine that operates according to its own inexorable laws, and persons are not mere objects tossed about by economic forces. Pope John Paul II has stated that "human work is a key, probably the essential key, to the whole social question."[50] The Pope's understand-

---

[50] *On Human Work*, 3.

ing of work includes virtually all forms of productive human activity: agriculture, entrepreneurship, industry, the care of children, the sustaining of family life, politics, medical care, and scientific research. Leisure, prayer, celebration, and the arts are also central to the realization of human dignity and to the development of a rich cultural life. It is in their daily work, however, that persons become the subjects and creators of the economic life of the nation.[51] Thus, it is primarily through their daily labor that people make their most important contributions to economic justice.

97.   All work has a threefold moral significance. First, it is a principal way that people exercise the distinctive human capacity for self-expression and self-realization. Second, it is the ordinary way for human beings to fulfill their material needs. Finally, work enables people to contribute to the well-being of the larger community. Work is not only for one's self. It is for one's family, for the nation, and indeed for the benefit of the entire human family.[52]

98.   These three moral concerns should be visible in the work of all, no matter what their role in the economy: blue collar workers, managers, homemakers, politicians, and others. They should also govern the activities of the many different, overlapping communities and institutions that make up society: families, neighborhoods, small businesses, giant corporations, trade unions, the various levels of government, international organizations, and a host of other human associations including communities of faith.

99.   Catholic social teaching calls for respect for the full richness of social life. The need for vital contributions from different human associations—ranging

---

[51] Ibid., 5, 6.
[52] Ibid., 6, 10.

in size from the family to government—has been clas-
sically expressed in Catholic social teaching in the
"principle of subsidiarity":

> Just as it is gravely wrong to take from individuals
> what they can accomplish by their own initiative and
> industry and give it to the community, so also it is
> an injustice and at the same time a grave evil and
> disturbance of right order to assign to a greater and
> higher association what lesser and subordinate or-
> ganizations can do. For every social activity ought of
> its very nature to furnish help (*subsidium*) to the mem-
> bers of the body social, and never destroy and absorb
> them.[53]

100.   This principle guarantees institutional pluralism. It provides space for freedom, initiative, and creativity on the part of many social agents. At the same
time, it insists that *all* these agents should work in
ways that help build up the social body. Therefore,
in all their activities these groups should be working
in ways that express their distinctive capacities for
action, that help meet human needs, and that make

---

[53] *Quadragesimo Anno*, 79. The meaning of this principle is not
always accurately understood. For studies of its interpretation in
Catholic teaching see: Calvez and Perrin in John F. Cronin, *Catholic
Social Principles*, (Milwaukee: Bruce, 1950), 328-342; Johannes Mess-
ner, "Freedom as a Principle of Social Order: An Essay in the
Substance of Subsidiary Function," *Modern Schoolman* 28 (1951): 97-
110; Richard E. Mulcahy, "Subsidiarity," *New Catholic Encyclopedia*
vol. 13 (New York: McGraw-Hill, 1966), 762; Franz H. Mueller,
"The Principle of Subsidiarity in Christian Tradition," *American
Catholic Sociological Review)* 4 (October 1943): 144-157; Oswald von
Nell-Breuning, "Zur Sozialreform, Erwagungen zum Subsidiari-
tatsprinzip," *Stimmen der Zeit* 157, Bd. 81 (1955-1956): 1-11; id.,
"Subsidiarity," *Sacramentum Mundi*, vol. 6 (New York: Herder and
Herder, 1970), 6, 114-116; Arthur Fridolin Utz, *Formen und Grenzen
des Subsidiaritatsprinzips* (Heidelberg: F. H. Kerle Verlag, 1956); id.,
"The Principle of Subsidiarity and Contemporary Natural Law,"
Natural Law Forum 3 (1958): 170-183; id., *Grundsatze der Sozialpolitik:
Solidaritat und Subsidiaritat in der Alterversicherung* (Stuttgart: Sewald
Verlag, 1969).

true contributions to the common good of the human community. The task of creating a more just U.S. economy is the vocation of all and depends on strengthening the virtues of public service and responsible citizenship in personal life and on all levels of institutional life.[54]

101.   Without attempting to describe the tasks of all the different groups that make up society, we want to point to the specific rights and duties of some of the persons and institutions whose work for justice will be particularly important to the future of the United States economy. These rights and duties are among the concrete implications of the principle of subsidiarity. Further implications will be discussed in Chapter IV of this letter.

1. Working People and Labor Unions

102.   Though John Paul II's understanding of work is a very inclusive one, it fully applies to those customarily called "workers" or "labor" in the United States. Labor has great dignity, so great that all who are able to work are obligated to do so. The duty to work derives both from God's command and from a responsibility to one's own humanity and to the common good.[55] The virtue of industriousness is also an expression of a person's dignity and solidarity with others. All working people are called to contribute to the common good by seeking excellence in production and service.

103.   Because work is this important, people have a right to employment. In return for their labor, workers have a right to wages and other benefits sufficient to sustain life in dignity. As Pope Leo XIII stated, every working person has "the right of securing things

---

[54] *Pastoral Constitution*, 31.
[55] *On Human Work*, 16.

to sustain life."[56] The way power is distributed in a free market economy frequently gives employers greater bargaining power than employees in the negotiation of labor contracts. Such unequal power may press workers into a choice between an inadequate wage and no wage at all. But justice, not charity, demands certain minimum guarantees. The provision of wages and other benefits sufficient to support a family in dignity is a basic necessity to prevent this exploitation of workers. The dignity of workers also requires adequate health care, security for old age or disability, unemployment compensation, healthful working conditions, weekly rest, periodic holidays for recreation and leisure, and reasonable security against arbitrary dismissal.[57] These provisions are all essential if workers are to be treated as persons rather than simply as a "factor of production."

104.   The Church fully supports the right of workers to form unions or other associations to secure their rights to fair wages and working conditions. This is a specific application of the more general right to associate. In the words of Pope John Paul II, "The experience of history teaches that organizations of this type are an indispensable element of social life, especially in modern industrialized societies."[58] Unions may also legitimately resort to strikes where this is the only available means to the justice owed to workers.[59] No one may deny the right to organize without attacking human dignity itself. Therefore, we firmly oppose organized efforts, such as those regrettably now seen in this country, to break existing unions and prevent workers from organizing. Migrant agricultural workers today are particularly in need of the

---

[56] *Rerum Novarum*, 62; see also 9.
[57] *On Human Work*, 19.
[58] Ibid., 20.
[59] Ibid.

protection, including the right to organize and bargain collectively. U.S. labor law reform is needed to meet these problems as well as to provide more timely and effective remedies for unfair labor practices.

105.   Denial of the right to organize has been pursued ruthlessly in many countries beyond our borders. We vehemently oppose violations of the freedom to associate, wherever they occur, for they are an intolerable attack on social solidarity.

106.   Along with the rights of workers and unions go a number of important responsibilities. Individual workers have obligations to their employers, and trade unions also have duties to society as a whole. Union management in particular carries a strong responsibility for the good name of the entire union movement. Workers must use their collective power to contribute to the well-being of the whole community and should avoid pressing demands whose fulfillment would damage the common good and the rights of more vulnerable members of society.[60] It should be noted, however, that wages paid to workers are but one of the factors affecting the competitiveness of industries. Thus, it is unfair to expect unions to make concessions if managers and shareholders do not make at least equal sacrifices.

107.   Many U.S. unions have exercised leadership in the struggle for justice for minorities and women. Racial and sexual discrimination, however, have blotted the record of some unions. Organized labor has a responsibility to work positively toward eliminating the injustice this discrimination has caused.

108.   Perhaps the greatest challenge facing United States workers and unions today is that of developing a new vision of their role in the United States economy of the future. The labor movement in the United States stands at a crucial moment. The dynamism of the

---

[60] Ibid.

unions that led to their rapid growth in the middle decades of this century has been replaced by a decrease in the percentage of U.S. workers who are organized. American workers are under heavy pressures today that threaten their jobs. The restrictions on the right to organize in many countries abroad make labor costs lower there, threaten American workers and their jobs, and lead to the exploitation of workers in these countries. In these difficult circumstances, guaranteeing the rights of U.S. workers calls for imaginative vision and creative new steps, not reactive or simply defensive strategies. For example, organized labor can play a very important role in helping to provide the education and training needed to help keep workers employable. Unions can also help both their own members and workers in developing countries by increasing their international efforts. A vital labor movement will be one that looks to the future with a deepened sense of global interdependence.

109. There are many signs that these challenges are being discussed by creative labor leaders today. Deeper and broader discussions of this sort are needed. This does not mean that only organized labor faces these new problems. All other sectors and institutions in the U.S. economy need similar vision and imagination. Indeed new forms of cooperation among labor, management, government, and other social groups are essential, and will be discussed in Chapter IV of this letter.

2. Owners and Managers

110. The economy's success in fulfilling the demands of justice will depend on how its vast resources and wealth are managed. Property owners, managers, and investors of financial capital must all contribute to creating a more just society. Securing economic

justice depends heavily on the leadership of men and women in business and on wise investment by private enterprises. Pope John Paul II has pointed out, "The degree of well-being which society today enjoys would be unthinkable without the dynamic figure of the business person, whose function consists of organizing human labor and the means of production so as to give rise to the goods and services necessary for the prosperity and progress of the community."[61] The freedom of entrepreneurship, business, and finance should be protected, but the accountability of this freedom to the common good and the norms of justice must be assured.

111.   Persons in management face many hard choices each day, choices on which the well-being of many others depends. Commitment to the public good and not simply the private good of their firms is at the heart of what it means to call their work a vocation and not simply a career or a job. We believe that the norms and priorities discussed in this letter can be of help as they pursue their important tasks. The duties of individuals in the business world, however, do not exhaust the ethical dimensions of business and finance. The size of a firm or bank is in many cases an indicator of relative power. Large corporations and large financial institutions have considerable power to help shape economic institutions within the United States and throughout the world. With this power goes responsibility and the need for those who manage it to be held to moral and institutional accountability.

112.   Business and finance have the duty to be faithful trustees of the resources at their disposal. No one can ever own capital resources absolutely or control

---

[61] Pope John Paul II, Address to Business Men and Economic Managers (Milan, May 22, 1983) in *L'Osservatore Romano*, weekly edition in English (June 20, 1983): 9:1.

their use without regard for others and society as a whole.[62] This applies first of all to land and natural resources. Short-term profits reaped at the cost of depletion of natural resources or the pollution of the environment violate this trust.

113.   Resources created by human industry are also held in trust. Owners and managers have not created this capital on their own. They have benefited from the work of many others and from the local communities that support their endeavors.[63] They are accountable to these workers and communities when making decisions. For example, reinvestment in technological innovation is often crucial for the long-term viability of a firm. The use of financial resources solely in pursuit of short-term profits can stunt the production of needed goods and services; a broader vision of managerial responsibility is needed.

114.   The Catholic tradition has long defended the right to private ownership of productive property.[64] This right is an important element in a just economic policy. It enlarges our capacity for creativity and initiative.[65] Small and medium-sized farms, businesses, and entrepreneurial enterprises are among the most creative and efficient sectors of our economy. They should be highly valued by the people of the United States, as are land ownership and home ownership. Widespread distribution of property can help avoid excessive concentration of economic and political power. For these reasons ownership should be made possible for a broad sector of our population.[66]

---

[62] Thomas Aquinas, *Summa Theologiae*, IIa, IIae, q. 66.

[63] As Pope John Paul II has stated: "This gigantic and powerful instrument—the whole collection of the means of production that in a sense are considered synonymous with 'capital'—is the result of work and bears the signs of human labor" *On Human Work*, 12.

[64] *Rerum Novarum*, 10, 15, 36.

[65] *Mater et Magistra*, 109.

[66] *Rerum Novarum*, 65, 66; *Mater et Magistra*, 115.

115.   The common good may sometimes demand that the right to own be limited by public involvement in the planning or ownership of certain sectors of the economy. Support of private ownership does not mean that anyone has the right to unlimited accumulation .of wealth. "Private property does not constitute for anyone an absolute or unconditioned right. No one is justified in keeping for his exclusive use what he does not need, when others lack necessities."[67] Pope John Paul II has referred to limits placed on ownership by the duty to serve the common good as a "social mortgage" on private property.[68] For example, these limits are the basis of society's exercise of eminent domain over privately owned land needed for roads or other essential public goods. The Church's teaching opposes collectivist and statist economic approaches. But it also rejects the notion that a free market automatically produces justice. Therefore, as Pope John Paul II has argued, "One cannot exclude the socialization, in suitable conditions, of certain means of production."[69] The determination of when such conditions exist must be made on a case by case basis in light of the demands of the common good.

116.   United States business and financial enterprises can also help determine the justice or injustice of the world economy. They are not all-powerful, but their real power is unquestionable. Transnational corporations and financial institutions can make positive contributions to development and global solidarity. Pope John Paul II has pointed out, however, that the desire to maximize profits and reduce the cost of natural resources and labor has often tempted these transnational enterprises to behavior that increases

---

[67] *On the Development of Peoples*, 23.
[68] Pope John Paul II, Opening Address at the Puebla Conference (Puebla, Mexico, January 28, 1979) in John Eagleson and Philip Scharper, eds., *Puebla and Beyond*, 67.
[69] *On Human Work*, 14.

inequality and decreases the stability of the international order.[70] By collaborating with those national governments that serve their citizens justly and with intergovernmental agencies, these corporations can contribute to overcoming the desperate plight of many persons throughout the world.

117.   Business people, managers, investors, and financiers follow a vital Christian vocation when they act responsibly and seek the common good. We encourage and support a renewed sense of vocation in the business community. We also recognize that the way business people serve society is governed and limited by the incentives which flow from tax policies, the availability of credit, and other public policies.

118.   Businesses have a right to an institutional framework that does not penalize enterprises that act responsibly. Governments must provide regulations and a system of taxation which encourage firms to preserve the environment, employ disadvantaged workers, and create jobs in depressed areas. Managers and stockholders should not be torn between their responsibilities to their organizations and their responsibilities toward society as a whole.

3. Citizens and Government

119.   In addition to rights and duties related to specific roles in the economy, everyone has obligations based simply on membership in the social community. By fulfilling these duties, we create a true commonwealth. Volunteering time, talent, and money to work for greater justice is a fundamental expression of Christian love and social solidarity. All who have more than they need must come to the aid of the poor. People with professional or technical skills needed to enhance the lives of others have a duty to share them.

---

[70] Ibid., 17.

And the poor have similar obligations: to work together as individuals and families to build up their communities by acts of social solidarity and justice. These voluntary efforts to overcome injustice are part of the Christian vocation.

120. Every citizen also has the responsibility to work to secure justice and human rights through an organized social response. In the words of Pius XI, "Charity will never be true charity unless it takes justice into account. . . . Let no one attempt with small gifts of charity to exempt himself from the great duties imposed by justice."[71] The guaranteeing of basic justice for all is not an optional expression of largesse but an inescapable duty for the whole of society.

121. The traditional distinction between society and the state in Catholic social teaching provides the basic framework for such organized public efforts. The Church opposes all statist and totalitarian approaches to socioeconomic questions. Social life is richer than governmental power can encompass. All groups that compose society have responsibilities to respond to the demands of justice. We have just outlined some of the duties of labor unions and business and financial enterprises. These must be supplemented by initiatives by local community groups, professional associations, educational institutions, churches, and synagogues. All the groups that give life to this society have important roles to play in the pursuit of economic justice.

122. For this reason, it is all the more significant that the teachings of the Church insist that *government has a moral function: protecting human rights and securing basic justice for all members of the commonwealth.*[72] Society as a whole and in all its diversity is responsible for building up the common good. But it is government's

[71] *Divini Redemptoris*, 49.
[72] *Peace on Earth*, 60-62.

role to guarantee the minimum conditions that make this rich social activity possible, namely, human rights and justice.[73] This obligation also falls on individual citizens as they choose their representatives and participate in shaping public opinion.

123.   More specifically, it is the responsibility of all citizens, acting through their government, to assist and empower the poor, the disadvantaged, the handicapped, and the unemployed. Government should assume a positive role in generating employment and establishing fair labor practices, in guaranteeing the provision and maintenance of the economy's infrastructure, such as roads, bridges, harbors, public means of communication, and transport. It should regulate trade and commerce in the interest of fairness.[74] Government may levy the taxes necessary to meet these responsibilities, and citizens have a moral obligation to pay those taxes. The way society responds to the needs of the poor through its public

---

[73] Vatican Council II, *Declaration on Religious Freedom (Dignitatis Humanae)*, 6. See John Courtney Murray, *The Problem of Religious Freedom*, Woodstock Papers, no. 7 (Westminster, Md.: Newman Press, 1965).

[74] *Peace on Earth*, 63-64. *Quadragesimo Anno*, 80. In *Rerum Novarum* Pope Leo XIII set down the basic norm that determines when government intervention is called for: "If, therefore, any injury has been done to or threatens either the common good or the interests of individual groups, which injury cannot in any other way be repaired or prevented, it is necessary for public authority to intervene" *Rerum Novarum*, 52. Pope John XXIII synthesized the Church's understanding of the function of governmental intervention this way: "The State, whose purpose is the realization of the common good in the temporal order, can by no means disregard the economic activity of its citizens. Indeed it should be present to promote in suitable manner the production of a sufficient supply of material goods, . . . contribute actively to the betterment of the living conditions of workers, . . . see to it that labor agreements are entered into according to the norms of justice and equity, and that in the environment of work the dignity of the human being is not violated either in body or spirit" *Mater et Magistra*, 20-21.

policies is the litmus test of its justice or injustice. The political debate about these policies is the indispensable forum for dealing with the conflicts and trade-offs that will always be present in the pursuit of a more just economy.

124.   The primary norm for determining the scope and limits of governmental intervention is the "principle of subsidiarity" cited above. This principle states that, in order to protect basic justice, government should undertake only those initiatives which exceed the capacity of individuals or private groups acting independently. Government should not replace or destroy smaller communities and individual initiative. Rather it should help them to contribute more effectively to social well-being and supplement their activity when the demands of justice exceed their capacities. This does not mean, however, that the government that governs least governs best. Rather it defines good government intervention as that which truly "helps" other social groups contribute to the common good by directing, urging, restraining, and regulating economic activity as "the occasion requires and necessity demands."[75] This calls for cooperation and consensus-building among the diverse agents in our economic life, including government. The precise form of government involvement in this process cannot be determined in the abstract. It will depend on an assessment of specific needs and the most effective ways to address them.

D. Christian Hope and the Courage To Act

125.   The Christian vision is based on the conviction that God has destined the human race and all creation

---

[75] *Quadragesimo Anno*, 79.

for "a kingdom of truth and life, of holiness and grace, of justice, love, and peace."[76] This conviction gives Christians strong hope as they face the economic struggles of the world today. This hope is not a naive optimism that imagines that simple formulas for creating a fully just society are ready at hand. The Church's experience through history and in nations throughout the world today has made it wary of all ideologies that claim to have the final answer to humanity's problems.[77] Christian hope has a much stronger foundation than such ideologies, for it rests on the knowledge that God is at work in the world, "preparing a new dwelling place and a new earth where justice will abide."[78]

126.   This hope stimulates and strengthens Christian efforts to create a more just economic order in spite of difficulties and setbacks.[79] Christian hope is strong and resilient, for it is rooted in a faith that knows that the fullness of life comes to those who follow Christ in the way of the Cross. In pursuit of concrete solutions, all members of the Christian community are called to an ever finer discernment of the hurts and opportunities in the world around them, in order to respond to the most pressing needs and thus build up a more just society.[80] This is a communal task calling for dialogue, experimentation, and imagination. It also calls for deep faith and courageous love.

---

[76] Preface for the Feast of Christ the King, *The Sacramentary of the Roman Missal*.
[77] *Octogesima Adveniens*, 26-35.
[78] *Pastoral Constitution*, 39.
[79] Ibid.
[80] *Octogesima Adveniens*, 42.

Chapter III

SELECTED
ECONOMIC POLICY ISSUES

127.   We have outlined this moral vision as a guide
to all who seek to be faithful to the Gospel in their
daily economic decisions and as a challenge to transform the economic arrangements that shape our lives
and our world. These arrangements embody and communicate social values and therefore have moral significance both in themselves and in their effects.
Christians, like all people, must be concerned about
how the concrete outcomes of their economic activity
serve human dignity; they must assess the extent to
which the structures and practices of the economy
support or undermine their moral vision.

128.   Such an assessment of economic practices,
structures, and outcomes leads to a variety of conclusions. Some people argue that an unfettered free-market economy, where owners, workers, and consumers
pursue their enlightened self-interest, provides the
greatest possible liberty, material welfare, and equity.
The policy implication of this view is to intervene in
the economy as little as possible because it is such a
delicate mechanism that any attempt to improve it is
likely to have the opposite effect. Others argue that
the capitalist system is inherently inequitable and
therefore contradictory to the demands of Christian
morality, for it is based on acquisitiveness, competi-

tion, and self-centered individualism. They assert that capitalism is fatally flawed and must be replaced by a radically different system that abolishes private property, the profit motive, and the free market.

129.   Catholic social teaching has traditionally rejected these ideological extremes because they are likely to produce results contrary to human dignity and economic justice.[1] Starting with the assumption that the economy has been created by human beings and can be changed by them, the Church works for improvement in a variety of economic and political contexts; but it is not the Church's role to create or promote a specific new economic system. Rather, the Church must encourage all reforms that hold out hope of transforming our economic arrangements into a fuller systemic realization of the Christian moral vision. The Church must also stand ready to challenge practices and institutions that impede or carry us farther away from realizing this vision.

130.   In short, the Church is not bound to any particular economic, political, or social system; it has lived with many forms of economic and social organization and will continue to do so, evaluating each according to moral and ethical principles: What is the impact of the system on people? Does it support or threaten human dignity?

131.   In this document we offer reflections on the particular reality that is the U.S. economy. In doing so we are aware of the need to address not only individual issues within the economy but also the larger question of the economic system itself. Our approach in analyzing the U.S. economy is pragmatic and evolutionary in nature. We live in a "mixed" economic system which is the product of a long history of reform and adjustment. It is in the spirit of this American pragmatic tradition of reform that we seek to continue

---

[1] *Octogesima Adveniens,* 26-41; and *On Human Work,* 7, 13.

the search for a more just economy. Our nation has many assets to employ in this quest—vast economic, technological, and human resources and a system of representative government through which we can all help shape economic decisions.

132.   Although we have chosen in this chapter to focus primarily on some aspects of the economy where we think reforms are realistically possible, we also emphasize that Catholic social teaching bears directly on larger questions concerning the economic system itself and the values it expresses—questions that cannot be ignored in the Catholic vision of economic justice.[2] For example, does our economic system place more emphasis on maximizing profits than on meeting human needs and fostering human dignity? Does our economy distribute its benefits equitably or does it concentrate power and resources in the hands of a few? Does it promote excessive materialism and individualism? Does is adequately protect the environment and the nation's natural resources? Does it direct too many scarce resources to military purposes? These and other basic questions about the economy need to be scrutinized in light of the ethical norms we have outlined. We urge continuing exploration of these systemic questions in a more comprehensive way than this document permits.

133.   We have selected the following subjects to address here: 1) employment, 2) poverty, 3) food and agriculture, and 4) the U.S. role in the global economy. These topics were chosen because of their relevance to both the economic "signs of the times" and the ethical norms of our tradition. Each exemplifies U.S. policies that are basic to the establishment of economic justice in the nation and the world, and each illustrates key moral principles and norms for action from Catholic social teaching. Our treatment of these issues does

---

[2] *Program of Social Reconstruction*, 33-40.

not constitute a comprehensive analysis of the U.S. economy. We emphasize that these are illustrative topics intended to exemplify the interaction of moral values and economic issues in our day, not to encompass all such values and issues. This document is not a technical blueprint for economic reform. Rather, it is an attempt to foster a serious moral analysis leading to a more just economy.

134. In focusing on some of the central economic issues and choices in American life in the light of moral principles, we are aware that the movement from principle to policy is complex and difficult and that although moral values are essential in determining public policies, they do not dictate specific solutions. They must interact with empirical data, with historical, social, and political realities, and with competing demands on limited resources. The soundness of our prudential judgments depends not only on the moral force of our principles, but also on the accuracy of our information and the validity of our assumptions.

135. Our judgments and recommendations on specific economic issues, therefore, do not carry the same moral authority as our statements of universal moral principles and formal church teaching; the former are related to circumstances which can change or which can be interpreted differently by people of good will. We expect and welcome debate on our specific policy recommendations. Nevertheless, we want our statements on these matters to be given serious consideration by Catholics as they determine whether their own moral judgments are consistent with the Gospel and with Catholic social teaching. We believe that differences on complex economic questions should be expressed in a spirit of mutual respect and open dialogue.[3]

---

[3] See *The Challenge of Peace: God's Promise and Our Response*, 9-10.

A. Employment

136.   Full employment is the foundation of a just economy. The most urgent priority for domestic economic policy is the creation of new jobs with adequate pay and decent working conditions. We must make it possible as a nation for every one who is seeking a job to find employment within a reasonable amount of time. Our emphasis on this goal is based on the conviction that human work has a special dignity and is a key to achieving justice in society.[4]

137.   Employment is a basic right, a right which protects the freedom of all to participate in the economic life of society. It is a right which flows from the principles of justice which we have outlined above. Corresponding to this right is the duty on the part of society to ensure that the right is protected. The importance of this right is evident in the fact that for most people employment is crucial to self-realization and essential to the fulfillment of material needs. Since so few in our economy own productive property, employment also forms the first line of defense against poverty. Jobs benefit society as well as workers, for they enable more people to contribute to the common good and to the productivity required for a healthy economy.

1. The Scope and Effects of Unemployment

138.   Joblessness is becoming a more widespread and deep-seated problem in our nation. There are about 8 million people in the United States looking for a job who cannot find one. They represent about

---

[4] *On Human Work,* 3.

7 percent of the labor force.[5] The official rate of unemployment does not include those who have given up looking for work or those who are working part-time, but want to work full-time. When these categories are added, it becomes clear that about one-eighth of the workforce is directly affected by unemployment.[6] The severity of the unemployment problem is compounded by the fact that almost three-fourths of those who are unemployed receive no unemployment insurance benefits.[7]

139.　　In recent years there has been a steady trend toward higher and higher levels of unemployment, even in good times. Between 1950 and 1980 the annual unemployment rate exceeded current levels only during the recession years of 1975 and 1976. Periods of economic recovery during these three decades brought unemployment rates down to 3 and 4 percent. Since 1979, however, the rate has generally been above 7 percent.

140.　　Who are the unemployed? Blacks, Hispanics, Native Americans, young adults, female heads of households, and those who are inadequately educated are represented disproportionately among the ranks of the unemployed. The unemployment rate among minorities is almost twice as high as the rate among whites. For female heads of households the unemployment rate is over 10 percent. Among black

[5] U.S. Department of Labor, Bureau of Labor Statistics, *The Employment Situation: April 1986* (May 1986).

[6] Full Employment Action Council, *Employment in America: Illusory Recovery in a Decade of Decline* (Washington, D.C., February 1985), 19. Calculations based on data from the U.S. Department of Labor's Bureau of Labor Statistics.

[7] U.S. Department of Labor, Bureau of Labor Statistics, *The Employment Situation: August 1985*; and U. S. Department of Labor, Employment and Training Administration, *Unemployment Insurance Claims*, Reference week of June 22, 1985.

teenagers, unemployment reaches the scandalous rate
of more than one in three.[8]

141.   The severe human costs of high unemployment levels become vividly clear when we examine
the impact of joblessness on human lives and human
dignity. It is a deep conviction of American culture
that work is central to the freedom and well-being of
people. The unemployed often come to feel they are
worthless and without a productive role in society.
Each day they are unemployed our society tells them:
We don't need your talent. We don't need your initiative. We don't need *you*. Unemployment takes a
terrible toll on the health and stability of both individuals and families. It gives rise to family quarrels,
greater consumption of alcohol, child abuse, spouse
abuse, divorce, and higher rates of infant mortality.[9]
People who are unemployed often feel that society
blames them for being unemployed. Very few people
survive long periods of unemployment without some
psychological damage even if they have sufficient
funds to meet their needs.[10] At the extreme, the strains

---

[8] *The Employment Situation: August 1985.*

[9] Brenner, "Fetal, Infant and Maternal Mortality during Periods
of Economic Instability," *International Journal of Health Services* (Sum-
mer 1973); P. H. Ellison, "Neurology of Hard Times," *Clinical Pe-
diatrics* (March 1977); S. V. Kasl and S. Cobb, "Some Mental Health
Consequences of Plant Closings and Job Loss," in L. Ferman and
J. P. Gordus, eds., *Mental Health and the Economy* (Kalamazoo, Mich.:
W. E. Upjohn Institute for Employment Research, 1979), 255-300;
L. E. Kopolow and F. M. Ochberg, "Spinoff from a Downward
Swing," *Mental Health* 59 (Summer 1975); D. Shaw, "Unemployment
Hurts More than the Pocketbook," *Today's Health* (March 1978).

[10] Richard M. Cohn, *The Consequences of Unemployment on Evaluation of Self*, Doctoral dissertation, Department of Psychology (University of Michigan, 1977); John A. Garraty, *Unemployment in History:
Economic Thought and Public Policy* (New York: Harper and Row,
1978); Harry Maurer, *Not Working: An Oral History of the Unemployed*
(New York: Holt, Rinehart, and Winston, 1979).

of job loss may drive individuals to suicide.[11]

142.   In addition to the terrible waste of individual talent and creativity, unemployment also harms society at large. Jobless people pay little or no taxes, thus lowering the revenues for cities, states, and the federal government. At the same time, rising unemployment requires greater expenditures for unemployment compensation, food stamps, welfare, and other assistance. It is estimated that in 1986, for every one percentage point increase in the rate of unemployment, there will be roughly a $40 billion increase in the federal deficit.[12] The costs to society are also evident in the rise in crime associated with joblessness. The Federal Bureau of Prisons reports that increases in unemployment have been followed by increases in the prison population. Other studies have shown links between the rate of joblessness and the frequency of homicides, robberies, larcenies, narcotics arrests, and youth crimes.[13]

143.   Our own experiences with the individuals, families, and communities that suffer the burdens of unemployment compel us to the conviction that as a nation we simply cannot afford to have millions of able-bodied men and women unemployed. We cannot afford the economic costs, the social dislocation, and the enormous human tragedies caused by unemployment. In the end, however, what we can least afford

---

[11] M. Harvey Brenner, *Estimating the Social Cost of National Economic Policy* (U.S. Congress, Joint Economic Committee, 1976); see Brenner, *Mental Illness and the Economy* (Cambridge, Mass.: Harvard University Press, 1973).

[12] Congressional Budget Office, *Economic and Budget Outlook: FY 1986—FY 1990* (Washington, D.C., February 1985), 75.

[13] *Correlation of Unemployment and Federal Prison Population* (Washington, D.C.: U.S. Bureau of Prisons, March 1975); M. Yeager, "Unemployment and Imprisonment," *Journal of Criminal Law and Criminology* 70:4 (1979); Testimony of M. H. Brenner in *Unemployment and Crime* (U.S. Congress, House Hearings, 1977,) 25.

is the assault on human dignity that occurs when millions are left without adequate employment. Therefore, we cannot but conclude that current levels of unemployment are intolerable, and they impose on us a moral obligation to work for policies that will reduce joblessness.

2. Unemployment in a Changing Economy

144.   The structure of the U.S. economy is undergoing a transformation that affects both the quantity and the quality of jobs in our nation. The size and makeup of the workforce, for example, have changed markedly in recent years. For a number of reasons, there are now more people in the labor market than ever before in our history. Population growth has pushed up the supply of potential workers. In addition, large numbers of women have entered the labor force not only in order to put their talents and education to greater use, but also out of economic necessity. Many families need two salaries if they are to live in a decently human fashion. Female-headed households often depend heavily on the mother's income to stay off the welfare rolls. Immigrants seeking a better existence in the United States have also added to the size of the labor force. These demographic changes, however, cannot fully explain the higher levels of unemployment.

145.   Technological changes are also having dramatic impacts on the employment picture in the United States. Advancing technology brings many benefits, but it can also bring social and economic costs, including the downgrading and displacement of workers. High technology and advanced automation are changing the very face of our nation's industries and occupations. In the 1970s, about 90 percent of all new jobs were in service occupations. By 1990, service industries are expected to employ 72 percent of the labor

force. Much of the job growth in the 1980s is expected to be in traditionally low-paying, high-turnover jobs such as sales, clerical, janitorial, and food service.[14] Too often these jobs do not have career ladders leading to higher skilled, higher paying jobs. Thus, the changing industrial and occupational mix in the U.S. economy could result in a shift toward lower paying and lower skilled jobs.

146.   Increased competition in world markets is another factor influencing the rate of joblessness in our nation. Many other exporting nations have acquired and developed up-to-the-minute technology, enabling them to increase productivity dramatically. Combined with very low wages in many nations, this has allowed them to gain a larger share of the U.S. market to cut into U.S. export markets. At the same time many corporations have closed plants in the United States and moved their capital, technology, and jobs to foreign affiliates.

147.   Discrimination in employment is one of the causes for high rates of joblessness and low pay among racial minorities and women. Beyond the normal problems of locating a job, blacks, Hispanics, Native Americans, immigrants, and other minorities bear this added burden of discrimination. Discrimination against women is compounded by the lack of adequate child care services and by the unwillingness of many employers to provide flexible employment or extend fringe benefits to part-time employees.

148.   High levels of defense spending also have an effect on the number of jobs in our economy. In our pastoral letter, *The Challenge of Peace*, we noted the serious economic distortions caused by the arms race and the disastrous effects that it has on society's ability to care for the poor and the needy. Employment is

---

[14] Committee on the Evolution of Work, AFL-CIO, *The Future of Work* (Washington, D.C.: AFL-CIO, 1983), 11.

one area in which this interconnection is very evident. The hundreds of billions of dollars spent by our nation each year on the arms race create a massive drain on the U.S. economy as well as a very serious "brain drain." Such spending on the arms race means a net loss in the number of jobs created in the economy, because defense industries are less labor-intensive than other major sectors of the economy.[15] Moreover, nearly half of the American scientific and engineering force works in defense-related programs and over 60 percent of the entire federal research and development budget goes to the military.[16] We must ask whether our nation will ever be able to modernize our economy and achieve full employment if we continue to devote so much of our financial and human resources to defense-related activities.

149.   These are some of the factors that have driven up the rate of unemployment in recent years. Although our economy has created more than 20 million new jobs since 1970,[17] there continues to be a chronic and growing job shortage. In the face of this challenge,

---

[15] Congressional Budget Office, *Defense Spending and the Economy* (Washington, D.C.: Government Printing Office, 1983). See also Michael Edelstein, *The Economic Impact of Military Spending* (New York: Council on Economic Priorities, 1977); and Robert De Grasse, Jr., *Military Expansion, Economic Decline* (New York: Council on Economic Priorities, 1983). See also U.S. Department of Labor, Bureau of Labor Statistics Report, "Structure of the U.S. Economy in 1980 and 1985" (Washington, D.C.: Government Printing Office, 1975); and Marion Anderson, *The Empty Pork Barrel* (Lansing, Mich.: Employment Research Associates, 1982).

[16] U.S. Office of Management and Budget, *Historical Tables*, Budget of the United States Government Fiscal Year 1986 (Washington, D.C.: U.S. Government Printing Office, 1985). Table 10.2, 10.2(3). See also, National Science Foundation Report, "Characteristics of Experienced Scientists and Engineers" (1978), Detailed Statistical Tables (Washington, D.C.: U.S. Government Printing Office, 1978).

[17] "Statistical Supplement to International Comparison of Unemployment," Bureau of Labor Statistics, (May 1984): 7. Unpublished.

our nation's economic institutions have failed to adapt adequately and rapidly enough. For example, failure to invest sufficiently in certain industries and regions, inadequate education and training for new workers, and insufficient mechanisms to assist workers displaced by new technology have added to the unemployment problem.

150.   Generating an adequate number of jobs in our economy is a complex task in view of the changing and diverse nature of the problem. It involves numerous trade-offs and substantial costs. Nevertheless, it is not an impossible task. Achieving the goal of full employment may require major adjustments and creative strategies that go beyond the limits of existing policies and institutions, but it is a task we must undertake.

3. Guidelines for Action

151.   We recommend that the nation make a major new commitment to achieve full employment. At present there is nominal endorsement of the full employment ideal, but no firm commitment to bringing it about. If every effort were now being made to create the jobs required, one might argue that the situation today is the best we can do. But such is not the case. The country is doing far less than it might to generate employment.

152.   Over the last decade, economists, policy makers, and the general public have shown greater willingness to tolerate unemployment levels of 6 to 7 percent or even more.[18] Although we recognize the

---

[18] Isabel V. Sawhill and Charles F. Stone state the prevailing view among economists this way: "High employment is usually defined as the rate of unemployment consistent with no additional inflation, a rate currently believed by many, but not all, economists to be in the neighborhood of 6 percent." "The Economy: The Key

complexities and trade-offs involved in reducing unemployment, we believe that 6 to 7 percent unemployment is neither inevitable nor acceptable. While
a zero unemployment rate is clearly impossible in an
economy where people are constantly entering the
job market and others are changing jobs, appropriate
policies and concerted private and public action can
improve the situation considerably, if we have the
will to do so. No economy can be considered truly
healthy when so many millions of people are denied
jobs by forces outside their control. The acceptance
of present unemployment rates would have been unthinkable twenty years ago. It should be regarded as
intolerable today.

153.   We must first establish a consensus that everyone has a right to employment. Then the burden of
securing full employment falls on all of us—policy
makers, business, labor, and the general public—to
create and implement the mechanisms to protect that
right. We must work for the formation of a new national consensus and mobilize the necessary political
will at all levels to make the goal of full employment
a reality.

154.   Expanding employment in our nation will require significant steps in both the private and public
sectors, as well as joint action between them. Private
initiative and entrepreneurship are essential to this
task, for the private sector accounts for about 80 percent of the jobs in the United States, and most new
jobs are being created there.[19] Thus, a viable strategy
for employment generation must assume that a large

---

to Success," in John L. Palmer and Isabel V. Sawhill, eds., *The
Reagan Record: An Assessment of America's Changing Domestic Priorities*
(Cambridge, Mass.: Bollinger, 1984), 72. See also Stanley Fischer
and Rudiger Dornbusch, *Economics* (New York: McGraw-Hill, 1983),
731-743.

[19] W. L. Birch, "Who Creates Jobs?," *The Public Interest* 65 (Fall
1981): 3-14.

part of the solution will be with private firms and small businesses. At the same time, it must be recognized that government has a prominent and indispensable role to play in addressing the problem of unemployment. The market alone will not automatically produce full employment. Therefore, the government must act to ensure that this goal is achieved by coordinating general economic policies, by job creation programs, and by other appropriate policy measures.

155.   Effective action against unemployment will require a careful mix of general economic policies and targeted employment programs. Taken together, these policies and programs should have full employment as their number one goal.

a. General Economic Policies

156.   The general or macroeconomic policies of the federal government are essential tools for encouraging the steady economic growth that produces more and better jobs in the economy. *We recommend that the fiscal and monetary policies of the nation—such as federal spending, tax, and interest rate policies—should be coordinated so as to achieve the goal of full employment.*

157.   General economic policies that attempt to expand employment must also deal with the problem of inflation.[20] The risk of inflationary pressures re-

---

[20] Martin Neil Baily and Arthur M. Okun, eds., *The Battle Against Unemployment and Inflation*, third edition (New York: Norton, 1982); and Martin Neil Baily, "Labor Market Performance, Competition and Inflation," in Baily, ed., *Workers, Jobs and Inflation* (Washington, D.C.: The Brookings Institution, 1982). See also, Lawrence Klein, "Reducing Unemployment Without Inflation"; and James Tobin, "Unemployment, Poverty, and Economic Policy," testimony before the Subcommittee on Economic Stabilization, U.S. House of Representatives Committee on Banking, Finance and Urban Affairs (March 19, 1985), serial no. 99-5 (Washington, D.C.: U.S. Government Printing Office, 1985), 15-18, 31-33.

sulting from such expansionary policies is very real. Our response to this risk, however, must not be to abandon the goal of full employment, but to develop effective policies that keep inflation under control.

158.   While economic growth is an important and necessary condition for the reduction of unemployment, it is not sufficient in and of itself. In order to work for full employment and restrain inflation, it is also necessary to adopt more specific programs and policies targeted toward particular aspects of the unemployment problem.[21]

b. Targeted Employment Programs

159.   (1) *We recommend expansion of job-training and apprenticeship programs in the private sector administered and supported jointly by business, labor unions, and government.* Any comprehensive employment strategy must include systematic means of developing the technical and professional skills needed for a dynamic and productive economy. Investment in a skilled work force is a prerequisite both for sustaining economic growth and achieving greater justice in the United States. The obligation to contribute to this investment falls on both the private and public sectors. Today business, labor, and government need to coordinate their efforts and pool their resources to promote a substantial increase in the number of apprenticeship programs and to expand on-the-job training programs. We recommend a national commitment to eradicate illiteracy and to provide people with the skills necessary to adapt to the changing demands of employment.

160.   With the rapid pace of technological change,

---

[21] Tobin, "Unemployment, Poverty, and Economic Policy"; and Klein, "Reducing Unemployment Without Inflation."

continuing education and training are even more important today than in the past. Businesses have a stake in providing it, for skilled workers are essential to increased productivity. Labor unions should support it, for their members are increasingly vulnerable to displacement and job loss unless they continue to develop their skills and their flexibility on the job. Local communities have a stake as well, for their economic well-being will suffer serious harm if local industries fail to develop and are forced to shut down.

161.   The best medicine for the disease of plant-closings is prevention. Prevention depends not only on sustained capital investment to enhance productivity through advanced technology but also on the training and retraining of workers within the private sector. In circumstances where plants are forced to shut down, management, labor unions, and local communities must see to it that workers are not simply cast aside. Retraining programs will be even more urgently needed in these circumstances.

162.   (2) *We recommend increased support for direct job creation programs targeted on the long-term unemployed and those with special needs.* Such programs can take the form of direct public service employment and also of public subsidies for employment in the private sector. Both approaches would provide jobs for those with low skills less expensively and with less inflation than would general stimulation of the economy.[22] The cost of providing jobs must also be balanced against the savings realized by the government through decreased welfare and unemployment insurance expenditures and increased revenues from the taxes paid by the newly employed.

163.   Government funds, if used effectively, can also stimulate private sector jobs for the long-term un-

---

[22] Robert H. Haveman, "Toward Efficiency and Equity through Direct Job Creation," *Social Policy* 11:1 (May/June 1980): 48.

employed and for groups particularly hard to employ. Experiments need to be conducted on the precise ways such subsidies would most successfully attract business participation and ensure the generation of permanent jobs.

164.   These job generation efforts should aim specifically at bringing marginalized persons into the labor force. They should produce a net increase in the number of jobs rather than displacing the burden of unemployment from one group of persons to another. They should also be aimed at long-term jobs and should include the necessary supportive services to assist the unemployed in finding and keeping jobs.

165.   Jobs that are created should produce goods and services needed and valued by society. It is both good common sense and sound economics to create jobs directly for the purpose of meeting society's unmet needs. Across the nation, in every state and locality, there is ample evidence of social needs that are going unmet. Many of our parks and recreation facilities are in need of maintenance and repair. Many of the nation's bridges and highways are in disrepair. We have a desperate need for more low-income housing. Our educational systems, day-care services, senior citizen services, and other community programs need to be expanded. These and many other elements of our national life are areas of unmet need. At the same time, there are more than 8 million Americans looking for productive and useful work. Surely we have the capacity to match these needs by giving Americans who are anxious to work a chance for productive employment in jobs that are waiting to be done. The overriding moral value of enabling jobless persons to achieve a new sense of dignity and personal worth through employment also strongly recommends these programs.

166.   These job creation efforts will require increased collaboration and fresh alliances between the

private and public sectors at all levels. There are already a number of examples of how such efforts can be successful.[23] We believe that the potential of these kinds of partnerships has only begun to be tapped.

c. Examining New Strategies

167.   In addition to the actions suggested above, we believe there is also a need for careful examination and experimentation with alternative approaches that might improve both the quantity and quality of jobs. More extensive use of job sharing, flex time, and a reduced work week are among the topics that should continue to be on the agenda of public discussion. Consideration should also be given to the possibility of limiting or abolishing compulsory overtime work. Similarly, methods might be examined to discourage the overuse of part-time workers, who do not receive fringe benefits.[24] New strategies also need to be explored in the area of education and training for the hard-to-employ, displaced workers, the handicapped, and others with special needs. Particular attention is needed to achieve pay equity between men and

---

[23] William H. McCarthy, *Reducing Urban Unemployment: What Works at the Local Level* (Washington, D.C.: National League of Cities, October 1985); William Schweke, "States that Take the Lead on a New Industrial Policy," in Betty G. Lall, ed., *Economic Dislocation and Job Loss* (New York: Cornell University, New York State School of Industrial and Labor Relations, 1985), 97-106; David Robinson, *Training and Jobs Programs in Action: Case Studies in Private Sector Initiatives for the Hard to Employ* (New York: Committee for Economic Development, 1978). See also ch. IV of this pastoral letter.

[24] Rudy Oswald, "The Economy and Workers' Jobs, The Living Wage and a Voice," in John W. Houch and Oliver F. Williams, eds., *Catholic Social Teaching and the U.S. Economy: Working Papers for a Bishops' Pastoral* (Washington, D.C.: University Press of America, 1984), 77-89. On the subject of shortening the work week, Oswald points out that in the first 40 years of this century, the average work week fell from 60 hours to 40 hours. However, the standard work week has been unchanged now for almost 50 years.

women, as well as upgrading the pay scale and working conditions of traditionally low-paying jobs. The
nation should renew its efforts to develop effective
affirmative action policies that assist those who have
been excluded by racial or sexual discrimination in
the past. New strategies for improving job placement
services at the national and local levels are also needed.
Improving occupational safety is another important
concern that deserves increased attention.

168.   Much greater attention also needs to be devoted to the long-term task of converting some of the
nation's military production to more peaceful and socially productive purposes. The nation needs to seek
more effective ways to retool industries, to retrain
workers, and to provide the necessary adjustment
assistance for communities affected by this kind of
economic conversion.

169.   These are among the avenues that need to be
explored in the search for just employment policies.
A belief in the inherent dignity of human work and
in the right to employment should motivate people
in all sectors of society to carry on that search in new
and creative ways.

B. Poverty

170.   More than 33 million Americans—about one
in every seven people in our nation—are poor by the
government's official definition. The norms of human
dignity and the preferential option for the poor compel
us to confront this issue with a sense of urgency.
Dealing with poverty is not a luxury to which our
nation can attend when it finds the time and resources. Rather, it is a moral imperative of the highest
priority.

171.   Of particular concern is the fact that poverty has increased dramatically during the last decade. Since 1973 the poverty rate has increased by nearly a third. Although the recent recovery has brought a slight decline in the rate, it remains at a level that is higher than at almost any other time during the last two decades.[25]

172.   As pastors we have seen firsthand the faces of poverty in our midst. Homeless people roam city streets in tattered clothing and sleep in doorways or on subway grates at night. Many of these are former mental patients released from state hospitals. Thousands stand in line at soup kitchens because they have no other way of feeding themselves. Millions of children are so poorly nourished that their physical and mental development are seriously harmed.[26] We have also seen the growing economic hardship and insecurity experienced by moderate-income Americans when they lose their jobs and their income due to forces beyond their control. These are alarming signs and trends. They pose for our nation an urgent moral and human challenge: to fashion a society where no one goes without the basic material necessities required for human dignity and growth.

173.   Poverty can be described and defined in many different ways. It can include spiritual as well as material poverty. Likewise, its meaning changes depending on the historical, social, and economic setting. Poverty in our time is different from the more severe deprivation experienced in earlier centuries in the U.S. or in Third World nations today. Our discussion of poverty in this chapter is set within the context of

---

[25] U.S. Bureau of the Census, Current Population Reports, Series P-60, no. 149, *Money Income and Poverty Status of Families in the United States: 1984* (Washington, D.C.: U.S. Government Printing Office, 1985).

[26] Massachusetts Department of Public Health, *Massachusetts Nutrition Survey* (Boston, Mass.: 1983).

present-day American society. By poverty, we are referring here to the lack of sufficient material resources
required for a decent life. We use the government's
official definition of poverty, although we recognize
its limits.[27]

1. Characteristics of Poverty

174.   Poverty is not an isolated problem existing
solely among a small number of anonymous people
in our central cities. Nor is it limited to a dependent
underclass or to specific groups in the United States.
It is a condition experienced at some time by many
people in different walks of life and in different circumstances. Many poor people are working but at

---

[27] There is considerable debate about the most suitable definition
of poverty. Some argue that the government's official definition
understates the number of the poor, and that a more adequate
definition would indicate that as many as 50 million Americans are
poor. For example, they note that the poverty line has declined
sharply as a percent of median family income—from 48% in 1959
to 35% in 1983. Others argue that the official indicators should be
reduced by the amount of in-kind benefits received by the poor,
such as food stamps. By some calculations that would reduce the
number counted as poor to about 12 million. We conclude that for
present purposes the official government definition provides a suitable middle ground. That definition is based on a calculation that
multiplies the cost of USDA's lowest cost food plan times three.
The definition is adjusted for inflation each year.
   Among other reasons for using the official definition is that it
allows one to compare poverty figures over time. For additional
readings on this topic see: L. Rainwater, *What Money Buys: Inequality
and the Social Meanings of Income* (New York: Basic Books, 1975); id.,
Persistent and Transitory Poverty: A New Look (Cambridge, Mass.:
Joint Center for Urban Studies, 1980); M. Orshansky, "How Poverty
is Measured," *Monthly Labor Review* 92 (1969): 37-41; M. Anderson,
Welfare (Stanford, Calif.: Hoover Institution Press, 1978); and Michael Harrington, *The New American Poverty* (New York: Holt, Rinehart, and Winston, 1984), 81-82.

wages insufficient to lift them out of poverty.[28] Others are unable to work and therefore dependent on outside sources of support. Still others are on the edge of poverty; although not officially defined as poor, they are economically insecure and at risk of falling into poverty.

175.   While many of the poor manage to escape from beneath the official poverty line, others remain poor for extended periods of time. Long-term poverty is concentrated among racial minorities and families headed by women. It is also more likely to be found in rural areas and in the South.[29] Of the long-term poor, most are either working at wages too low to bring them above the poverty line or are retired, disabled, or parents of preschool children. Generally they are not in a position to work more hours than they do now.[30]

---

[28] Of those in poverty, 3 million work year-round and are still poor. Of the 22.2 million poor who are 15 years or over, more than 9 million work sometime during the year. Since 1979, the largest increases of poverty in absolute terms have been among those who work and are still poor. U.S. Bureau of the Census, *Money, Income and Poverty*.

[29] U.S. Bureau of the Census, Current Population Reports, series P-60, no. 149, 19. Blacks make up about 12% of the entire population but 62% of the long-term poor. Only 19% of the overall population live in families headed by women, but they make up 61% of the long-term poor. Twenty-eight percent of the nation's total population reside in nonmetropolitan areas, but 34% of the nation's poor live in these areas.

[30] G. J. Duncan et al., *Years of Poverty, Years of Plenty: The Changing Economic Fortunes of American Workers and Their Families* (Ann Arbor, Mich.: Institute for Social Research, The University of Michigan, 1984). This book is based on the Panel Study of Income Dynamics, a survey of 5,000 American families conducted annually by the Survey Research Center of the University of Michigan. See G. J. Duncan and J. N. Morgan, *Five Thousand American Families—Patterns of Economic Progress* vol. III (Ann Arbor: University of Michigan, 1975).

a. Children in Poverty

176.   Poverty strikes some groups more severely than others. Perhaps most distressing is the growing number of children who are poor. Today one in every four American children under the age of six, and one in every two black children under six, are poor. The number of children in poverty rose by four million over the decade between 1973 and 1983, with the result that there are now more poor children in the United States than at any time since 1965.[31] The problem is particularly severe among female-headed families, where more than half of all children are poor. Two-thirds of black children and nearly three-quarters of Hispanic children in such families are poor.

177.   Very many poor families with children receive no government assistance, have no health insurance, and cannot pay medical bills. Less than half are immunized against preventable diseases such as diphtheria and polio.[32] Poor children are disadvantaged even before birth; their mothers' lack of access to high quality prenatal care leaves them at much greater risk of premature birth, low-birth weight, physical and mental impairment, and death before their first birthday.

b. Women and Poverty

178.   The past twenty years have witnessed a dramatic increase in the number of women in poverty.[33]

---

[31] Congressional Research Service and Congressional Budget Office, *Children in Poverty* (Washington, D.C., May 22, 1985), 57. This recent study also indicates that children are now the largest age group in poverty. We are the first industrialized nation in the world in which children are the poorest age group. See Daniel Patrick Moynihan, *Family and Nation* (New York: Harcourt, Brace, Jovanovich, 1986), 112.

[32] Children's Defense Fund, *American Children in Poverty* (Washington, D.C., 1984).

[33] This trend has been commonly referred to as the "feminization

This includes women raising children alone as well as women with inadequate income following divorce, widowhood, or retirement. More than one-third of all female-headed families are poor. Among minority families headed by women the poverty rate is over 50 percent.[34]

179.   Wage discrimination against women is a major factor behind these high rates of poverty. Many women are employed but remain poor because their wages are too low. Women who work outside their homes full-time and year-round earn only 61 percent of what men earn. Thus, being employed full-time is not by itself a remedy for poverty among women. Hundreds of thousands of women hold full-time jobs but are still poor. Sixty percent of all women work in only ten occupations, and most new jobs for women are in areas with low pay and limited chances of advancement. Many women suffer discrimination in wages, salaries, job classifications, promotions, and other areas.[35] As a result, they find themselves in jobs that have low status, little security, weak unionization, and few fringe benefits. Such discrimination is immoral and efforts must be made to overcome the effects of sexism in our society.

180.   Women's responsibilities for childrearing are another important factor to be considered. Despite the many changes in marriage and family life in recent decades, women continue to have primary respon-

---

of poverty." This term was coined by Dr. Diana Pierce in the *1980 Report to the President* of the National Advisory Council on Economic Opportunity to describe the dramatic increase in the proportion of the poor living in female-headed households.

[34] U.S. Bureau of the Census, Technical Paper 55, *Estimates of Poverty Including the Value of Non-Cash Benefits: 1984* (Washington, D.C., August 1985), 5, 23.

[35] Barbara Raskin and Heidi Hartmann, *Women's Work, Men's Work, Sex Segregation on the Job*, National Academy of Sciences (Washington, D.C.: National Academy Press, 1986), pp. 10–126.

sibility in this area. When marriages break up, mothers typically take custody of the children and bear the major financial responsibility for supporting them. Women often anticipate that they will leave the labor force to have and raise children, and often make job and career choices accordingly. In other cases they are not hired or promoted to higher paying jobs because of their childrearing responsibilities. In addition, most divorced or separated mothers do not get child support payments. In 1983, less than half of women raising children alone had been awarded child support, and of those, only half received the full amount to which they were entitled. Even fewer women (14 percent) are awarded alimony, and many older women are left in poverty after a lifetime of homemaking and childrearing.[36] Such women have great difficulty finding jobs and securing health insurance.

c. Racial Minorities and Poverty

181.   Most poor people in our nation are white, but the rates of poverty in our nation are highest among those who have borne the brunt of racial prejudice and discrimination. For example, blacks are about three times more likely to be poor than whites. While one out of every nine white Americans is poor, one of every three blacks and Native Americans and more than one of every four Hispanics are poor.[37] While some members of minority communities have suc-

---

[36] U.S. Bureau of the Census, series P-23, no. 124, *Special Study Child Support and Alimony: 1981 Current Population Report* (Washington, D.C., 1981).

[37] U.S. House of Representatives Subcommittee on Oversight and Public Assistance and Unemployment Compensation, Committee on Ways and Means, *Background Material on Poverty* (Washington, D.C., October, 1983). See also Committee on Ways and Means, U.S. House of Representatives, *Children in Poverty*, 3.

cessfully moved up the economic ladder, the overall picture indicates that black family income is only 55 percent of white family income, reflecting an income gap that is wider now than at any time in the last fifteen years.[38]

182.   Despite the gains which have been made toward racial equality, prejudice and discrimination in our own time as well as the effects of past discrimination continue to exclude many members of racial minorities from the mainstream of American life. Discriminatory practices in labor markets, in educational systems, and in electoral politics create major obstacles for blacks, Hispanics, Native Americans, and other racial minorities in their struggle to improve their economic status.[39] Such discrimination is evidence of the continuing presence of racism in our midst. In our pastoral letter, *Brothers and Sisters to Us*, we have described this racism as a sin—"a sin that divides the human family, blots out the image of God among specific members of that family, and violates the fundamental human dignity of those called to be children of the same Father."[40]

2. Economic Inequality

183.   Important to our discussion of poverty in America is an understanding of the degree of economic inequality in our nation. Our economy is marked by a very uneven distribution of wealth and income. For example, it is estimated that 28 percent of the total net wealth is held by the richest 2 percent of families in the United States. The top ten percent holds 57

---

[38] The National Urban League, *The Status of Black America 1984* (New York, January 1984).

[39] Ibid.

[40] NCCB, *Brothers and Sisters to Us* Pastoral Letter on Racism in Our Day (Washington, D.C.: USCC Office of Publishing and Promotion Services, 1979).

percent of the net wealth.[41] If homes and other real estate are excluded, the concentration of ownership of "financial wealth" is even more glaring. In 1983, 54 percent of the total net financial assets were held by 2 percent of all families, those whose annual income is over $125,000. Eighty-six percent of these assets were held by the top 10 percent of all families.[42]

184.   Although disparities in the distribution of income are less extreme, they are still striking. In 1984 the bottom 20 percent of American families received only 4.7 percent of the total income in the nation and the bottom 40 percent received only 15.7 percent, the lowest share on record in U.S. history. In contrast, the top one-fifth received 42.9 percent of the total income, the highest share since 1948.[43] These figures are only partial and very imperfect measures of the inequality in our society.[44] However, they do suggest that the degree of inequality is quite large. In comparison with other industrialized nations, the United States is among the more unequal in terms of income

---

[41] Federal Reserve Board, "Survey of Consumer Finances, 1983: A Second Report," reprint from the *Federal Reserve Bulletin* (Washington, D.C., December 1984), 857-868. This survey defines net worth as the difference between gross assets and gross liabilities. The survey's estimates include all financial assets, equity in homes and other real property, as well as all financial liabilities such as consumer credit and other debts.

[42] Ibid., 863-864.

[43] U.S. Bureau of the Census, series P-60, no. 149, 11.

[44] Income distribution figures give only a static picture of income shares. They do not reflect the significant movement of families into and out of different income categories over an extended period of time. See *Years of Poverty, Years of Plenty*, 13. It should also be noted that these figures reflect pre-tax incomes. However, since the national tax structure is proportional for a large segment of the population, it does not have a significant impact on the distribution of income. See Joseph Pechman, *Who Paid Taxes, 1966-85?* (Washington, D.C.: The Brookings Institution, 1985), 51.

distribution.[45] Moreover, the gap between rich and poor in our nation has increased during the last decade.[46] These inequities are of particular concern because they reflect the uneven distribution of power in our society. They suggest that the level of participation in the political and social spheres is also very uneven.

185.   Catholic social teaching does not require absolute equality in the distribution of income and wealth. Some degree of inequality not only is acceptable, but also may be considered desirable for economic and social reasons, such as the need for incentives and the provision of greater rewards for greater risks. However, unequal distribution should be evaluated in terms of several moral principles we have enunciated: the priority of meeting the basic needs of the poor and the importance of increasing the level of participation by all members of society in the economic life of the nation. These norms establish a strong presumption against extreme inequality of income and wealth as long as there are poor, hungry, and homeless people in our midst. They also suggest that extreme inequalities are detrimental to the development of social solidarity and community. In view of these norms we find the disparities of income and wealth in the United States to be unacceptable. Justice requires that all members of our society work for economic, political, and social reforms that will decrease these inequities.

3. Guidelines for Action

186.   Our recommendations for dealing with poverty in the United States build upon several moral

---

[45] Lars Osberg, *Economic Inequality in the United States* (New York: M. E. Sharpe, Inc., 1984), 24-28.
[46] U.S. Bureau of the Census, series P-60, no. 149, 11.

principles that were explored in chapter two of this letter. The themes of human dignity and the preferential option for the poor are at the heart of our approach; they compel us to confront the issue of poverty with a real sense of urgency.

187.   The principle of social solidarity suggests that alleviating poverty will require fundamental changes in social and economic structures that perpetuate glaring inequalities and cut off millions of citizens from full participation in the economic and social life of the nation. The process of change should be one that draws together all citizens, whatever their economic status, into one community.

188.   The principle of participation leads us to the conviction that the most appropriate and fundamental solutions to poverty will be those that enable people to take control of their own lives. For poverty is not merely the lack of adequate financial resources. It entails a more profound kind of deprivation, a denial of full participation in the economic, social, and political life of society and an inability to influence decisions that affect one's life. It means being powerless in a way that assaults not only one's pocketbook but also one's fundamental human dignity. Therefore, we should seek solutions that enable the poor to help themselves through such means as employment. Paternalistic programs which do too much *for* and too little *with* the poor are to be avoided.

189.   The responsibility for alleviating the plight of the poor falls upon all members of society. As individuals, all citizens have a duty to assist the poor through acts of charity and personal commitment. But private charity and voluntary action are not sufficient. We also carry out our moral responsibility to assist and empower the poor by working collectively through government to establish just and effective public policies.

190.   Although the task of alleviating poverty is complex and demanding, we should be encouraged by examples of our nation's past successes in this area. Our history shows that we can reduce poverty. During the 1960s and early 1970s, the official poverty rate was cut in half, due not only to a healthy economy, but also to public policy decisions that improved the nation's income transfer programs. It is estimated, for example, that in the late 1970s federal benefit programs were lifting out of poverty about 70 percent of those who would have otherwise been poor.[47]

191.   During the last twenty-five years, the Social Security Program has dramatically reduced poverty among the elderly.[48] In addition, in 1983 it lifted out of poverty almost 1.5 million children of retired, deceased, and disabled workers.[49] Medicare has enhanced the life expectancy and health status of elderly and disabled people, and Medicaid has reduced infant mortality and greatly improved access to health care for the poor.[50]

---

[47] "Poverty in the United States: Where Do We Stand Now?" *Focus* (University of Wisconsin: Institute for Research on Poverty, Winter 1984). See also Danzinger and Gottschalk, "The Poverty of Losing Ground," *Challenge* 28:2 (May/June 1985). As these studies indicate, the slowing of the economy after 1969 tended to push more people into poverty, a trend that was offset to a great extent by the broadening of federal benefit programs. Likewise, the cutbacks in federal programs for the poor in recent years have contributed to the increase in poverty. For other analyses of the causes and cures of poverty see Charles Murray, *Losing Ground: American Social Policy 1950-1980* (New York: Basic Books, Inc., 1984); Ben J. Wattenberg, *The Good News Is the Bad News Is Wrong* (New York: Simon and Shuster, 1984); and Michael Harrington, *The New American Poverty* (New York: Holt, Rinehart, and Winston, 1984).

[48] *Family and Nation*, 111-113.

[49] Committee on Ways and Means, *Children In Poverty*. Calculation based on Tables 6-1 and 6-2, 180-181; and estimates of social insurance transfers on 221-222.

[50] Paul Starr, *The Social Transformation of American Medicine* (New York: Basic Books, Inc., 1982), 373.

192.   These and other successful social welfare programs are evidence of our nation's commitment to
social justice and a decent life for everyone. They also
indicate that we have the capacity to design programs
that are effective and provide necessary assistance to
the needy in a way that respects their dignity. Yet it
is evident that not all social welfare programs have
been successful. Some have been ill-designed, ineffective, and wasteful. No one has been more aware
of this than the poor themselves, who have suffered
the consequences. Where programs have failed, we
should discard them, learn from our mistakes, and
fashion a better alternative. Where programs have
succeeded, we should acknowledge that fact and build
on those successes. In every instance, we must summon a new creativity and commitment to eradicate
poverty in our midst and to guarantee all Americans
their right to share in the blessings of our land.

193.   Before discussing directions for reform in public policy, we must speak frankly about misunderstandings and stereotypes of the poor. For example,
a common misconception is that most of the poor are
racial minorities. In fact, about two-thirds of the poor
are white.[51] It is also frequently suggested that people
stay on welfare for many years, do not work, could
work if they wanted to, and have children who will
be on welfare. In fact, reliable data show that these
are not accurate descriptions of most people who are
poor and on welfare. Over a decade people move on
and off welfare, and less than 1 percent obtain these
benefits for all ten years.[52] Nor is it true that the rolls
of Aid to Families with Dependent Children (AFDC)
are filled with able-bodied adults who could but will
not work. The majority of AFDC recipients are young

---

[51] U.S. Bureau of the Census, series P-60, no. 149, 11.
[52] *Years of Poverty, Years of Plenty*, 13.

children and their mothers who must remain at home.[53] These mothers are also accused of having more children so that they can raise their allowances. The truth is that 70 percent of AFDC families have only one or two children and that there is little financial advantage in having another. In a given year, almost half of all families who receive AFDC include an adult who has worked full or part-time.[54] Research has consistently demonstrated that people who are poor have the same strong desire to work that characterizes the rest of the population.[55]

194.   We ask everyone to refrain from actions, words, or attitudes that stigmatize the poor, that exaggerate the benefits received by the poor, and that inflate the amount of fraud in welfare payments.[56] These are symptoms of a punitive attitude towards the poor. The belief persists in this country that the poor are poor by choice or through laziness, that anyone can escape poverty by hard work, and that welfare programs make it easier for people to avoid work. Thus, public attitudes toward programs for the poor tend to differ sharply from attitudes about other benefits and programs. Some of the most generous sub-

---

[53] Center on Social Welfare Policy and Law, *Beyond the Myths: The Families Helped by the AFDC Program* (New York, 1985).

[54] Ibid. This booklet cites Census Bureau data showing that in 1980 about 45% of those families who received AFDC also had earned income during that year, and that the average number of weeks worked during the year was 32.1.

[55] Leonard Goodwin, *Causes and Cures of Welfare* (Lexington, Mass.: Lexington Books, 1983), ch. 1. See also Leonard Goodwin, "Can Workfare Work?" *Public Welfare* 39 (Fall 1981): 19-25.

[56] *Beyond the Myths*. With respect to error and fraud rates in AFDC, this booklet notes that erroneous payments in the AFDC program account for less than 10% of the benefits paid. No more than 8.1% of the families on AFDC received overpayments as a result of client error. In less than 4.5% of all AFDC cases nationally are questions of fraud raised. Moreover, in over 40% of these cases, a review of the facts indicated that there was insufficient evidence to support an allegation of fraud.

sidies for individuals and corporations are taken for
granted and are not even called benefits but entitle-
ments.[57] In contrast, programs for the poor are called
handouts and receive a great deal of critical attention,
even though they account for less than 10 percent of
the federal budget.[58]

195.   We now wish to propose several elements
which we believe are necessary for a national strategy
to deal with poverty. We offer this not as a comprehensive list but as an invitation for others to join the
discussion and take up the task of fighting poverty.

196.   a. *The first line of attack against poverty must be
to build and sustain a healthy economy that provides employment opportunities at just wages for all adults who are
able to work.* Poverty is intimately linked to the issue
of employment. Millions are poor because they have
lost their jobs or because their wages are too low. The
persistent high levels of unemployment during the
last decade are a major reason why poverty has increased in recent years.[59] Expanded employment especially in the private sector would promote human
dignity, increase social solidarity, and promote self-
reliance of the poor. It should also reduce the need
for welfare programs and generate the income necessary to support those who remain in need and cannot work: elderly, disabled, and chronically ill people,
and single parents of young children. It should also
be recognized that the persistence of poverty harms
the larger society because the depressed purchasing
power of the poor contributes to the periodic cycles
of stagnation in the economy.

---

[57] P. G. Peterson, "No More Free Lunch for the Middle Class,"
New York Times Magazine (January 17, 1982).

[58] Interfaith Action for Economic Justice, *End Results: The Impact
of Federal Policies Since 1980 on Low-Income Americans* (Washington,
D.C.), 2.

[59] "The Poverty of Losing Ground," 32-38.

197.   In recent years the minimum wage has not been adjusted to keep pace with inflation. Its real value has declined by 24 percent since 1981. We believe Congress should raise the minimum wage in order to restore some of the purchasing power it has lost due to inflation.

198.   While job creation and just wages are major elements of a national strategy against poverty, they are clearly not enough. Other more specific policies are necessary to remedy the institutional causes of poverty and to provide for those who cannot work.

199.   b. *Vigorous action should be undertaken to remove barriers to full and equal employment for women and minorities.* Too many women and minorities are locked into jobs with low pay, poor working conditions, and little opportunity for career advancement. So long as we tolerate a situation in which people can work full-time and still be below the poverty line—a situation common among those earning the minimum wage—too many will continue to be counted among the "working poor." Concerted efforts must be made through job training, affirmative action, and other means to assist those now prevented from obtaining more lucrative jobs. Action should also be taken to upgrade poorer paying jobs and to correct wage differentials that discriminate unjustly against women.

200.   c. *Self-help efforts among the poor should be fostered by programs and policies in both the private and public sectors.* We believe that an effective way to attack poverty is through programs that are small in scale, locally based, and oriented toward empowering the poor to become self-sufficient. Corporations, private organizations, and the public sector can provide seed money, training and technical assistance, and organizational support for self-help projects in a wide variety of areas such as low-income housing, credit unions, worker cooperatives, legal assistance, and neighborhood and community organizations. Efforts that enable the poor

to participate in the ownership and control of economic resources are especially important.

201.   Poor people must be empowered to take charge of their own futures and become responsible for their own economic advancement. Personal motivation and initiative, combined with social reform, are necessary elements to assist individuals in escaping poverty. By taking advantage of opportunities for education, employment, and training, and by working together for change, the poor can help themselves to be full participants in our economic, social, and political life.

202.   d. *The tax system should be continually evaluated in terms of its impact on the poor.* This evaluation should be guided by three principles. First, the tax system should raise adequate revenues to pay for the public needs of society, especially to meet the basic needs of the poor. Secondly, the tax system should be structured according to the principle of progressivity, so that those with relatively greater financial resources pay a higher rate of taxation. The inclusion of such a principle in tax policies is an important means of reducing the severe inequalities of income and wealth in the nation. Action should be taken to reduce or offset the fact that most sales taxes and payroll taxes place a disproportionate burden on those with lower incomes. Thirdly, families below the official poverty line should not be required to pay income taxes. Such families are, by definition, without sufficient resources to purchase the basic necessities of life. They should not be forced to bear the additional burden of paying income taxes.[60]

203.   e. *All of society should make a much stronger commitment to education for the poor.* Any long-term solution to poverty in this country must pay serious attention

---

[60] The tax reform legislation of 1986 did a great deal to achieve this goal. It removed from the federal income tax rules virtually all families below the official poverty line.

to education, public and private, in school and out of school. Lack of adequate education, especially in the inner city setting, prevents many poor people from escaping poverty. In addition, illiteracy, a problem that affects tens of millions of Americans, condemns many to joblessness or chronically low wages. Moreover, it excludes them in many ways from sharing in the political and spiritual life of the community.[61] Since poverty is fundamentally a problem of powerlessness and marginalization, the importance of education as a means of overcoming it cannot be overemphasized.

204.   Working to improve education in our society is an investment in the future, an investment that should include both the public and private school systems. Our Catholic schools have the well-merited reputation of providing excellent education, especially for the poor. Catholic inner-city schools provide an otherwise unavailable educational alternative for many poor families. They provide one effective vehicle for disadvantaged students to lift themselves out of poverty. We commend the work of all those who make great sacrifices to maintain these inner-city schools. We pledge ourselves to continue the effort to make Catholic schools models of education for the poor.

205.   We also wish to affirm our strong support for the public school system in the United States. There can be no substitute for quality education in public schools, for that is where the large majority of all students, including Catholic students, are educated. In Catholic social teaching, basic education is a fundamental human right.[62] In our society a strong public school system is essential if we are to protect that right and allow everyone to develop to their maximum ability. Therefore, we strongly endorse the recent calls

---

[61] Jonathan Kozol, *Illiterate America* (New York: Anchor Press/ Doubleday, 1985).
[62] *Peace on Earth*, 13.

for improvements in and support for public education, including improving the quality of teaching and enhancing the rewards for the teaching profession.[63] At all levels of education we need to improve the ability of our institutions to provide the personal and technical skills that are necessary for participation not only in today's labor market but also in contemporary society.

206.   f. *Policies and programs at all levels should support the strength and stability of families, especially those adversely affected by the economy.* As a nation, we need to examine all aspects of economic life and assess their effects on families. Employment practices, health insurance policies, income security programs, tax policy, and service programs can either support or undermine the abilities of families to fulfill their roles in nurturing children and caring for infirm and dependent family members.

207.   We affirm the principle enunciated by John Paul II that society's institutions and policies should be structured so that mothers of young children are not forced by economic necessity to leave their chil-

---

[63] These reports and studies include: E. Boyer, *High School: A Report on Secondary Education in America* (Princeton: Carnegie Foundation for the Advancement of Teaching, 1983); P. Cusick, *The American High School and the Egalitarian Ideal* (New York: Longman, 1983); J. I. Goodlad, *A Place Called School: Prospects for the Future* (New York: McGraw-Hill, 1983); The National Commission on Excellence in Education, *A Nation at Risk: The Imperative for Educational Reform* (Washington, D.C.: U.S. Department of Education, 1983); D. Ravitch, *The Troubled Crusade: American Education, 1945-1980* (New York: Basic Books, 1983); T. R. Sizer, *Horace's Compromise: The Dilemma of the American High School* (Boston: Houghton Mifflin, 1984); Task Force on Education for Economic Growth, *Action for Excellence: A Comprehensive Plan to Improve our Nation's Schools* (Denver: Education Commission of the States, 1983); and The Twentieth Century Fund Task Force on Federal Elementary and Secondary Education Policy, *Making the Grade* (New York: Twentieth Century Fund, 1983). For a discussion of the issues raised in these reports see *Harvard Educational Review* 54:1 (February 1984): 1-31.

dren for jobs outside the home.[64] The nation's social welfare and tax policies should support parents' decisions to care for their own children and should recognize the work of parents in the home because of its value for the family and for society.

208. For those children whose parents do work outside the home, there is a serious shortage of affordable, quality day care. Employers, governments, and private agencies need to improve both the availability and the quality of child care services. Likewise, families could be assisted by the establishment of parental leave policies that would assure job security for new parents.

209. The high rate of divorce and the alarming extent of teenage pregnancies in our nation are distressing signs of the breakdown of traditional family values. These destructive trends are present in all sectors of society: rich and poor; white, black, and brown; urban and rural. However, for the poor they tend to be more visible and to have more damaging economic consequences. These destructive trends must be countered by a revived sense of personal responsibility and commitment to family values.

210. g. *A thorough reform of the nation's welfare and income-support programs should be undertaken.* For millions of poor Americans the only economic safety net is the public welfare system. The programs that make up this system should serve the needs of the poor in a manner that respects their dignity and provides adequate support. In our judgment the present welfare system does not adequately meet these criteria.[65] We

---

[64] The Vatican, *Charter of the Rights of the Family* (Washington, D.C.: USCC Office of Publishing and Promotion Services, 1983). See also *On Human Work*, 19; *Familiaris Consortio*, 23, 81; and "Christian Solidarity Leads to Action," Address to Austrian Workers (Vienna, September 1983) in *Origins* 13:16 (September 29, 1983): 275.

[65] H. R. Rodgers, Jr., *The Cost of Human Neglect: America's Welfare* (Armonk, N.Y.: W. E. Sharpe, Inc., 1982); C. T. Waxman, *The Stigma*

believe that several improvements can and should be made within the framework of existing welfare programs. However, in the long run, more far-reaching reforms that go beyond the present system will be necessary. Among the immediate improvements that could be made are the following:

211.   (1) *Public assistance programs should be designed to assist recipients, wherever possible, to become self-sufficient through gainful employment.* Individuals should not be worse off economically when they get jobs than when they rely only on public assistance. Under current rules, people who give up welfare benefits to work in low-paying jobs soon lose their Medicaid benefits. To help recipients become self-sufficient and reduce dependency on welfare, public assistance programs should work in tandem with job creation programs that include provisions for training, counseling, placement, and child care. Jobs for recipients of public assistance should be fairly compensated so that workers receive the full benefits and status associated with gainful employment.

212.   (2) *Welfare programs should provide recipients with adequate levels of support.* This support should cover basic needs in food, clothing, shelter, health care, and other essentials. At present only 4 percent of poor families with children receive enough cash welfare benefits to lift them out of poverty.[66] The combined benefits of AFDC and food stamps typically come to less than three-fourths of the official poverty level.[67]

of Poverty, second edition (New York: Pergamon Press, 1983), especially ch. 5; and S. A. Levitan and C. M. Johnson, *Beyond the Safety Net: Reviving the Promise of Opportunity in America* (Cambridge, Mass.: Ballinger, 1984).

[66] *Children in Poverty.*

[67] U.S. House of Representatives Committee on Ways and Means, *Background Materials and Data on Programs Within the Jurisdiction of the Committee on Ways and Means* (Washington, D.C., February 22, 1985), 345-346.

Those receiving public assistance should not face the prospect of hunger at the end of the month, homelessness, sending children to school in ragged clothing, or inadequate medical care.

213.   (3) *National eligibility standards and a national minimum benefit level for public assistance programs should be established.* Currently welfare eligibility and benefits vary greatly among states. In 1985 a family of three with no earnings had a maximum AFDC benefit of $96 a month in Mississippi and $558 a month in Vermont.[68] To remedy these great disparities, which are far larger than the regional differences in the cost of living, and to assure a floor of benefits for all needy people, our nation should establish and fund national minimum benefit levels and eligibility standards in cash assistance programs.[69] The benefits should also be indexed to reflect changes in the cost of living. These changes reflect standards that our nation has already put in place for aged and disabled people and veterans. Is it not possible to do the same for the children and their mothers who receive public assistance?

214.   (4) *Welfare programs should be available to two-parent as well as single-parent families.* Most states now limit participation in AFDC to families headed by single parents, usually women.[70] The coverage of this program should be extended to two-parent families so that fathers who are unemployed or poorly paid do not have to leave home in order for their children

---

[68] Ibid., 347-348.

[69] In 1982, similar recommendations were made by eight former Secretaries of Health, Education, and Welfare (now Health and Human Services). In a report called "Welfare Policy in the United States," they suggested a number of ways in which national minimal standards might be set and strongly urged the establishment of a floor for all states and territories.

[70] Committee on Ways and Means, *Background Materials and Data on Programs.*

to receive help. Such a change would be a significant step toward strengthening two-parent families who are poor.

4. Conclusion

215.   The search for a more human and effective way to deal with poverty should not be limited to short-term reform measures. The agenda for public debate should also include serious discussion of more fundamental alternatives to the existing welfare system. We urge that proposals for a family allowance or a children's allowance be carefully examined as a possible vehicle for ensuring a floor of income support for all children and their families.[71] Special attention is needed to develop new efforts that are targeted on long-term poverty, which has proven to be least responsive to traditional social welfare programs. The "negative income tax" is another major policy proposal that deserves continued discussion.[72] These and other proposals should be part of a creative and ongoing effort to fashion a system of income support for the poor that protects their basic dignity and provides the necessary assistance in a just and effective manner.

---

[71] France adopted a "family" or "children's" allowance in 1932, followed by Italy in 1936, The Netherlands in 1939, the United Kingdom in 1945, and Sweden in 1947. Arnold Heidenheimer, Hugh Heclo, and Carolyn Teich Adams, *Comparative Public Policy: The Politics of Social Choice in Europe and America* (New York: St. Martin's Press, 1975), 189, 199. See Also Robert Kuttner, *The Economic Illusion* (Boston: Houghton Mifflin Co., 1984), 243-246; and Joseph Piccione, *Help for Families on the Front Lines: The Theory and Practice of Family Allowances* (Washington, D.C.: The Free Congress Research and Education Foundation, 1983).

[72] Milton Friedman, *Capitalism and Freedom* (University of Chicago Press, 1962), 190-195.

C. Food and Agriculture

216.   The fundamental test of an economy is its ability to meet the essential human needs of this generation and future generations in an equitable fashion. Food, water, and energy are essential to life; their abundance in the United States has tended to make us complacent. But these goods—the foundation of God's gift of life—are too crucial to be taken for granted. God reminded the people of Israel that "the land is mine; for you are strangers and guests with me" (Lv 25:23, RSV). Our Christian faith calls us to contemplate God's creative and sustaining action and to measure our own collaboration with the Creator in using the earth's resources to meet human needs. While Catholic social teaching on the care of the environment and the management of natural resources is still in the process of development, a Christian moral perspective clearly gives weight and urgency to their use in meeting human needs.

217.   No aspect of this concern is more pressing than the nation's food system. We are concerned that this food system may be in jeopardy as increasing numbers of farm bankruptcies and foreclosures result in increased concentration of land ownership.[73] We are likewise concerned about the increasing damage to natural resources resulting from many modern agricultural practices: the overconsumption of water, the depletion of topsoil, and the pollution of land and water. Finally, we are concerned about the stark reality of world hunger in spite of food surpluses. Our food production system is clearly in need of evaluation and reform.

---

[73] *The Current Financial Condition of Farmers and Farm Lenders*, Ag. Info. Bulletin no. 490 (Washington, D.C.: U.S. Department of Agriculture Economic Research Service, March 1985), viii-x.

1. U.S. Agriculture—Past and Present

218.   The current crisis has to be assessed in the context of the vast diversity of U.S. crops and climates. For example, subsistence farming in Appalachia, where so much of the land is absentee-owned and where coal mining and timber production are the major economic interests, has little in common with family farm grain production in the central Midwest or ranching in the Great Plains. Likewise, large-scale irrigated fruit, vegetable, and cotton production in the central valley of California is very different from dairy farming in Wisconsin or tobacco and peanut production in the Southeast.

219.   Two aspects of the complex history of U.S. land and food policy are particularly relevant. First, the United States entered this century with the ownership of productive land widely distributed. The Preemption Acts of the early 19th century and the Homestead Act of 1862 were an important part of that history. Wide distribution of ownership was reflected in the number and decentralization of farms in the United States, a trend that reached its peak in the 1930s. The U.S. farm system included nearly 7 million owner-operators in 1935.[74] By 1983 the number of U.S. farms had declined to 2.4 million, and only about 3 percent of the population were engaged in producing food.[75] Second, U.S. food policy has had a parallel goal of keeping the consumer cost of food low. As a result, Americans today spend less of their disposable income on food than people in any other industrialized country.[76]

---

[74] Data on farms and farm population are drawn from *Agricultural Statistics*, annual reports of the U.S. Department of Agriculture, Washington, D.C.

[75] Irma T. Elo and Calvin L. Beale, *Rural Development, Poverty, and Natural Resources* (Washington, D.C.: National Center for Food and Agricultural Policy, Resources for the Future, 1985).

[76] *National Food Review*, USDA, no. 29 (Winter/Spring 1985). In

220.   These outcomes require scrutiny. First of all, the loss of farms and the exodus of farmers from the land have led to the loss of a valued way of life, the decline of many rural communities, and the increased concentration of land ownership. Secondly, while low food prices benefit consumers who are left with additional income to spend on other goods, these pricing policies put pressure on farmers to increase output and hold down costs. This has led them to replace human labor with cheaper energy, expand farm size to employ new technologies favoring larger scale operations, neglect soil and water conservation, underpay farmworkers, and oppose farmworker unionization.[77]

221.   Today nearly half of U.S. food production comes from the 4 percent of farms with over $200,000 in gross sales.[78] Many of these largest farms are no longer operated by families, but by managers hired by owners.[79] Nearly three-quarters of all farms, accounting for only 13 percent of total farm sales, are comparatively small. They are often run by part-time farmers who derive most of their income from off-farm employment. The remaining 39 percent of sales comes from the 24 percent of farms grossing between $40,000 and $200,000. It is this group of farmers, located throughout the country and caught up in the

---

1984 Americans were spending 15.1% of their disposable income on food. This is an average figure. Many low-income people spent a good deal more and others much less.

[77] Luther Tweeten, *Causes and Consequences of Structural Change in the Farming Industry* (Washington, D.C.: National Planning Association, 1984), 7.

[78] *Economic Indicators of the Farm Sector: Income and Balance Sheet Statistics, 1983*, ECIFS 3-3 (Washington, D.C.: U.S. Department of Agriculture Economic Research Service, September 1984).

[79] Marion Clawson, *Ownership Patterns of Natural Resources in America: Implications for Distribution of Wealth and Income* (Washington, D.C.: Resources for the Future, Summer 1983).

long-term trend toward fewer and larger farms, who
are at the center of the present farm crisis.

222.   During the 1970s new markets for farm exports created additional opportunities for profit and
accelerated the industrialization of agriculture, a process already stimulated by new petroleum-based, large-
scale technologies that allowed farmers to cultivate
many more acres. Federal tax policies and farm programs fostered this tendency by encouraging too much
capital investment in agriculture and overemphasiz-
ing large-scale technologies.[80] The results were greater
production, increases in the value of farmland, and
heavy borrowing to finance expansion. In the 1980s,
with export markets shrinking and commodity prices
and land values declining, many farmers cannot repay
their loans.

223.   Their situation has been aggravated by certain
"external" factors: persistent high interest rates that
make it difficult to repay or refinance loans, the heavy
debt burden of food-deficient countries, the high value
of the dollar, dramatically higher U.S. budget and
trade deficits, and generally reduced international trade
following the worldwide recession of the early 1980s.
The United States is unlikely to recapture its former
share of the world food and fiber trade, and it is not
necessarily an appropriate goal to attempt to do so.
Exports are not the solution to U.S. farm problems.
Past emphasis on producing for overseas markets has
contributed to the strain on our natural resource base
and has also undermined the efforts of many less
developed countries in attaining self-reliance in feeding their own people. In attempting to correct these
abuses, however, we must not reduce our capability
to help meet emergency food needs.

---

[80] *Causes and Consequences,* 7; and *A Time to Choose: Summary
Report on the Structure of Agriculture* (Washington, D.C.: U.S. Department of Agriculture, January 1981).

224.   Some farmers face financial insolvency because of their own eagerness to take advantage of what appeared to be favorable investment opportunities. This was partly in response to the encouragement of public policy incentives and the advice of economists and financiers. Nevertheless, farmers should share some responsibility for their current plight.

225.   Four other aspects of the current situation concern us: first, land ownership is becoming further concentrated as units now facing bankruptcy are added to existing farms and nonfarm corporations. Diversity of ownership and widespread participation are declining in this sector of the economy as they have in others. Since differing scales of operation and the investment of family labor have been important for American farm productivity, this increasing concentration of ownership in almost all sectors of agriculture points to an important change in that system.[81] Of particular concern is the growing phenomenon of "vertical integration" whereby companies gain control of two or three of the links in the food chain: as suppliers of farm inputs, landowners, and food processors. This increased concentration could also adversely affect food prices.

226.   Second, diversity and richness in American society are lost as farm people leave the land and rural communities decay. It is not just a question of coping with additional unemployment and a need for retraining and relocation. It is also a matter of maintaining opportunities for employment and human

---

[81] The nature of this transformation and its implications have been addressed previously by the USCC Committee on Social Development and World Peace in a February 1979 statement *The Family Farm* and again in May 1980 by the bishops of the Midwest in a joint pastoral letter *Strangers and Guests: Toward Community in the Heartland*.

development in a variety of economic sectors and cultural contexts.

227.   Third, although the United States has set a world standard for food production, it has not done so without cost to our natural resource base.[82] On nearly one-quarter of our most productive cropland, topsoil erosion currently exceeds the rate at which it can be replaced by natural processes. Similarly, underground water supplies are being depleted in areas where food production depends on irrigation. Furthermore, chemical fertilizers, pesticides, and herbicides, considered now almost essential to today's agriculture, pollute the air, water, and soil, and pose countless health hazards. Finally, where the expansion of residential, industrial, and recreational areas makes it rewarding to do so, vast acreages of prime farmland, three million acres per year by some estimates, are converted to nonfarm use. The continuation of these practices, reflecting short-term investment interests or immediate income needs of farmers and other landowners, constitutes a danger to future food production because these practices are not sustainable.

228.   Farm owners and farmworkers are the immediate stewards of the natural resources required to produce the food that is necessary to sustain life. These resources must be understood as gifts of a generous God. When they are seen in that light and when the human race is perceived as a single moral community, we gain a sense of the substantial responsibility we bear as a nation for the world food system. Meeting

---

[82] *Soil Conservation in America: What Do We Have To Lose?* (Washington, D.C.: American Farmland Trust, 1984); E. Philip LeVeen, "Domestic Food Security and Increasing Competition for Water," in Lawrence Busch and William B. Lacy, eds., *Food Security in the United States* (Boulder, Colo.: Westview Press, 1984), 52. See also *America's Soil and Water: Condition and Trends* (Washington, D.C.: U.S. Department of Agriculture Soil Conservation Service, 1981).

human needs today and in the future demands an increased sense of stewardship and conservation from owners, managers, and regulators of all resources, especially those required for the production of food.

229.   Fourth, the situation of racial minorities in the U.S. food system is a matter of special pastoral concern. They are largely excluded from significant participation in the farm economy. Despite the agrarian heritage of so many Hispanics, for example, they operate only a minute fraction of America's farms.[83] Black-owned farms, at one time a significant resource for black participation in the economy, have been disappearing at a dramatic rate in recent years,[84] a trend that the U.S. Commission on Civil Rights has warned "can only serve to further diminish the stake of blacks in the social order and reinforce their skepticism regarding the concept of equality under the law."[85]

230.   It is largely as hired farm laborers rather than farm owners that minorities participate in the farm economy. Along with many white farmworkers, they are, by and large, the poorest paid and least benefited of any laboring group in the country. Moreover, they are not as well protected by law and public policy as other groups of workers; and their efforts to organize and bargain collectively have been systematically and vehemently resisted, usually by farmers themselves. Migratory field workers are particularly susceptible to exploitation. This is reflected not only in their characteristically low wages but also in the low standards of housing, health care, and education made available to these workers and their families.[86]

---

[83] *1982 Census of Agriculture.*

[84] U.S. Commission on Civil Rights, *The Decline of Black Farming in America* (Washington, D.C.: U.S. Commission on Civil Rights, February 1982), esp. 65-69 regarding their property.

[85] Ibid., 8.

[86] U.S. Department of Labor, *Hearings Concerning Proposed Full Sanitation Standards,* document no. H-308 (Washington, D.C., 1984).

2. Guidelines for Action

231.   We are convinced that current trends in the
food sector are not in the best interests of the United
States or of the global community. The decline in the
number of moderate-sized farms, increased concentration of land ownership, and the mounting evidence
of poor resource conservation raise serious questions
of morality and public policy. As pastors, we cannot
remain silent while thousands of farm families caught
in the present crisis lose their homes, their land, and
their way of life. We approach this situation, however,
aware that it reflects longer-term conditions that carry
consequences for the food system as a whole and for
the resources essential for food production.

232.   While much of the change needed must come
from the cooperative efforts of farmers themselves,
we strongly believe that there is an important role for
public policy in the protection of dispersed ownership
through family farms, as well as in the preservation
of natural resources. We suggest three guidelines for
both public policy and private efforts aimed at shaping
the future of American agriculture.

233.   *First, moderate-sized farms operated by families on
a full-time basis should be preserved and their economic
viability protected.* Similarly, small farms and part-time
farming, particularly in areas close to cities, should
be encouraged. As we have noted elsewhere in this
pastoral letter,[87] there is genuine social and economic
value in maintaining a wide distribution in the ownership of productive property. The democratization
of decision making and control of the land resulting
from wide distribution of farm ownership are protections against concentration of power and a consequent
possible loss of responsiveness to public need in this

---

[87] Ch. II, para. 112.

crucial sector of the economy.[88] Moreover, when those who work in an enterprise also share in its ownership, their active commitment to the purpose of the endeavor and their participation in it are enhanced. Ownership provides incentives for diligence and is a source of an increased sense that the work being done is one's own. This is particularly significant in a sector as vital to human well-being as agriculture.

234.   Furthermore, diversity in farm ownership tends to prevent excessive consumer dependence on business decisions that seek maximum return on invested capital, thereby making the food system overly susceptible to fluctuations in the capital markets. This is particularly relevant in the case of nonfarm corporations that enter agriculture in search of high profits. If the return drops substantially, or if it appears that better profits can be obtained by investing elsewhere, the corporation may cut back or even close down operations without regard to the impact on the community or on the food system in general. In similar circumstances full-time farmers, with a heavy personal investment in their farms and strong ties to the community, are likely to persevere in the hope of better times. Family farms also make significant economic and social contributions to the life of rural communities.[89] They support farm suppliers and other local merchants, and their farms support the tax base needed to pay for roads, schools, and other vital services.

235.   This rural interdependence has value beyond the rural community itself. Both Catholic social teaching and the traditions of our country have emphasized the importance of maintaining the rich plurality of social institutions that enhances personal freedom and

---

[88] *A Time to Choose*, 148.
[89] Luther Tweeten, "The Economics of Small Farms," *Science* vol. 219 (March 4, 1983): 1041.

increases the opportunity for participation in community life. Movement toward a smaller number of very large farms employing wage workers would be a movement away from this institutional pluralism. By contributing to the vitality of rural communities, full-time residential farmers enrich the social and political life of the nation as a whole. Cities, too, benefit soundly and economically from a vibrant rural economy based on family farms. Because of out-migration of farm and rural people, too much of this enriching diversity has been lost already.

236.   *Second, the opportunity to engage in farming should be protected as a valuable form of work.* At a time when unemployment in the country is already too high, any unnecessary increase in the number of unemployed people, however small, should be avoided. Farm unemployment leads to further rural unemployment as rural businesses lose their customers and close down. The loss of people from the land also entails the loss of expertise in farm and land management and creates a need for retraining and relocating another group of displaced workers.

237.   Losing any job is painful, but losing one's farm and having to leave the land can be tragic. It often means the sacrifice of a family heritage and a way of life. Once farmers sell their land and their equipment, their move is practically irreversible. The costs of returning are so great that few who leave ever come back. Even the small current influx of people into agriculture attracted by lower land values will not balance this loss. Society should help those who would and could continue effectively in farming.

238.   *Third, effective stewardship of our natural resources should be a central consideration in any measures regarding U.S. agriculture.* Such stewardship is a contribution to the common good that is difficult to assess in purely economic terms, because it involves the care of resources entrusted to us by our Creator for the

benefit of all. Responsibility for the stewardship of these resources rests on society as a whole. Since farmers make their living from the use of this endowment, however, they bear a particular obligation to be caring stewards of soil and water. They fulfill this obligation by participating in soil and water conservation programs, using farm practices that enhance the quality of the resources, and maintaining prime farmland in food production rather than letting it be converted to nonfarm uses.

3. Policies and Actions

239.   The human suffering involved in the present situation and the long-term structural changes occurring in this sector call for responsible action by the whole society. A half-century of federal farm-price supports, subsidized credit, production-oriented research and extension services, and special tax policies for farmers have made the federal government a central factor in almost every aspect of American agriculture.[90] No redirection of current trends can occur without giving close attention to these programs.

240.   A prime consideration in all agricultural trade and food assistance policies should be the contribution our nation can make to global food security. This means continuing and increasing food aid without depressing Third World markets or using food as a weapon in international politics. It also means not subsidizing exports in ways that lead to trade wars and instability in international food markets.

241.   We offer the following suggestions for governmental action with regard to the farm and food sector of the economy.

---

[90] U.S. Department of Agriculture, *History of Agricultural Price-Support and Adjustment Programs, 1933-1984,* Ag. Info. Bulletin no. 485 (Washington, D.C.: U.S. Department of Agriculture Economic Research Service, December 1984).

242.   a. The current crisis calls for special measures
to assist otherwise viable family farms that are threatened with bankruptcy or foreclosure. Operators of
such farms should have access to emergency credit,
reduced rates of interest, and programs of debt restructuring. Rural lending institutions facing problems because of nonpayment or slow payment of large
farm loans should also have access to temporary assistance. Farmers, their families, and their communities will gain immediately from these and other short-
term measures aimed at keeping these people on the
land.

243.   b. Established federal farm programs, whose
benefits now go disproportionately to the largest
farmers,[91] should be reassessed for their long-term
effects on the structure of agriculture. Income-support
programs that help farmers according to the amount
of food they produce or the number of acres they farm
should be subject to limits that ensure a fair income
to all farm families and should restrict participation
to producers who genuinely need such income assistance. There should also be a strict ceiling on price-
support payments which assist farmers in times of
falling prices, so that benefits go to farms of moderate
or small size. To succeed in redirecting the benefits
of these programs while holding down costs to the
public, consideration should be given to a broader
application of mandatory production control programs.[92]

244.   c. We favor reform of tax policies which now
encourage the growth of large farms, attract invest-

---

[91] *The Distribution of Benefits from the 1982 Federal Crop Programs*
(Washington, D.C.: U.S. Senate Committee on the Budget, November 1984).

[92] "The Great Debate on Mandatory Production Controls" in
*Farm Policy Perspectives: Setting the Stage for 1985 Agricultural Legis-
lation* (Washington, D.C.: U.S. Senate Committee on Agriculture,
Nutrition, and Forestry, April 1984).

ments into agriculture by nonfarmers seeking tax shelters, and inequitably benefit large and well-financed farming operations.[93] Offsetting nonfarm income with farm "losses" has encouraged high-income investors to acquire farm assets with no intention of depending on them for a living as family farmers must. The ability to depreciate capital equipment faster than its actual decline in value has benefited wealthy investors and farmers. Lower tax rates on capital gains have stimulated farm expansion and larger investments in energy-intensive equipment and technologies as substitutes for labor. Changes in estate tax laws have consistently favored the largest estates. All of these results have demonstrated that reassessment of these and similar tax provisions is needed.[94] We continue, moreover, to support a progressive land tax on farm acreage to discourage the accumulation of excessively large holdings.[95]

245. d. Although it is often assumed that farms must grow in size in order to make the most efficient and productive use of sophisticated and costly technologies, numerous studies have shown that medium-sized commercial farms achieve most of the technical cost efficiencies available in agriculture today. We, therefore, recommend that the research and extension resources of the federal government and the nation's land grant colleges and universities be redirected toward improving the productivity of small and medium-sized farms.[96]

---

[93] *A Time to Choose*, 91.

[94] Richard Dunford, *The Effects of Federal Income Tax Policy on U.S. Agriculture* (Washington, D.C.: Subcommittee on Agriculture and Transportation of the Joint Economic Committee of the Congress of the United States, December 21, 1984).

[95] This proposal was put forward thirteen years ago in *Where Shall the People Live? A Special Message of the United States Catholic Bishops* (Washington, D.C.: USCC Office of Publishing and Promotion Services, 1972).

[96] Thomas E. Miller, et al., *Economies of Size in U.S. Field Crop*

246.   e. Since soil and water conservation, like other efforts to protect the environment, are contributions to the good of the whole society, it is appropriate for the public to bear a share of the cost of these practices and to set standards for environmental protection. Government should, therefore, encourage farmers to adopt more conserving practices and distribute the costs of this conservation more broadly.

247.   f. Justice demands that worker guarantees and protections such as minimum wages and benefits and unemployment compensation be extended to hired farmworkers on the same basis as all other workers. There is also an urgent need for additional farmworker housing, health care, and educational assistance.

4. Solidarity in the Farm Community

248.   While there is much that government can and should do to change the direction of farm and food policy in this country, that change in direction also depends upon the cooperation and good will of farmers. The incentives in our farm system to take risks, to expand farm size, and to speculate in farmland values are great. Hence, farmers and ranchers must weigh these incentives against the values of family, rural community, care of the soil, and a food system responsive to long-term as well as short-term food needs of the nation and the world. The ever present temptation to individualism and greed must be countered by a determined movement toward solidarity in the farm community. Farmers should approach farming in a cooperative way, working with other farmers in the purchase of supplies and equipment and in the marketing of produce. It is not necessary for every farmer to be in competition against every other farmer.

Farming (Washington, D.C.: U.S. Department of Agriculture Economic Research Service, July 1981).

Such cooperation can be extended to the role farmers play through their various general and community organizations in shaping and implementing governmental farm and food policies.[97] Likewise, it is possible to seek out and adopt technologies that reduce costs and enhance productivity without demanding increases in farm size. New technologies are not forced on farmers; they are chosen by farmers themselves.

249.   Farmers also must end their opposition to farmworker unionization efforts. Farmworkers have a legitimate right to belong to unions of their choice and to bargain collectively for just wages and working conditions. In pursuing that right they are protecting the value of labor in agriculture, a protection that also applies to farmers who devote their own labor to their farm operations.

5. Conclusion

250.   The U.S. food system is an integral part of the larger economy of the nation and the world. As such this integral role necessitates the cooperation of rural and urban interests in resolving the challenges and problems facing agriculture. The very nature of agricultural enterprise and the family farm traditions of this country have kept it a highly competitive sector with a widely dispersed ownership of the most fundamental input to production, the land. That competitive, diverse structure, proven to be a dependable source of nutritious and affordable food for this country and millions of people in other parts of the world, is now threatened. The food necessary for life, the land and water resources needed to produce that food, and the way of life of the people who make the land productive are at risk. Catholic social and ethical traditions attribute moral significance to each of these.

---

[97] See ch. IV.

Our response to the present situation should reflect a sensitivity to that moral significance, a determination that the United States will play its appropriate role in meeting global food needs, and a commitment to bequeath to future generations an enhanced natural environment and the same ready access to the necessities of life that most of us enjoy today. To farmers and farm workers who are suffering because of the farm crisis, we promise our solidarity, prayers, counseling and the other spiritual resources of our Catholic faith.

D. The U.S. Economy and the Developing Nations: Complexity, Challenge, and Choices

1. The Complexity of Economic Relations in an Interdependent World

251.   The global economy is made up of national economies of industrialized countries of the North and the developing countries of the South, together with the network of economic relations that link them. It constitutes the framework in which the solidarity we seek on a national level finds its international expression. Traditional Catholic teaching on this global interdependence emphasizes the dignity of the human person, the unity of the human family, the universally beneficial purpose of the goods of the earth, the need to pursue the international common good, as well as the good of each nation, and the imperative of distributive justice. The United States plays a leading role in the international economic system, and we are concerned that U.S. relations with all nations—Can-

ada, Europe, Japan, and our other trading partners, as well as the socialist countries—reflect this teaching and be marked by fairness and mutual respect.

252.　　　　Nevertheless, without in the least discounting the importance of these linkages, our emphasis on the preferential option for the poor moves us to focus our attention mainly on U.S. relations with the Third World. Unless conscious steps are taken toward protecting human dignity and fostering human solidarity in these relationships, we can look forward to increased conflict and inequity, threatening the fragile economies of these relatively poor nations far more than our own relatively strong one. Moreover, equity requires, even as the fact of interdependence becomes more apparent, that the *quality* of interdependence be improved, in order to eliminate "the scandal of the shocking inequality between the rich and the poor"[98] in a world divided ever more sharply between them.

253.　　　　Developing countries, moreover, often perceive themselves more as *dependent* on the industrialized countries, especially the United States, because the international system itself, as well as the way the United States acts in it, subordinates them. The prices at which they must sell their commodity exports and purchase their food and manufactured imports, the rates of interest they must pay and the terms they must meet to borrow money, the standards of economic behavior of foreign investors, the amounts and conditions of external aid, etc., are essentially determined by the industrialized world. Moreover, their traditional cultures are increasingly susceptible to the aggressive cultural penetration of Northern (especially U.S.) advertising and media programing. The developing countries are junior partners at best.

---

[98] *Instruction on Certain Aspects of the Theology of Liberation*, I:6. See also *Peace on Earth*, 130-131; and *On Human Work*, 11.

254.   The basic tenets of church teaching take on a
new moral urgency as we deepen our understanding
of how disadvantaged large numbers of people and
nations are in this interdependent world. Half the
world's people, nearly two and a half billion, live in
countries where the annual per capita income is $400
or less.[99] At least 800 million people in those countries
live in absolute poverty, "beneath any rational definition of human decency."[100] Nearly half a billion are
chronically hungry, despite abundant harvests worldwide.[101] Fifteen out of every 100 children born in those
countries die before the age of five, and millions of
the survivors are physically or mentally stunted. No
aggregate of individual examples could portray adequately the appalling inequities within those desperately poor countries and between them and our own.
And their misery is not the inevitable result of the
march of history or of the intrinsic nature of particular
cultures, but of human decisions and human institutions.

255.   On the international economic scene three
main sets of actors warrant particular attention: individual nations, which retain great influence; multilateral institutions, which channel money, power,
ideas, and influence; transnational corporations and
banks, which have grown dramatically in number,
size, scope, and strength since World War II.[102] In less

---

[99] Overseas Development Council, *U.S. Policy and the Third World: Agenda 1985-1986.*

[100] Robert S. McNamara, *Address to the Board of Governors of the World Bank* (Washington, D.C.: World Bank, September 30, 1980).

[101] U.N./Food and Agricultural Organization, *Dimensions of Need*, E 9 (Rome, 1982). The U.N. World Food Council uses this figure consistently, most recently at its 11th annual meeting in Paris.

[102] Joseph Greenwald and Kenneth Flamm, *The Global Factory* (Washington, D.C.: The Brookings Institution, 1985); see also Ron-ald Muller and Richard Barnet, *Global Reach* (New York: Simon and Schuster, 1974); Raymond Vernon, *The Economic and Political Con-sequences of Multinational Enterprise* (Cambridge, Mass.: Harvard

identifiable ways trade unions, popular movements, private relief and development agencies, and regional groupings of nations also affect the global economy. The interplay among all of them sets the context for policy choices that determine whether genuine interdependence is promoted or the dependence of the disadvantaged is deepened.

256.　　　In this arena, where fact and ethical challenges intersect, the moral task is to devise rules for the major actors that will move them toward a just international order. One of the most vexing problems is that of reconciling the transnational corporations' profit orientation with the common good that they, along with governments and their multilateral agencies, are supposed to serve.

257.　　　The notion of interdependence erases the fading line between domestic and foreign policy. Many foreign policy decisions (for example, on trade, investment, and immigration) have direct and substantial impact on domestic constituencies in the United States. Similarly, many decisions thought of as domestic (for example, on farm policy, interest rates, the federal budget, or the deficit) have important consequences for other countries. This increasingly recognized link of domestic and foreign issues poses new empirical and moral questions for national policy.

2. The Challenge of Catholic Social Teaching

258.　　　Catholic teaching on the international economic order recognizes this complexity, but does not provide specific solutions. Rather, we seek to ensure that moral considerations are taken into account. All of the elements of the moral perspective we have

---

University Press, 1972); the United Nations Center on Transnational Corporations maintains current data on these institutions.

outlined above have important implications for international relationships. (1) The demands of *Christian love* and *human solidarity* challenge all economic actors to choose community over chaos. They require a definition of political community that goes beyond national sovereignty to policies that recognize the moral bonds among all people. (2) *Basic justice* implies that all peoples are entitled to participate in the increasingly interdependent global economy in a way that ensures their freedom and dignity. When whole communities are effectively left out or excluded from equitable participation in the international order, basic justice is violated. We want a world that works fairly for all. (3) *Respect for human rights*, both political and economic, implies that international decisions, institutions, and policies must be shaped by values that are more than economic. The creation of a global order in which these rights are secure for all must be a prime objective for all relevant actors on the international stage. (4) *The special place of the poor* in this moral perspective means that meeting the basic needs of the millions of deprived and hungry people in the world must be the number one objective of international policy.

259.   These perspectives constitute a call for fundamental reform in the international economic order. Whether the problem is preventing war and building peace, or addressing the needs of the poor, Catholic teaching emphasizes not only the individual conscience, but also the political, legal, and economic structures through which policy is determined and issues are adjudicated.[103] We do not seek here to evaluate the various proposals for international economic reform or deal here with economic relations between the United States and other industrialized countries. We urge, as a basic and overriding consideration, that

---

[103] *Peace on Earth*, 56–63.

both empirical and moral evidence, especially the precarious situation of the developing countries, calls for the renewal of the dialogue between the industrialized countries of the North and the developing countries of the South, with the aim of reorganizing international economic relations to establish greater equity and help meet the basic human needs of the poor majority.[104]

260.   *Here, as elsewhere, the preferential option for the poor is the central priority for policy choice.* It offers a unique perspective on foreign policy in whose light U.S. relationships, especially with developing countries, can be reassessed. Standard foreign policy analysis deals with calculations of power and definitions of national interest; but the poor are, by definition, not powerful. If we are to give appropriate weight to their concerns, their needs, and their interests, we have to go beyond economic gain or national security as a starting point for the policy dialogue. We want to stand with the poor everywhere, and we believe that relations between the U.S. and developing nations should be determined in the first place by a concern for basic human needs and respect for cultural traditions.

3. The Role of the United States in the Global Economy: Constructive Choices

261.   As we noted in *The Challenge of Peace*, recent popes have strongly supported the United Nations as a crucial step forward in the development and organization of the human community; we share their regret that no political entity now exists with the responsibility and power to promote the global common good, and we urge the United States to support UN

---

[104] *On the Development of Peoples*, 44, 58-63; quoted also by Pope John Paul II, *Origins* 14:16 (October 4, 1984): 247.

efforts to move in that direction. Building a just world economic order in the absence of such an authority demands that national governments promote public policies that increase the ability of poor nations and marginalized people to participate in the global economy. Because no other nation's economic power yet matches ours, we believe that this responsibility pertains especially to the United States; but it must be carried out in cooperation with other industrialized countries as in the case of halting the rise of the dollar. This is yet another evidence of the fact of interdependence. Joint action toward these goals not only promotes justice and reduces misery in the Third World, but also is in the interest of the United States and other industrialized nations.

262.   Yet in recent years U.S. policy toward development in the Third World has become increasingly one of selective assistance based on an East-West assessment of North-South problems, at the expense of basic human needs and economic development. Such a view makes national security the central policy principle.[105] Developing countries have become largely testing grounds in the East-West struggle; they seem to have meaning or value mainly in terms of this larger geopolitical calculus. The result is that issues of human need and economic development take second place to the political-strategic argument. This tendency must be resisted.

263.   Moreover, U.S. performance in North-South negotiations often casts us in the role of resisting developing-country proposals without advancing realistic ones of our own.[106] North-South dialogue is bound

---

[105] President's Commission on Security and Economic Assistance (Carlucci Commission), *A Report to the Secretary of State* (Washington, D.C., November 1983).

[106] For example: After a dozen years of negotiations, during which nearly all of the issues were resolved to U.S. satisfaction, the United States refused to sign the Law of the Seas treaty; only

to be complex, protracted, and filled with symbolic and often unrealistic demands; but the situation has now reached the point where the rest of the world expects the United States to assume a reluctant, adversarial posture in such discussions. The U.S. approach to the developing countries needs urgently to be changed; a country as large, rich, and powerful as ours has a moral obligation to lead in helping to reduce poverty in the Third World.

264.　　　　We believe that U.S. policy toward the developing world should reflect our traditional regard for human rights and our concern for social progress. In economic policy, as we noted in our pastoral letter on nuclear war, the major international economic relationships of aid, trade, finance, and investment are interdependent among themselves and illustrate the range of interdependence issues facing U.S. policy. All three of the major economic actors are active in all these relationships. Each relationship offers us the possibility of substantial, positive movement toward increasing social justice in the developing world; in each, regrettably, we fall short. It is urgent that immediate steps be taken to correct these deficiencies.

265.　　　　a. *Development Assistance:* The official development assistance that the industrialized and the oil-producing countries provide the Third World in the form of grants; low-interest, long-term loans; commodities; and technical assistance is a significant contribution to their development. Although the annual share of U.S. gross national product (GNP) devoted to foreign aid is now less than one-tenth of that of the Marshall Plan, which helped rebuild devastated but advanced European economies, we remain the largest donor country. We still play a central role in

the United States failed to support the U.N. infant formula resolution; the United States has not ratified the two UN Covenants on Human Rights, etc.

these resource transfers, but we no longer set an example for other donors. We lag proportionately behind most other industrial nations in providing resources and seem to care less than before about development in the Third World. Our bilateral aid has become increasingly militarized and security-related and our contributions to multilateral agencies have been reduced in recent years.[107] Not all of these changes are justifiable. The projects of the International Development Agency, for example, seem worthy of support.

266.   This is a grave distortion of the priority that development assistance should command. We are dismayed that the United States, once the pioneer in foreign aid, is almost last among the seventeen industrialized nations in the Organization for Economic Cooperation and Development (OECD) in percentage of GNP devoted to aid. Reduction of the U.S. contribution to multilateral development institutions is particularly regrettable, because these institutions are often better able than the bilateral agencies to focus on the poor and reduce dependency in developing countries.[108] This is also an area in which, in the past, our leadership and example have had great influence. A more affirmative U.S. role in these institutions, which we took the lead in creating, could improve their performance, send an encouraging signal of U.S. intentions, and help reopen the dialogue on the growing poverty and dependency of the Third World.

---

[107] U.S. Agency for International Development, *Congressional Presentation, Fiscal Year 1986, Main Volume* (Washington, D.C., 1985).

[108] The clients of the International Development Association, the "soft loan window" of the World Bank, are the poorest countries. The United States insisted upon—and obtained—a 25% reduction in IDA's current (seventh) replenishment. Taking inflation into account, this meant a 40% drop in real terms at exactly the moment when developing-country debt levels are punishingly high and the prices of their export commodities are almost at rock bottom.

267.   b. *Trade:* Trade continues to be a central component of international economic relations. It contributed in a major way to the rapid economic growth of many developing countries in the 1960s and 1970s and will probably continue to do so, though at a slower rate. The preferential option for the poor does not, by itself, yield a trade policy; but it does provide a frame of reference. In particular, an equitable trading system that will help the poor should allocate its benefits fairly and ensure that exports from developing countries receive fair prices reached by agreement among all trading partners. Developing nations have a right to receive a fair price for their raw materials that allows for a reasonable degree of profit.

268.   Trade policy illustrates the conflicting pressures that interdependence can generate: claims of injustice from developing countries denied market access are countered by claims of injustice in the domestic economies of industrialized countries when jobs are threatened and incomes fall. Agricultural trade and a few industrial sectors present particularly acute examples of this.

269.   We believe the ethical norms we have applied to domestic economic questions are equally valid here.[109] As in other economic matters, the basic questions are: Who benefits from the particular policy measure? How can any benefit or adverse impact be equitably shared? We need to examine, for example, the extent to which the success in the U.S. market of certain imports is derived from exploitative labor conditions in the exporting country, conditions that in some cases have attracted the investment in the first place. The United States should do all it can to ensure that the trading system treats the poorest segments of developing countries' societies fairly and does not lead to human rights violations. In particular the United

---

[109] See ch. II.

States should seek effective special measures under the General Agreement on Tariffs and Trade (GATT)[110] to benefit the poorest countries.

270.   At the same time, U.S. workers and their families hurt by the operation of the trading system must be helped through training and other measures to adjust to changes that advance development and decrease poverty in the Third World. This is a very serious, immediate, and intensifying problem. In our judgment, adjustment assistance programs in the United States have been poorly designed and administered, and inadequately funded. A society and an economy such as ours can better adjust to trade dislocations than can poverty-ridden developing countries.

271.   c. *Finance:* Aid and trade policies alone, however enlightened, do not constitute a sufficient approach to the developing countries; they must also be looked at in conjunction with international finance and investment. The debtor-creditor relationship well exemplifies both the interdependence of the international economic order and its asymmetrical character, i.e., the *dependence* of the developing countries. The aggregate external debt of the developing countries now approaches $1 trillion,[111] more than one-third of their combined GNP; this total doubled between 1979 and 1984 and continues to rise. On average, the first 20 percent of export earnings goes to service that debt without significantly reducing the principal; in some countries debt service is nearly 100

---

[110] The GATT, third of the Bretton Woods "institutions" (with the World Bank and the IMF) is in fact a treaty, monitored and supported by a secretariat located in Geneva, Switzerland. Periodic "rounds" of negotiations among its several score members, North and South, modify and extend its provisions and regulations.

[111] Debt figures have been compiled from data published by the World Bank, the IMF, and the Bank for International Settlements.

percent of such earnings, leaving scant resources available for the countries' development programs.

272.   The roots of this very complex debt crisis are both historic and systemic. *Historically,* the three major economic actors share the responsibility for the present difficulty because of decisions made and actions taken during the 1970s and 1980s. In 1972 the Soviet Union purchased the entire U.S. grain surplus, and grain prices trebled. Between 1973 and 1979, the Organization of Petroleum Exporting Countries raised the price of oil eightfold and thereafter deposited most of the profits in commercial banks in the North. In order to profit from the interest-rate spread on these deposits, the banks pushed larger and larger loans on eager Third World borrowers needing funds to purchase more and more expensive oil. A second doubling of oil prices in 1979 forced many of these countries to refinance their loans and borrow more money at escalating interest rates. A global recession beginning in 1979 caused the prices of Third World export commodities to fall and thus reduced the ability to meet the increasingly burdensome debt payments out of export earnings.

273.   The global *system* of finance, development, and trade established by the Bretton Woods Conference in 1944—the World Bank, the International Monetary Fund (IMF), and the GATT—was created by the North to prevent a recurrence of the economic problems that were perceived to have led to World War II. Forty years later that system seems incapable, without basic changes, of helping the debtor countries—which had no part in its creation—manage their increasingly untenable debt situation effectively and equitably. The World Bank, largest of these institutions, has been engaged primarily in lending for specific projects rather than for general economic health. The IMF was intended to be a short-term lender that would help out with temporary balance of payments, or cash-flow

problems; but in the current situation it has come to the fore as a monitor of commercial financial transactions and an evaluator of debtors' creditworthiness—and therefore the key institution for resolving these problems. The GATT, which is not an institution, had been largely supplanted, as trade monitor for the developing countries, by UNCTAD[112] in which the latter have more confidence.

274.   This crisis, however, goes beyond the system; it affects people. It afflicts and oppresses large numbers of people who are already severely disadvantaged. That is the scandal: it is the poorest people who suffer most from the austerity measures required when a country seeks the IMF "seal of approval" which establishes its creditworthiness for a commercial loan (or perhaps an external aid program). It is these same people who suffer most when commodity prices fall, when food cannot be imported or they cannot buy it, and when natural disasters occur. Our commitment to the preferential option for the poor does not permit us to remain silent in these circumstances. Ways must be found to meet the immediate emergency—moratorium on payments, conversion of some dollar-denominated debt into local-currency debt, creditors' accepting a share of the burden by partially writing-down selected loans, capitalizing interest, or perhaps outright cancellation.

---

[112] The United Nations Conference on Trade and Development (UNCTAD) originated in Geneva in 1964 at a meeting convened by the U.N. to discuss trade, development, and related problems of low-income countries. It established a quadrennial meeting and created permanent machinery in the U.N. to deal with these problems. A Trade and Development Board (TDB), with standing committees, meets every two years; and there is a small secretariat to staff it. UNCTAD is viewed as representing the developing countries' continuing effort to have a larger voice in international decisions affecting trade and development and to secure more favorable terms of trade.

275.   The poorest countries, especially those in sub-Saharan Africa which are least developed, most afflicted by hunger and malnutrition, and most vulnerable to commodity price declines, are in extremely perilous circumstances.[113] Although their aggregate debt of more than $100 billion (much of it owed to multilateral institutions), is about one-quarter that of Latin America, their collateral (oil, minerals, manufactures, grain, etc.) is much less adequate, their ability to service external debt much weaker, and the possibility of their rescheduling it very small. For low-income countries like these, the most useful immediate remedies are longer payment periods, lower interest rates, and modification of IMF adjustment requirements that exacerbate the already straitened circumstances of the poor.[114] Especially helpful for some African countries would be cancellation of debts owed to governments, a step already taken by some creditor nations.

276.   Better off debtor countries also need to be able to adjust their debts without penalizing the poor. Although the final policy decisions about the allocation of adjustment costs belong to the debtor government, internal equity considerations should be taken into account in determining the conditions of debt rescheduling and additional lending; for example, wage reductions should not be mandated, basic public services to the poor should not be cut, and measures should be required to reduce the flight of capital. Since

---

[113] *U.S. Policy and the Third World*, Table B-5.

[114] When the IMF helps a country adjust to balance-of-payments problems (e.g., by assisting in the rescheduling of its external debt), it negotiates certain conditions with the debtor country in order to improve its immediate financial position. In general, these require the borrowing country to earn and save more. The adjustments, usually referred to as "conditionality," tend to fall most heavily on the poor through reduction of government spending on consumer subsidies and public services, and often of wages.

this debt problem, like most others, is systemic, a case-by-case approach is not sufficient: lending policies and exchange-rate considerations are not only economic questions, but are thoroughly and intensely political.

277.   Beyond all this, the growing external debt that has become the overarching economic problem of the Third World also requires systemic change to provide immediate relief and to prevent recurrence. The Bretton Woods institutions do not adequately represent Third World debtors, and their policies are not dealing effectively with problems affecting those nations. These institutions need to be substantially reformed and their policies reviewed at the same time that the immediate problem of Third World debt is being dealt with. The United States should promote, support, and participate fully in such reforms and reviews. Such a role is not only morally right, but is in the economic interest of the United States; more than a third of this debt is owed to U.S. banks. The viability of the international banking system (and of those U.S. banks) depends in part on the ability of debtor countries to manage those debts. Stubborn insistence on full repayment could force them to default—which would lead to economic losses in the United States. In this connection, we should not overlook the impact of U.S. budget and trade deficits on interest rates. These high interest rates exacerbate the already difficult debt situation. They also attract capital away from investment in economic development in Third World countries.

278.   d. *Foreign Private Investment:* Although direct private investment in the developing countries by U.S.-based transnational corporations has declined in recent years, it still amounts to about $60 billion and accounts for sizeable annual transfers. Such investment in developing countries should be increased, consistent with the host country's development goals and with benefits equitably distributed. Particular efforts should be made to encourage investments by

medium-sized and small companies, as well as to joint ventures, which may be more appropriate to the developing country's situation. For the foreseeable future, however, private investment will probably not meet the infrastructural needs of the poorest countries—roads, transportation, communications, education, health, etc.— since these do not generally show profits and therefore do not attract private capital. Yet without this infrastructure, no real economic growth can take place.

279.   Direct foreign investment, risky though it may be for both the investing corporation and the developing country, can provide needed capital, technology, and managerial expertise. Care must be taken lest such investment create or perpetuate dependency, harming especially those at the bottom of the economic ladder. Investments that sustain or worsen inequities in a developing country, that help to maintain oppressive elites in power, or that increase food dependency by encouraging cash cropping for export at the expense of local needs, should be discouraged. Foreign investors, attracted by low wage rates in less developed countries, should consider both the potential loss of jobs in the home country and the potential exploitation of workers in the host country.[115] Both the products and the technologies of the investing firms should be appropriate to the developing country, neither catering just to a small number of high-income consumers, nor establishing capital-intensive processes that displace labor, especially in the agricultural sector.[116]

280.   Such inequitable results, however, are not necessary consequences of transnational corporate activ-

---

[115] North American Coalition for Human Rights in Korea, *Testimony before the U. S. Trade Representative,* June 24, 1985.

[116] E. F. Schumacher, *Small Is Beautiful: Economics As If People Mattered* (New York: Harper and Row, 1973).

ity. Corporations can contribute to development by attracting and training high-caliber managers and other personnel, by helping organize effective marketing systems, by generating additional capital, by introducing or reinforcing financial accountability, and by sharing the knowledge gained from their own research and development activities. Although the ability of the corporations to plan, operate, and communicate across national borders without concern for domestic considerations makes it harder for governments to direct their activities toward the common good, the effort should be made; the Christian ethic is incompatible with a primary or exclusive focus on maximization of profit. We strongly urge U.S. and international support of efforts to develop a code of conduct for foreign corporations that recognizes their quasi-public character and encourages both development and the equitable distribution of their benefits. Transnational corporations should be required to adopt such a code, and to conform their behavior to its provisions.

281.   e. *The World Food Problem—A Special Urgency:* These four resource transfer channels—aid, trade, finance, and investment—intersect and overlap in all economic areas, but in none more clearly than in the international food system. The largest single segment of development assistance support goes to the agricultural sector and to food aid for short-term emergencies and vulnerable groups; food constitutes one of the most critical trade sectors; developing countries have borrowed extensively in the international capital markets to finance food imports; and a substantial portion of direct private investment flows into the agricultural sector.

282.   The development of U.S. agriculture has moved the United States into a dominant position in the international food system. The best way to meet the responsibilities this dominance entails is to design and

implement a U.S. food and agriculture policy that contributes to increased food security—that is, access by everyone to an adequate diet. A world with nearly half a billion hungry people is not one in which food security has been achieved. The problem of hunger has a special significance for those who read the Scriptures and profess the Christian faith. From the Lord's command to feed the hungry, to the Eucharist we celebrate as the Bread of Life, the fabric of our faith demands that we be creatively engaged in sharing the food that sustains life. There is no more basic human need. The gospel imperative takes on new urgency in a world of abundant harvests where hundreds of millions of people face starvation. Relief and prevention of their hunger cannot be left to the arithmetic of the marketplace.[117]

283.   The chronic hunger of those who live literally from day to day is one symptom of the underlying problem of poverty; relieving and preventing hunger is part of a larger, coordinated strategy to attack poverty itself. People must be enabled either to grow or to buy the food they need, without depending on an indefinite dole; there is no substitute for long-term agricultural and food-system development in the nations now caught in the grip of hunger and starvation. Most authorities agree that the key to this development is the small farmers, most of whom are prevented from participating in the food system by the lack of a market incentive resulting from the poverty of the bulk of the populations and by the lack of access to productive agricultural inputs, especially land, resulting mainly from their own poverty. In these poor, food-deficit countries, no less than in our own, the small family farm deserves support and protection.

284.   But recognizing the long-term problem does not dissolve the short-term obligation of the world's

---

[117] *On the Development of Peoples,* 44, 58-63.

major food-exporting nation to provide food aid sufficient to meet the nutritional needs of poor people,
and to provide it not simply to dispose of surpluses
but in a way that does not discourage local food production. There can be no successful solution to the
problem of hunger in the world without U.S. participation in a cooperative effort that simultaneously increases food aid and launches a long-term program
to help develop food self-reliance in food-deficit developing countries.

285.   Hunger is often seen as being linked with the
problem of population growth, as effect to cause. While
this relationship is sometimes presented in oversim-
plified fashion, we cannot fail to recognize that the
earth's resources are finite and that population tends
to grow rapidly. Whether the world can provide a
truly human life for twice as many people or more as
now live in it (many of whose lives are sadly deficient
today) is a matter of urgent concern that cannot be
ignored.[118]

286.   Although we do not believe that people are
poor and hungry primarily because they have large
families, the Church fully supports the need for all to
exercise responsible parenthood. Family size is heavily dependent on levels of economic development,
education, respect for women, availability of health
care, and the cultural traditions of communities.
Therefore, in dealing with population growth we
strongly favor efforts to address these social and economic concerns.

287.   Population policies must be designed as part
of an overall strategy of integral human development.
They must respect the freedom of parents and avoid
coercion. As Pope Paul VI has said concerning population policies: "It is true that too frequently an accelerated demographic increase adds its own

---

[118] Ibid., 37; *Pastoral Constitution*, 87.

difficulties to the problems of development: the size of the population increases more rapidly than available resources, and things are found to have reached apparently an impasse. From that moment the temptation is great to check the demographic increase by means of radical measures. It is certain that public authorities can intervene, within the limit of their competence, by favoring the availability of appropriate information and by adopting suitable measures, provided that these be in conformity with the moral law and that they respect the rightful freedom of married couples. Where the inalienable right to marriage and procreation is lacking, human dignity has ceased to exist."[119]

4. U.S. Responsibility for Reform in the International Economic System

288.　　　The United States cannot be the sole savior of the developing world, nor are Third World countries entirely innocent with respect to their own failures or totally helpless to achieve their own destinies. Many of these countries will need to initiate positive steps to promote and sustain development and economic growth—streamline bureaucracies, account for funds, plan reasonable programs, and take further steps toward empowering their people. Progress toward development will surely require them to take some tough remedial measures as well: prevent the flight of capital, reduce borrowing, modify price discrimination against rural areas, eliminate corruption in the use of funds and other resources, and curtail spending on inefficient public enterprises. The pervasive U.S. presence in many parts of our interdependent world, however, also creates a responsibility for us to increase

---

[119] *On the Development of Peoples,* 37.

the use of U.S. economic power—not just aid—in the service of human dignity and human rights, both political and economic.

289.　　　In particular, as we noted in our earlier letter, *The Challenge of Peace*, the contrast between expenditures on armaments and on development reflects a shift in priorities from meeting human needs to promoting "national security" and represents a massive distortion of resource allocations. In 1982, for example, the military expenditures of the industrialized countries were seventeen times larger than their foreign assistance; in 1985 the United States alone budgeted more than twenty times as much for defense as for foreign assistance, and nearly two-thirds of the latter took the form of military assistance (including subsidized arms sales) or went to countries because of their perceived strategic value to the United States.[120] *Rather than promoting U.S. arms sales, especially to countries that cannot afford them, we should be campaigning for an international agreement to reduce this lethal trade.*

290.　　　In short, the international economic order, like many aspects of our own economy, is in crisis; the gap between rich and poor countries and between rich and poor people within countries is widening. The United States represents the most powerful single factor in the international economic equation. But even as we speak of crisis, we see an opportunity for the United States to launch a worldwide campaign for justice and economic rights to match the still incomplete, but encouraging, political democracy we have achieved in the United States with so much pain and sacrifice.

291.　　　To restructure the international order along lines of greater equity and participation and apply the preferential option for the poor to international eco-

---

[120] Ruth Leger Sivard, *World Military and Social Expenditures 1983* (Washington D.C.: World Priorities, 1983), 23.

nomic activity will require sacrifices of at least the scope of those we have made over the years in building our own nation. We need to call again upon the qualities of leadership and vision that have marked our history when crucial choices were demanded. As Pope John Paul II said during his 1979 visit to the United States, "America, which in the past decades has demonstrated goodness and generosity in providing food for the hungry of the world, will, I am sure, be able to match this generosity with an equally convincing contribution to the establishing of a world order that will create the necessary economic and trade conditions for a more just relationship between all the nations of the world."[121]

292.　　　We share his conviction that most of the policy issues generally called economic are, at root, moral and therefore require the application of moral principles derived from the Scriptures and from the evolving social teaching of the Church and other traditions.[122] We also recognize that we are dealing here with sensitive international issues that cross national boundaries. Nevertheless, in order to pursue justice and peace on a global scale, *we call for a U.S. international economic policy designed to empower people everywhere and enable them to continue to develop a sense of their own worth, improve the quality of their lives, and ensure that the benefits of economic growth are shared equitably.*

E. Conclusion

293.　　　None of the issues we have addressed in this chapter can be dealt with in isolation. They are

---

[121] Pontifical Commission Justitia et Pax, *The Social Teaching of John Paul II*, 6 (October 6, 1979).

[122] *On the Development of Peoples*, 44, 58-63.

interconnected, and their resolution requires difficult
trade-offs among competing interests and values. The
changing international economy, for example, greatly
influences efforts to achieve full employment in the
United States and to maintain a healthy farm sector.
Similarly, as we have noted, policies and programs
to reduce unemployment and poverty must not ignore
a potential inflationary impact. These complexities and
trade-offs are real and must be confronted, but they
are not an excuse for inaction. They should not par-
alyze us in our search for a more just economy.

294.   Many of the reforms we have suggested in this
chapter would be expensive. At a time when the United
States has large annual deficits some might consider
these costs too high. But this discussion must be set
in the context of how our resources are allocated and
the immense human and social costs of failure to act
on these pressing problems. We believe that the question of providing adequate revenues to meet the needs
of our nation must be faced squarely and realistically.
Reforms in the tax code which close loopholes and
generate new revenues, for example, are among the
steps that need to be examined in order to develop a
federal budget that is both fiscally sound and socially
responsible. The cost of meeting our social needs must
also be weighed against the $300 billion a year allo-
cated for military purposes. Although some of these
expenditures are necessary for the defense of the nation, some elements of the military budget are both
wasteful and dangerous for world peace.[123] Careful
reductions should be made in these areas in order to

---

[123] See "Testimony on U. S. Arms Control Policy," *Origins* 14:10
(August 9, 1984): 154ff.

free up funds for social and economic reforms. In the end, the question is not whether the United States can provide the necessary funds to meet our social needs, but whether we have the political will to do so.

Chapter IV

A NEW AMERICAN EXPERIMENT: PARTNERSHIP FOR THE PUBLIC GOOD

295.   For over two hundred years the United States has been engaged in a bold experiment in democracy. The founders of the nation set out to establish justice, promote the general welfare, and secure the blessings of liberty for themselves and their posterity. Those who live in this land today are the beneficiaries of this great venture. Our review of some of the most pressing problems in economic life today shows, however, that this undertaking is not yet complete. Justice for all remains an aspiration; a fair share in the general welfare is denied to many. In addition to the particular policy recommendations made above, a long-term and more fundamental response is needed. This will call for an imaginative vision of the future that can help shape economic arrangements in creative new ways. We now want to propose some elements of such a vision and several innovations in economic structures that can contribute to making this vision a reality.

296.   Completing the unfinished business of the American experiment will call for new forms of cooperation and partnership among those whose daily work is the source of the prosperity and justice of the nation. The United States prides itself on both its competitive sense of initiative and its spirit of teamwork. Today a greater spirit of partnership and team-

work is needed; competition alone will not do the job. It has too many negative consequences for family life, the economically vulnerable, and the environment. Only a renewed commitment by all to the common good can deal creatively with the realities of international interdependence and economic dislocations in the domestic economy. The virtues of good citizenship require a lively sense of participation in the commonwealth and of having obligations as well as rights within it.[1] The nation's economic health depends on strengthening these virtues among all its people, and on the development of institutional arrangements supportive of these virtues.[2]

297.   The nation's founders took daring steps to create structures of participation, mutual accountability, and widely distributed power to ensure the political rights and freedoms of all. We believe that similar steps are needed today to expand economic participation, broaden the sharing of economic power, and make economic decisions more accountable to the common good. As noted above, the principle of subsidiarity states that the pursuit of economic justice must occur on all levels of society. It makes demands on communities as small as the family, as large as the

---

[1] *Octogesima Adveniens*, 24.

[2] For different analyses along these lines with quite different starting points see Martin Carnoy, Derek Shearer, and Russell Rumberger, *A New Social Contract* (New York: Harper and Row, 1983); Amatai Etzioni, *An Immodest Agenda: Reconstructing America before the Twenty-First Century* (New York: McGraw-Hill, 1983); Charles E. Lindblom, *Politics and Markets* (New York: Basic Books, 1977), esp. 346-348; George C. Lodge, *The New American Ideology* (New York: Alfred A. Knopf, 1975); Douglas Sturm, "Corporations, Constitutions, and Covenants," *Journal of the American Academy of Religion*, 41 (1973): 331-55; Lester Thurow, *The Zero-Sum Society* (New York: Basic Books, 1980), esp. ch. 1; Roberto Mangabeira Unger, *Knowledge and Politics* (New York: Free Press, 1975); George F. Will, *Statecraft as Soulcraft: What Government Does* (New York: Simon and Schuster, 1982), esp. ch. 6.

global society and on all levels in between. There are a number of ways to enhance the cooperative participation of these many groups in the task of creating this future. Since there is no single innovation that will solve all problems, we recommend careful experimentation with several possibilities that hold considerable hope for increasing partnership and strengthening mutual responsibility for economic justice.

A. Cooperation within Firms and Industries

298.   A new experiment in bringing democratic ideals to economic life calls for serious exploration of ways to develop new patterns of partnership among those working in individual firms and industries.[3] Every business, from the smallest to the largest, including farms and ranches, depends on many different persons and groups for its success: workers, managers, owners or shareholders, suppliers, customers, creditors, the local community, and the wider society. Each makes a contribution to the enterprise, and each has a stake in its growth or decline. Present structures of accountability, however, do not acknowledge all these contributions or protect these stakes. A major challenge in today's economy is the development of new institutional mechanisms for accountability that also preserve the flexibility needed to respond quickly to a rapidly changing business environment.[4]

---

[3] *Pastoral Constitution*, 68. See *Mater et Magistra*, 75-77.

[4] Charles W. Powers provided a helpful discussion of these matters in a paper presented at a conference on the first draft of this pastoral letter sponsored by the Harvard University Divinity School and the Institute for Policy Studies, Cambridge, Massachusetts, March 29-31, 1985.

299.   New forms of partnership between workers and managers are one means for developing greater participation and accountability within firms.[5] Recent experience has shown that both labor and management suffer when the adversarial relationship between them becomes extreme. As Pope Leo XIII stated, "Each needs the other completely: capital cannot do without labor, nor labor without capital."[6] The organization of firms should reflect and enhance this mutual partnership. In particular, the development of work patterns for men and women that are more supportive of family life will benefit both employees and the enterprises they work for.

300.   Workers in firms and on farms are especially in need of stronger institutional protection, for their jobs and livelihood are particularly vulnerable to the decisions of others in today's highly competitive labor market. Several arrangements are gaining increasing support in the United States: profit sharing by the workers in a firm; enabling employees to become company stockholders; granting employees greater participation in determining the conditions of work; cooperative ownership of the firm by all who work within it; and programs for enabling a much larger number of Americans, regardless of their employment status, to become shareholders in successful corporations. Initiatives of this sort can enhance productivity, increase the profitability of firms, provide greater

---

[5] See John Paul II, "The Role of Business in a Changing Workplace," 3, *Origins* 15 (February 6, 1986): 567.

[6] *Rerum Novarum*, 28. For an analysis of the relevant papal teachings on institutions of collaboration and partnership, see John Cronin, *Catholic Social Principles: The Social Teaching of the Catholic Church Applied to American Economic Life* (Milwaukee: Bruce, 1950), ch. VII; Oswald von Nell-Breuning, *Reorganization of Social Economy: The Social Encyclical Developed and Explained*, trans. Bernard W. Dempsey (Milwaukee: Bruce, 1936), chs. X-XII; Jean-Yves Calvez and Jacques Perrin, *The Church and Social Justice*, trans. J. R. Kirwan (Chicago: Regnery, 1961), ch. XIX.

job security and work satisfaction for employees, and reduce adversarial relations.[7] In our 1919 Program of Social Reconstruction, we observed "the full possibilities of increased production will not be realized so long as the majority of workers remain mere wage earners. The majority must somehow become owners, at least in part, of the instruments of production."[8] We believe this judgment remains generally valid today.

301.   None of these approaches provides a panacea, and all have certain drawbacks. Nevertheless we believe that continued research and experimentation with these approaches will be of benefit. Catholic social teaching has endorsed on many occasions innovative methods for increasing worker participation within firms.[9] The appropriateness of these methods will depend on the circumstances of the company or industry in question and on their effectiveness in actually increasing a genuinely cooperative approach to shaping

---

[7] Michael Conte, Arnold S. Tannenbaum, and Donna Mc-Culloch, *Employee Ownership*, Research Report Series, Institute for Social Research (Ann Arbor, Mich.: University of Michigan, 1981); Robert A. Dahl, *A Preface to Economic Democracy* (Berkeley: University of California Press, 1985); Harvard Business School, "The Mondragon Cooperative Movement," case study prepared by David P. Ellerman (Cambridge, Mass.: Harvard Business School, n.d.); Robert Jackall and Henry M. Levin, eds., *Worker Cooperatives in America* (Berkeley: University of California Press, 1984); Derek Jones and Jan Svejnar, eds., *Participatory and Self-Managed Firms: Evaluating Economic Performance* (Lexington, Mass.: D. C. Heath, 1982); Irving H. Siegel and Edgar Weinberg, *Labor-Management Cooperation: The American Experience* (Kalamazoo, Mich.: W. E. Upjohn Institute for Employment Research, 1982); Stuart M. Speiser, "Broadened Capital Ownership—The Solution to Major Domestic and International Problems," *Journal of Post Keynesian Economics* VIII (1985): 426-434; Jaroslav Vanek, ed., *Self-Management: Economic Liberation of Man* (London: Penguin, 1975); Martin L. Weitzman, *The Share Economy* (Cambridge, Mass.: Harvard University Press, 1984).

[8] *Program of Social Reconstruction* in *Justice in the Marketplace*, 381.

[9] *Mater et Magistra*, 32, 77, 85-103; *On Human Work*, 14.

decisions. The most highly publicized examples of such efforts have been in large firms facing serious financial crises. If increased participation and collaboration can help a firm avoid collapse, why should it not give added strength to healthy businesses? Cooperative ownership is particularly worthy of consideration in new entrepreneurial enterprises.[10]

302.   Partnerships between labor and management are possible only when both groups possess real freedom and power to influence decisions. This means that unions ought to continue to play an important role in moving toward greater economic participation within firms and industries. Workers rightly reject calls for less adversarial relations when they are a smokescreen for demands that labor make all the concessions. For partnership to be genuine it must be a two-way street, with creative initiative and a willingness to cooperate on all sides.

303.   When companies are considering plant closures or the movement of capital, it is patently unjust to deny workers any role in shaping the outcome of these difficult choices.[11] In the heavy manufacturing sector today, technological change and international competition can be the occasion of painful decisions leading to the loss of jobs or wage reductions. While such decisions may sometimes be necessary, a collaborative and mutually accountable model of industrial organization would mean that workers not be expected to carry all the burdens of an economy in transition. Management and investors must also ac-

---

[10] For examples of worker-owned and operated enterprises supported by the Campaign for Human Development's revolving loan fund see CHD's *Annual Report* (Washington, D.C.: USCC).

[11] *Quadragesimo Anno* states the basic norm on which this conclusion is based: "It is wholly false to ascribe to property alone or to labor alone whatever has been obtained through the combined effort of both, and it is wholly unjust for either, denying the efficacy of the other, to arrogate to itself whatever has been produced" (53).

cept their share of sacrifices, especially when management is thinking of closing a plant or transferring capital to a seemingly more lucrative or competitive activity. The capital at the disposal of management is in part the product of the labor of those who have toiled in the company over the years, including currently employed workers.[12] As a minimum, workers have a right to be informed in advance when such decisions are under consideration, a right to negotiate with management about possible alternatives, and a right to fair compensation and assistance with retraining and relocation expenses should these be necessary. Since even these minimal rights are jeopardized without collective negotiation, industrial cooperation requires a strong role for labor unions in our changing economy.

304.   Labor unions themselves are challenged by the present economic environment to seek new ways of doing business. The purpose of unions is not simply to defend the existing wages and prerogatives of the fraction of workers who belong to them, but also to enable workers to make positive and creative contributions to the firm, the community, and the larger society in an organized and cooperative way.[13] Such

---

[12] *On Human Work*, 12.

[13] Ibid., 20. This point was well made by John Cronin twenty-five years ago: "Even if most injustice and exploitation were removed, unions would still have a legitimate place. They are the normal voice of labor, necessary to organize social life for the common good. There is positive need for such organization today, quite independently of any social evils which may prevail. Order and harmony do not happen; they are the fruit of conscious and organized effort. While we may hope that the abuses which occasioned the rise of unions may disappear, it does not thereby follow that unions will have lost their function. On the contrary, they will be freed from unpleasant, even though temporarily necessary, tasks and able to devote all their time and efforts to a better organization of social life" *Catholic Social Principles*, 418. See also AFL-CIO Committee on the Evolution of Work, *The Future of Work* (Washington, D.C.: AFL-CIO, 1983).

contributions call for experiments with new directions in the U.S. labor movement.

305.   The parts played by managers and shareholders in U.S. corporations also need careful examination. In U.S. law, the primary responsibility of managers is to exercise prudent business judgment in the interest of a profitable return to investors. But morally this legal responsibility may be exercised only within the bounds of justice to employees, customers, suppliers, and the local community. Corporate mergers and hostile takeovers may bring greater benefits to shareholders, but they often lead to decreased concern for the well-being of local communities and make towns and cities more vulnerable to decisions made from afar.

306.   Most shareholders today exercise relatively little power in corporate governance.[14] Although shareholders can and should vote on the selection of corporate directors and on investment questions and other policy matters, it appears that return on investment is the governing criterion in the relation between them and management. We do not believe this is an adequate rationale for shareholder decisions. The question of how to relate the rights and responsibilities of shareholders to those of the other people and communities affected by corporate decisions is complex and insufficiently understood. We, therefore, urge serious, long-term research and experimentation in this area. More effective ways of dealing with these questions are essential to enable firms to serve the common good.

---

[14] For a classic discussion of the relative power of managers and shareholders see A. A. Berle and Gardiner C. Means, *The Modern Corporation and Private Property* (New York, Macmillan, 1932).

B. Local and Regional Cooperation

307.　　　　The context within which U.S. firms do business has direct influence on their ability to contribute to the common good. Companies and indeed whole industries are not sole masters of their own fate. Increased cooperative efforts are needed to make local, regional, national, and international conditions more supportive of the pursuit of economic justice.

308.　　　　In the principle of subsidiarity, Catholic social teaching has long stressed the importance of small- and intermediate-sized communities or institutions in exercising moral responsibility. These mediating structures link the individual to society as a whole in a way that gives people greater freedom and power to act.[15] Such groups include families, neighborhoods, church congregations, community organizations, civic and business associations, public interest and advocacy groups, community development corporations, and many other bodies. All these groups can play a crucial role in generating creative partnerships for the pursuit of the public good on the local and regional level.

309.　　　　The value of partnership is illustrated by considering how new jobs are created. The development of new businesses to serve the local community is key to revitalizing areas hit hard by unemployment.[16] The cities and regions in greatest need of these new jobs face serious obstacles in attracting enterprises that can provide them. Lack of financial resources, limited entrepreneurial skill, blighted and unsafe environments, and a deteriorating infrastructure create a vicious cycle

---

[15] Peter L. Berger and Richard John Neuhaus, *To Empower People: The Role of Mediating Structures in Public Policy* (Washington, D.C.: American Enterprise Institute, 1977).

[16] United States Small Business Administration, *1978 Annual Report* (Washington, D.C.: Government Printing Office, 1979).

that makes new investment in these areas more risky and therefore less likely.

310. Breaking out of this cycle will require a cooperative approach that draws on all the resources of the community.[17] Community development corporations can keep efforts focused on assisting those most in need. Existing business, labor, financial, and academic institutions can provide expertise in partnership with innovative entrepreneurs. New cooperative structures of local ownership will give the community or region an added stake in businesses and even more importantly give these businesses a greater stake in the community.[18] Government on the local, state, and national levels must play a significant role, especially through tax structures that encourage investment in hard hit areas and through funding aimed at conservation and basic infrastructure needs. Initiatives like these can contribute to a multilevel response to the needs of the community.

311. The Church itself can work as an effective partner on the local and regional level. First-hand knowledge of community needs and commitment to the protection of the dignity of all should put Church leaders in the forefront of efforts to encourage a community-wide cooperative strategy. Because churches

---

[17] For recent discussion from a variety of perspectives see: Robert Friedman and William Schweke, eds., *Expanding the Opportunity to Produce: Revitalizing the American Economy through New Enterprise Development: A Policy Reader* (Washington, D.C.: Corporation for New Enterprise Development, 1981); Jack A. Meyer, ed., *Meeting Human Needs: Toward a New Public Philosophy* (Washington, D.C.: American Enterprise Institute, 1982); Committee for Economic Development, *Jobs for the Hard-to-Employ: New Directions for a Public-Private Partnership* (New York: Committee for Economic Development, 1978); Gar Alperovitz and Jeff Faux, *Rebuilding America: A Blueprint for the New Economy* (New York: Pantheon Books, 1984).

[18] Christopher Mackin, *Strategies for Local Ownership and Control: A Policy Analysis* (Somerville, Mass.: Industrial Cooperative Association, 1983).

include members from many different parts of the community, they can often serve as mediator between groups who might otherwise regard each other with suspicion. We urge local church groups to work creatively and in partnership with other private and public groups in responding to local and regional problems.

C. Partnership in the Development of National Policies

312.   The causes of our national economic problems and their possible solutions are the subject of vigorous debate today. The discussion often turns on the role the national government has played in creating these problems and could play in remedying them. We want to point to several considerations that could help build new forms of effective citizenship and cooperation in shaping the economic life of our country.

313.   First, while economic freedom and personal initiative are deservedly esteemed in our society, we have increasingly come to recognize the inescapably social and political nature of the economy. The market is always embedded in a specific social and political context. The tax system affects consumption, saving, and investment. National monetary policy, domestic and defense programs, protection of the environment and worker safety, and regulation of international trade all shape the economy as a whole. These policies influence domestic investment, unemployment rates, foreign exchange, and the health of the entire world economy.

314.   The principle of subsidiarity calls for government intervention when small or intermediate groups in society are unable or unwilling to take the steps needed to promote basic justice. Pope John XXIII observed that the growth of more complex relations of

interdependence among citizens has led to an increased role for government in modern societies.[19] This role is to work *in partnership with* the many other groups in society, helping them fulfill their tasks and responsibilities more effectively, not replacing or destroying them. The challenge of today is to move beyond abstract disputes about whether more or less government intervention is needed, to consideration of creative ways of enabling government and private groups to work together effectively.

315.   It is in this light that we understand Pope John Paul II's recommendation that "society make provision for overall planning" in the economic domain.[20] Planning must occur on various levels, with the government ensuring that basic justice is protected and also protecting the rights and freedoms of all other agents. In the Pope's words:

> In the final analysis this overall concern weighs on the shoulders of the state, but it cannot mean one-sided centralization by the public authorities. Instead what is in question is a just and rational coordination within the framework of which the initiative of individuals, free groups, and local work centers and complexes must be safeguarded.[21]

316.   We are well aware that the mere mention of economic planning is likely to produce a strong negative reaction in U.S. society. It conjures up images of centralized planning boards, command economies, inefficient bureaucracies, and mountains of government paperwork. It is also clear that the meaning of "planning" is open to a wide variety of interpretations and takes very different forms in various nations.[22]

---

[19] *Mater et Magistra,* 59, 62.
[20] *On Human Work,* 18.
[21] Ibid.
[22] For examples and analysis of different meanings of economic planning see Naomi Caiden and Aaron Wildavsky, *Planning and*

The Pope's words should not be construed as an endorsement of a highly centralized form of economic planning, much less a totalitarian one. His call for a "just and rational coordination" of the endeavors of the many economic actors is a call to seek creative new partnership and forms of participation in shaping national policies.

317.   There are already many forms of economic planning going on within the U.S. economy today. Individuals and families plan for their economic future. Management and labor unions regularly develop both long- and short-term plans. Towns, cities, and regions frequently have planning agencies concerned with their social and economic future. When state legislatures and the U.S. Congress vote on budgets or on almost any other bill that comes before them, they are engaged in a form of public planning. Catholic social teaching does not propose a single model for political and economic life by which these levels are to be institutionally related to each other. It does insist that reasonable coordination among the different parts of the body politic is an essential condition for achieving justice. This is a moral precondition of good citizenship that applies to both individual and institutional actors. In its absence no political structure can guarantee justice in society or the economy. Effective decisions in these matters will demand greater cooperation among all citizens. To encourage our fellow citizens to consider more carefully the appropriate

---

Budgeting in Poor Countries (New York: Wiley, 1974); Robert Dahl and Charles E. Lindblom, *Politics, Economics and Welfare: Planning and Politico-Economic Systems Resolved into Basic Social Processes* (Chicago: University of Chicago Press, 1976); Stephen S. Cohen, *Modern Capitalist Planning: The French Model* (Berkeley: University of California Press, 1977); Albert Waterston, *Development Planning: Lessons of Experience* (Baltimore: Johns Hopkins Press, 1965); *Rebuilding America*, chs. 14, 15.

balance of private and local initiative with national economic policy, we make several recommendations.

318.   *First, in an advanced industrial economy like ours, all parts of society, including government, must cooperate in forming national economic policies.* Taxation, monetary policy, high levels of government spending, and many other forms of governmental regulation are here to stay. A modern economy without governmental interventions of the sort we have alluded to is inconceivable. These interventions, however, should help, not replace, the contributions of other economic actors and institutions and should direct them to the common good. The development of effective new forms of partnership between private and public agencies will be difficult in a situation as immensely complex as that of the United States in which various aspects of national policy seem to contradict one another.[23] On the theoretical level, achieving greater coordination will make demands on those with the technical competence to analyze the relationship among different parts of the economy. More practically, it will require the various subgroups within our society to sharpen their concern for the common good and moderate their efforts to protect their own short-term interests.

319.   *Second, the impact of national economic policies on the poor and the vulnerable is the primary criterion for judging their moral value.* Throughout this letter we have stressed the special place of the poor and the vulnerable in any ethical analysis of the U. S. economy. National economic policies that contribute to

---

[23] For example, many students of recent policy point out that monetary policy on the one hand and fiscal policies governing taxation and government expenditures on the other have been at odds with each other, with larger public deficits and high interest rates as the outcome. See Alice M. Rivlin, ed., *Economic Choices 1984* (Washington, D.C.: The Brookings Institution, 1984), esp. ch. 2.

building a true commonwealth should reflect this by
standing firmly for the rights of those who fall through
the cracks of our economy: the poor, the unemployed,
the homeless, the displaced. Being a citizen of this
land means sharing in the responsibility for shaping
and implementing such policies.

320.   *Third, the serious distortion of national economic
priorities produced by massive national spending on defense
must be remedied.* Clear-sighted consideration of the
role of government shows that government and the
economy are already closely intertwined through military research and defense contracts. Defense-related
industries make up a major part of the U.S. economy
and have intimate links with both the military and
civilian government; they often depart from the competitive model of free-market capitalism. Moreover,
the dedication of so much of the national budget to
military purposes has been disastrous for the poor
and vulnerable members of our own and other nations. The nation's spending priorities need to be revised in the interests of both justice and peace.[24]

321.   We recognize that these proposals do not provide a detailed agenda. We are also aware that there
is a tension between setting the goals for coherent
policies and actually arriving at them by democratic
means. But if we can increase the level of commitment
to the common good and the virtues of citizenship in
our nation, the ability to achieve these goals will greatly
increase. It is these fundamental moral concerns that
lead us as bishops to join the debate on national priorities.

---

[24] *The Challenge of Peace*, 270-271.

D. Cooperation at the International Level

322.   If our country is to guide its international economic relationships by policies that serve human dignity and justice, we must expand our understanding of the moral responsibility of citizens to serve the common good of the entire planet. Cooperation is not limited to the local, regional, or national level. Economic policy can no longer be governed by national goals alone. The fact that the "social question has become worldwide"[25] challenges us to broaden our horizons and enhance our collaboration and sense of solidarity on the global level. The cause of democracy is closely tied to the cause of economic justice. The unfinished business of the American experiment includes the formation of new international partnerships, especially with the developing countries, based on mutual respect, cooperation, and a dedication to fundamental justice.

323.   The principle of subsidiarity calls for government to intervene in the economy when basic justice requires greater social coordination and regulation of economic actors and institutions. In global economic relations, however, no international institution provides this sort of coordination and regulation. The U.N. system, including the World Bank, the International Monetary Fund, and the General Agreement on Tariffs and Trade, does not possess the requisite authority. Pope John XXIII called this institutional weakness a "structural defect" in the organization of the human community. The structures of world order, including economic ones, "no longer correspond to

---

[25] *On the Development of Peoples*, 3.

the objective requirements of the universal common good."[26]

324.   Locked together in a world of limited material resources and a growing array of common problems, we help or hurt one another by the economic policies we choose. All the economic agents in our society, therefore, must consciously and deliberately attend to the good of the whole human family. We must all work to increase the effectiveness of international agencies in addressing global problems that cannot be handled through the actions of individual countries. In particular we repeat our plea made in *The Challenge of Peace* urging "that the United States adopt a stronger supportive leadership role with respect to the United Nations."[27] In the years following World War II, the United States took the lead in establishing multilateral bodies to deal with postwar economic problems. Unfortunately, in recent years this country has taken steps that have weakened rather than strengthened multilateral approaches. This is a shortsighted policy and should be reversed if the long-term interests of an interdependent globe are to be served.[28] In devising more effective arrangements for pursuing international economic justice, the overriding problem is how to get from where we are to where we ought to be. Progress toward that goal demands positive and often difficult action by corporations, banks, labor unions, governments, and other major actors on the international stage. But whatever the difficulty, the need to give priority to alleviating poverty in developing countries is undeniable; and the cost of continued inaction can be counted in human lives lost or stunted, talents wasted, opportunities foregone, misery and suffering prolonged, and injustice condoned.

---

[26] *Peace on Earth*, 134-135.

[27] *The Challenge of Peace*, 268.

[28] See Robert O. Keohane and Joseph S. Nye, Jr., "Two Cheers for Multilateralism," *Foreign Policy* 60 (Fall 1985): 148-167.

325.   Self-restraint and self-criticism by all parties
are necessary first steps toward strengthening the international structures to protect the common good.
Otherwise, growing interdependence will lead to conflict and increased economic threats to human dignity.
This is an important long-term challenge to the economic future of this country and its place in the emerging world economic community.

Chapter V

A COMMITMENT
TO THE FUTURE

326.   Because Jesus' command to love our neighbor is universal, we hold that the life of each person on this globe is sacred. This commits us to bringing about a just economic order where all, without exception, will be treated with dignity and to working in collaboration with those who share this vision. The world is complex and this may often tempt us to seek simple and self-centered solutions; but as a community of disciples we are called to a new hope and to a new vision that we must live without fear and without oversimplification. Not only must we learn more about our moral responsibility for the larger economic issues that touch the daily life of each and every person on this planet, but we also want to help shape the Church as a model of social and economic justice. Thus, this chapter deals with the Christian vocation in the world today, the special challenges to the Church at this moment of history, ways in which the themes of this letter should be followed up, and a call to the kind of commitment that will be needed to reshape the future.

A. The Christian Vocation in the World Today

327.   This letter has addressed many matters commonly regarded as secular, for example, employment rates, income levels, and international economic relationships. Yet, the affairs of the world, including economic ones, cannot be separated from the spiritual hunger of the human heart. We have presented the biblical vision of humanity and the Church's moral and religious tradition as a framework for asking the deeper questions about the meaning of economic life and for actively responding to them. But words alone are not enough. The Christian perspective on the meaning of economic life must transform the lives of individuals, families, in fact, our whole culture. The Gospel confers on each Christian the vocation to love God and neighbor in ways that bear fruit in the life of society. That vocation consists above all in a change of heart: a conversion expressed in praise of God and in concrete deeds of justice and service.

1. Conversion

328.   The transformation of social structures begins with and is always accompanied by a conversion of the heart.[1] As disciples of Christ each of us is called to a deep personal conversion and to "action on behalf of justice and participation in the transformation of the world."[2] By faith and baptism we are fashioned into a "new creature"; we are filled with the Holy Spirit and a new love that compels us to seek out a new profound relationship with God, with the human

---

[1] *Reconciliation and Penance*, 13.
[2] *Justice in the World*, 6.

family, and with all created things.[3] Renouncing self-centered desires, bearing one's daily cross, and imitating Christ's compassion, all involve a personal struggle to control greed and selfishness, a personal commitment to reverence one's own human dignity and the dignity of others by avoiding self-indulgence and those attachments that make us insensitive to the conditions of others and that erode social solidarity. Christ warned us against attachments to material things, against total self-reliance, against the idolatry of accumulating material goods and seeking safety in them. We must take these teachings seriously and in their light examine how each of us lives and acts towards others. But personal conversion is not gained once and for all. It is a process that goes on through our entire life. Conversion, moreover, takes place in the context of a larger faith community: through baptism into the Church, through common prayer, and through our activity with others on behalf of justice.

2. Worship and Prayer

329.   Challenging U.S. economic life with the Christian vision calls for a deeper awareness of the integral connection between worship and the world of work. Worship and common prayer are the wellsprings that give life to any reflection on economic problems and that continually call the participants to greater fidelity to discipleship. To worship and pray to the God of the universe is to acknowledge that the healing love of God extends to all persons and to every part of existence, including work, leisure, money, economic and political power and their use, and to all those practical policies that either lead to justice or impede it. Therefore, when Christians come together in prayer,

---

[3] Medellin Documents: *Justice* (1968), 4.

they make a commitment to carry God's love into all these areas of life.

330.   The unity of work and worship finds expression in a unique way in the Eucharist. As people of a new covenant, the faithful hear God's challenging word proclaimed to them—a message of hope to the poor and oppressed—and they call upon the Holy Spirit to unite all into one body of Christ. For the Eucharist to be a living promise of the fullness of God's Kingdom, the faithful must commit themselves to living as redeemed people with the same care and love for all people that Jesus showed. The body of Christ which worshipers receive in Communion is also a reminder of the reconciling power of his death on the Cross. It empowers them to work to heal the brokenness of society and human relationships and to grow in a spirit of self-giving for others.

331.   The liturgy teaches us to have grateful hearts: to thank God for the gift of life, the gift of this earth, and the gift of all people. It turns our hearts from self-seeking to a spirituality that sees the signs of true discipleship in our sharing of goods and working for justice. By uniting us in prayer with all the people of God, with the rich and the poor, with those near and dear, and with those in distant lands, liturgy challenges our way of living and refines our values. Together in the community of worship, we are encouraged to use the goods of this earth for the benefit of all. In worship and in deeds for justice, the Church becomes a "sacrament," a visible sign of that unity in justice and peace that God wills for the whole of humanity.[4]

---

[4] *Dogmatic Constitution on the Church,* 1; *Pastoral Constitution,* 42, 45; *Constitution on the Liturgy,* 26; *Decree on the Church's Missionary Activity,* 5; *Liturgy and Social Justice,* ed. by Mark Searle, (Collegeville, Minn.: Liturgical Press, 1980); National Conference of Catholic Bishops, *The Church at Prayer* (Washington, D.C.: USCC Office of Publishing and Promotion Services, 1983).

3. Call to Holiness in the World

332.   Holiness is not limited to the sanctuary or to moments of private prayer; it is a call to direct our whole heart and life toward God and according to God's plan for this world. For the laity holiness is achieved in the midst of the world, in family, in community, in friendships, in work, in leisure, in citizenship. Through their competency and by their activity, lay men and women have the vocation to bring the light of the Gospel to economic affairs, "so that the world may be filled with the Spirit of Christ and may more effectively attain its destiny in justice, in love, and in peace."[5]

333.   But as disciples of Christ we must constantly ask ourselves how deeply the biblical and ethical vision of justice and love permeates our thinking. How thoroughly does it influence our way of life? We may hide behind the complexity of the issues or dismiss the significance of our personal contribution; in fact, each one has a role to play, because every day each one makes economic decisions. Some, by reason of their work or their position in society, have a vocation to be involved in a more decisive way in those decisions that affect the economic well-being of others. They must be encouraged and sustained by all in their search for greater justice.

334.   At times we will be called upon to say no to the cultural manifestations that emphasize values and aims that are selfish, wasteful, and opposed to the Scriptures. Together we must reflect on our personal and family decisions and curb unnecessary wants in order to meet the needs of others. There are many questions we must keep asking ourselves: Are we becoming ever more wasteful in a "throw-away" so-

---

[5] *Dogmatic Constitution on the Church*, 36.

ciety? Are we able to distinguish between our true needs and those thrust on us by advertising and a society that values consumption more than saving? All of us could well ask ourselves whether as a Christian prophetic witness we are not called to adopt a simpler lifestyle, in the face of the excessive accumulation of material goods that characterizes an affluent society.

335.   Husbands and wives, in particular, should weigh their needs carefully and establish a proper priority of values as they discuss the questions of both parents working outside the home and the responsibilities of raising children with proper care and attention. At times we will be called as individuals, as families, as parishes, as Church, to identify more closely with the poor in their struggle for participation and to close the gap of understanding between them and the affluent. By sharing the perspectives of those who are suffering, we can come to understand economic and social problems in a deeper way, thus leading us to seek more durable solutions.

336.   In the workplace the laity are often called to make tough decisions with little information about the consequences that such decisions have on the economic lives of others. Such times call for collaborative dialogue together with prayerful reflection on Scripture and ethical norms. The same can be said of the need to elaborate policies that will reflect sound ethical principles and that can become a part of our political and social system. Since this is a part of the lay vocation and its call to holiness, the laity must seek to instill a moral and ethical dimension into the public debate on these issues and help enunciate the ethical questions that must be faced. To weigh political options according to criteria that go beyond efficiency and expediency requires prayer, reflection, and dialogue on all the ethical norms involved. Holiness for the laity will involve all the sacrifices needed to lead

such a life of prayer and reflection within a worshiping and supporting faith community. In this way the laity will bridge the gap that so easily arises between the moral principles that guide the personal life of the Christian and the considerations that govern decisions in society in the political forum and in the market-place.

4. Leisure

337.   Some of the difficulty in bringing Christian faith to economic life in the United States today results from the obstacles to establishing a balance of labor and leisure in daily life. Tedious and boring work leads some to look for fulfillment only during time off the job. Others have become "workaholics," people who work compulsively and without reflection on the deeper meaning of life and their actions. The quality and pace of work should be more human in scale enabling people to experience the dignity and value of their work and giving them time for other duties and obligations. This balance is vitally important for sustaining the social, political, educational, and cul-tural structures of society. The family, in particular, requires such balance. Without leisure there is too little time for nurturing marriages, for developing parent-child relationships, and for fulfilling commit-ments to other important groups: the extended family, the community of friends, the parish, the neighbor-hood, schools, and political organizations. Why is it one hears so little today about shortening the work week, especially if both parents are working? Such a change would give them more time for each other, for their children, and for their other social and po-litical responsibilities.

338.   Leisure is connected to the whole of one's value system and influenced by the general culture one lives in. It can be trivialized into boredom and

laziness, or end in nothing but a desire for greater consumption and waste. For disciples of Christ, the use of leisure may demand being countercultural. The Christian tradition sees in leisure, time to build family and societal relationships and an opportunity for communal prayer and worship, for relaxed contemplation and enjoyment of God's creation, and for the cultivation of the arts which help fill the human longing for wholeness. Most of all, we must be convinced that economic decisions affect our use of leisure and that such decisions are also to be based on moral and ethical considerations. In this area of leisure we must be on our guard against being swept along by a lack of cultural values and by the changing fads of an affluent society. In the creation narrative God worked six days to create the world and rested on the seventh (Gn 2:1-4). We must take that image seriously and learn how to harmonize action and rest, work and leisure, so that both contribute to building up the person as well as the family and community.

B. Challenges to the Church

339.   The Church is all the people of God, gathered in smaller faith communities, guided and served by a pope and a hierarchy of bishops, ministered to by priests, deacons, religious, and laity, through visible institutions and agencies. Church is, thus, primarily a communion of people bonded by the Spirit with Christ as their Head, sustaining one another in love, and acting as a sign or sacrament in the world. By its nature it is people called to a transcendent end; but, it is also a visible social institution functioning in this world. According to their calling, members participate in the mission and work of the Church and share, to

varying degrees, the responsibility for its institutions and agencies.[6]

At this moment in history, it is particularly important to emphasize the responsibilities of the whole Church for education and family life.

1. Education

340.   We have already emphasized the commitment to quality education that is necessary if the poor are to take their rightful place in the economic structures of our society. We have called the Church to remember its own obligation in this regard and we have endorsed support for improvements in public education.

341.   The educational mission of the Church is not only to the poor but to all its members. We reiterate our 1972 statement: "Through education, the Church seeks to prepare its members to proclaim the Good News and to translate this proclamation into action. Since the Christian vocation is a call to transform oneself and society with God's help, the educational efforts of the Church must encompass the twin purposes of personal sanctification and social reform in the light of Christian values."[7] Through her educational mission the Church seeks: to integrate knowledge about this world with revelation about God; to understand God's relationship to the human race and its ultimate destiny in the Kingdom of God; to build up human communities of justice and peace; and to teach the value of all creation. By inculcating these values the educational system of the Church contributes to society and to social justice. Economic questions are, thus, seen as a part of a larger vision of the human

---

[6] *Justice in the World*, 41.

[7] National Conference of Catholic Bishops, *To Teach as Jesus Did*, A Pastoral Message on Education (Washington, D.C.: USCC Office of Publishing and Promotion Services, 1972), 7.

person and the human family, the value of this created earth, and the duties and responsibilities that all have toward each other and toward this universe.

342.   For these reasons the Church must incorporate into all levels of her educational system the teaching of social justice and the biblical and ethical principles that support it. We call on our universities, in particular, to make Catholic social teaching, and the social encyclicals of the popes a part of their curriculum, especially for those whose vocation will call them to an active role in U.S. economic and political decision making. Faith and technological progress are not opposed one to another, but this progress must not be channeled and directed by greed, self-indulgence, or novelty for its own sake, but by values that respect human dignity and foster social solidarity.

343.   The Church has always held that the first task and responsibility for education lies in the hands of parents: they have the right to choose freely the schools or other means necessary to educate their children in the faith.[8] The Church also has consistently held that public authorities must ensure that public subsidies for the education of children are allocated so that parents can freely choose to exercise this right without incurring unjust burdens. This parental right should not be taken from them. We call again for equitable sharing in public benefits for those parents who choose private and religious schools for their children. Such help should be available especially for low-income parents. Though many of these parents sacrifice a great deal for their children's education, others are effectively deprived of the possibility of exercising this right.

---

[8] Cf. Vatican Council II, *Declaration on Christian Education*, 3, 6. See also, *Charter of the Rights of the Family*, 5b; *Instruction on Christian Freedom and Liberation*, 94.

2. Supporting the Family

344.   Economic life has a profound effect on all social structures and particularly on the family. A breakdown of family life often brings with it hardship and poverty. Divorce, failure to provide support to mothers and children, abandonment of children, pregnancies out of wedlock, all contribute to the amount of poverty among us. Though these breakdowns of marriage and the family are more visible among the poor, they do not affect only that one segment of our society. In fact, one could argue that many of these breakdowns come from the false values found among the more affluent—values which ultimately pervade the whole of society.

345.   More studies are needed to probe the possible connections between affluence and family and marital breakdowns. The constant seeking for self-gratification and the exaggerated individualism of our age, spurred on by false values often seen in advertising and on television, contribute to the lack of firm commitment in marriage and to destructive notions of responsibility and personal growth.[9]

346.   With good reason, the Church has traditionally held that the family is the basic building block of any society. In fighting against economic arrangements that weaken the family, the Church contributes to the well-being of society. The same must be said of the Church's teaching on responsible human sexuality and its relationship to marriage and family. Economic

---

[9] Pope John Paul II, *On the Family* (Washington, D.C.: USCC Office of Publishing and Promotion Services, 1981), 6. See also Robert N. Bellah, Richard Madsen, William M. Sullivan, Ann Swidler, Steven M. Tipton, *Habits of the Heart: Individualism and Commitment in American Life* (Berkeley: University of California Press, 1985); *The Family Today and Tomorrow: The Church Addresses Her Future* (Boston, Mass.: The Pope John Center, 1985).

arrangements must support the family and promote its solidity.

3. The Church as Economic Actor

347.   Although all members of the Church are economic actors every day in their individual lives, they also play an economic role united together as Church. On the parish and diocesan level, through its agencies and institutions, the Church employs many people; it has investments; it has extensive properties for worship and mission. *All the moral principles that govern the just operation of any economic endeavor apply to the Church and its agencies and institutions; indeed the Church should be exemplary.* The Synod of Bishops in 1971 worded this challenge most aptly: "While the Church is bound to give witness to justice, she recognizes that anyone who ventures to speak to people about justice must first be just in their eyes. Hence, we must undertake an examination of the modes of acting and of the possessions and lifestyle found within the Church herself."[10]

348.   Catholics in the United States can be justly proud of their accomplishments in building and maintaining churches and chapels, and an extensive system of schools, hospitals, and charitable institutions. Through sacrifices and personal labor our immigrant ancestors built these institutions. For many decades religious orders of women and men taught in our schools and worked in our hospitals with very little remuneration. Right now, we see the same spirit of generosity among the religious and lay people even as we seek to pay more adequate salaries.

349. We would be insincere were we to deny a need for renewal in the economic life of the Church itself

---

[10] *Justice in the World*, 40.

and for renewed zeal on the part of the Church in examining its role in the larger context of reinforcing in U.S. society and culture those values that support economic justice.[11]

350.   We select here five areas for special reflection: (1) wages and salaries, (2) rights of employees, (3) investments and property, (4) works of charity, and (5) working for economic justice.

351.   We bishops commit ourselves to the principle that those who serve the Church—laity, clergy, and religious—should receive a sufficient livelihood and the social benefits provided by responsible employers in our nation. These obligations, however, cannot be met without the increased contributions of all the members of the Church. We call on all to recognize their responsibility to contribute monetarily to the support of those who carry out the public mission of the Church. Sacrificial giving or tithing by all the People of God would provide the funds necessary to pay these adequate salaries for religious and lay people; the lack of funds is the usual underlying cause for the lack of adequate salaries. The obligation to sustain the Church's institutions—education and health care, social service agencies, religious education programs, care of the elderly, youth ministry, and the like—falls on all the members of the community because of their baptism; the obligation is not just on the users or on those who staff them. Increased resources are also needed for the support of elderly members of religious communities. These dedicated women and men have not always asked for or received the stipends and pensions that would have assured their future. It would be a breach of our obligations to them to let them or their communities face retirement without adequate funds.

---

[11] *Dogmatic Constitution on the Church*, 8.

352.   Many volunteers provide services to the Church and its mission which cannot be measured in dollars and cents. These services are important to the life and vitality of the Church in the United States and carry on a practice that has marked the history of the Church in this country since its founding. In this tradition, we ask young people to make themselves available for a year or more of voluntary service before beginning their training for more specific vocations in life; we also recommend expanding voluntary service roles for retired persons; we encourage those who have accepted this challenge.

353.   All church institutions must also fully recognize the rights of employees to organize and bargain collectively with the institution through whatever association or organization they freely choose.[12] In the light of new creative models of collaboration between labor and management described earlier in this letter, we challenge our church institutions to adopt new fruitful modes of cooperation. Although the Church has its own nature and mission that must be respected and fostered, we are pleased that many who are not of our faith, but who share similar hopes and aspirations for the human family, work for us and with us in achieving this vision. In seeking greater justice in wages, we recognize the need to be alert particularly to the continuing discrimination against women throughout Church and society, especially reflected in both the inequities of salaries between women and men and in the concentration of women in jobs at the lower end of the wage scale.

354.   Individual Christians who are shareholders and those responsible within church institutions that own stocks in U.S. corporations must see to it that

---

[12] National Conference of Catholic Bishops, *Health and Health Care* (Washington, D.C.: USCC Office of Publishing and Promotion Services, 1981), 50.

the invested funds are used responsibly. Although it
is a moral and legal fiduciary responsibility of the
trustees to ensure an adequate return on investment
for the support of the work of the Church, their stewardship embraces broader moral concerns. As part-
owners, they must cooperate in shaping the policies
of those companies through dialogue with management, through votes at corporate meetings, through
the introduction of resolutions, and through participation in investment decisions. We praise the efforts
of dioceses and other religious and ecumenical bodies
that work together toward these goals. We also praise
efforts to develop alternative investment policies, especially those which support enterprises that promote
economic development in depressed communities and
which help the Church respond to local and regional
needs.[13] When the decision to divest seems unavoidable, it should be done after prudent examination and
with a clear explanation of the motives.

355.   The use of church property demands special
attention today. Changing demographic patterns have
left many parishes and institutions with empty or
partially used buildings. The decline in the number
of religious who are teaching in the schools and the
reduction in the number of clergy often result in large
residences with few occupants. In this regard, the
Church must be sensitive to the image the possession
of such large facilities often projects, namely, that it
is wealthy and extravagant in the use of its resources.
This image can be overcome only by clear public accountability of its financial holdings, of its properties
and their use, and of the services it renders to its
members and to society at large. We support and
encourage the creative use of these facilities by many
parishes and dioceses to serve the needs of the poor.

---

[13] See ch. IV of this pastoral letter.

356.　　　　　　The Church has a special call to be a servant of the poor, the sick, and the marginalized, thereby becoming a true sign of the Church's mission—a mission shared by every member of the Christian community. The Church now serves many such people through one of the largest private human services delivery systems in the country. The networks of agencies, institutions, and programs provide services to millions of persons of all faiths. Still we must be reminded that in our day our Christian concerns must increase and extend beyond our borders, because everyone in need is our neighbor. We must also be reminded that charity requires more than alleviating misery. It demands genuine love for the person in need. It should probe the meaning of suffering and provoke a response that seeks to remedy causes. True charity leads to advocacy.

357.　　　　　　Yet charity alone is not a corrective to all economic social ills. All citizens, working through various organizations of society and through government, bear the responsibility of caring for those who are in need. The Church, too, through all its members individually and through its agencies, must work to alleviate injustices that prevent some from participating fully in economic life. Our experience with the Campaign for Human Development confirms our judgment about the validity of self-help and empowerment of the poor. The campaign, which has received the positive support of American Catholics since it was launched in 1970, provides a model that we think sets a high standard for similar efforts. We bishops know of the many faithful in all walks of life who use their skills and their compassion to seek innovative ways to carry out the goals we are proposing in this letter. As they do this, they *are* the Church acting for economic justice. At the same time, we hope they will join together with us and their priests to influence our society so that even more steps can be taken to alleviate injustices. Grassroots efforts by the poor themselves, helped by community support, are indispensable. The entire Christian community can learn much from the way our deprived brothers and sisters assist each other in their struggles.

358.   In addition to being an economic actor, the Church is a significant cultural actor concerned about the deeper cultural roots of our economic problems. As we have proposed a new experiment in collaboration and participation in decision making by all those affected at all levels of U. S. society, so we also commit the Church to become a model of collaboration and participation.

C. The Road Ahead

359.   The completion of a letter such as this one is but the beginning of a long process of education, discussion and action; its contents must be brought to all members of the Church and of society.

360.   In this respect we mentioned the twofold aim of this pastoral letter: to help Catholics form their consciences on the moral dimensions of economic decision making and to articulate a moral perspective in the general societal and political debate that surrounds these questions. These two purposes help us to reflect on the different ways the institutions and ministers of the Church can assist the laity in their vocation in the world. Renewed emphasis on Catholic social teaching in our schools, colleges, and universities; special seminars with corporate officials, union leaders, legislators, bankers, and the like; the organization of small groups composed of people from different ways of life to meditate together on the Gospel and ethical norms; speakers' bureaus; family programs; clearinghouses of available material; pulpit aids for

priests; diocesan television and radio programs; research projects in our universities—all of these are appropriate means for continued discussion and action. Some of these are done best on the parish level, others by the state Catholic conferences, and others by the National Conference of Catholic Bishops. These same bodies can assist the laity in the many difficult decisions that deal with political options that affect economic decisions. Where many options are available, it must be the concern of all in such debates that we as Catholics do not become polarized. All must be challenged to show how the decisions they make and the policies they suggest flow from the ethical moral vision outlined here. As new problems arise, we hope through our continual reflection that we will be able to help refine Catholic social teaching and contribute to its further development.

361.   We call upon our priests, in particular, to continue their study of these issues, so that they can proclaim the gospel message in a way that not only challenges the faithful but also sustains and encourages their vocation in and to the world. Priestly formation in our seminaries will also have to prepare candidates for this role.

362.   We wish to emphasize the need to undertake research into many of the areas this document could not deal with in depth and to continue exploration of those we have dealt with. We encourage our Catholic universities, foundations, and other institutions to assist in these necessary projects. The following areas for further research are merely suggestive, not exhaustive: the impact of arms production and large military spending on the domestic economy and on culture; arms production and sales as they relate to Third World poverty; tax reforms to express the preferential option for the poor; the rights of women and minorities in the work force; the development of communications technology and its global influences; ro-

botics, automation, and reduction of defense industries
as they will affect employment; the economy and the
stability of the family; legitimate profit versus greed;
securing economic rights; environmental and ecological questions; future roles of labor and unions; international financial institutions and Third World debt;
our national deficit; world food problems; "full employment" and its implementation; plant closings and
dealing with the human costs of an evolving economy;
cooperatives and new modes of sharing; welfare reform and national eligibility standards; income support systems; concentration of land ownership;
assistance to Third World nations; migration and its
effects; population policies and development; the effects of increased inequality of incomes in society.

D. Commitment to a Kingdom of Love and Justice

363.   Confronted by this economic complexity and
seeking clarity for the future, we can rightly ask ourselves one single question: How does our economic
system affect the lives of people—*all* people? Part of
the American dream has been to make this world a
better place for people to live in; at this moment of
history that dream must include everyone on this
globe. Since we profess to be members of a "catholic"
or universal Church, we all must raise our sights to
a concern for the well-being of everyone in the world.
Third World debt becomes our problem. Famine and
starvation in sub-Saharan Africa become our concern.
Rising military expenditures everywhere in the world
become part of our fears for the future of this planet.
We cannot be content if we see ecological neglect or
the squandering of natural resources. In this letter we
bishops have spoken often of economic interdepen-

dence; now is the moment when all of us must confront the reality of such economic bonding and its consequences and see it as a moment of grace—a *kairos*—that can unite all of us in a common community of the human family. We commit ourselves to this global vision.

364.   We cannot be frightened by the magnitude and complexity of these problems. We must not be discouraged. In the midst of this struggle, it is inevitable that we become aware of greed, laziness, and envy. No utopia is possible on this earth; but as believers in the redemptive love of God and as those who have experienced God's forgiving mercy, we know that God's providence is not and will not be lacking to us today.

365.   The fulfillment of human needs, we know, is not the final purpose of the creation of the human person. We have been created to share in the divine life through a destiny that goes far beyond our human capabilities and before which we must in all humility stand in awe. Like Mary in proclaiming her *Magnificat*, we marvel at the wonders God has done for us, how God has raised up the poor and the lowly and promised great things for them in the Kingdom. God now asks of us sacrifices and reflection on our reverence for human dignity—in ourselves and in others—and on our service and discipleship, so that the divine goal for the human family and this earth can be fulfilled. Communion with God, sharing God's life, involves a mutual bonding with all on this globe. Jesus taught us to love God and one another and that the concept of neighbor is without limit. We know that we are called to be members of a new covenant of love. We have to move from our devotion to independence, through an understanding of interdependence, to a commitment to human solidarity. That challenge must find its realization in the kind of com-

munity we build among us. Love implies concern for all—especially the poor—and a continued search for those social and economic structures that permit everyone to share in a community that is a part of a redeemed creation (Rom 8:21-23).

Index